9/2/2010

THE LAST OF THE
IMPERIOUS RICH

|||||||||||||||||||||||||||||||||||||||||||||||||||||||

THE LAST OF THE

IMPERIOUS

RICH

Lehman Brothers,
1844–2008

Peter Chapman

PORTFOLIO / PENGUIN

PORTFOLIO PENGUIN
Published by the Penguin Group
Penguin Group (USA) Inc., 375 Hudson Street, New York, New York 10014, U.S.A. • Penguin Group (Canada),
90 Eglinton Avenue East, Suite 700, Toronto, Ontario, Canada M4P 2Y3 (a division of Pearson Penguin Canada Inc.) •
Penguin Books Ltd, 80 Strand, London WC2R 0RL, England • Penguin Ireland, 25 St Stephen's Green, Dublin 2, Ireland
(a division of Penguin Books Ltd) • Penguin Books Australia Ltd, 250 Camberwell Road, Camberwell, Victoria 3124,
Australia (a division of Pearson Australia Group Pty Ltd) • Penguin Books India Pvt Ltd, 11 Community Centre, Panchsheel
Park, New Delhi – 110 017, India • Penguin Group (NZ), 67 Apollo Drive, Rosedale, North Shore 0632, New Zealand
(a division of Pearson New Zealand Ltd) • Penguin Books (South Africa) (Pty) Ltd, 24 Sturdee Avenue, Rosebank,
Johannesburg 2196, South Africa

Penguin Books Ltd, Registered Offices:
80 Strand, London WC2R 0RL, England

First published in 2010 by Portfolio,
a member of Penguin Group (USA) Inc.

10 9 8 7 6 5 4 3 2 1

LIBRARY OF CONGRESS CATALOGING-IN-PUBLICATION DATA
Chapman, Peter, 1948–
    The last of the imperious rich : Lehman Brothers, 1844–2008 / Peter Chapman.
        p. cm.
    Includes bibliographical references and index.
    ISBN 978-1-59184-309-2
        1. Lehman Brothers—History.   2. Stockbrokers—United States.   3. Investment banking—New York (State)—
New York—History.   4. Finance—New York (State)—New York—History.   5. Bankruptcy—United States.
6. Business failures—United States.   I. Title.

    HG5129.N5C43 2010
    332.660973—dc22   2010013787

Printed in the United States of America
Designed by Carla Bolte • Set in Warnock

To Marie, Alex, and Pepito

Grabbing and greed can go on for just so long,
but the breaking point is bound to come sometime.

—HERBERT LEHMAN,
partner at Lehman Brothers, 1908–28;
governor of New York, 1933–42; senator from New York, 1949–57

CONTENTS

THE LAST OF THE
IMPERIOUS RICH

1

Alabama Fever

Henry Lehman arrived in New York on a ship from Europe on September 11, 1844. The activity and noise that greeted him often shocked immigrants as they approached Manhattan Island after weeks on the open sea. Steam-driven ferries plowed across the harbor, traveling to and from Brooklyn, Staten Island, and Hoboken, New Jersey. Rowboats and sailboats swarmed the area, their handlers shouting offers to passengers of any incoming ship to come with them and avoid waiting until their ship had docked. Innkeepers climbed on board touting the charms of the accommodation they had to offer onshore. Reporters came too, armed with notebooks and pencils, seeking stories from the Old World.

Friedrich Gerstäcker, a twenty-seven-year-old immigrant who had arrived in America from Germany seven years before Henry, recorded his first impressions of New York in a letter to his mother in Leipzig. "Delicious was the sight of the land shining in fresh green, with lush forests and splendid houses," he wrote. "With forts to the right and left, protecting the harbor, above us a friendly blue sky, beneath us softly murmuring waves."

When Henry arrived, there was no single place that handled newcomers. The old fort of Castle Garden at the southern tip of Manhattan did not become an immigrant receiving center until 1855, and Ellis Island did not replace it until thirty-seven years after that. Henry landed at one of the passenger receiving docks on the three- to four-mile stretch along the East and Hudson rivers. Immigration procedures were lax. The federal government left the administration of such tasks to the individual states and only required that a ship's captain present a list of the people he had brought with him. Henry arrived aboard a ship called the *Burgundy* and was one on a list of 149 passengers. Two of his fellow travelers apparently failed to complete the journey; crosses are marked near their names, in the column "Died on the Voyage."

The *Burgundy* passenger list named him as Heyum Lehmann, but in America he became the far more anglicized Henry. Whether as a result of a spelling mistake by an immigration official or by his own choice, his family name took on a less German look by dropping the final "n." At some stage its pronunciation also changed, from the Germanic "Lay-man" to its common form in America, "Lee-man."

Henry was far from alone in seeking a new life in America, and with the inflow of migrants, the population was rising quickly. In 1840, the twenty-six states of the Union had a population of seventeen million; by 1850 America would have thirty states and over twenty-three million people, an increase of more than a third. The United States was mainly an agricultural country, and cotton, its principal export, was grown in the South. But the rise of industry attracted many migrants to the cities. New York was the largest, its population about three hundred thousand in 1840. Brooklyn, which lies to the east and was, at the time, considered a separate city, was the seventh largest, with a population of thirty-six thousand. In the 1840s, New York's population rose by two thirds and Brooklyn's far more than doubled.

All the new migrants came with their hopes and dreams and helped in their own ways in building modern America. Henry would contribute more than most. As the first of the Lehman family to arrive in the United States, he would set up an enterprise that became one of the world's most reputable banks. It would last for 158 years, and over that time its history mirrored the ascent to wealth and world leadership of the United States. Its story, furthermore, would provide a precise reflection of the ebbs and flows, and the rises and falls, of the American Dream.

For most migrants their immediate dream was to shed their past and start again. Most were making their escape from Europe's despotic princes and kings. Henry came from Bavaria, which, though now part of Germany, was then a separate state run by King Ludwig I, an autocrat with a penchant for mistresses—and for the restoration of old monasteries that had fallen into disuse and taxing his people to pay for them. The United States provided a sense of protected separateness that suited the new immigrants. In 1823, President James Monroe had declared the Monroe Doctrine, which instructed foreign regimes to keep out of the Americas.

This was aimed at the monarchies of Spain, France, Russia, and Prussia, which in Monroe's time were thought to be hatching plans to help Spain regain the empire it had lost in South America. Spain still controlled Cuba and Puerto Rico in the Caribbean. Given that the new immigrants had no fondness for the governments they had left behind, they found common cause with American citizens of longer standing who, with their collective memory of throwing out the British in 1776, similarly valued their autonomy.

As the United States expanded west and south, the nation concentrated its plans for territorial growth on the American continent. In 1844 the government in Washington debated whether to annex the independent Republic of Texas—which had broken away from Mexico—as the twenty-seventh state. While the politicians talked, Florida beat Texas to the punch and won statehood six months after Henry arrived. Spain had ceded Florida to the United States in 1821, and after more than twenty years of running battles with the Seminole Indians, Washington deemed it safe to enter the Union.

The United States also spied opportunities beyond the Americas. In July 1844 it had signed the Treaty of Wanghia with China, with the aim of beginning trade between the two countries. Until two years before, China had shunned all commerce with the outside world and had only changed its mind when the British launched the Opium War, which forced China to buy British opium from India. With the opening of the Chinese market, the United States feared that the established Great Powers of Britain, France, Russia, and Prussia would grab the bounty. President John Tyler dispatched a mission to China led by Caleb Cushing, a Massachusetts lawyer. It took 208 days to sail to China, and he waited for weeks in Macau, the territory near the British redoubt of Hong Kong, before Chinese government representatives would meet him.

As expansion of trade caused the world to shrink, so did astounding advances in communications. A little less than four months before Henry Lehman came to America, on May 24, 1844, Samuel Morse successfully tested his telegraph system. He had tried it two years earlier via a cable laid in New York harbor, but a ship's propeller had cut the cable. Morse worked to overcome the vulnerabilities of technology and eventually managed to send a message between Washington, DC, and Baltimore. His words had an ominous tone: "What hath God wrought?"

In social affairs, Sojourner Truth had in 1843 become America's first famous black woman orator when she traveled widely throughout New England and the Midwest to speak out against slavery. In literature, Herman Melville returned to Boston three months after Henry's arrival, following several years abroad. His tales from the world's distant whaling zones inspired his epic work of American literature, *Moby-Dick*, which was published in 1851.

Henry Lehman probably stepped on land to the customary melee that greeted new arrivals. Boardinghouse runners attempted to lure immigrants to decrepit lodgings where they would be charged exorbitant rates. Immigrant societies, Germans, Irish, and others, would have representatives on hand to greet newcomers. They would buttonhole anyone whose provenance they recognized and urge them to move on and out of this pitiless city.

None of them need have wasted their effort on Henry. He was new to this place but not naively "just off the boat." He had been a cattle dealer and wine merchant in Bavaria and so had the haggling skills required to get a fair price for a room. He was twenty-two years old, unmarried, and, according to Roland Flade, a German journalist who chronicled the Lehman family in his book *The Lehmans, From Rimpar to the New World: A Family History*, probably traveling with two friends, Meyer and Arnold Goldschmidt, who were of similar age and disposition. The three did not intend to stick around New York for long. Meyer, twenty-four, and Arnold, eighteen, were from a village a few miles from the small town of Rimpar where Henry had lived, and they were on their way to see relatives in the South. A Goldschmidt family member had moved there from Bavaria a few years before and set up business as a merchant under his changed name of Goldsmith in Mobile, Alabama.

As they waited for their boat to Mobile, Henry and his companions may well have had some time to spare in New York. They possibly visited or even stayed in the area north of what is now Division Street and east of the Bowery, where a large number of Germans lived. It was known as Kleindeutschland, "Little Germany." Despite its ethnic makeup, the area was quite unlike the environment that Henry came from in Germany. Rimpar was in an area of hills covered by fields, gardens, and vineyards, while Kleindeutschland was very much urban New York. Tenements five stories high housed sometimes more than twenty families. Just the year before, in 1843, the Association for Improving Conditions of the Poor described the tenements as "generally defective in size, arrangement, supplies of water, warmth and ventilation." In about fifty years' time one of Henry's nephews, Herbert H. Lehman (the H stands for "Henry"), would take a great interest in such districts of the city and work in them as a community organizer. Later in the 1920s and '30s he would be President Franklin D. Roosevelt's right-hand man, assigned to create the reform and welfare programs of the New Deal.

By 1840 New York's northern perimeter had stretched to Fourteenth Street. Immigrants had flooded in to occupy the old downtown areas of the Lower East Side, and established city dwellers had expanded the city's boundaries to the north and west. Low-lying land-filled areas of Manhattan near the East River were known as "the swamp." They were not conducive to healthy living, especially in warmer months, and richer and middle-class families hastened to the city's outskirts. Epidemics helped chase them away, including a yellow fever outbreak that occurred about two decades before Henry came.

People who traveled into town from the city's edges used omnibuses, horse-drawn communal passenger vehicles that followed fixed routes and were often painted colorfully. Their owners gave them names like George Washington and Lady Washington. Men commuted in them to work and women to shops on lower Broadway in them. When they finished, they left quickly. Only the poor stayed downtown at night. The famed gangs of New York had not achieved their renown of later years, but that would come by the end of the decade, when local resentments and large-scale Irish immigration led to battles between gangs such as the Bowery Boys, the Plug Uglies, and the Dead Rabbits.

Aside from the shopping expeditions of the middle class, very few women were seen in the streets. On Wall Street, the central banking area, they were a rarity at any time. The sight was enough to rouse traders from their posts to gawk and bring the stock market to a halt. Further on—after the crash of 2008—some people commented that had Wall Street, the City of London, and other financial centers employed more women, the average testosterone levels might have been sufficiently lowered to prevent the disaster. Lehman Brothers possibly would never have disappeared had it been "Lehman Sisters," suggested Neelie Kroes, the European Union's equality commissioner. If that were true, the rot in New York's financial district had set in by the 1840s.

When Henry Lehman first saw New York, it was still many years before skyscrapers were a feature of city architecture. But Trinity Church, at the west end of Wall Street, was in the process of becoming an important part of the skyline. Severe snow in the winter of 1838–39 had damaged the church badly, and reconstruction was under way. Completed in 1846, Trinity's spire became the highest point in New York, at 281 feet.

Whether his first impressions of America made Henry homesick for Bavaria is uncertain, but they probably did not make him regret leaving. Rimpar was located halfway between Nuremberg and Munich and a few miles from Würzburg, the largest town in the area. Rimpar's most prominent feature was Grumbach Castle in the heart of town, built in 1600. With a rounded turret at one end, Grumbach looked less like a traditional four-square castle with a surrounding moat than an overbearing cathedral. This was perhaps no coincidence given that the local potentates who initially occupied it—before it passed into the ownership of the Bavarian king in the eighteenth century—were officially known as prince-bishops. Rimpar, indeed Bavaria, lived in the despotic shadow of both the local monarchy and the Roman Catholic Church.

The town's 120 Jews—out of a total population of 1,300—lived there at the sufferance of Rimpar's royal rulers and their ecclesial counterparts. Both were glad to have them around as taxpayers; the Jewish community paid as much for the welfare of the Roman Catholic priest, for example, as for the upkeep of the Jewish cemetery. But law dictated where Jews lived, and that only the oldest boy of a family could remain in the town into adulthood. Henry was the sixth of ten children and the second-oldest brother. He was always going to have to leave.

Abraham and Eva Lehmann, Henry's parents, had given him a broad education. Like his brothers and sisters, Henry attended Rimpar's Jewish school in the morning and Roman Catholic school in the afternoon. He learned how to assimilate and inherited commercial skills from his family's merchant background. Seligmann Löw, his grandfather, had been a *Kleinhändler*, a "petty trader" or retailer, traveling the highways of Germany. He sold grain, skins, and wool that he bought from farmers, as well as luxuries such as spices that he purchased at trade fairs in cities like Leipzig and Frankfurt. He rose to be a member of the Jewish upper middle class. Henry's father was able to lead a more settled existence as a cattle trader and wine merchant. Henry started working for him as soon as he left school at the age of fourteen.

Henry had the breeding to travel and incentive to go beyond the petty world of Bavaria and its fellow German fiefdoms. There was, as yet, no grand German design or Count Otto von Bismarck of Prussia to unify the German states as one nation. This Bismarck would eventually do by waging war in the 1860s and '70s. From Berlin, its capital, Prussia was the strongest of the states, but Germany itself remained little more than a geographical expression. Each of its component states was rigidly stuck in its sense of *Heimat*, or homeland, and Jews were not part of it.

Bavaria was also torn between being a German state and its attachment to Austria, its southern neighbor. Culturally and linguistically, as well as geographically, the two were close. But Austria's old imperial regime was in a state of collapse; political movements in the 1840s in parts of the Austrian empire such as Hungary demanded independence. So, too, did those in Germany. In 1844 Ludwig I's cravings for money led to his putting a tax on beer, which set off riots in many areas of Bavaria. The signs also pointed to a bad harvest that year and poor prospects for the countryside in general. Henry made his decision to go.

Stories had traveled back from the New World of its possibilities and wide-open spaces. The Oregon Trail had recently opened, with the frontiersman Kit Carson making a name for himself thanks to his explorations in such areas as Colorado, California, and the Pacific Northwest. But German people had been learning about America's promise for years. In 1829 Gottfried Duden, a German graduate in law and medicine who had settled in the territory of Missouri, had his book *Report on a Journey to the Western States of North America and a Stay of Several Years Along the Missouri (During the Years 1824, '25, '26, and 1827)* published, his account of a democratic life free of the kind of restrictions suffered by individuals in Germany. In 1837 *Die Allegemeine Zeitung des Judentums*, a new Jewish periodical in Germany, reported on groups that had left for America and how they were getting on.

Rimpar was a river settlement on the Main, which linked to the Rhine, and from there the way was open to the sea. More travel agents had set themselves up to take advantage of a growing business opportunity as people left for America. Increasing trade between Europe and America also helped; ships like the *Burgundy* that took Henry were sailing ships coming to Europe from the Americas laden with cotton, tobacco, and other products. They had space available in their holds for migrants wanting to make the westward trip.

Henry would be the first person to leave Rimpar for America, though from all around Germany the tide of migrants was rising. Leopold Sonnemann, founder of the German newspaper *Frankfurter Zeitung*, witnessed the departure of people like Henry. "[E]migration became a mass phenomenon," he wrote in his memoirs. He watched parents say good-bye to their grown-up children on sad, sun-drenched summer evenings in villages and towns being denuded of their youth: "[P]robably the most skillful and vigorous elements of the population" were leaving. He observed how brave they were. Migrants like Henry lived a long way from the sea and were journeying into what for them was the complete unknown. "[T]o the inlander," wrote Sonnemann, "the trips seemed like what a North Pole expedition would be today."

Having sailed from Rimpar to Mainz, Henry took another boat to Rotterdam in the Netherlands, and yet another along the north European coast to the French port of Le Havre. He boarded the *Burgundy* in late July for a transatlantic crossing that took between five and six weeks. Journeys were cramped, dark, stuffy, and miserable. Storms, sometimes hurricanes, had to be braved. Deaths onboard and burials at sea were common. Whole families might travel, including young children and the elderly. Later and sentimental characterizations of these people as "poor" and "huddled masses" did them no service. They were proud and dignified, the enterprising ones and the risk takers. Anything less and they would have stayed at home.

Henry Lehman probably knew that going to America amounted to a tough bargain: You might never complete the journey; once there you might not make a success of yourself and go under. But if you worked you had every chance of making it. And who would not work? Why would anyone make the effort of pulling up his roots and getting on a boat to the unknown if his intention was to cruise through life on the other side?

The American Dream was not a romantic notion for the likes of Henry. You did not ask for much and were grateful for what you got. Work would bring its own reward, and there would be no chance of its being stripped away at the whim of feudal princes. That was the great thing about the

United States—there were few nuances, no weird signals or moods to be read that might presage some officially sanctioned pogrom. Matters were practical, solid; you could build on this kind of foundation.

It is not known when exactly, but Henry and the Goldschmidts—probably now the anglicized Goldsmiths—boarded a ship in New York bound for Mobile. Sailing down the eastern seaboard, the vessel ran the often stormy seas off Cape Hatteras, rounded Florida into the Gulf of Mexico, and headed for the coast of Alabama. Henry and his friends would have had a mounting feeling of excitement—and apprehension. Alabama: The word itself had an alliterative ring and a sense of driving on. Add an exclamation mark and it was almost a war cry.

Henry Lehman provided no written account of his journey to America, but there were a number of possible factors that drew him to the South. It was a rural area and he came from a farming background. He also had contacts there through the Goldsmiths. But doubtless he was drawn by cotton. This was the time when cotton production dominated the South. Cotton exports from the Southern states had flooded into Europe, including Germany. The German city of Mainz, not far along the Main from Rimpar, had been a textile center since the Middle Ages; Johannes Gutenberg had developed his printing press there in the fifteenth century using compressed fabric for paper. Cotton was a familiar commodity in Bavaria, and many Jewish cotton weavers worked in Rimpar and its surrounding villages.

Cotton was the lifeblood of America as far as its trade with the outside world was concerned. When Henry arrived in Mobile, he would have seen the docks piled with bales awaiting shipment to mills in Europe or the American Northeast. Mobile dispatched much of the cotton that went to Germany. The city had experienced remarkable growth, and with a population of twelve thousand was by far the largest settlement in Alabama; "a place of trade and nothing else," wrote a traveler cited by Roland Flade in *The Lehmans*. "[T]he quays are crowded with shipping, and in amounts of exports it is inferior only to New Orleans."

Alabama had entered the Union in 1819, and from the 1820s "Alabama fever" had gripped the Southern states. People from elsewhere in the South—notably Kentucky and the Carolinas—had seen their lands steadily exhausted and found themselves drawn by the allure of Alabama's rich soil. Caravans of slaves, mules, household goods, and their owners had clogged the roads and minor trails into the state. Many of the new entrants settled in the Black Belt, an area across the center of Alabama so named for its dark, fertile soil.

Henry could have stayed in Mobile with the Goldsmiths, but instead he headed inland. He was used to being landlocked, being from Bavaria, but he was also a river person who had lived most of his life on the Main. From Mobile the steamers ran on the Alabama River toward Montgomery, the Black Belt's main city. They carried grain, lumber, flour, liquor, tobacco, and an array of other everyday and luxury goods. The interior of the state clearly did good business. Henry may have bought supplies on credit from the Goldsmiths; certainly, he headed out along the roads by the Alabama River to sell to its plantations and other scattered settlements.

He was an itinerant peddler. He sold farmers' and household goods— tools, seeds, glassware, crockery. "Dry goods" was another line: basic haberdashery, cotton sheets, and the like. Thousands of peddlers worked the byways of America at this time, many of them immigrants and some destined to do very well: The Gimbels, the Goldmans, and the Guggenheims were among them. Henry may have had a horse-drawn wagon. The alternatives were to strap his wares to the back of a horse, or to his own. Stephen Birmingham, in his book *Our Crowd* (which chronicles the history of New York's wealthy Jewish families), wrote that to later generations this kind of ancestral detail was important. "[S]tarting on foot showed a certain physical stamina," he wrote. "Starting with a wagon, on the other hand, might indicate superior business acumen." The Lehman family placed Henry and itself in the latter category: "[M]ost Lehmans feel strongly that the Lehmans started with a wagon."

Kenneth Libo in his book *Lots of Lehmans* stresses the educational advantages of peddling. It had an important schooling function for new immigrants who took to the trade and, furthermore, was an important breeding ground for the American tradition of entrepreneurship. "Peddling was the Harvard Business School of that day," wrote Libo.

Henry Lehman had to acquire a rapid familiarity with a territory and its inhabitants, but he had the advantage of knowing how to deal with farmers and their needs. The work required diplomatic and negotiation skills, patience and stamina; on a long and hot day—of which Alabama had many—tiredness could ruin a sales pitch. Henry must have had a considerable ability to communicate, though his English would still have been minimal. The Southern accent, meanwhile, was not the easiest to understand, being akin to the English accent around the time of Shakespeare. He was probably a skilled user of sign language.

The work could also create its own problems. Men sometimes resented peddlers' intrusions, especially seductive sales pitches aimed at their wives. In this, German Jewish peddlers may have enjoyed an advantage over their American counterparts, given that they had not yet developed their English enough to have the gift of gab. They also gradually displaced salesmen from the Yankee North, who were often regarded with suspicion. Amid fears of slave insurrections fueled by Northerners, Yankee peddlers were more likely seen as the enemy among us, as it were, than their German Jewish competitors, who were new to the social mores of America and unlikely to have been peddling abolition.

Little if any discrimination stood in the way of Henry's progress. As a Jew he would have been ready for it, but he was white and part of a pecking order that placed him some way up the local scale. Oscar Straus, a close friend of the Lehmans who became a leading politician, spoke of this in his memoir, *Under Four Administrations, From Cleveland to Taft*, when writing of his father Lazarus's life as a peddler in the South: The "white visitor [had] a status of equality that probably otherwise he would not have enjoyed to such a degree." From a peddling start, the Strauses went on to own Macy's, the New York department store.

Henry prospered because he had what people wanted. A peddler provided a valued function in such areas as the Alabama River valley. Many of its outposts lacked the convenience of a local store. Straus wrote that plantation owners greeted "as an honored guest" any peddler who "conscientiously treated his customers with fairness and made no misrepresentation regarding his wares." They were happy to buy what Henry had to sell. He understood the value of a good deal and reaped the reward from providing something of simple but real value. Peddlers of lesser wares did not fare well. By some swampland telegraph—of lower technology but comparable effectiveness to that recently invented by Samuel Morse—one plantation owner would find out from another when a rotten deal had been done.

Lehman took to this place. The Alabama River meandered like the

Main and the Rhine around Mainz and Bingen, although without its cooling mists or Lorelei heights to provide refuge from the heat. Some farmhouses took passersby in at night and for twenty-five cents offered supper and breakfast as well as lodging. Or he slept out, grabbing food where he could, reconciled to compromising the dictates of kosher law. "Thousands of peddlers wander around America," wrote one observer cited by H. G. Reissner in his book *The German-American Jews (1800–1850):* "[T]hey pray neither on working days, nor on the Sabbath." Henry would make amends for this later.

As he sold so he reordered by way of the riverboats heading back to Mobile. In a little less than a year he reached Montgomery, a distance of 120 miles as the crow flies from Mobile and quite a few more as the peddler travels. He had spent the months selling, fending for himself, and somehow sleeping while guarding his money and other possessions. He was most likely exhausted.

Montgomery sat in its amphitheater of hills. Travelers approached it on plank roads—roads with planks of wood stretched across them, a common feature in preasphalt days. The planks deteriorated into rutted, unpaved streets in Montgomery's town center, which, in turn, was reduced to rivers of mud when it rained. The town was only a quarter of a century old and had a population of four thousand free and two thousand enslaved people. Its sole rail link was with Atlanta. Open sewers ran between basic wooden houses, storefronts, and odorous livery stables and down to the river and its lines of ramshackle piers. Swarms of flies filled the air. Yellow fever was endemic.

Lehman saw something of promise. Those livery stables were "crowded, hub to hub, with cotton wagons," recorded *A Centennial*, an in-house history published by Lehman Brothers in 1950 to mark the firm's hundred-year anniversary. And "[s]teamboats fought for space against the rickety wharves." Montgomery was growing fast and had become a warehouse for cotton heading to Mobile and New Orleans. Some speculative ventures suggested the city had a future. "[I]nvestors, their confidence in cotton supreme, had built the Exchange Hotel, Madison House, Dexter House and other hotels far beyond the needs and the means of the Montgomery of that day," it was reported in *A Centennial*.

Henry rented one of the wooden houses near the town center on Commerce Street and opened a general store. On bare wood shelving he laid out his wares, the same goods for farm and home that he had sold from his wagon. He put up a sign outside, a single shingle. It read H. LEHMAN.

|||||||||

The firm that would eventually become Lehman Brothers began life because of a failed bank. Shortly before Henry Lehman arrived in Montgomery, the state government in Tuscaloosa, Alabama's capital at that time, decided to close the Alabama state bank. It had collapsed, and people who had arrived at the bank's doors seeking the funds they had entrusted to it were informed that the coffers were empty. Many Alabamians had lost their life savings.

So-called wildcat banking was behind the collapse. Individual states had been allowed to set up their own banks and issue their own "wildcat currency." Alabama's bank, chartered in 1823 by state governor Israel Pickens, was one of many in the early 1800s to issue notes and coins. The federal government had set up the Bank of the United States to regulate the banks and maintain restrictions on the amount of currency they could issue, but the extent to which the government should be involved in such activities had been argued over virtually since independence from the British.

Andrew Jackson came to the presidency in 1829, exemplifying the spirit of the banks and emphasizing that the states be allowed to run their own affairs. The government's regulators had perhaps unwisely referred to the Bank of the United States as being based on the "English model"—a model that Jackson in general vehemently opposed. The son of poor Scotch-Irish immigrants, as a boy Jackson had been struck by a king's officer's sword and bore the scars on his arms and head. He gained revenge when in 1815 he led American forces to defeat the British army at the battle of New Orleans and remained critical of anything resembling an "English model."

Jackson, who hailed from the Carolinas, argued that the Bank of the United States was a corrupt monopoly set up to favor the interests of the political establishment in the Northeast of the country. Because of its controls, farmers and pioneers in the South and the West complained that they could not get enough credit. The president refused the bank's charter in 1836, whereupon the state banks, in a far less restrained fashion than before, began producing quantities of their own currency. Ten weeks before the end of Jackson's presidency, the economy collapsed, and he left the White House in 1837 with America's finances in a shocking state.

When Henry Lehman came to America, the debate over whether or not a central bank should exist remained a live one. President Tyler had taken office in April 1841, having been vice president to William Harrison. Harrison had caught a chill on the day of his inauguration and died a month later of pneumonia. His supporters had believed that Tyler would reintroduce the central bank idea as a rock on which to steady the economy. Shortly after Tyler took office, however, he, a Southern Democrat averse to interference by federal authorities in the nation's affairs, refused to do so. As a result, a mob marched on the White House, stoned and broke many of its windows, and threatened to storm the building. Tyler issued guns to the White House staff and ordered them to stand firm. Having satisfied themselves with burning an effigy of the president, the mob went away. Some seventy or so years later, in 1913 President Woodrow Wilson finally did create a central bank, the U.S Federal Reserve, and Lehman Brothers provided advisers to the government in setting it up.

At the time Henry set up his store, however, there was little confidence at all in money. Cash had been exposed as a myth—it was merely useless metal or paper if no one had faith in it. The greater faith of Alabama's cotton farmers and others was also under pressure. The state bank's financial failure had been followed by droughts, the devastation of crops, and outbreaks of yellow fever.

Farmers had very little spare cash at the best of times, and generally had to deal in credit. They borrowed on the promise to repay debts when their crops came in. Antebellum farmers in the South had long felt that bankers much preferred not to lend to them—the creators of material things and material wealth—but to merchants, the middlemen, who circulated such wealth as there was, making sure to take a good slice for themselves.

Henry Lehman, therefore, presented himself as the farmers' friend. He exchanged his goods for cash here and there but mainly for the goods the farmers had to offer. He bartered, he dealt—skills that he had brought with him from the Bavarian countryside. The farmers saw that they were getting a fair deal—trade in kind. They paid in cotton. The origin of the business that eventually became Lehman Brothers was solid practical goods that you could see and touch.

Lehman's gamble in deciding to settle in Montgomery paid off. A few months after he opened his store, the city was pronounced the capital of Alabama, thanks to the rise in its wealth. Someone must have known this was going to happen; someone like the people who had had all those hotels built. Montgomery set about improving itself as a showpiece and voted to allot seventy-five thousand dollars to build a new capitol building. It commissioned Stephen Button, a Philadelphia architect, to supervise its construction in the style of the Capitol in Washington, DC. The brick building, covered with stucco and with a gleaming white dome, was built in the area of the city known as Goat Hill.

Henry worked long hours and lived in one room behind his store, where he pored over his accounts late into the night by the light of a whale-oil lamp. He led a celibate existence, and locals regarded him as something of an oddball. According to Birmingham in *Our Crowd*, they called him "our little monk." The nighttime solitude amid the heat and proliferation of bugs he had not been used to in Germany may have encouraged him to worry about his health. "There is money to be made here," he wrote back home, "if the Fever does not get me first."

Its cause unknown, yellow fever worried everyone. Suspicion fell upon the recent innovation of the postal delivery service, and people wondered whether the improving communication system was carrying the virus. Henry and others in Montgomery walked around awkwardly, with blocks of sulfur in their shoes, and put sponges soaked in carbolic acid on their windowsills at night. No one yet knew that mosquitoes carried the disease.

Henry set about building a circle of friends. There was no doubting that he worked hard, but he allotted time for other responsibilities; "[n]o Jewish community was there to embrace Henry Lehman upon his arrival in Montgomery," wrote Roland Flade. Lehman and the dozen other Jewish men who lived in the city, all of them of German origin, set up a community, rented halls, and held services. Some of the men had families. Babies were born, and in about 1846 Montgomery witnessed its first circumcision. Henry's group bought land to use as a Jewish cemetery. Jews from nearby towns such as Selma attended celebrations and services on occasions including the Jewish New Year and Yom Kippur. Non-Jews participated in social events organized by the Jewish community.

Lehman appears to have been a main influence in its work. Flade writes that although the circle he joined had already discussed how to organize the city's Jews, much seems to have happened after his arrival. In 1846 the community grew to sixteen and founded the Hevra Mavaker Holim, a society aimed at "a close union of the members of the ancient faith" and the "proper observation of our religion." Henry redeemed himself for all those nonkosher meals on the road. The society began charity work, raising money to provide "nurses and support for the sick and distressed."

The U.S. crisis of the earlier part of the decade had given way to the "fabulous forties." President James Polk replaced the oil lamps and candles at the White House with new gaslights. Doubts existed, however, as to his vision. The son of a rich farmer and land speculator from Tennessee, Polk favored slavery and immediately annexed Texas. Northern politicians had agonized over accepting slave states such as Texas into the Union, fearing that would swing the balance of power in the United States toward the Southern states.

While Henry settled into amicable dealings with local cotton farmers, Alabama's fortunes surged. Demand from the mills of the U.S. Northeast and Europe for the South's "white gold" rapidly increased. Elias Howe's invention of the sewing machine had stepped up the mass production of clothing and the need for cotton. Lehman had worked to get some of his younger brothers to America, and his dispatches of money home enabled his brother Mendel to join him in 1847. Mendel was five years younger than Henry, and once in America he changed his name to Emanuel.

A year later the brothers moved to larger premises on Court Square, in the center of town and opposite the Exchange Hotel, the venture that had paid off as thriving Montgomery welcomed more visitors. Not all were welcomed, however. Outside the hotel stood the wooden platform, or "block," where the city auctioned its slaves. Court Square, as such, was a prime position in town and, as far as the Lehmans were concerned, a real indication of arrival. They put up a new sign: H. LEHMAN AND BRO.

For some people, these were the hopeful times at the end of the Mexican-American War. The Jewish community had grown to thirty and decided to set up Kahl Montgomery, a formal Montgomery congregation. It had a constitution, bylaws, and minutes recorded in German. In 1849, the congregation voted Henry as its first vice president and Emanuel as secretary. The Lehmans did not hesitate to put themselves in positions of responsibility and move themselves toward the top table.

Montgomery began to look the part of the state capital, and was as pleasant a place to live as any in the South. It had some handsomely built timber houses with hand-carved mantels and paneled stairs. It called itself a "city of flowers," with blossoming dogwood trees and gardens blooming with yellow jasmine, pinks, and azaleas. Cherokee rose hedges defined those gardens, and wisteria climbed the walls of the better-kept houses.

Montgomery had theaters and concerts. In addition to church—or in the Lehmans' case, the Kahl Montgomery—its citizens flocked to political rallies. Fiery Southern orators guided their secular thought. William Lowndes Yancey, a local newspaper owner and a member of the U.S. Congress, was among the most popular. The city asserted itself as a center of Southern feeling, and in 1848 stood against the tide of change when Yancey proclaimed the Alabama Platform. This was a response to what the South viewed as Northern interference in its affairs. As the United States had advanced into new areas like Texas, Northern politicians demanded that slavery be outlawed in them. The Alabama Platform declared that Washington had no right to do any such thing, and that the Democratic Party, then the majority in the South, should seek only presidential and vice presidential candidates who supported slavery.

In 1848 anger also exploded across Europe, though of a different political flavor. Liberal revolution demanding the emancipation of peoples swept from France into Germany and beyond. Just south of Bavaria, independence movements threatened the Austrian empire. According to the *Universal Jewish Encyclopedia*, Henry and Emanuel's youngest brother, Maier, played an active part in campaigning and stirring up the unrest. At first it appeared as if the effort had paid off. In 1849 the lower house of the Bavarian parliament passed a bill granting complete equality between Christians and Jews. Amid anti-Semitic protests, however, the upper house threw out the bill in February 1850. In Würzburg, the nearest large town to Rimpar, the *Neue Fränkische Zeitung*, the local newspaper, ran an article saying Bavarian Jews should seek emancipation through emigration to the United States.

Maier took the advice. He was twenty at the time and with all of life's prospects ahead of him. A radical in his own land, he had too many of the wrong type of friends. America, on the other hand, accepted people of a liberal mind. He set sail from Hamburg in May 1850 and arrived in Montgomery later that summer.

||||||||||

The turmoil surrounding the 1848 revolutions in Europe greatly added to the attractiveness of the United States as a place of refuge. In the 1850s, nearly one million Germans arrived in America. Most came to make a living after a number of bad harvests and because of poor European economic prospects in general, but Maier came as a political exile. From the outset, incidentally, his name became Mayer, though this may have had less to do with a wish to sound anglicized than simply being easier for most Americans to pronounce.

Others who came to America around this time and played important roles in U.S. life included Carl Schurz, a student revolutionary from the Rhineland and a member of the same liberal group as Mayer. Such groups embraced Christians and Jews alike, and Schurz was Christian. He had escaped from Germany to Switzerland and spent periods in Paris and London during what in Europe were tumultuous political times. The political hierarchies of several countries seemed, and felt, on the brink of overthrow. Schurz sailed for New York in 1852. In the United States he joined the Republican Party, and became a passionate supporter of President Abraham Lincoln and a Union army general during the Civil War. In his youth the authorities in Europe had regarded Schurz's views as a danger to security; on the contrary, in 1877 President Rutherford B. Hayes appointed him secretary of the interior.

In Germany and America, the Lehmans were friends of the Straus family. The father of the family, Lazarus Straus, took part in the German revolution in 1848 and later came to America to begin his working life there as a peddler. Oscar, his son and a good friend of Mayer's, went on to be the first Jewish member of a U.S. cabinet when, in 1907, Theodore Roosevelt made him commerce and labor secretary. Comfortably spanning any cultural differences between Jews and Muslims, he became Washington's man in Constantinople and ambassador to the Ottoman Empire. The Oscar Straus memorial, a marble fountain near the White House, commemorates his life. His grandsons, Isidor, who died on the

Titanic in 1912, and Nathan, co-owned Macy's. Some years hence, Lehman Brothers and Macy's would enjoy a profitable partnership.

Looking for better prospects than Europe could offer, Marcus Goldman in 1848 also emigrated to America. At age twenty-seven, Goldman came from Trappstadt in Bavaria, about thirty miles north of Rimpar. In the same year, Joseph Sachs emigrated to America from a village near Rimpar. Eventually the Goldmans and Sachses intermarried and set up the banking firm of Goldman Sachs, which at varying times would be in partnership and rivalry with Lehman Brothers.

Mayer Lehman retained the liberal beliefs that he brought with him from Germany. His son Herbert H. Lehman inherited them and put them to use in his work for Franklin D. Roosevelt's New Deal, to combat the Great Depression of the 1930s. By then, the philosophy of Adam Smith, the Scotsman and acknowledged father of economics, had guided American thinking since independence. Smith's book *The Wealth of Nations*, in which he laid out his principles, had appeared in 1776, the year of America's Revolution. Smith believed in the free market, that market forces should be left free of government intervention. Given that despots and nothing like modern democracy ruled in Smith's day, it was little wonder he felt like this. A deeply religious man, he believed the economy found its own equilibrium; its path was guided by God or, as Smith mysteriously put it, an "invisible hand." In 1848, while Europe was embroiled in revolution of its own, Karl Marx published his *Communist Manifesto*, rejecting religion and saying Smith's economics amounted to capitalist exploitation of the working class. With Mayer's son Herbert in a lead role, the New Deal would attempt to find a middle ground between the extremes of Smith and Marx.

Europe's problems in the mid-nineteenth century had grown under the mounting strains of industrialization. In the rural American South, meanwhile, industry played little part. Poor white sharecropping farmers lived in feudal conditions, indebted to those from whom they rented land or to those from whom they had borrowed the funds to till it. More primitive still were the living conditions of half the Southern population: the slaves who worked the plantations of cotton, tobacco, and sugar and tended to the family affairs of those who dictated their lives from the big house.

When Mayer Lehman arrived in Montgomery, cotton was providing a fine platform for the increase of wealth. Alabama supplied most of

America's cotton, and America supplied most of the world's. Henry and Emanuel gave Mayer a two-year apprenticeship and put him to work in a progressively busier office. They rustled up another sign for outside the door: LEHMAN BROTHERS.

Founded in 1850, Lehman Brothers came into existence in the same year that, out in the distant west, California gained statehood. California had had its gold rush the year before, and over the coming years Lehman Brothers and California symbolized the two contrasting business models of American life. California's was the get-rich-quick, high-risk, bet-the-farm model of the gold-rushing forty-niners. The life of Lehman Brothers, at least in the days when the family or family partners ran the firm, followed the more gradual and deliberative course portrayed by the old American maxim "Another day, another dollar." They still made more than enough money to go around.

With his brothers alongside him, Henry eased up a little and defined his priorities. In November 1849, at age twenty-seven, he married Rosa Wolf in Montgomery. Not a great deal is known about her, although her name indicates that she came from a German background. She also got on well with Emanuel and Mayer, to whom she was their "beloved aunt Rosa." Within six years, she and Henry had had four children, the oldest and youngest boys, with two girls in the middle.

Stephen Birmingham writes that the three Lehman brothers became part of Montgomery's social crowd and assimilated into Alabama life. Despite their Jewish heritage, they even enjoyed the state's passion for pork. He suggests that they acquired Southern accents, although Herbert Lehman remembers his father, Mayer, when the family later moved to New York, speaking with an enduring Teutonic lilt. Maybe in the 1850s they spoke in a mix of Alabamian and Bavarian dialects, which would have been worth recording for posterity had the technology been at hand. Whether all three Lehmans became men-about-town in Montgomery is uncertain: Henry had his family and Emanuel was quite reserved. Mayer, the most flamboyant, would have been up to the part.

One area in which the Lehmans fully assimilated was business. Religion again had to find its place. There was no financial sense in adhering to the Jewish Sabbath by closing early on Fridays and staying shut on Saturdays, the days that cotton farmers came to town. The Montgomery city directory listed Henry and his brothers as "grocers," but by now their general store played second string to the city's main line of trade. Robert Rosen in his book *The Jewish Confederates* cites a traveler of the day who described Montgomery's citizens as thinking, eating, drinking, and dreaming cotton. As they led cotton lives, so "they marry cotton wives and unto them are born cotton children."

Soon the brothers advertised themselves as "Agents for the Sale of Leading Southern Domestics," domestics meaning cotton items used around the house: "osnaburgs, sheetings, shirtings, yarn, cotton rope, and ball thread." Osnaburgs were heavy, coarse fabrics used for grain sacks, upholstery, and drapery. In old Germany the Lehmans had lived in a land of vassals and princes. They had successfully made their escape, though to a place ruled, in the phrase of the day, by "King Cotton."

They moved more and more into cotton broking. Brokers provided the link between the sellers—the farmers—and the buyers—the industrialists and exporters. Brokers "read" the market. Their job was to know before anyone else the figures on how much farmers had grown that season and how much the industry and export people might want to buy. They studied the data, the sacred texts, and made their own story of them. Brokers were commercial versions of priests—the Bible was open to everyone to read, but the priests had the Latin.

Some people were just better placed than others to interpret the market's apparent mysteries. The Lehman Brothers' craft adhered to the philosophical dictum "Only connect." They connected the parts and, acting as go-betweens, took their share for having carried out this service. The French, of course, had the word for it: *entrepreneur*. Henry Lehman may have heard this term on his now regular travels to the important cotton port of New Orleans.

The Lehmans branched out and got around. As a family man, Henry confined his journeys to the Old South, mainly to New Orleans' cotton docks and warehouses. Emanuel took frequent trips to New York to speak to textile factory owners and exporters. He also had to check on the increasing sums of money paid by these people to Lehman Brothers through New York banks.

Mayer stayed at home in Montgomery to run the office. Once the apprentice, he became the family's chief cotton expert: "mastering every intricacy and nuance of the trade with the same patience and persistence his ancestors had applied to the Talmud," wrote Kenneth Libo. He had the chance to indulge his fancy for being the man-about-town. Mayer was not only the gregarious brother but also the most political, and he managed to mix with all the right people.

Not much, it seemed, could go wrong for Lehman Brothers. The brothers had worked the firm into a position where its future was as assured as the rising price of cotton. But in 1855 tragedy took revenge on the brothers for such presumption. A yellow fever epidemic hit Montgomery, which caused Henry great anxiety. His brothers urged him to escape it by going to New Orleans. He went, but the fever pursued him. In sync with his fears, Henry contracted it.

Not until the Spanish-American War at the end of the century did anyone learn that mosquitoes spread the disease, and this long-sought knowhow came fifty years too late for Henry. The disease ran its course: First came headaches and fever, which would sometimes pass and cause victims to believe they were on the road to recovery. Then the skin turned yellow and their gums began to bleed. Again, this might pass amid claims that the worst was past. Then delirium took over and victims fell into a coma from which there was no escape. Henry Lehman did not make it back to Montgomery and was buried in New Orleans in November 1855.

Devastated as they were, the brothers—Emanuel, twenty-nine, and Mayer, twenty-six—had to move on and build on Henry's foundations. Their course faced north. While Mayer took care of affairs in Montgomery, Emanuel moved to New York. Cotton was America's most important raw material and New York its largest city, the business capital of a rapidly growing nation. Henry's death had shown that while you needed friends and family around you, that might not be enough in the event of disaster. With the migrant's instinct, the Lehman brothers built into their thinking the essential element of any business plan: always make sure to have an exit route.

2

"It's All Over"

In 1854, the year before Henry died, the Lehmans bought a slave. The deed confirming the sale was in the name of H. Lehman & Brother, even though the third brother, Mayer, had already come to America and joined the business. The person they bought was named Martha, age fourteen. The deed confirmed she was "sound in body and mind" and a "slave for life," and that the purchase price was nine hundred dollars (about twenty-one thousand dollars in today's terms).

After Henry died and Emanuel moved to New York, Mayer Lehman would eventually have seven slaves, four women and three men. Some were household workers. Roland Flade points out that others may have been used in the firm, presumably to do general work in and around the office. While the majority of slaves in the South worked on the plantations or as household servants, their owners employed them in various ways, including as office workers.

Mayer had fought for freedom in Germany yet accepted slavery in the American South. From his location in the family office in Court Square, he would have seen the buying and selling of slaves taking place outside the Exchange Hotel. W. H. Russell, a correspondent from the London *Times*, visited the town and recorded his thoughts on July 13, 1861, during the Civil War, for *Harper's Weekly* magazine. He witnessed the sale of a young man in his midtwenties for $975. Russell, who declared himself not to be a "sentimentalist," had seen slave markets in Asia and wrote that the atmosphere of those "deprived them of the disagreeable harshness and matter-of-fact character of the transaction before me. . . . Here it grated on my ear to listen to the familiar tones of the English tongue as the medium by which the transfer was effected."

As well-educated people who had seen something of the world, both

Mayer and Emanuel could hardly have ignored what was happening in the country. *Uncle Tom's Cabin*, by Harriet Beecher Stowe, which portrayed the horrors of slavery, became a bestseller after its publication in 1852. In the western territory of Kansas, proslavers and abolitionists had fought in violent hand-to-hand combat. In 1856, John Brown, a bitter opponent of slavery, was at the center of several bloody battles in the state, leading newspapers to coin the moniker "Bleeding Kansas."

But Mayer and Emanuel remained ardent Southern Democrats. "Jews wanted to acclimate themselves in every way to their environment," wrote Bertram Wallace Korn in his essay "Jews and Negro Slavery in the Old South, 1789–1865." "[I]n both a social and psychological sense, they needed to be accepted as equals by their fellow citizens." Oscar Straus noted that whatever people in the South thought about slavery, they "would not, except in rare instances, speak against it; and even then in the most private and guarded way." In keeping with this custom, the Lehman family kept its head down on the subject. Possibly on the credit side, at least two of the former slaves, as freed people, followed Mayer and his family when they eventually moved north after the Civil War. One, a woman, helped bring up several of the Lehman children in New York.

In the late 1850s, the Lehmans stayed out of the melee and kept their eyes on the economy, which was showing signs of going out of control. Congress had made large areas of federal land available for the thrusting progress of the railroads. Prices of the land rose dramatically, as did the price of shares churned out by railroad companies. The real value of the railroad companies—as measured by their land and other assets—did not justify the issue of so many shares. The government, meanwhile, printed a lot of money to keep people buying them and to maintain the pace of the economy in general. There was not enough tangible wealth—in particular, gold—to back the money; the gold standard still operated, and people had the right to swap their paper dollars for gold. When, in 1857, a boat bringing gold from the prospecting fields of California sank, it set off a bank and stock market panic in the East.

The Lehmans were not marred by this. They operated according to their own, if unofficial, standard—the cotton standard. They had large quantities of the commodity in their warehouses and began to set themselves up as commercial bankers. Depositors lodged their money with them knowing that it was as safe as the Lehmans' cotton reserves. In

New York, Emanuel established the firm's first office without any set-backs from the panic of 1857. At 119 Liberty Street, the office was only a short walk from the pandemonium of the stock exchange and the area that, in the next century, would become the home of the World Trade Center. It was modestly sized, and before long, Emanuel would be looking for larger premises.

The brothers got along very well, though their characters were different. Emanuel was the more cautious. Mayer, it was said, was all "buy, buy," Emanuel, "sell, sell." According to family tradition, wrote Kenneth Libo, "Mayer made the money; Emanuel made sure they didn't lose it." Mayer was a natural salesman, a socializer and contact maker. *A Centennial* characterized him as the firm's "Mr. Outside"; Emanuel was its "Mr. Inside," who quietly held the firm together. Lehman Brothers began and grew as a balanced, tightly run, and carefully managed enterprise.

Mayer married in 1858 shortly before his twenty-eighth birthday. He had taken over Henry's duties of traveling to New Orleans, where some of the Goldsmith family had moved from Mobile. He married Babette New-gass of New Orleans, a relative of the Goldsmiths, who also hailed from Bavaria. She had arrived in the United States about four years after Mayer, around 1854. She was eight years younger, though that never inhibited her in her relationship with Mayer: "[S]he advised him constantly," wrote Allan Nevins in his biography of Mayer's son Herbert. One possible interpretation of that is that Babette bossed Mayer around. If so, Nevins added, she did it "with such practical keenness that he never took an important business step without consulting her." They had eight children over the next two decades, four born in the South and four in the North.

In 1859, Emanuel married Pauline Sondheim, a young New York woman with whom he would have five children. Of the oldest and youngest, Milton and Albert, very little is recorded in any Lehman family histories. Philip, the second-eldest, went on to become senior partner in the firm. Harriet, the oldest daughter, married her cousin Sigmund. Her sister, Evelyn, married Jules Ehrich, proprietor of Ehrich Bros. department store at Sixth Avenue and Twenty-third Street.

Emanuel's was a fully New York family. He rented a brownstone in one of the city's best neighborhoods, Murray Hill, which was marked by the mansions of the wealthy. The Lehmans' house was close to that of Joseph Seligman, founder of J.&W. Seligman, one of New York's leading banks—*the* bank of the Jewish community. Emanuel placed himself and the family close to the Seligmans because he thought of them as good models. They, too, had come from Bavaria and risen from peddlers to financiers, though faster than the Lehmans. Emanuel may have wanted to study their methods.

In Montgomery, Babette and Mayer had their first child, Sigmund, in 1859. Hattie, Lisette, and Benjamin followed at two-year intervals, though Benjamin, born near the end of the Civil War in 1865, died in infancy. The family lived in a house that covered most of a city block. It was an imposing two-and-a-half-story structure, finely designed with elements of Italianate and Greek Revival architecture. The house spoke of the growing confidence of Montgomery and of the Lehmans; it was just across from the office, and the firm's clerks came to eat with the family at lunchtime.

Mayer and Babette enjoyed themselves as popular members of the city community. "My mother used to tell us," recalled Herbert Lehman, the youngest of their eight children, that "they entered into the social life very well." Mayer communed with friends and colleagues at the Exchange Hotel and frequented newspaper offices, whether to pick up the latest gossip or contribute to it.

The dome of the capitol building on Goat Hill rose almost a hundred feet above the well-tended lawns. During the buildup to the Civil War, Montgomery's population of nine thousand—half of which were slaves—was about half that of Mobile, but it was the political center of Alabama and to a considerable extent that of the South. Mayer's circle of friends and contacts included a succession of state governors, senators, and other legislators. He knew Jefferson Davis, the U.S. senator for Mississippi who would soon be declared president of the Confederate states.

Mayer continued his brothers' tradition of working for the city's Jewish community. In 1859 he and five others had formed a committee to build a synagogue; Mayer was the treasurer, and donations came from as far away as New Orleans. The committee bought land for it at the corner of Catoma and Church streets, a few blocks from the capitol. Completed in 1862, it was a sober red-brick construction in Romanesque style, with a double-stone staircase and decorative wrought-iron railings leading up to its tripartite facade. Local historians believe it was the only synagogue built in the South during the Civil War.

Mayer gained acceptance beyond the Jewish community. He and Babette were invited to the houses of other successful business families, and by 1860 he had become a member of the city's Masonic lodge. In joining this organization, whose members were drawn from Montgomery's social elite, Mayer gained "the definite seal of civic approval," wrote Roland Flade. A family that had emerged from a Jewish ghetto in small-town Bavaria had, in America, friendships and alliances that cut across ethnic and religious lines.

As the Lehmans emerged, however, the South was disappearing into a ghettoized world of its own making. It made great profits but with little thought given to its general direction. On a practical level, it was dangerously dependent on one item—cotton. In the 1850s, a number of Alabama entrepreneurs had tried to develop the state's industry. To them it seemed a good idea to have more railroads or more factories making iron. Their ideas gained little traction. The organizers of the annual state fair in Montgomery had made an earnest bid to diversify the local economy in 1856. Thousands of people turned up to see exhibits of livestock, cereal crops, vegetables, and fruit, and experts offered farmers advice on how to produce them. Then everyone went away and carried on with the business of cotton. They believed they would lose money doing anything else.

Cotton had given the South an exaggerated sense of its own power. As producers of so much of the world's cotton, Alabama and the other Southern states were beginning to believe they should seize control of their destiny. One point that the Lehmans grasped but most other Southerners did not was that an important part of that control was already embedded elsewhere. The factories of the American Northeast and England and other parts of Europe provided the main sources of demand for cotton. New York was progressively becoming the link to them and effectively the economic capital of the South. Lehman Brothers had a foot in each U.S. camp, North and South, while the South hared off into a world of its own.

The first of the Southern states to secede from the Union, South Carolina, did so in December 1860, right after President Lincoln's election. Soon the focus shifted to Alabama. On February 4, 1861, Montgomery's cannons roared and bells rang out as the delegates of the, by now, six seceding states met in the city to form a Confederate government. Later in the month large crowds gathered on the lawns of Goat Hill to witness Jefferson Davis being sworn in as president on the balcony of the capitol.

A few days later Davis was to be found on another balcony, that of the Exchange Hotel, where, *A Centennial* reported, he stood "to accept the wild acclaim of throngs in Court Square." Excited members of Mayer Lehman's family and staff would have been close at hand, whether in the exuberant crowd or watching from the firm's offices across the way.

Montgomery became the first Confederate capital, and Alabama was proclaimed the "Cradle of the Confederacy." Over the next couple of months, Montgomery was "a seething depot for troops and provisions, loud with war activities." Davis and his family occupied what was known as the First White House of the Confederacy, a modest two-story frame house painted white with green shutters at the corner of Bibb and Lee streets. Young men immodestly dashed off to war. Their only fear was that they would not reach the front before the South won—they just knew they could not lose.

Emanuel Lehman acquired a quite different view of events from New York. Lincoln's blockade of the Southern states from April 1861 cut the flow of Southern cotton to the North and Lehman Brothers' income from Northern textile makers. Southern cotton would have to run the blockade if it was to get across the Atlantic to its other markets in England and continental Europe. As business seized up, a desperate Emanuel realized that the product of many years of effort could rapidly be lost. Maybe, privately, he allowed himself the indulgence of questioning how his Southern compatriots—even his brother—had allowed this chaos to happen. The South had been in a jubilant "buy, buy" mood in the political market, when Emanuel would have chosen to "sell, sell." He saw the latest developments in apocalyptic terms. In Lehman Brothers' offices on Liberty Street, he reached instinctively back to his mother tongue to express his emotions. He scrawled on a notepad, *"Alles ist beendet"* ("It's all over").

It was not over in the complete manner that Emanuel feared. Once he calmed down, and he and Mayer took stock of the circumstances, the situation was less grim than he had imagined. During the Civil War the trading of cotton fell sharply but did not stop. The South desperately needed to sell cotton to pay for the war, and the North required cotton, not least for the factories churning out uniforms for the Union army.

In their early thirties when the war broke out, Emanuel and Mayer could have joined the Confederate army, but they put their particular skills to better use. They became blockade-runners—not exactly kosher Rhett

Butlers, but respectable and bearded versions of him. Mayer maneuvered whatever cotton he could through the blockade, and Emanuel sold it to an eager market in New York. Some cotton from the South that went to New York had to travel via England to evade the blockade, completing two crossings of the Atlantic.

Matters may have eased when the Northern navy took control of New Orleans in May 1862. That year, Mayer moved part of Lehman Brothers' business there and went into partnership with Benjamin Newgass, Babette's brother. If it was at all possible to get more cotton out through the blockade—through diplomacy, delicate negotiations, and conceivably even bribes—then Lehman Brothers was well placed to do so.

Emanuel made trips to England during the war. On one occasion in late 1863, he also took his family to Germany. On the surface, this was a way of getting his wife, children, and himself back in touch with their roots. Then again, this was not exactly the time for a comfortable jaunt around Europe. In Prussia, Count Otto von Bismarck, the chancellor and power behind the throne of Kaiser Wilhelm I, was preparing for the wars that would unite the German states. In the 1860s and early 1870s he would launch military exercises against Denmark, Austria, and France for this purpose. The Prussian army, therefore, needed a lot of uniforms, and the price of cotton would have been good. Emanuel, the practical Lehman brother, was unlikely to have conducted such a trip for tourist and sentimental purposes alone.

Mayer Lehman suggested to Emanuel that on his trips to England he act as an agent for the sale of Confederate bonds. Bonds are debt. Borrowers sell bonds to a lender with the agreement that they will pay back money after a specific period. On top of the repayment is a fixed rate of interest, the lender's profit from the exercise. During the early stages of the war, Emanuel found Europe was keener to buy bonds from the South than those hawked around at the same time by Northern salesmen. England especially favored the Southern cause, thanks to the good business it did with the South in the cotton trade.

On one embarrassing occasion in a London office, Emanuel was selling Southern bonds when he came across Joseph Seligman attempting to sell bonds for the North. Emanuel had intended to keep his eye on Seligman, his Murray Hill neighbor, but in New York rather than London. "Their manner toward each other was cool, reserved," writes Birmingham in

Our Crowd. But although both men were loyal to their causes, they were not really in the business of fighting a war: "[T]hey were in the business of making money."

Back in Montgomery, Mayer strengthened the firm's position when in 1863 he went into partnership with John Wesley Durr, a leading cotton merchant. They formed Lehman, Durr & Co. and bought the Alabama Warehouse Company, one of Montgomery's main centers for storing and selling cotton. Durr, who was not Jewish, also held the important political position of city alderman.

Toward the end of the war, and with matters not going at all the South's way, Mayer planned a grand coup that might have worked wonderfully well but proved totally naive. His aim was to exploit his political connections to get cotton worth half a million dollars through to the North and use the proceeds to clothe and feed desperate Alabamian prisoners of war in Northern jails. Mayer took his idea to Thomas Hill Watts, the Alabama governor and a friend, and then to Jefferson Davis in Richmond, Virginia. The Confederacy had switched its base from Montgomery to Richmond, as Virginia, one of the oldest American states, was viewed as a more prestigious place for a capital. Mayer handed Davis a letter of reference from Watts: "I have appointed Mr. Mayer Lehman as the agent of the State," wrote the Alabama governor, describing Mayer as "one of the best Southern patriots." Though "a foreigner," he added, Lehman had "been here fifteen years and is thoroughly identified with us."

Davis gave the go-ahead, and in January 1865 Mayer wrote a letter explaining the idea to, of all people, General Ulysses S. Grant, commander of the Northern forces: "General: We have the honor to announce to you that the Legislature of the State of Alabama has appropriated $500,000 for the relief of prisoners from that State held by the United States." Mayer detailed how, with the general's permission, a Northern ship would carry cotton of that value from Mobile to New York "for the purposes of supplying the prisoners from that State with blankets, clothing and other such things as may be necessary for their comfort." Mayer asked for Grant's approval to pass through the battle lines between the two sides in order to supervise the plan's execution from the North. He concluded: "We make this request with confidence, assured that your sympathies for the unfortunate brave will lead you to do all in your power to promote the benevolent design entrusted to us by the State of Alabama."

The scheme showed how out of touch with reality Mayer and the South were. It had been a bloody war, and while the South might have entered it as a battle between country gentlemen, this was not the North's perspective. Grant ignored the letter. Mayer waited in a chilly Richmond for a response, and even wrote a reminder. He appended a copy of the original as if the initial version might have been lost in the general's in-box. Mayer finally gave up and went home, possibly reflecting that Grant wasn't nicknamed "Unconditional Surrender" for nothing.

Montgomery escaped lightly from the war. Just to the west, in Selma, fighting continued for several days after General Robert E. Lee, the South's leader, signed the surrender at Appomattox Court House on April 9, 1865. The Lehmans suffered some damage, although this was self-inflicted. Retreating Confederate troops set fire to the Alabama Warehouse in order to keep the cotton it held out of enemy hands. Mayer was assessing the damage when some fourteen thousand Union cavalry entered Montgomery on April 12, with "flags flying, bands playing, spurs and swords jingling," wrote Allan Nevins. "[N]ot a word was uttered to offend the people," although Mayer's family "doubtless shared the general apprehension as this force rode in from the west." The people of Montgomery, the Lehmans among them, "witnessed the spectacle from doors and windows in melancholy silence."

Even now the Lehmans came out of things well, and their alliance with the Durr family proved to be a particular advantage. Mayer and John Wesley Durr had saved a considerable sum of money during the war and changed it into gold. As the Northern army searched the town, the Lehmans and Durrs decided that one of the few safe places to hide it was beneath Mrs. Durr's skirts. As uncivilized as people in the Confederacy believed Northern troops to be, the Lehmans and Durrs imagined that they would stop short of searching the underwear of a mature lady. Their supposition was correct, and when the troops had moved from the Durr household to other premises, the gold was intact. This story was told years later by Virginia Durr, John Wesley Durr's granddaughter-in-law, a friend of Martin Luther King, Jr., the civil rights leader, and herself a passionate advocate of civil rights.

Montgomery's capitol building was shabby, the city's houses dilapidated and unpainted, and much of the railroad line to West Point ripped up to salvage iron for the war effort. The wharves were falling into the Alabama River. Yet by summer the Lehman offices were doing brisk business.

Everyone still needed cotton. By 1866, New Orleans was shipping a third of all the cotton coming from American ports, and much of it was being handled by the Lehman Brothers office there run by Babette's brother, Benjamin.

In New York, Emanuel moved into larger business premises. By 1868, he was at 133–135 Pearl Street, a block or so from Wall Street and just off Hanover Square, where the main cotton brokers of the city had their offices. Lehman Brothers had, with new vibrancy, started up again.

|||||||||

In the Reconstruction period after the war, Lehman Brothers took on a large part of the task of getting Alabama moving. Much of the state was left devastated, with houses destroyed, fields abandoned, cotton gins and ironworks burned. Mobile, the main port, was in ruins, and the state's railroad system had been destroyed.

Some of the most important initial steps to be taken were political, and in November 1867 Alabama staged its first constitutional convention to begin its return to the Union. The state could not pay for the meeting, and Lehman Brothers provided one hundred thousand dollars for the purpose. It is not clear whether any other benefactors put up money, but at the time, a hundred thousand dollars would have gone a long way toward organizing the whole event.

Alabama appointed Lehman Brothers to be its fiscal agent, the firm's chief task being to raise money for the state and manage its debt. To an extent this was a continuation of Emanuel Lehman's work during the war: Lehman Brothers sold Alabama's bonds to raise money that was vital to the process of transforming Alabama from a slave state of the old agrarian South to an industrial part of a truly capitalist United States. Given Alabama's and the South's low credit rating after the war, however, selling the bonds was not easy. Lehman Brothers also managed Alabama's repayments of its debt and interest charges from the limited funds that the state had available.

With responsibilities of this kind, Lehman Brothers took a further step from being simply a commodity broker dealing in cotton toward a business more akin to that of a bank. It was no doubt exhausting work, and it is not known how large a staff Mayer had to help him cope with the task.

In 1867 he took Babette and their three children to Germany to visit their families and, quite possibly, to impress them with their success in the new world. A photograph taken during the trip in Würzburg shows Mayer against a Victorian backdrop of drawing room curtains. Dressed in a suit complete with a watch chain and buttoned waistcoat, he leans nonchalantly on an amply cushioned chair. He seems, in every way, to embody the confident nineteenth-century businessman. The picture may have belied the truth, though, because circumstances back in Alabama were deteriorating.

The state government fell under the control of carpetbaggers and scalawags. Carpetbaggers were politicians and businessmen from the North seeing what they could pick up amid the ruins of the South. Scalawags were their Southern counterparts, out to profit from the South's fall. With the old social structure broken down, security deteriorated in Montgomery and other cities. There were a rising number of attacks and robberies. "No woman was safe on the streets," complained Mary Powell, one of the Lehmans' city neighbors. "[L]ife became almost unendurable."

Roland Flade notes that Mayer wanted to get away from the racial and political strife. The Ku Klux Klan, the Knights of the White Camelia, and other white supremacist groups fought the social and political changes that followed the end of the war, most notably the emancipation of slaves. Such groups found ready support among younger rural whites and former slave owners. The KKK and others were also no fans of foreigners, wealthy businessmen, or Jews. Mayer fit all three categories.

He had an exit route. Emanuel was doing well in the North. The management of the Montgomery side of the business could be left with the Durrs and that in New Orleans with Benjamin Newgass. In 1868, therefore, Mayer made his departure from the South. He initially came to New York alone, but he was followed later by Babette, their three children, and the family employees who had formerly been slaves. Some years later Babette told her youngest son, Herbert, of the tough nature of the journey, particularly in its early stages. "For some time after the war, there was very little communication between the South and Washington," Herbert later recalled. "The railroads had been destroyed. She told us that when she got to the Potomac, there was a bridge across, but there was no railroad connection." Babette completed the journey without harm, however, and thus the family was reunited in the North.

For Lehman Brothers as a business the move was a convenient one. Mayer could concentrate on the cotton side of the enterprise, while Emanuel had already branched out into buying and selling other things, such as petroleum, coffee, and sugar. In 1870, along with 130 or so other cotton merchants, Mayer organized the New York Cotton Exchange in a building in Hanover Square. Previously, buying and selling had gone on between the brokers scattered in their various offices, but now the process was brought into one central trading forum.

The exchange was a "futures" market, which meant that buyers and sellers bought and sold ahead of when the cotton was ready in the fields or needed in the factories. Other futures markets had existed for some time. Japan had had a rice exchange for two hundred years; Chicago, out by the nation's breadbasket and plains of the Midwest, had its grain market. The cotton exchange was the first such market for so-called commodities in New York.

The futures market was important not least because farmers needed money upfront in order to buy machinery, fertilizers, and other necessities so that they could deliver their product later. In part, cotton buyers put up the money; customers such as factory owners used the market to commit to buying in the future at a price they could agree on in the present. This helped them plan their budgets and their production schedules. But a good deal of the money came from traders buying and selling contracts on the cotton exchange. This helped provide the pool of "liquidity"—cash—from which a farmer coming to market to sell his future harvest would be paid.

Traders traded contracts, not actual cotton; they traded the right to buy the cotton rather than the cotton itself. The contract, therefore, was an early form of derivative—it was an investment that was one step removed from the cotton and not directly related to the commodity. Hence, it was "derived." Another way to put it is that it is a kind of side bet on the market: Most of those who traded the contracts were gambling on which way the price of cotton would move.

Traders are fast thinkers. One of them might hear some quiet word of scant rains in Mississippi and a likely poor crop come harvesttime. He would therefore buy a contract now, at an agreed price, giving him the right to take delivery of cotton at some future time. He would know that when the rest of the market soon heard the weather outlook, other traders would scramble to do the same. Hence the price of cotton would rise and he would be able to sell the contract for profit. A trader's task is to deal in the short term: How cheaply can I buy this contract for now and how much can I sell it for as quickly as possible?

Mayer Lehman was on the first board of governors of the cotton exchange and took charge of its finances. After the one for cotton, New York opened other exchanges for cheese, butter, and eggs. Lehman Brothers joined the coffee exchange in the early 1880s; it was the patriotic drink and a good market to be in; tea, of Boston Harbor fame, was the tipple of the English colonizers of old. Lehman Brothers also joined other exchanges, such as the one for sugar and, in 1884, the new petroleum exchange. Oil was vital for industry and home heating; cars remained some way off.

Together Emanuel and Mayer were part of the New York scene: "[F]amiliar on the streets of downtown Manhattan were the two Lehman brothers," wrote Stephen Birmingham. They were well liked and generally in such good humor that friends called them "the Cheeryble Brothers," after the twins Charles and Ned Cheeryble, the wealthy and humanitarian merchants in Charles Dickens's novel *Nicholas Nickleby*. Emanuel and Mayer, although not twins, looked alike, with high foreheads, bright eyes, and full beards. In their frock coats and gray-black striped trousers, they could give the impression of being in two places at the same time. Their characters did remain different, though; as Nevins wrote, photographs show "the optimistic Mayer with a gay bow tie, the conservative Emanuel with a sober cravat."

But it was a different kind of community from the one Mayer and Emanuel had been used to in the South. In 1870, about eighty thousand Jews lived in New York, comprising just under a tenth of the population. Its richer members lived in midtown Manhattan, and many, like the Lehmans, had emigrated from Germany. Some, again like the Lehmans, had accumulated wealth in other parts of the United States and moved to New York during or soon after the Civil War. The Lehmans had enjoyed free and easy relations with the gentile elite in Montgomery, but they did not in New York.

Non-Jewish banks, law firms, and hospitals would not accept Jewish partners or directors. Wealthy New York German Jewish families, therefore, also segregated themselves and inhabited "a universe parallel to that from which they had been excluded," observed Kenneth Libo in *Lots of Lehmans*. The heads of the families met at the synagogue and served on the same boards of hospitals and charities. The white Anglo-Saxon Protestants, or WASPs, stood on one side of a gaping social divide and the Jews of *Our Crowd* on the other.

Mayer, with his social skills, soon adapted to the circumstances as he found them, though he probably toned down his politics, at least in public in the early years after the Civil War. The North's hero, Ulysses S. Grant, with whom Mayer had had his one-sided correspondence during the conflict, was elected president in 1868. Although Mayer remained a Democrat, these were times when diplomacy was called for. People with his party loyalties had to deal not only with being on the losing side in the recent war but also on the one identified with slavery. Besides, Mayer had family life to get on with. Babette gave birth to their fourth child, Clara, in 1870.

As for Emanuel, he had been a Southern patriot but not as political a person as Mayer. He concentrated on business. In the Jewish community, many people specialized in retail, wholesale, or manufacturing, but the banking members saw themselves as a cut above. As Birmingham points out, a shop or a factory had to be shut one day a week, or at least overnight; a banker's money loaned out at interest never stopped working. In 1873 Emanuel took a clear step into banking, his first of several on behalf of Lehman Brothers: He helped set up the Queens County Bank in Long Island and took a seat on its board of directors.

A steady hand was needed, since a lot of wild speculation was going on both in banking and on the stock markets, largely due to vicious competition for control of the railroads. Key participants, like Jay Gould, James Fisk, and Daniel Drew, became known as "robber barons," and carried out various issues of dubious shares on the stock market. They fought for railroad domination with such characters as Cornelius Vanderbilt, originally a shipping entrepreneur who now pursued the profit motive on dry land.

F. Scott Fitzgerald would later memorialize Jay Gould as Jay Gatsby in his 1925 novel *The Great Gatsby*. In one of his conspiracies, Gould had tried to buy all the available gold in New York City and thereby cause a shortage; he would then have sold it at grossly inflated prices. He was only prevented from doing so when President Grant ordered a fast release of federal gold onto the market to ease prices. At one stage Gould admitted to the title of "the most hated man in America." But while he was happy to hog the attention, he had a partner in his schemes: Joseph Seligman. Upstanding *Our Crowd* figure though he appeared to be, Seligman had another side. He was so trusted in high circles that Grant offered him the post of treasury secretary. Seligman refused the honor; he was making far more money teaming up with Gould.

The stock market collapsed on September 19, 1873, "Black Friday." With Wall Street destabilized by railroad speculation, a run on the stock exchange in Vienna, Austria, was enough to send the New York exchange into a spin. Then, as now, the world was truly a global economy. Several large U.S. banks collapsed, badly affecting town and country areas alike. Congress demanded that Grant—recently elected for a second term—put more money into circulation to ease the crisis, but the president would not. The Republicans were the party of sound money, and he was not going to start throwing dollars around.

How long the effects of the 1873 collapse lasted is a matter of historical debate. Some say about four years, while others argue that the recession turned into a great "long depression" that continued for over twenty years, into the mid-1890s. Improved communications—shipping, railroads, and so on—brought down the costs of producing things and contributed to a protracted period of price deflation. Farmers were hit badly as the price of imported food fell. Their homegrown goods could not compete.

An event of great relevance to Lehman Brothers was the opening of the Suez Canal in Egypt in 1869. Egyptian cotton was a high-class alternative to American cotton. The canal also meant large parts of the Western world could get their cotton more quickly than before from distant places like India.

The firm decided to spread its activities from businesses based on agriculture to others connected to industry. This was largely thanks to Emanuel, who had moved on from the rural ways of the Old South. His Lehman Brothers, for example, organized a syndicate of New York investors to back Samuel Noble, an iron and steel expert originally from Cornwall in southwest England. Noble had set up business in Georgia but moved across the state line to northern Alabama, an area that proved to have large reserves of coal, limestone, and iron ore, the minerals required to make steel. Supported by Lehman Brothers, Noble began his Woodstock Iron Company in Anniston, Alabama, in 1873. Once the worst effects of that year's crash had passed, the city of Birmingham, sixty miles to the southwest, took the cue and turned the region into one of America's main iron and steel centers.

As the United States celebrated its hundredth birthday in 1876, Mayer and Babette marked the occasion with the birth of another child, Irving, and the construction of a new house: a five-story brownstone near Central Park at 5 East Sixty-second Street. They needed the living space; another son, Arthur, had arrived in 1873 and Herbert would follow in 1878. The house "had the characteristic Victorian ungainliness of the period," wrote Herbert's biographer, Nevins, "long stairs, airless central rooms, and gloomy furniture." The most attractive room was the long parlor, which was "furnished with late Victorian pieces, upholstered in light gold satin so as to produce a bright effect." The boys were not allowed in there and spent a lot of time in the library.

Proof that Lehman Brothers had spotted the historical trends came when America staged the great Centennial Exhibition of 1876. Held in the spring and summer and across vast fairgrounds in Philadelphia, the event signified America's arrival into the world's select group of industrialized countries. News from the Little Big Horn in Montana of Lieutenant Colonel George Custer's demise at the end of June added a sour note to the July Fourth celebrations, but such battles in the territories were of a passing era. The invention of barbed wire in 1873 had tamed large parts of the West, and a railroad now crossed the country. At the great Centennial event, huge turbines on show noiselessly provided power for the entire exhibition, and cooling cascades of water from roof to floor gave visitors relief from the worst of the summer heat. The Prussian ambassador, representing the recently unified German nation, commented on how limited Germany's machines were by comparison.

The Centennial Exhibition also showed the remarkable inventiveness of the United States. A large and growing nation, with few people in many of its areas and vast spaces to cross, the United States had developed a fascination and talent for technology. Alexander Graham Bell, a Scotsman though lately of Boston, exhibited his telephone, Thomas Edison, his latest refinements to the telegraph system. Visitors saw other inventions, such as the typewriter, for the first time. "The American invents as the Greek sculpted and the Italian painted," wrote a reporter from the London *Times*. "[I]t is genius."

Rutherford B. Hayes, a Republican, entered the White House in 1877. With the effects of the economic collapse four years earlier still apparent, Hayes stood for calm and sobriety. His wife, Lucille, refused to serve alcohol at White House receptions and became popularly styled as "Lemonade Lucy." The president denied appeals to print money to ease the economic crisis, nor would he put more gold and silver into circulation. Americans had the world before them but still had to live within their means.

Increased trade union activity, however, indicated that average Americans felt their means were rather stretched. The president dispatched federal troops to break a lengthy strike on the railroads that began in July 1877 in Martinsburg, West Virginia, and over forty-five days spread from city to city. Troops and strikers clashed in bloody battles in Baltimore, Pittsburgh, Chicago, and other cities. Hayes, however, had plenty of military muscle at hand; when he came into office he had declared the end of Reconstruction and withdrawn federal troops from the South.

Lehman Brothers pursued the logic of the president's thinking: It was safe, he was suggesting, to go back into the South. The North, meanwhile, was troublesome, with workers demanding better money and conditions. Southerners, by contrast, would be glad to have work. Lehman Brothers, with a foot on both sides of the Mason-Dixon Line, set about providing it.

Cotton was a prime candidate for industrial development. For decades, the North had bought Southern cotton cheaply (and the Lehmans had sold it to them). The mills of New York State and New England had then processed it into clothes and other textile goods and sold it at a great profit. Lehman Brothers would now, on both its own and the South's behalf, claim some of that benefit.

In 1878 Mayer and Emanuel set up the Tallassee Falls Manufacturing Company near Montgomery with themselves and John Wesley Durr on the board of directors. The company became an important part of the expanding Southern textile economy. The Lehmans also bought another mill, Lane Cotton Mills of Louisiana, and installed themselves on the board again. Thus, Lehman Brothers initiated the gradual migration of American cotton mills from the North to the South over the next century.

Having already invested in Southern iron and steel, Mayer and Emanuel considered the jump into the railroad industry a natural one. Although at first the North's railroads had been dominated by the likes of Jay Gould and other barons, beginning in the 1870s J. P. Morgan and his banking house had moved into financing them; to Morgan's considerable chagrin he had then been joined by the bank Kuhn Loeb. Jacob Schiff, the chief partner of Kuhn Loeb, was an *Our Crowd* eminence and a hero of the German Jewish community in battling the forces of industrial WASPishness exemplified by Morgan. Schiff matched him in taste and style and always traveled in his own private rail coach, along with his family and a retinue. Schiff, too, incidentally, was chipping away at the dominance of Seligman. In addition to his dodgy dealings with Jay Gould, which called his reputation into question, Seligman had also sloppily handled some railroad interests of his own. Schiff was known to be thorough in all his dealings, and the Seligman star was falling. The Lehmans were among those ascending to fill its place in the heavens.

All the speculation by the likes of Morgan and Schiff left the Northern railroad market relatively full, but in the South, Lehman Brothers had the terrain to itself. It developed the Southern railroad system through the 1880s and '90s. *A Centennial* records that Emanuel became a director of the Richmond & Danville Railroad and Mayer chairman of the stockholders' committee of the Montgomery, Tuscaloosa & Memphis Railway Company. Others it had an important interest in were the Savannah & Western and the Louisville, Evansville, & St. Louis—not to mention the Georgia Central and the Richmond & West Point Terminal Railway and Warehouse Company.

Though Lehman Brothers had fled the South after the Civil War, the firm had returned stronger than ever and armed with an array of steelworks, cotton mills, and railroads. The once-lauded members of Montgomery's elite had returned home to rebuild the South and bring it into the industrial age.

|||||||||

In 1881 the ill-fated James A. Garfield, another Republican, ascended to the presidency. Garfield was from Ohio and the last president born in a log cabin. In this new era, electric light on the streets replaced the fading gas lamps, but technology could still disappoint. On July 2, four months into office, Garfield was shot by Charles J. Guiteau, a malcontent bitter at the president for not appointing him to the post of U.S. consul to Paris. As Garfield lay for eighty days with a bullet lodged near his spine, his doctors summoned Alexander Graham Bell to find it with an electrical device of his own invention. Bell failed, and Garfield's agony ended in death.

Vice President Chester A. Arthur of Vermont took over and saw a new landscape before him. He was the first president to show an interest in travel, and he took sightseeing trips to Florida and Yellowstone National Park. The American diet improved: In the early 1880s European scientists had discovered that germs cause disease, with the result that a passion for domestic science bloomed among American wives and mothers who wanted to provide better and cleaner food for their families. The growth of an urban middle class also led to people buying more than just the basics. Literacy was on the rise, as was the number of newspapers and magazines available. Americans were less like cogs in the wheels of production and more like consumers.

The world had witnessed its first skyscraper, the Home Insurance Building in Chicago. In New York the population had surpassed one million, and the Brooklyn Bridge opened in 1883. With its span of nearly sixteen hundred feet, the longest in the world at the time, it connected the city's major parts and was clogged for much of the day with horse-drawn traffic.

Lehman Brothers expanded, taking on new partners. No non–blood members of the family, however, were allowed to be partners. Given that in the South the Lehmans had partners who were not blood relatives, it is possible that they thought that in New York the family was the only place where they could find trustworthy people.

In New York the firm had managed with a staff of about half a dozen. Their late brother Henry's son Meyer H. Lehman (not to be confused with his uncle Mayer) had worked in the office for a number of years and became a partner in 1880. Sigmund, Mayer's oldest son, had joined the firm at twenty-five dollars a week, which was by no means a bad salary in 1878, and become a partner four years later. Philip, the only one of Emanuel's children to come into the business, began at twenty dollars a week in 1882. It was not clear why he started at a lower rate than Sigmund, but in two years he was up to forty dollars a week. In 1885 he made partner at the age of twenty-four. Of this new generation, Philip was the one to watch.

Partners bought a share of the firm, which they would withdraw—that is to say, cash in—on leaving or retiring. Henry's boy Meyer H. and Mayer's son Sigmund each had a 12 percent share of the firm, and Emanuel's son Philip 10 percent. The value of such shares was made apparent when Sigmund decided to retire in 1908, at age forty-nine. He took his money, and he and his wife, Harriet, set off on a more or less continuous jaunt for the rest of their lives on the world's finest cruise ships. Blessedly, they were not on the *Titanic* in 1912, and Sigmund died in Paris in 1930. They were staying at the Ritz, one of their customary hostelries. He still left an estate worth $4 million, the majority of which went to Harriet and their two sons, Allan and Harold, with $100,000 each for his and Harriet's four grandchildren.

Founding partners Mayer and Emanuel had between them a 65 percent share of the business. They trusted each other so much that they shared the same bank account, which either could draw on without consulting the other. In their dealings with others, too, they were reliably fastidious and fair. A friend of Emanuel's later recalled a time when the brothers had some construction work done. The contractor had underestimated the cost of the project and, on telling the brothers with some embarrassment, was asked to provide new figures. When he was asked whether these gave him any profit and he said no, he was told to revise them again: "[N]o one works for Lehman Brothers for nothing," they informed him.

Of the two, more is known about Mayer, given that his youngest son, Herbert, went on to become an important politician and in his memoirs left reminiscences of his father. Mayer's easygoing nature meant that Babette ran the house. She scolded her maids (though Herbert recalled none ever leaving her) and her boys with the same severity. Mayer, wrote Nevins, "seldom needed scolding," possibly because he had learned better than the others how to keep his nose clean. Without being glaringly ostentatious, Mayer and Babette enjoyed their wealth. Mayer kept a team of horses at a nearby stable on Park Avenue and in the morning, having had his carriage brought to the door, would take the reins himself and drive the boys through Central Park. Though not on school days: "Now, Mayer," his wife reminded him, "you'll make them late."

When he took the family on trips to Europe, Mayer insisted that they sail with Cunard, the British shipping line. He felt the British knew the most about ships. Herbert had been to Europe twice by the time he was ten, including in 1887 to the Golden Jubilee in London that marked Queen Victoria's fifty years on the throne. In Britain the Lehmans visited relatives involved in the cotton business in Liverpool and London and traveled on to meet other family in Germany. Mayer guarded his health, and on his European trips liked to "take the cure" in Carlsbad, today the spa town of Karlovy Vary in the Czech Republic. Later he regarded the waters of Saratoga, New York, more highly and regularly went there to take them. Herbert and some of his brothers smoked, and their father offered them the high sum of one thousand dollars to forsake the habit. None felt inclined or impoverished enough to take up his offer.

During some summers, the Lehmans, like many wealthy Jewish families, spent lengthy periods at large beach houses in the resort of Elberon, New Jersey. Apart from the sun and the sea, Elberon had gambling houses and, inland, the Monmouth racetrack. Peggy Guggenheim, later the eminent art collector, hated the place and described it as a "kind of ghetto." Stephen Birmingham in *Our Crowd* portrayed Elberon as the Jewish equivalent of the WASPish resort of Newport, Rhode Island. The men of the family worked in the city and, in addition to the weeks they might take as vacation, joined the women and children there on the weekends. Jacob Schiff of Kuhn Loeb contrived for himself the best arrangement: He had his own stateroom on the Manhattan ferry and commuted to and from Wall Street as he wished.

Lots of Lehmans says that in the 1890s, Emanuel's daughters Harriet and Evelyn bought the camp and lodge of Kildare in the Adirondacks from the Vanderbilts. Technically, this may not have been correct, since in his will, Sigmund left a half share of the ownership to Harriet, which suggests that he, and possibly Evelyn's husband, Jules Ehrich, had actually bought Kildare. To the family, however, Harriet and Evelyn appeared to be the owners. During meals, each would sit at opposite ends of a long dining room table that could accommodate thirty guests; the sisters' conversations, according to William Mayer, Harriet's grandson, often involved "rivalries" (whether between themselves or members of the family he did not say) and were enough to cause all other table talk to cease as people looked down at their plates.

Kildare covered some ten thousand acres, a "dense wilderness," said William Mayer, with its center point a large log cabin "clubhouse." It had multiple fireplaces and bedrooms, a large dining room and a "billiard room," which for some reason was the name given to the living room. The grounds had cottages for various members of the family, with outdoor space left over for tents during the summer overflow. A staff composed of a superintendent, his wife, and their relatives organized hunting and fishing parties.

Mayer and Emanuel steeped themselves in charity work. Emanuel was president of the Hebrew Orphan Asylum. Mayer supported Mount Sinai Hospital and the Montefiore Home for Chronic Invalids, among other charities. He spent hours walking the wards at nights and on the weekends, often taking his children with him. Herbert remembered his father being religious and, at Passover and other holidays, reading prayers at the table in Hebrew—the children would giggle. Once Orthodox, Mayer had turned Reform. Temple Emanu-El, the synagogue used by the family, held services in German, and women worshipped alongside men rather than in a separate gallery in the Orthodox manner.

Politically, most members of the family drifted away from their Democratic Party allegiances, with Mayer the rare exception. Eventually he revealed his colors again after the subdued years following the Civil War and during a succession of Republican administrations. Herbert said that when he was a six-year-old, he remembered his father returning from a torchlight procession for Grover Cleveland's victorious 1884 election. Old politicians from the South visited the family home to talk of old times and new. Hilary Herbert, whom Herbert had been named after, was a regular visitor. The Montgomery attorney had been a Confederate army colonel who fought at Antietam and Gettysburg. A great enthusiast of Lehman Brothers' efforts to industrialize the South, he went on to be a congressman and secretary of the navy when Cleveland, after a four-year gap, won the election for a second term in 1892.

Edward Douglass White, Jr., a jovial Louisiana attorney, was a family friend. White combined the courtliness of the Old South with a higher education gained in Jesuit schools. Cleveland elevated him to the Supreme Court in 1894. From a wealthy background—his father was both a planter and a lawyer and had also sat ten years in Congress—White had married an equally wealthy wife. He passed his family fortune to Mayer to manage when Lehman Brothers set about building a reputation for the safe handling of rich people's money.

Emanuel Lehman pushed ahead with his interests on the more grimy industrial side. He saw opportunities in the growing area of public utilities, and in 1890 joined the board of the East River Gas Company. *A Centennial* recorded that he bought a sizable financial interest in the Brooklyn Ferry Company and East River ferry companies. Finely printed share certificates of the old New York and New Jersey Ferry Company, described as "rare," are for sale on the Internet and signed by company president Emanuel Lehman in his clear and sloping hand. He involved Lehman Brothers in streetcar and other transport companies; he was on the board of directors of New York's Third Avenue Railroad Company.

Another collapse overtook the economy soon after Cleveland began his second term in 1893. Standard economic theories that the system worked toward a sublime equilibrium said these downturns were an aberration. But they happened with such regularity as to make them the norm. Railroads, again, and a run on gold caused the upheaval. Too many railroad companies had engaged in sharing too few passengers, and too many banks had financed them. Some six hundred banks failed, fifteen thousand businesses went bankrupt, and four million people lost their jobs. Some western states outlawed bankers; Texas did so for the next ten years.

The depressing effects of the 1893 collapse lasted three years. The nineteenth century's long depression maintained its grip around the world, and those who lived off the land took the brunt of it. Peasant farmers left their homes in Eastern Europe in droves and took the boat to America. Ellis Island opened in 1892 to accommodate them. The U.S. election campaign the following year, between the Republican candidate William McKinley and the Democrat William Jennings Bryan, was fought bitterly. Though McKinley won the contest, it was best remembered for the speeches made by Bryan, a small-town lawyer, congressman, and lay preacher from Nebraska. He made his pitch for the votes of ordinary people. When the Democrats nominated him at their 1896 party convention in Chicago, Bryan said, "[T]he man who is employed for wages is as much a businessman as his employer," and that man had as much right to a living as the "magnates, who, in a back room, corner the money of the world."

Bryan demanded the relaxing of the gold standard. If there was too little gold to support the release of more dollars into the economy to get the system going again, then the government should release silver coins instead. The western states of Colorado and Nevada had discovered large quantities of silver. Bryan concluded his famous convention speech with a half appeal, half threat to those in charge of the nation's purse strings: "[Y]ou shall not crucify mankind upon a cross of gold." This election marked the moment that the Democratic Party turned from the party that had lost the Civil War, wrote Simon Schama, a British historian, into "the party that would embody the cause of the Common Man in tough times." Some years later, Robert Lehman, better known as Bobbie and the future and most lauded head of the Lehman Brothers, would marry a granddaughter of William Jennings Bryan.

Mayer Lehman died on June 21, 1897, at the age of sixty-seven, after an operation for gangrene. During the funeral three days later at Temple Emanu-El, the New York Cotton Exchange shut for an hour, the first time it let such a mark of respect interfere with its business. Louis R. Ehrich, a friend, wrote a eulogy for Mayer: "A noble, manly, wide-beloved man! . . . He slowly added to his well-earned wealth. . . . Nor did his wealth beget false pride or stir . . . the promptings of vain conceit." Mayer left $5 million in his will.

Emanuel continued developing the business in an industrial direction. The emerging idea in the last years of the nineteenth century was the "road locomotive," "horseless carriage," or as more prosaically styled, the "automobile." Lehman Brothers shunned the idea of a gasoline-powered vehicle in favor of electricity and invested in a company called the Electric Vehicle Company. Fellow investors included P. A. B. Widener, the trolley car and street railway millionaire of Philadelphia. Many people's imaginations about electric automobiles had been captured by John Jacob Astor IV, whose 1894 science fiction novel, *A Journey in Other Worlds*, had imagined the world in 2088, when the United States was a world superpower: People communicated using a world telephone network, traveled through air and space, and used solar power. Astor, of the New York family that by the 1830s had made its enormous fortune from trading in fur, real estate, and opium, also wrote of a vehicle that would carry people to their destinations noiselessly, using a "battery with insignificant weight, compact form, and great capacity."

In 1899, the inventor Thomas Edison began research into creating a long-lasting battery for cars, though eventually he abandoned it. Of the 4,192 cars produced in the United States in 1900, nearly a third were powered by electricity. The Electric Vehicle Company made electric taxicabs, and at one stage it had a fleet of 2,000 on the streets of New York, Chicago, Philadelphia, Boston, and Washington. Gasoline power drove electric vehicles out of business in the early years of the twentieth century.

The electric cars were deemed inefficient because their batteries were not long-lasting enough for them to go long distances and, with oil production increasing, gasoline was readily available.

The idea of the electric vehicle was revived late in the first decade of the twenty-first century. Alas, Lehman Brothers was no longer around to see whether its hunch of a century or so earlier had been right all along.

3

Stuff of Dreams

As the twentieth century approached, a new force appeared on the world stage. In the Spanish-American War of 1898, the United States briskly ejected Spain from the Caribbean islands of Cuba and Puerto Rico and from the Philippines in the Pacific. The United States also annexed Hawaii, where it had used Pearl Harbor as a naval base for some time. The world was moving toward "the American century," and there was an imperial feel in the air—a sense that America was destined to lead. When President William McKinley received word that dissidents in the Philippines objected to American forces occupying the islands in place of the Spaniards, his answer was emphatic: "[T]here was nothing left for us to do but to take them all, and to educate the Filipinos, and uplift and civilize and Christianize them."

The United States was also exercising its economic muscle. In 1899 the United Fruit Company began its reign over wide areas of Central America and the Caribbean. Based in Boston, it was a large banana-growing and trading company formed from the merger that year of the Boston Fruit Company and the Tropical Trading Company of New Orleans. United Fruit had huge plantations in such countries as Costa Rica, Panama, Colombia, and Cuba. In 1890, the Sherman Anti-Trust Act had come into force in an attempt to curb the monopolistic practices of large companies, which in those days were often called "trusts." The act took measures to prevent large companies from dominating markets and fixing prices to their advantage, but it gave Congress no power to stop American companies from acting in a monopolistic fashion abroad. Over the next thirty years, United Fruit would widen its influence in the Caribbean—over Honduras, Guatemala, and Jamaica, among others. Lehman Brothers would become involved in the banana business beginning in the 1920s, and it would eventually be the banker of the United Fruit Company.

Recent gold strikes in the Yukon and Alaska meant that at the turn of the century, America was a richer place. Its population of seventy-six million had tripled since Lehman Brothers' founding in 1850, and for a people and nation of ambition there was more money around than ever. When William Jennings Bryan ran again for the presidency against McKinley in the 1900 election, his arguments for releasing more silver coins into the economy were no longer relevant. Lehman Brothers itself had invested in gold mines in Utah and Nevada.

A note of warning came from the world of literature. L. Frank Baum's book *The Wonderful Wizard of Oz* appeared in 1900. At first glance it was a tale of optimism, as a group of different characters, with their varied strengths and weaknesses, set off along the yellow brick road; Baum was writing from South Dakota, which in the Black Hills a quarter of a century before had seen its own gold rush. To many people the book spoke for the nation as it headed with great hope into the American century, but Baum addressed other themes. The wizard, a cheery scoundrel, possibly bore some relation to the snake-oil salesmen and other such types Baum would have seen around South Dakota, a distant frontier location that had become a state only eleven years before. The characters in the book also happened upon the Emerald City, whose occupants wore glasses that tinted their surroundings green, the color of money. Baum's tale was conceivably therefore one in which optimism encountered delusion.

Virtually with his dying words President McKinley urged his countrymen to look outward. An anarchist's bullet claimed him in 1901 as he visited the Pan-American Exposition in Buffalo, New York. The "period of exclusiveness is past," he had said in a speech the day before. The world was expanding, and the United States should enjoy "sensible trade relations" with it. McKinley had lately been warning the "Great Powers," such as Britain, France, and Germany, that America wanted more of the market in China. His message to Americans was to make sure that they did not lapse into isolation.

His vice president, Theodore "Teddy" Roosevelt, took over, and took up the call. Roosevelt had made his name both as governor of New York in the 1890s and as a soldier leading the charge of his company, the Rough Riders, up San Juan Hill in the victorious Spanish-American War. In 1903

Roosevelt helped engineer the insurrection of Panamanian nationalists that won Panama independence from Colombia. He was assisted by the United Fruit Company, which shipped supplies to the insurrectionists. The Panamanians immediately gave the United States the right to build the Panama Canal that Colombia had denied.

Teddy Roosevelt saw America's world role as a matter of destiny— "determined for us by fate"—but received a lot of criticism for his Panamanian escapade. Cartoons depicted him, a rotund character, as the overbearing Rough Rider bearing down on poor little Colombia. This kind of activity was typical of the empires and potentates of Europe from which Americans had made their escape. Imperialism was for the British and others who hoodwinked their people with delusional glories of empire. The message to Roosevelt from his critics appeared to be rather that Americans wanted to look inward on their path to development; with their newfound wealth, Americans wanted material goods—the true stuff of dreams. This Lehman Brothers found itself handily placed to provide.

Philip Lehman, Emanuel's son, emerged as the leader of the firm. Emanuel had carried on for three or four years after Mayer's death, then passed power to the new generation. On Mayer's side, Arthur joined as a partner in 1902, while Sigmund, the oldest of Mayer's sons, had let it be known he would retire in 1908 before he turned fifty. Philip was born in New York in 1861 during the Civil War, when Emanuel was away on one of his Confederate bond missions. He would remain senior partner until the mid-1920s, when he handed control to his son Bobbie, though he remained in the firm until his death in 1947.

Philip Lehman "unleashed his generation's quest for progress," wrote Kenneth L. Fisher in his *100 Minds That Made the Market*, speaking of the general urge for progress in America at the time. Philip had a "sense of dignity, a sense of aristocracy, a restrained manner and intellectual brain," Fisher added. There were, however, other views. Birmingham in *Our Crowd* quotes an unnamed friend of Philip's who called him "rough" and a real horse trader. An unnamed family member added that "at anything he did, Philip *had* to win," and an anonymous friend of the family referred to him as "dull and bankerish." Whatever the truth, Philip had a vision for Lehman Brothers and knew where he wanted to take it.

The firm had invested well. Hedging its electric vehicle bets, it put money into the Rubber Tire Wheel Company at the turn of the century.

The company was the only maker of the pneumatic tire, without which automobile journeys were uncomfortable. Lehman Brothers kept its shares in Rubber Tire Wheel, which, having changed names to the Kelly-Springfield Tire Company, was bought by the Goodyear Tire & Rubber Company in 1935 at a good profit for existing shareholders. The firm also backed the Maine Steamship Company, since shipping was an excellent area to invest in as more goods were transported around the country and abroad. Ships linked with the railroads and, again at good profit, Maine Steamship was eventually sold to the New York, New Haven and Hartford Railroad.

Lehman Brothers had moved into the profitable field of advising on mergers and acquisitions. Good money could be made from counseling companies on how to take over or merge with others. Accounts had to be scrutinized, potential costs and savings identified. Only a few firms claimed expertise in such matters, and they could dictate their fees. Lehman Brothers advised in the lucrative merger of several midwestern gas and electric companies to form the American Light and Traction Company, one of the first big American utility companies.

Crucially, Philip wanted Lehman Brothers to move into the role of underwriting the issuance of a company's shares. There were good fees in this field. Companies issued shares to raise capital to improve their business, and an underwriter guaranteed a market for a company's shares by buying them itself. It then sold them to its contacts. The risk for a company was that if the underwriter could not sell the shares, no other underwriter would take the risk of selling shares for the company in the future. The underwriter ran the risk of ending up with a lot of unsold shares of an unloved company on its hands. For that risk it charged the company 20 percent or more of the value of the shares.

Until now Lehman Brothers' activities had been confined mainly to markets, in particular the buying and selling of commodities. The WASP-ish banking elite of New York rather shunned markets; they were mucky places full of people to-ing and fro-ing and haggling face-to-face with one another. Those who made their living in markets bore a stigma similar to that attached by the British ruling classes to anyone involved in commerce, or "trade." Somehow it was beneath proper banking, which was a matter of guiding and advising firms on their future progress.

Of course, Philip Lehman was not part of the WASPish elite, but he had every ambition of breaking into the fold. Joseph Seligman had made inroads with his railroad alliances with the scurrilous Jay Gould. Jacob Schiff had stood toe-to-toe with J. P. Morgan in underwriting shares for railroad companies. Surely there was room for another member of the Jewish community to elbow his way in, though Philip had ideas of finding his own niche rather than one, like the railroads, in which WASP bankers and a rare few like the Seligmans and Schiffs already dominated.

Underwriting was a potential means of transforming Lehman Brothers from an old commodities brokerage trading mainly in cotton—a product that in the United States was no longer as lucrative as it used to be—into a modern "house of issue" (referring to the issue of shares). In searching for his niche, Philip Lehman homed in on the rather quaint view that big WASPish banks had of the economy: They saw it predominantly as a producers' economy of large companies like the railroads or steel companies run by people such as Andrew Carnegie. WASPs liked to deal in large and obvious things, such as huge mills, steam engines, and thousands of miles of railroad track stretching off to the western horizon.

Paradoxically, American capitalists had a view of the economy rather similar to that of Communists. After the revolution in Russia a decade or so later, the Communists would build statues of heroic workers at their furnaces and lathes hammering out lengths of white-hot steel. These were the kinds of workers engaged in the kinds of businesses that were uppermost in American capitalists' minds. The WASPish banks issued shares on the stock market for companies of the heavy industrial variety. An underwriting firm could see the tangible value that lay behind the shares that it was taking on and expecting to sell. Share buyers, too, could visualize where their funds were going. But there were a lot of companies out there whose value was not so easy to see. They did not have huge and visible assets and, as such, were not candidates to get the money to expand and grow by launching themselves on the stock market. A lot of these companies were in retail, the distribution of goods aimed at millions of American consumers, and many also happened to be owned by Jews, which was another reason the WASPs would not do business with them.

If WASPish banks were only interested in the large-scale producer economy, then Philip Lehman saw his opportunity in the smaller-scale consumer economy. It was a revelation at the time; he just needed an ally of like mind with whom to set out on his new enterprise. He found one in the most homespun way imaginable—across the garden fence.

In Elberon, Philip's large summer home shared a boundary with his backyard neighbor Samuel Sachs, son of Joseph Sachs, who had emigrated to America from Bavaria in the late 1840s. A chief partner in the Wall Street banking firm of Goldman Sachs, Samuel Sachs introduced Philip to his fellow partner Henry Goldman. If Philip was a rough horse trader, then Goldman was an "intense, high-strung, didactic man." Perhaps strangely, they got on well, and as the women and servants of the family took the children to the beach, they discussed their affairs on the porch and worked out a course of action.

Both were creatures of the swamp. The Lehmans had emerged from the vaporous mists of the South and had a sense of mystery about them. They had made money down there; no one knew quite how much except themselves, but they had made it and done well since their move north. The Goldmans had been known around those streets near the East River—the "swamp"—for a far longer time; there was no mystery about them, but they knew the right people.

Henry Goldman's late father, Marcus, was an itinerant peddler in Pennsylvania before making his way to New York. The businessmen he knew ran such concerns as small factories making leather goods and textiles. WASPish banks uptown would not lend to them on the small scale that they required, but Marcus Goldman would. For a loan of, say, one thousand dollars he would give nine hundred; the one-hundred-dollar difference would be the interest rate, his lending fee. The agreement was scrawled on a piece of paper and stuffed in the inner band of Goldman's stovepipe hat, the fashion of those times.

Marcus Goldman was a money lender, a local entrepreneur, and a venture capitalist, and those pieces of paper were IOUs. In the financial world they acquired the more posh title of "commercial paper." In basic terms, once Goldman had a sufficient collection of, say, ten pieces of commercial paper for loans totaling $10,000—for which he had paid $9,000— he would take a horse-drawn cab to a bank uptown and sell the loans to the bank, in a single bundle, for perhaps $9,500. Everyone was happy: The small businessman had a loan for his business; the bank would eventually get $10,000 for its payment to Goldman of $9,500. And he would be left with a profit of $500 of his own, plus more cash from the bank now to begin the process over again.

Marcus Goldman was estimated to have a turnover of $5 million a year. That is to say, he handled loans of $5 million annually; if we assume a 5 percent profit from this, he was earning $250,000 a year, which was a very substantial income in those times. Some people, of course, might not repay, but the problem of such bad debts occurring would be alleviated to a great extent by the fact that Goldman knew the district and its people. Anyone who did not repay would never get money again, and their reputations would be such that they might as well leave the area.

In this way, Goldman Sachs built its foundation as a merchant banking firm. Some of the Goldmans married some of the Sachses. The Sachses had good international contacts in Europe, principally in England with the Kleinwort family, which was also engaged in banking. The Kleinworts had originally made their money in Cuba but moved to establish themselves as a prestigious banking house in the City of London.

Goldman Sachs had built up its contacts over the years among businesses that WASP banks would not touch—the retailers, distributors, and small industrialists of the Jewish community. Lehman Brothers had fewer contacts but more wealth, or at least it was perceived to have more wealth. The element of mystique was important; successful underwriting required prestige if potential buyers of shares were to have faith in the goods on offer. Lehman Brothers enjoyed such a distinction; it had been something significant in the South. Goldman Sachs had been nothing much in the North, where it had pulled itself up from the gutter. Street wisdom was its key quality.

Still, Philip Lehman got the better end of the deal. Goldman and Lehman chose not to have a formal partnership; they would keep their day jobs and see how their joint business fared. As informal partners they agreed to share the proceeds of any deal fifty-fifty, but Goldman Sachs would do more of the work. Goldman had bigger facilities—about twenty people working six-day weeks in its New York office, plus others in branch offices in Chicago and Boston.

Lehman Brothers had been turning itself into a fully New York firm for some time, and at the turn of the century, according to *A Centennial*, Emanuel wrote to his partners in Montgomery to say that their joint business had become "more or less unprofitable." The process of dissolution, however, was gradual and not completed until 1912. At the time of the incipient partnership with Goldman, Lehman Brothers had, in effect, only its one office in New York and about ten people working for the firm. Philip Lehman, therefore, quite deftly arranged matters so that Goldman Sachs would execute most of the partnership's dog work—the close study of a client's accounts, for example, to assess what the price of its shares should be when pitched to the market. It was a tricky matter: too low and you would not get value; too high and no one would buy them. The Goldman side of the operation would also sell most of the shares, leaving Lehman Brothers to assume the aristocratic position of putting up its capital, sitting back, and watching the money roll in.

Philip Lehman and Henry Goldman met each day for lunch at Delmonico's, a popular restaurant among the financial community at the corner of William and Beaver streets and two short blocks from Wall Street. The miasma of cigar smoke around them may have pointed the two friends in the direction of their first venture. Since the end of the Spanish-American War, American investors had poured money into Cuba, particularly into tobacco—Cuban cigars were at a high point of popularity.

Cuba exported 258 million cigars in 1906, all of them hand rolled. Its chief tobacco-growing region of Vuelta Abajo, in the northwest of the island, had a soil that when combined with the Havana tobacco seed, provided the basic material of a cigar with a flavor variously described as strong and full, spicy and aromatic. It was soon found that the Havana seed could be grown productively in the Connecticut River valley, but, as good as the resulting cigars might have been, Connecticut could never quite match Cuba for mystique.

A large number of relatively small American companies competed for the business. Henry Goldman knew Jake Wertheim, the chief executive of the United Cigar Manufacturers' Company. Wertheim wanted to expand and Goldman and Lehman suggested an issue of shares to raise the capital. How much should they pitch for? In the September 5, 1905, issue of the *Saturday Evening Post*, United Cigar ran an advertisement for its Isle of Pines brand of small cigars. Cuba's Isla de Pinos was on the southwest rather than northwest side of the island, where most of the tobacco was grown, but the name and the swaying palms depicted on its box tapped into the Cuban fantasy: "Send $1.25 for fifty," directed the ad. "Delicious short smokes . . . no ifs or buts." People could send for them at 319 Flatiron

Building, New York. United Cigar, it said, was the largest cigar retailer in the world, operating over three hundred stores.

United Cigar's capital assets added up to $2 million. Lehman, Goldman, and Wertheim decided that the company needed to raise more than that for its expansion. A railroad or steel company with its machinery, iron, and other solid reserves could win the confidence of the market to raise vast amounts of money, but a cigar company did not have much in the way of background assets: a few machines, some vehicles for deliveries, and perhaps a warehouse or two.

So Lehman and Goldman made a shift in thinking from the tangible to the intangible. United Cigar had the benefit, they assessed, of what it could expect to earn in future sales. This was surely an asset; today it would be known by the common accounting term "goodwill," but it was far less recognized then. To move into the realm of intangible assets like this involved an obvious element of risk, but in Lehman and Goldman's case it was one based on a hard assessment of their client's worth. They studied its value and took a position based on their own judgment and years of experience, whether their own or that gained from their families. They took a risk, but were measured about it. It was their money that they stood to lose.

Lehman and Goldman calculated they would underwrite a share issue for United Cigar worth $4.5 million. They sold these shares for $5.6 million, a 20 percent profit. With share buyers skeptical about this idea of "goodwill," it took ninety days of hard selling to get the shares out to the market. The Goldman Sachs office did most of that selling. In London, the Kleinworts, the Sachs family's banking friends, sold quite a few of the shares to their European connections.

The work paid off as United Cigar's business grew strong and full-bodied for quite some years. In 1920 Americans consumed 8.5 billion cigars. The product's image suffered during the 1920s gangster era, however, thanks to Hollywood and cigar-chomping stars like Edward G. Robinson. According to *Cigars* magazine, the industry did not regain its prestige until Winston Churchill, Britain's cigar-loving prime minister, popularized them in the 1940s and '50s.

Lehman and Goldman's next deal fell into their hands almost immediately. Julius Rosenwald, who owned one third of Sears, Roebuck, the mail-order company, was a distant relative of the Sachs family. He had stayed with Sam Sachs and his wife about a decade before, just after he arrived as an immigrant from Germany. They had found him "crude and uncultured," as Charles D. Ellis described in his book *The Partnership*, but they kept their own counsel. Rosenwald headed west to make a decent retail fortune and a bigger one when he joined forces with Richard Sears. Sears, Roebuck now wanted to raise money to build a large storage plant in Chicago from where it could send its merchandise across much of America. Rosenwald came and asked for a $5 million loan.

Philip Lehman and Henry Goldman suggested a better idea: Take $10 million. This would be in the form of shares, however, rather than debt; in short, Sears, Roebuck should "go public." Rosenwald would never have thought of asking for such a thing. The old and established banks would never have given it to him, because they would not touch a mail-order company. Mail order was a phenomenon of the wide-open spaces of the West and Midwest that was barely known or understood around the East Coast. Lehman and Goldman cashed in on the fact that most Americans still lived on or near farms and could not easily get into town to shop. Sears called itself the "Cheapest Supply House on Earth"; its catalog mixed the kind of down-home earthiness of rural areas with a degree of material luxury. The company offered almost everything, from work clothes and farm tools to household furniture, organs, and pianos.

The market was more skeptical about the Sears, Roebuck deal than it had been about the United Cigar one. It took nine months of selling — compared with ninety days — to prize out the goodwill of share buyers. Again, Kleinwort sold a lot of the issue in Europe. It worked, however, and Sears built its facility in Chicago, paid off its bank loans, and had some cash in hand. Sales rose sixfold over the next fifteen years. Sears opened its first retail outlet in 1925 in Chicago, and by the end of the decade it had 324 of them. The company caught on to the rising popularity of the automobile and was the first to have free parking lots next to its stores.

In the 1940s Sears, Roebuck expanded abroad to open stores in Cuba and Mexico. After World War II, when it became clear that the cold war with communism was setting in, the Moscow bureau chief of the Associated Press news agency wrote that the most influential American propaganda in the Soviet Union was the Sears catalog. If the Russian people needed to know what they were missing, they had to look no further than there.

Between 1906 and 1925 Lehman Brothers and Goldman Sachs acted as underwriters on share issues of more than one hundred companies, many of which became household names: Continental Can; Underwood Typewriter; Brown Shoe; Jewel Tea, the nationwide supplier of tea, coffee, spices and its own baking powder; and S. H. Kress, the five-and-dime chain, among them. The most world famous was Woolworth's. It was another five-and-dime and the first Lehman and Goldman dealt with. Frank Woolworth, the boss of the company formally named F. W. Woolworth, came to them in 1912 and asked for the same kind of deal that they had given Sears.

Initially, they balked at the idea, wondering if it was a step too far. While Sears had some pretense of luxury, Woolworth's clearly catered to the masses. It vigorously undercut the prices of local merchants. It made agreements behind the scenes with friendly rivals—that is to say, it formed illegal cartels in order to present a united front to suppliers and forced them to cut their prices. At the same time it literally kept in friendlier touch with its customers—it was one of the first retailers to display merchandise so that people could touch it before deciding whether or not to buy. At other stores only salesclerks were allowed to do so.

Frank Woolworth needed capital to merge six hundred stores in the United States and Canada under the Woolworth banner. He offered Lehman and Goldman 20 percent of any share offering free of charge if they would act as underwriters. They went ahead and offered the shares to investors at $50 each, for a total value estimated at $65 million. By now, stock market devotees had identified Lehman and Goldman as a good proposition, and so many people wanted to buy Woolworth shares that their price increased to $80 each on their first day on the market. This made the share offering worth a little under $80 million, of which Lehman and Goldman's share was worth near $16 million.

With part of the proceeds, Frank Woolworth paid for the construction of the Woolworth Building at 233 Broadway in Manhattan. In granite and limestone, with a setback Gothic tower 792 feet high, work on it was finished in 1913, and it remained the tallest building in the world for seventeen years. Only the construction boom leading up to the Wall Street crash of 1929 saw it overtaken by the likes of the Chrysler and Empire State buildings.

With their art deco facades, Woolworth stores became a feature of almost every American downtown area. The company's lunch counters were a place to gather and the forerunners of the food courts of modern shopping malls. Curiously, this experiment was first tried in Liverpool, England, before Woolworth introduced the idea to the United States. As effective a tool of propaganda as the Sears catalog, the fame of Woolworth's stores had spread abroad as well. In the gray and sometimes smoggy London of the 1950s, they were one of the most exciting places to be—they had hot dogs, which were barely known elsewhere, and piped background pop music that, when it wasn't playing Perry Como, promised the advent of the sixties.

On February 1, 1960, the lunch counter in the Woolworth's on South Elm Street in Greensboro, North Carolina, became a focus of the civil rights movement. Refused service at the segregated counter, African American students staged a sit-in that led to six months of protests and became a milestone for the cause. An eight-foot section of the Greensboro lunch counter was moved in 1993 to the Smithsonian Institution in Washington, DC. By this time, many branches of Woolworth's had disappeared from Main Street, America. In Britain they lingered into the new millennium, struggling to maintain the appearance of a vibrant business. Many people claimed Woolworth's as their favorite store, though far fewer managed to use it. Woolworth's finally disappeared at the end of 2008 in the wake of the crisis caused by the end of Lehman Brothers itself.

But some ninety-five years before, Philip Lehman and Henry Goldman became the hottest underwriting team on Wall Street. Suddenly they were no longer the outsiders they had been in a WASP-dominated environment. Partners of the two firms got into the spirit of things, wrote Ellis, and began to boast that the companies Lehman and Goldman brought to market bore the two firms' "hallmark." Previously that hallmark had been one of businesses no one else had wanted to touch. Now other underwriters followed their lead and launched companies onto the market that were previously thought unworthy. The stock market itself, therefore, expanded into something more akin to that of modern times.

Before Lehman and Goldman pooled their social, financial, and intellectual resources, people undeniably consumed. The Philip and Henry initiative, however, began the transformation of the United States' production economy into a consumption one. Their joint efforts had a profound effect on the way Americans spent their money, and eventually many other people around the world followed suit. For good or ill, Philip Lehman and Henry Goldman rank among the principal architects of our consumer society.

|||||||||

In 1908 President Theodore Roosevelt approached the end of his second term with the economy still recovering from the financial panic of 1907. The stock market collapsed in the fall of that year after an extended period of speculation, particularly in metal stocks. Copper was of great interest given the increased use of electricity in daily life and the metal's use as a conductor. One of the factors that sparked the market's crash was that J. P. Morgan, the banker, and others were rumored to have found new deposits of copper in outlying reaches of the country, and that the increased supply of the metal would see its price fall. Lots of people rushed, therefore, to sell their shares in copper and other metals.

A number of other reasons were behind the crash. Investors had borrowed heavily from banks to buy shares. In turn, they used these shares as security to borrow more money to invest in yet more shares. Shares were used as collateral—a guarantee—for as much as half the bank loans in New York City. This was "an extremely shaky base for the system," wrote Ron Chernow in *The House of Morgan*. Many of these shares were very poor collateral given that their prices could drop at any minute. And many did in 1907.

So-called trust companies bore some of the guilt. Traditionally, these firms handled wills and estates, by and large an unexciting but necessary business. Though their names were similar, they were not to be confused with the trusts—the large corporations, like the oil, steel, and railroad companies—that the Sherman Anti-Trust Act of 1890 had been introduced to combat. In one regard, though, the trusts and the trust companies had shown that they had something in common: They could not be trusted to serve much more than their own interests.

The trust companies that handled wills and estates had once been cautious investors, but that had changed by 1907. With the aspiration of being big market players, they had "exploited enough legal loopholes to become highly speculative," wrote Chernow. A century later, handlers of mortgages, another once cautious business, decided they wanted to be high-risk speculators, and their actions would be among the causes of the crash of 2008 that bankrupted Lehman Brothers. In 1907, the trust companies used their investors' funds to borrow heavily and plunge headlong into the markets.

So-called bucket shops also played a key role in the crash. These were betting shops where people could gamble on the stock market. There is confusion as to where the term "bucket shop" comes from, though it may have derived from the ancient and lower-class alehouses of London that collected the alcoholic leftovers of classier bars by the bucketful and then sold them. Bucket shops lived off the stock market but were not part of it. Their proliferation on the streets of American cities largely catered to small-time bettors who put money on the movements up or down of a stock or collection of stocks in, say, a particular industry they had a strong interest in, like metals. But big-time bettors joined in too, and contributed to the crash.

An important aspect of this practice was that the sums of money in play at the bucket shops were not investments in company shares themselves. An investor buying shares on the stock market acquired part ownership of the company he was investing in. A bucket shop gamble, by contrast, was a side bet rather like that made with a bookie on a horse; such a bet does not give the gambler partial ownership of the horse any more than bucket-shop bets give partial ownership of a company.

The bet in a bucket shop, therefore, was another early form of derivative. That is to say, it was not an investment directly in a company itself but an indirect, or "derived," gamble on the company's future. But bucket shops were very popular. Through the early part of the century, as the nation's wealth grew, many people wanted to be involved in the prosperity of the financial markets even though they may have lacked the funds or knowledge to get directly involved by buying shares. Many thousands of people gambled in the many thousands of bucket shops, and cumulatively this represented a huge amount of money that was outside the market yet could influence its movements; the market might react to a large rush of money put on particular stocks at the bucket shops, for example, causing lurches and instability in prices.

The stock market of the day had some limited supervision by later standards of regulation, but the bucket shops were unregulated by any central authority. There was no stipulation, for example, as to how much capital they should hold to guarantee that successful gamblers would get a payout. In the event of big losses they could simply close. They also had the capacity to move markets directly; many of them owned blocks of stocks. In the event of bettors' gambling on a stock price's rising, the shops could sell the stock on the market in sufficient quantity to bring a fall in price; hence the bettors would lose. If gamblers bet on a fall in price, bucket shops could buy on the market and cause the stock price to rise. Those who used these shops were often sold nothing but useless pieces of paper.

In 1908 New York banned bucket shops, and as other states followed suit, they disappeared from the streets of America. A century later, however, their spirit returned. In the crash of 2008, derivatives played a major part. The 2008 counterpart of a bet in a bucket shop was the so-called credit default swap. These were huge side gambles on, for example, whether Lehman Brothers would survive or whether its ill-advised investments in mortgage bonds would fail. Credit default swaps were subject to only minimal regulation and amounted to many billions, even trillions, of dollars. They were placed through such willing takers as AIG (American International Group), the large and prestigious insurance company that had in effect turned itself into a glorified bucket shop. The crash of 2008 would turn out to be a lesson not learned a hundred years before.

Wall Street blamed Teddy Roosevelt's antibusiness policies for the 1907 crash. Since he, a Republican, had taken office in 1901, he had spoken of introducing greater controls over large corporations; in one instance, he curbed the powers of J. P. Morgan to control some western railroads. More recently, in 1906 he had read *The Jungle*, Upton Sinclair's novel that exposed unsanitary conditions in the meatpacking industry; the president promptly pushed Congress to introduce the first food and drug laws. Then, before the 1907 panic, he had also spoken in uncompromising tones at the Gridiron Club in Washington, DC. The club, founded in 1885, had as its members the editors of the leading newspapers and magazines, and it annually invited the nation's president to dinner to air his views. Roosevelt chose as his theme what he called the "malefactors of great wealth." Wall Street said this undermined market confidence.

The panic led Roosevelt to threaten stricter regulation, and J. P. Morgan took on the challenge of convincing the world that financiers could clean up their house without outside intervention. He strode along Wall Street rallying support and, in its major offices, banged heads together to raise money to get the market going again. Huge crowds gathered outside his office window to cheer his efforts. Arguably Morgan was the first of the street's "masters of the universe," albeit a term not coined until Tom Wolfe's book *The Bonfire of the Vanities* appeared in 1987. For good measure, Morgan, an avid churchgoer who at the time of the panic's start was attending a conference in Philadelphia to make revisions to the *English Book of Common Prayer*, also called on church leaders to have their congregations pray for the market's recovery.

Teddy Roosevelt was not deterred. He began deliberations on setting up a central bank as a way to supervise and stabilize American financial life. President Andrew Jackson had abandoned the idea in the 1830s. Roosevelt called in Jacob Schiff as an adviser, and Lehman Brothers also joined the discussions, which were held in secret. Since Jackson, a central bank had been regarded as a foreign idea, and the involvement of Jewish bankers would have tapped into a "strong anti-Semitic undercurrent in the country," wrote Charles Geisst in his book *The Last Partnerships*. He added that, apart from thinking that emergencies should not be left to Morgan to sort out, critics of Wall Street worried that the financial community manufactured panics—or at least was not averse to them—"so that it could make money on the bailouts." Geisst's book, by the way, was published in 2001, several years before the huge bailouts following the 2008 crash.

After Roosevelt left office in 1909, his successor, William Taft, continued the central bank discussions. Senator Nelson Aldrich of Rhode Island organized one clandestine meeting in 1910 on Jekyll Island, tucked away off the coast of Georgia. Lehman Brothers stayed part of the consultation process and, finally, President Woodrow Wilson introduced the Federal Reserve in 1913. J. P. Morgan coincidentally died the same year.

Herbert Lehman, meanwhile, had joined the family firm as a partner in 1908. He took the place of his oldest brother, Sigmund, who had left to sail around the world. As Sigmund found the freedom of the seas, Herbert entered Lehman Brothers' offices in the Farmers' Loan & Trust Building at 16 William Street, one of several dark and narrow lanes within a block or so of Wall Street.

He had come from J. Spencer Turner Co., a textile company in Brooklyn owned by a friend of Mayer, his father. "Whatever knowledge I have had of business came much more from my ten years' experience in a merchandising house than from the investment banking business," Herbert said later. In 1906, by the age of twenty-eight, he had risen to the position of vice president, having begun as a "duck" salesman—duck being the coarse, strong fabric used for tarpaulins, tents, and other such durable wares as tennis shoes and butchers' aprons. His first weekly pay was five dollars, from which he took a two-dollar bill and framed it. He did not need the cash; his father had left him four hundred thousand dollars.

Herbert had graduated in 1899 from Williams College in Massachusetts with a reputation more for reliability than academic brilliance. He scored a lot of Bs and Cs. His only A was in oratory, although few who heard his speeches when he later became governor of, and then senator from, New York would have compared his eloquence to that of his friend and contemporary in public affairs, Franklin D. Roosevelt.

He was known for his persistence, tact, and good nature. He said he had a suspicion of crowds, something he had gained from an experience at Williams, in which he had joined a mob of students on campus as they hounded one of the deans. The dean had been a disciplinarian but "really a nice man," according to Lehman, who was ashamed to admit that he had joined the crowd. The incident led to the dean's resigning from the school.

Frank Erwin, a teacher at Herbert Lehman's high school, the Sachs Collegiate Institute in New York, had recommended Williams to Lehman's parents. Erwin had been there himself; other notable alumni included William Lowndes Yancey, the defiant Southern orator of the late 1840s, and President James Garfield, who had fallen to an assassin's bullet in 1881.

Herbert was the last of Mayer and Babette Lehman's seven surviving children, and his parents had not known quite what to do with him. For no obvious reason they had imagined he was a mining engineer in the making; metals, after all, represented good and solid wealth. But Herbert had no gift for the vocation and, not least, little grasp of mathematics. Of his brothers nearest him in age, Arthur was destined for the family business and Irving for a distinguished career in the law. (Irving would eventually become chief judge of the New York Court of Appeals in 1940, at the age of sixty-four, and serve in the position until his death in 1945.)

Even before Williams, Erwin helped steer Lehman onto another path. Herbert was twelve in 1890 when Erwin escorted his class on a school journey that, although not far away geographically, took the boys a million miles from the world they knew socially. The privileged boys from midtown Manhattan, wearing bowler hats, starched collars, neat dark suits, and high-polished shoes, took the Third Avenue elevated train to the Lower East Side and the ghetto areas of the Bowery. In the time of Herbert's late uncle Henry, this was the district in and around Kleindeutschland. Now it was peopled by immigrants from farther afield than Germany. Herbert heard Russian and Polish spoken as the boys visited squalid tenements with windowless rooms, no sewer connections, and no space for recreation. The area suffered a high rate of tuberculosis. "I was shocked," Lehman later said. "I'm sure I couldn't have described my feelings to anybody."

Most of the German Jewish community had moved on from their humble beginnings in America. Some, like the Lehmans, had even made their fortune. A large number of the later immigrants were also Jews who had run away from pogroms in Russia and Poland in the 1880s and '90s. Yet more would flee in the early part of the twentieth century. Many of those whose homes Herbert Lehman saw worked in the textile sweatshops that some of the German Jews ran.

He started devouring the writings of Jacob Riis, the Danish American social reformer and journalist. *Scribner's* magazine had run Riis's article "How the Other Half Lives," about the New York tenements in 1889, and he later published a book of the same name. Herbert began working with Lillian Wald, a nurse who had helped set up and ran the Henry Street Settlement on the Lower East Side. It trained people in home nursing, cooking, and sewing and provided recreation in music, drama, and art. Financial help came from the Loeb and Schiff banking families. Mayer and Babette Lehman also became friendly with Wald, and Herbert did volunteer work with groups of local teenage boys.

In his job at Spencer Turner he had developed skills in sales, accounting, and negotiation. Having traveled widely since he was a boy, he was especially interested in export but found his enthusiasm not widely shared. Turner had tried to sell a large part of its denims, work shirts, canvases, and yarns in China and the Middle East, where Britain and Japan had well-established trade links. Turner sought cooperation from American companies similar to itself but found them "too . . . indifferent to study alien tastes," said Nevins, reflecting Herbert Lehman's views. They would not pay attention to the different patterns, sizes, colors, and textures except when the home market was in a slump and they needed urgently to sell elsewhere. This "spasmodic alternation of inattention and frenzied interest," Nevins wrote, explained why American exports in many fields lagged behind those of Britain, Germany, and Japan.

One of Herbert's first jobs at Lehman Brothers was to sort out the affairs of Studebaker, the automobile company. Two of the three founding Studebaker brothers began in business in a blacksmith's shop in the 1850s in South Bend, Indiana. The third returned from building a useful fortune of eight thousand dollars making wheelbarrows for prospectors in the California gold rush. He invested it in the business, which the brothers converted into making wagons for the U.S. Army and European pioneers heading west. The company in its early days had played a significant role in the settlement of the American frontier; between a quarter and a half of the vehicles in the midcentury wagon trains were estimated to be Studebakers.

Studebaker earned the distinction of being the only manufacturer to switch from horse-drawn to gasoline-powered vehicles. En route, and like Lehman Brothers, it initially drove into the cul-de-sac occupied by the electric car, though by the time Herbert arrived to be installed as a member of the Studebaker board, the company was gambling on a low-priced vehicle to compete with Ford's Model T. It had taken over several companies that had not survived the new and overcrowded automobile market—one, named EMF, had such a mixed reputation for reliability that it became known as "every mechanical fault." Lehman installed a new quality controller and turned its fortunes around. Over two to three years he spent weeks at a time at the company's Midwest headquarters preparing it for launch on the stock market. Studebaker's first public offering of shares in 1911 was a success, and twelve years later the company's South Bend car plant laid claim to being the largest in the world.

In 1910 Herbert married a young woman named Edith Altschul. While a love match, it was also usefully strategic. In keeping with the *Our Crowd* tradition, the Lehmans had made other such matches: Sigmund from Mayer's side had married his cousin Harriet from Emanuel's, a fail-safe method of wealth containment; Arthur had married Adele Lewisohn (which was "of prime importance" wrote Birmingham, "for it brought the Lewisohn mining enterprises under the Lehman wing"). The Altschuls, like the Lehmans, were generally well connected in the banking world, and Edith's father, Charles, was head of the New York branch of Lazard Frères, the French merchant bank.

Edith and Herbert honeymooned in Europe, which was still in good prewar spirits. Back home they bought a house in rural Westchester, in the small community of Purchase. They lived during summers and week-ends at the house and in winter in a midtown Manhattan hotel, either the Gotham or the Ambassador. It was hard work at the family firm, but their lives were not obviously overburdened with cares.

Herbert did not discover he had an interest in politics until the elec-tion of 1912, which was won by Woodrow Wilson. As governor of New Jersey, Wilson had introduced improvements in education and mea-sures against political corruption in a state that had some reputation for it. He was the last American president to ride to his inauguration in a horse-drawn carriage, and in another nod toward sentimentality, made William Jennings Bryan his first secretary of state. Thereafter he embarked on reform. Carter Glass, his treasury secretary, introduced the bill that created the Federal Reserve to supervise the banking system. Wilson brought in laws to police monopolistic practices by big business and impose restrictions on the hours worked by children. Herbert recalled his father's background—the torchlight processions for Grover Cleveland, the old Southern politicians who dropped around to visit—and decided that he, too, was a Democrat.

Meanwhile, Philip Lehman's chief distraction from his business affairs was a passion for art, of which he became a major collector. He made regu-lar trips with his wife, Caroline, and their children Bobbie and Pauline to Europe, where they visited Italy, France, and elsewhere buying paintings, tapestries, and furniture. Philip had top art dealers and experts looking out for him, among them Bernard Berenson, the art historian and author of the acclaimed book *The Florentine Painters of the Renaissance*. Philip and the family visited Berenson at his villa I Tatti in the Etruscan town of Fiesole near Florence.

Philip kept his collection at his mansion at 7 West Fifty-fourth Street, which he had moved into in 1900. It was one of six numbered 5 to 15 that went up from 1896 to 1900 on land opposite the single brownstone at number 4 occupied by John D. Rockefeller. Philip had the house built in a "rich Beaux-Arts style," wrote Christopher Gray in the *New York Times* in 2006, looking back a century or so: "The deep recesses between the courses of limestone and details like the triple circular windows at the top floor—called oculi—set it apart from most midtown mansions." Actually, elegant as the house no doubt is, it is not set apart at all. Held in a viselike grip by its neighbors, it looks squeezed in. This may reflect how keen Philip was to edge into WASPish terrain. The strip of luxury dwellings of which Philip's was one is today opposite the Museum of Modern Art.

One of the reasons that may have led Philip to start his art collection was that it provided that extra bit of class; an ancient painting made relatively new wealth look like old money. Collecting had become a fashionable occupation of the well-to-do: Andrew Carnegie, the steel magnate did it, as did Henry Clay Frick, coke supplier to Carnegie's furnaces, and Andrew Mellon, the banker and future treasury secretary in the Hoover administration at the time of the Wall Street crash in 1929. Philip numbered them among his friends.

All such people, however, had to rely on the leading art dealers of the time, and the market could be treacherous: You might easily end up with a fake. Renaissance art, Berenson's specialty, was particularly fashionable, and Berenson had become a wealthy man on his commissions. How else, Philip might have wondered, could he have paid for that villa?

Philip, therefore, pursued the Lehman Brothers' principle of keeping it in the family. In 1913 his son Bobbie graduated from Yale, where he had included art among his studies, and his father awarded him the near-perfect job: wandering around Paris, London, Florence, Rome, and anywhere else he wanted to buy art on his father's behalf. Money was no object. Bobbie would cable home from Aix-en-Provence or Siena or wherever with the name of the painter, the title of the work, and the price to be paid. The reply was invariably "money sent STOP all well STOP father."

For quite some time as he traveled in Europe, Bobbie seemed blissfully unaware of the situation around him. World War I broke out in the summer of 1914, yet on November 23, 1915, he wrote home from Europe on a postcard of Piero della Francesca's *The Nativity*, reporting "Lots of nice pictures to be seen." By that time, Germany had started its naval blockade of Britain, the Germans had used poison gas in the second battle of Ypres in Belgium, and, more than six months earlier, a German submarine had sunk the *Lusitania*, the American liner, off Cork on the south coast of Ireland, with a terrible loss of life.

In 1915, Bobbie sent another postcard from the Ritz in Paris indicating that he had been in London and that "good Chinese paintings" were coming to America. "Laurence Binyon of the British Museum told me so." Binyon was the Western expert on Chinese and Japanese art and had published the first book on the subject in any European language, *Painting in the Far East.*

Binyon also happened to be a friend of Ezra Pound and Robert Frost, the American poets, and himself would become if not one of the most famous poets in the world, then certainly one of its most quoted. In September 1914 he had completed his work "For the Fallen," the poem that begins, "They shall not grow old, as we that are left grow old" and builds to the famous line, "At the going down of the sun and in the morning/ We will remember them." Today Binyon's poem is read at annual commemorations of the dead of World War I and other wars in Britain, the countries of the former British empire, and in many other parts of the world. When he wrote it, he could not have guessed the millions who would die in the war that lasted until November 1918.

Thanks to the contacts that his son was acquiring, Philip Lehman was able to make informed speculations in the world of art. As for Bobbie, he was en route to building America's most famous private art collection, though in time he would have to combine that with the lesser joys of running Lehman Brothers.

|||||||||

On June 28, 1914, Archduke Franz Ferdinand of Austria was shot dead in the Bosnian capital, Sarajevo, by a member of the Black Hand, a nationalist group seeking Serbian independence from the Austro-Hungarian Empire. Through a line of entangled alliances, one after the other of the European powers went to war. The United States kept out until the spring of 1917, taking the view that this was an old European affair between competing monarchies and empires.

Wall Street, however, suffered its first casualty almost immediately—the reputation of Goldman Sachs. It turned out that Philip Lehman's partner, Henry Goldman, was a supporter of Germany, while almost all the leading banking houses and Goldman's partners from the Sachs family were not. The Sachses wanted to join in an effort being orchestrated by the J. P. Morgan bank to raise a loan for $500 million for the wartime allies Britain and France. In fact, the Sachses had assured their friends the Kleinworts in London that Goldman Sachs would back the loan. Henry disagreed and vetoed the idea.

To an extent Goldman was only picking up a ball already put in play by Jacob Schiff. European bankers had approached Schiff's bank, Kuhn Loeb, to raise the loan for Britain and France, but Schiff would not agree to it because some of the money might make its way to Russia, which was an ally of France. The Russian pogroms had caused many hundreds of thousands of Jews to flee to the United States, and Schiff was not prepared to raise one cent to back the regime of Czar Nicholas II. Schiff's refusal to endorse the loan prompted one newspaper to headline "Kuhn Loeb, German Bankers, Refuse to Aid Allies."

Schiff, nonetheless, was an elder statesman whose opinions evoked respectful thought, if not agreement. Henry Goldman had no such advantages, and his views also went further. He thought Germany under Bismarck, and more recently under a new Prussian monarch, Kaiser Wilhelm II, had reformed itself from a group of disparate principalities and kingdoms into a modern nation-state. He was a fan of Prussianism, a synonym for discipline and organization. He would quote the German philosopher Friedrich Nietzsche, who among his many works had written on man's conflicting desires for order and disorder. As an advocate of Prussian ways, Goldman preferred the former.

Several members of the Goldman and Sachs families were intermarried, and the divisions between them proved irreparable. Charles Ellis, in *The Partnership*, wrote that one dinnertime conversation on foreign affairs at the Astor Hotel erupted into a fight. The Sachses were especially mortified, given their assurances to the Kleinworts, and hastened to contribute one hundred thousand dollars of their own to the Anglo-French loan.

For years after, Goldman Sachs bore the stigma around Wall Street of being the "German firm." Henry Goldman left and pulled his money out of it—a "sizable" sum, said Ellis—which sharply reduced its capital and ability to operate as a bank. The firm also lost his dynamism and leadership and struggled for years to replace him.

Henry's departure from Goldman Sachs posed a dilemma for Philip. It was because of Henry's leading position in the firm that Goldman Sachs had taken on the idea of doing most of the work involved in the informal partnership with Lehman Brothers. The alliance continued into the late 1920s but was never the same again.

Elsewhere in the family, Herbert Lehman had been angered by President Wilson's initially neutral stance on the war. Herbert's views on Prussianism were the opposite of Goldman's. He hated the autocracy and militarism. Once, while visiting family in Würzburg, he was walking along a street with one of his older sisters when three Prussian officers coming in the opposite direction simply marched straight toward them and crowded him and the girl into the gutter. "I was mad enough to fight the whole German army," he said. He was about nine years old at the time.

Herbert nonetheless maintained his support for the president in the 1916 election, which Wilson looked likely to lose up until the last moment. On election night Wilson went to bed with his declared number of votes cast trailing those of Charles Evans Hughes, the Republican candidate. Having to meet early deadlines, some of the next morning's newspapers would bring word of Wilson's defeat. Lehman, however, had gone to Democratic headquarters in midtown Manhattan to await the results. They trickled in, mostly on the telegraph system; America had had its first telephone line between New York and San Francisco installed only the year before. By five in the morning it became clear that the outcome hinged on California, where it was felt the Democrats might have a narrow margin of four thousand votes in their favor. Around the party's HQ there were fears that the Republicans, who held state power in California, might steal the election. "Money was needed instantly to hire guards over the ballot boxes," wrote Nevins, "and nobody knew where to find it."

Lehman family connections came into play. Herbert telegraphed Isaias Hellman, an uncle in California who was married to his mother's sister. Hellman was president of the Wells Fargo Nevada National Bank in San Francisco. He was also a Republican, but deeper ties prevailed as Herbert asked him for five thousand dollars, which the Democrats would guarantee, to be ready when the bank opened. Ballot box guards were hired, and the Democrats won the state by a little under four thousand votes. Had the guards been necessary? No one knew, but the organizers of Wilson's campaign in California were highly appreciative of Lehman's efforts, and Wilson rode to his inauguration in 1917 to the strains of bands playing "I Love You, California," the state's official song.

Wilson took America into World War I in April 1917 after Germany increased attacks with its submarines on Atlantic shipping, U.S. ships included. The president declared that "the world must be made safe for democracy" to a wave of patriotic fervor. Hollywood answered the call with such stars of the silent screen as Mary Pickford, Douglas Fairbanks, and Charlie Chaplin appearing at huge rallies to sell savings bonds to the public to help pay for the war. World War I was the first occasion on which the U.S. government used savings bonds to raise money, and they became known as Liberty Loans or, more widely, Liberty Bonds.

Herbert Lehman was disappointed with the limits placed on his own contribution to the war effort. Having undergone army officer training, he was deemed too old—at thirty-nine—for an officer's commission. He joined the navy, but this offered no obvious prospect of frontline action. With his textile background, the navy put him into the Bureau of Supplies and Accounts, the department that clothed the service. Wartime America increased the number of sailors sixfold to three hundred thousand men, so he had plenty to do. He also worked as a chief assistant to the undersecretary of the navy, Franklin D. Roosevelt.

Lehman liked Roosevelt's no-nonsense attitude. The undersecretary delegated well, and the two got along. While Roosevelt had trained as a lawyer, he rose above the detail and saw the bigger picture. A medium that promised to be part of it was radio. It had no public function; there were no such things as news broadcasts or entertainment programs. Radio's importance was strategic, particularly in the movement of ships, and vital in times of war. The year 1919 saw Wilson's being the first president to broadcast on radio when he spoke from one ship to others bringing soldiers back from Europe. This was quite possibly at the recommendation of Roosevelt, who, when he became president himself in the 1930s, regularly spoke to the American people on the radio in what became known as his "fireside chats."

The American radio system was in the hands of Marconi, a private British company. Roosevelt directed the transfer of Marconi's U.S. holdings into a new venture run by General Electric and other U.S. companies with a close interest in the field. These included the United Fruit Company, which used radio to direct its large fleet of banana boats. The new venture was called the Radio Corporation of America (RCA). Thus, American radio, from which television eventually came, was the result of enlightened cooperation between public and private enterprise.

Herbert Lehman handled the negotiations with companies that supplied textile goods to the navy. Some struggled to balance the conflicting demands of patriotism and profit. One character whom Lehman sus-pected of overcharging was William "Billy" Wood, boss of the American Woolen Company in the mill town of Lawrence, Massachusetts, who boasted ownership of the largest woolen mill in the world. In the case of one contract, when Wood refused to adjust his price to what Lehman knew to be fair, Herbert suggested that he order a check of the company's books to find out how much Wood had paid for the goods. Wood promptly cut his price to Lehman's original offer.

Herbert continued his volunteer work. He and his brother Arthur, part-ner at Lehman Brothers, were leading organizers of the American Jew-ish Joint Distribution Committee. Its head was Jacob Schiff, now in his seventies. The committee organized relief for several million people left homeless and starving by the war in Belgium, Russia, Austria-Hungary, and elsewhere in Europe.

The army soon decided to commission Lehman as an officer after all. He pushed to serve overseas but again found himself responsible for textile supplies and negotiating with manufacturers. His commanding officers told him he was "indispensable." Although the hours were long, there were benefits. In Washington, Lehman had a social life. He and his wife, Edith, had adopted their first child, Peter, who was born in 1917. The friends the Lehmans made, like the Roosevelts, also had young families.

With war under way, Herbert received an anxious telegram from Bob-bie, his first cousin once removed, now stationed at Fort Oglethorpe, Georgia. Bobbie had come back to America from his art jaunts in Europe to join the army, and he had an officer's commission. But with America's entry into the war seen likely to bring a quick conclusion to the conflict, Bobbie felt he might miss out on the action. He wanted to get to the Euro-pean front and asked whether Herbert, with his contacts in Washington, could do something to help: "[F]oreign languages may be an asset," Bobbie wrote, a reminder that he was versed in French and Italian.

Herbert telegraphed back on June 2, 1917, to "Lt R Lehman" that he would help as long as Bobbie had the assent of higher authority: "I feel too close to your parents to accept moral responsibility." This may give some indication of how firm Lehman family bonds were, though also that Her-bert did not want it on his head that a young member of the Lehman clan, for whom much was planned, was scheming a potentially deadly tour of Flanders and Picardy without parental permission. But "if your father is willing," he added, "I will run my legs off to do anything I can for you here and your anxiety for early service is certainly most praiseworthy."

Bobbie's parents proved willing, or at least felt they could not hold him back amid the war fever of the times, and Bobbie went to serve with the American forces in Europe. He became a captain in the 318th Field Artillery in the Eighty-first, or "Wildcat," Division. The Wildcats took part in the biggest operation by U.S. forces in the war, the Meuse-Argonne Offensive near the town of Verdun on the approaches to Paris. Colonel George C. Marshall, future general in World War II and later organizer of the Marshall Plan, designed to help rebuild Europe, directed the offensive. Meuse-Argonne began in late September 1918 and continued to the final day of the war, on November 11. Not knowing of the armistice, the division was still fighting for several hours after hostilities officially ceased. The Eighty-first Division suffered 1,100 casualties in the war, including 248 dead. Bobbie saw action and survived unharmed.

Herbert Lehman carried on working in Washington. After the war he had a mass of military-supply contracts to conclude and mountains of surplus materials to sell off. He worked closely with John Hancock, a fellow assistant to navy undersecretary Roosevelt. After World War I, a lot of companies wanted Hancock's services and, through his acquaintance with Herbert, he went to Lehman Brothers in 1919; in 1924 he would become the first partner to come from outside the family. Herbert also worked in Washington with Paul Mazur, a Harvard-trained economist and the nation's acknowledged expert in the retail trade, a specialty of the firm since it had launched Sears, Roebuck and Woolworth's. Mazur, too, would join Lehman Brothers.

In no rush to return to the family firm himself, Herbert enjoyed the work in Washington and felt it had contributed to the victory. He had risen to the rank of colonel and won the Distinguished Service Medal— just in time for him to show it to Babette, his mother, on the day before she died in the spring of 1919; she and Mayer had not thought he would amount to much. Herbert stayed on in the capital looking for a political position. He inquired after that of assistant secretary of war, which had become vacant, but it had been promised to someone else.

For a Democrat, this was not the best time to be around the capital, where the political tide had turned. In Europe, ecstatic crowds greeted Wilson, the first president to cross the Atlantic while in office, as he rode through the streets of Paris in December 1918. In London he stayed at Buckingham Palace, and in Rome he met the pope—Benedict XV—another first for a sitting American president. But affairs at home did not work out as Wilson wished. His political enemies raged against his plan for the League of Nations, a body intended to maintain world peace, with America in the leading role. Wilson's foes saw it as an unwarranted involvement in the affairs of the great beyond, a corrupt and ungodly world in which the United States had no part. After Wilson suffered a paralytic stroke in October 1919, from which he never recovered, Congress rejected the idea of the United States joining the League of Nations. Without the world's most vibrant economic and military power as a member, the league did not have a chance of success.

America withdrew into its shell. For the 1920 elections, the Democrats nominated governor James M. Cox of Ohio as their candidate, with Franklin D. Roosevelt running for the vice presidency. They campaigned for membership in the League of Nations and failed to interest the electorate, losing by a wide margin to Republican senator Warren G. Harding of Ohio and governor Calvin Coolidge of Massachusetts.

The Democrats would not return to power in Washington for thirteen years. For his part, Herbert Lehman felt he had no option but to go back to Wall Street.

4

Flying

Bobbie Lehman had led a privileged life of travel and adventure. He had walked the hill towns of Tuscany, haunted the auction houses and ateliers of France, and, at his leisure, discussed life with leading characters of the art world in London, Paris, and Rome. He had also recently returned as a young infantry officer from a brief and triumphant war in Europe. Now he had to face the reality of buckling down to a life in the family firm.

He joined Lehman Brothers in 1919 in his late twenties, having probably known that this was to be his fate for a long time. "To you and me this may be a mysterious realm, art and finance," a friend told the *New York Times* many years later, "but you've got to remember that Bobbie Lehman was born to it. Every night when he sat down to supper that was what he heard. Bobbie ate art and drank finance."

Nonetheless, the change would take some getting used to. First there was the comparatively restricted nature of the business that Lehman Brothers did. Bobbie had been accustomed to comparing the qualities of Tintoretto—or Jacopo Robusti, the Venetian artist's real name, as Bobbie would remind people—with those of Titian—or, as Bobbie with his grasp of Italian would have called him, Tiziano. Now he was more likely to find himself in discussions with clients chewing over the merits of issuing common or preferred stock. Then there were the people. Wall Street types were not a cosmopolitan bunch in comparison with those Bobbie had met in the capitals of Europe. Many had never been abroad much, if at all, and had no interest in going. Most were thoroughly steeped in the ethic of money.

As for Wall Street itself, it was like a cavern that swallowed anyone who entered. Walking along the street even on pleasant days could feel like being in a closed room. Its workers disappeared into buildings that disgorged them at particular times. On dark winter's days it was miserable. Bobbie doubtless pined for some of the journeys he had taken along the roads of Europe, the approaches to Siena and Florence, perhaps, with their views of cathedrals and ancient towers.

Finding himself on Wall Street while not exactly of it, Bobbie threw himself into sports. Doctors to whom he later complained about his health would sound nonplussed, describing him as a "vigorous athlete." Not tall at five feet seven inches, he was always trim. He liked wading in rushing streams as he fished for salmon at the exclusive Restigouche Salmon Club on the border of New Brunswick and Quebec in Canada. He regularly went duck shooting. His favorite sport was polo. Bobbie had his own string of ponies and played at the Meadowbrook Polo Club in Old Westbury, Long Island.

Averell Harriman, a friend from Yale, was a fellow player. Son of E. H. Harriman, a railroad magnate of the late nineteenth century, Averell ran Brown Brothers Harriman, the family bank. His father was generally thought a miserable character, and Averell had his own laconic side. He eventually went into politics and diplomacy, serving in various posts such as ambassador to Britain under FDR, secretary of commerce to Harry Truman, and head of the Paris peace talks on the Vietnam War in the late 1960s under President Lyndon B. Johnson. Harriman was a negotiator and could sit for hours without twitching a muscle.

Bobbie was laconic too. Many people would ask his business secrets, and his responses, while always polite, were rarely expansive: "I bet on the man," he was known to reply, when asked about what projects and people he invested in. "If I see something I like, I buy it," he said of his ways of purchasing art. He and Harriman remained lifelong business partners and friends. At the Meadowbrook they played with the Vanderbilts and the Whitneys. Since the Civil War, New York's elite had settled in the Old Westbury area, where they enjoyed pursuits such as fox hunting. Thomas Hitchcock, founder of the Meadowbrook, was a landowner in the area, and his son Thomas Hitchcock, Jr., would later be a partner in Lehman Brothers. Bobbie Lehman had no trouble with the split between WASPish New York and the Jewish *Our Crowd*. Socially, he flew with the WASPs.

After World War I, there was a question of which direction the United States would take. Should it spread its wings overseas or concentrate on home? The United States had the world to play with. Before the war it depended on striking gold and silver in various remote locations of the country or raising capital abroad in order to grow. Now everyone needed U.S. capital. Europe had ground to a halt after the war, and much of it was in ruins. The world had to come to America as it replaced Britain as the world's most powerful economy.

Lehman Brothers' ventures abroad were limited. The firm helped finance some department stores in Germany run mainly by Jewish interests; Adolf Hitler seized these in the 1930s. In the early twenties the firm also had one hundred thousand dollars in German marks deposited in a German bank, but Germany's hyperinflation of 1922–23 wiped it out. The inflation was an early sign that Germany's moderate Social Democratic government might not be able to survive for long. With Germany economically ruined and owing large reparations to France and its other World War I enemies, the German mark moved from 200 to the dollar in 1922 to 4 billion to the dollar the following year. When Lehman Brothers asked its German bank why it had not mailed a statement of account to New York for some time, the bank replied that a stamp on a letter "costs more than the whole account is now worth."

The firm's decision to concentrate mainly on domestic business reflected the American mood. Warren Harding, who took over as president in 1921, came from Ohio in the Midwest and had little interest in foreign affairs, let alone visions like Wilson's League of Nations. After American involvement in World War I, Harding campaigned on the slogan of a "return to normalcy." The word appeared to break new linguistic ground, as if the president had meant to say "normality" but garbled his words. His defenders, with their eyes on the ancient lexicon, responded that "normalcy" dated back to the mid-nineteenth century. In any case, it captured the imagination of an electorate that had had enough of the outside world's wars and sacrilegious ways.

In 1920 Congress had voted for Prohibition, the banning of the sale and consumption of alcohol. Voices also rose in disapproval at the teaching of evolution in schools, which reached a catharsis in 1925 when John T. Scopes, a public school teacher in Tennessee, went on trial for teaching evolution. The prosecuting counsel was William Jennings Bryan, who, in addition to being a passionate orator and politician, was a religious fundamentalist. The defense was represented by Clarence Darrow, the famed lawyer and member of the American Civil Liberties Union. Bryan won the case.

Harding brought to Washington a number of political friends, known as the Ohio Gang. Harry M. Daugherty, his attorney general, was a deft political strategist who had guided Harding's career. They had been together since Harding's early days in state politics, when Daugherty had spotted in Harding qualities that he believed might make a future leader. Harding was affable and had won a reputation as a man of the people. This contrasted well with Woodrow Wilson, his predecessor, who was seen as an aloof East Coast intellectual.

Where Wilson had been an economic interventionist, Harding was of the laissez-faire, or leave it alone, school. According to this theory, the economy followed its own path in line with the movements of the heavens. Paradoxically, Herbert Hoover, who as Harding's commerce secretary was in charge of economic affairs, did favor some limited government tinkering. America's economy, though healthier than others, suffered a sharp recession in 1920–21. During the war, farmers had provided food for the home front when German U-boats off the coast had stopped many overseas products from getting into America. With the war over, cheaper food arrived from abroad, forcing American farmers' prices and incomes down. Many could not repay their loans to banks, causing many banks to go bust; the effects spread to the economy as a whole and five million people lost their jobs. Hoover helped pull matters around. He summoned experts to a conference for the unemployed and urged bosses to maintain wage levels so that workers had money to spend. He supported public works programs to boost the number of jobs. Much as a result, the recession ended quickly in 1921, and America soon forgot about it.

Lehman Brothers patiently built its business and looked to some of the basics of life to do so. The firm lent its support, for example, to the idea of condensed soup when in the early 1920s it organized the stock market launch of Campbell Soup. The company became a long-term client, a condensed soup "pioneer," as a Lehman Brothers' internal memorandum later put it. The memo added that Campbell's had stolen a march on its main rival, H. J. Heinz, which had apparently turned its nose up at its competitor's gooey product and stuck to producing the noncondensed variety. Heinz finally realized in the 1940s that, as a result of its disdain, it had for years been "shipping a lot of water around the country."

As the economy began to pick up in the first half of the twenties, Lehman Brothers saw the opportunities this presented in retail, a strongpoint of the firm dating back to its ventures with Sears, Roebuck and Woolworth's. Many Americans again had more money in their pockets to spend in the stores, and several top department stores were working hard to attract the American shoppers' attentions.

Lehman Brothers threw itself into the famous rivalry between the New York department stores R. H. Macy's and Gimbel Brothers. For many people the two were the Coke and Pepsi of early American shopping. Macy's claimed it was the "largest department store in the world" and, with its Palladian facade the dominant feature of New York's Herald Square, reveled in attracting the right type of people (that is, customers with money and class). It would not deal in credit: "[N]o one is in debt to Macy's," it said. Gimbel Brothers, on the other side of the street, was not to be outdone. It used the slogan "Select, Don't Settle," which basically meant "Come to us and don't just take the merchandise they're offering you across the way."

From the early twenties, Gimbels staged a Thanksgiving Day parade in Philadelphia, its other flagship city. Macy's shoplifted the idea and brought it to New York. Gimbels advertised its procession as the "oldest parade in the country." Macy's was soon calling its event *the* Thanksgiving parade.

The Lehman family had been friends for many years with the Straus family, owners of Macy's. Lazarus Straus had, like Henry Lehman, come from Bavaria in the mid-1800s, peddled wares along the byways of America, and settled in the South. From Georgia, he moved to New York. Of his three sons, Oscar had fled Germany for political reasons, as had his friend Mayer Lehman. Nathan Straus, another son, had a daughter who married Irving, Mayer Lehman's son, who became a leading New York judge. Isidor, the best known of the Straus sons, died with Ida, his wife, on the *Titanic* in 1912. They both refused the chance to take to the lifeboats, stayed together, and Hollywood immortalized them in various movies about the *Titanic* disaster in years to come.

Macy's wanted to expand and, under advice from Lehman Brothers, raised the money from the stockholding public. In 1922 the store made its first public offering of shares on the market and opened more branches in New York and Long Island. The Gimbel family was determined to match its rival and overcome the fact that it had always been looked down upon by the Jewish community. One department store family in its midst was enough, wrote Stephen Birmingham of the prevailing *Our Crowd* view. New York Jewish society, it appeared, had a prejudice against retail similar to that held by WASPs. The Gimbels were mere "storekeepers," whereas the Strauses somehow had managed not to be. If Lehman Brothers had such prejudices, however, it rose above them and took Gimbels to the stock market in the 1920s.

Macy's claimed to be classier, yet Gimbels beat it at making a move uptown when it bought Saks Fifth Avenue, one of the biggest and most prestigious New York department stores. Gimbels was a good self-advertiser and among the first stores to have its own radio station, WGBS in New York, and others in Philadelphia and Pittsburgh. It used in-store radio to encourage customers to take a look at the full wonders of what it had to offer, not just what was on their shopping lists.

As it progressed with Lehman Brothers' help, Gimbels answered Macy's architectural grandeur with an elegant art deco bridge between its buildings near Herald Square. The walkway was three stories high and made of copper. Its architects, Richmond Shreve and William Lamb, won sufficient acclaim to be offered a role in designing the new Empire State Building commissioned in the building boom at the end of the twenties.

It was Lehman Brothers that spanned the divide between the two famous stores. For several decades a phrase captured their rivalry: "Does Macy's tell Gimbels?" It implied the utmost secrecy, as if to say, "Would you really expect me to tell you that?" In one key sense the competition between the two was itself a grand facade. Macy's and Gimbels revealed their innermost secrets and plans, their budgets and hopes for the future, to a mutual party they trusted. Would Macy's tell Gimbels? Probably not, but both told Lehman Brothers.

Even at this stage of its growing prosperity, Lehman Brothers kept a tight rein on its expenses and its operations in general. It ran only a small office. The exact number is not known, but it is reasonable to assume that the firm employed about twenty people, a dozen or so staff plus partners. Bobbie had become a partner in the early twenties, and two other family members had recently been made partners—Allan and Harold Lehman, the sons of oceangoing Sigmund and Harriet. Allan and Harold would play an undoubtedly useful but quiet role in Lehman Brothers' future development.

The most senior partner after Philip was Arthur, his cousin, who was twelve years younger. Arthur was a great friend of Herbert's, as well as being his broker. There was also nothing to suggest that Arthur and Philip did not get along very well. Arthur had a firm grounding in the business; after he graduated from Harvard in the latter years of the nineteenth century, he had spent a year in the cotton trade with a company in New Orleans and worked in a New York bank before joining the firm. Pictures show Arthur as an Edwardian businessman: bowler hat, starched high-collar shirt, velvet-collared overcoat, leather gloves, and umbrella. He wore an ever-present white carnation. Arthur's children told Kenneth Libo for *Lots of Lehmans* that they had not known him very well because he spent so much time at work. "He was just a man with a moustache who had a jovial voice," said his daughter Frances. "He was kind and never got excited."

John Hancock, recently recruited to the firm, exemplified solid Lehman Brothers growth. One of the first tasks of this friend of Herbert's from wartime Washington was to sort out the affairs of Jewel Tea, the nationwide grocer that Lehman Brothers had launched on the stock market in the Philip Lehman–Henry Goldman years. The company had sixteen hundred stores from Hoboken to San Francisco, but its profit margins had crumbled after many of its salesmen went off to the war. It had since struggled to regain momentum. Hancock came in, cut the number of its stores, closed plants, and abolished obsolete delivery routes. He thus turned the fortunes of Jewel Tea around, and its grateful board of directors made him president of the company.

A little later, Lehman Brothers felt it was time to end its policy of relying on blood members of the family by elevating Hancock to partner in 1924. Its business was growing, and the firm needed reliable new people. Hancock was "tall, burly, restless," wrote Nevins. "[A] strong gust of the Dakota prairies came into the office with this big, direct, and dynamic man." Apparently he also enjoyed big-game hunting in the Canadian Rockies. Hancock sustained a Lehman Brothers tradition of serving on the boards of its clients. A board of directors decided a company's strategic direction, and Hancock not only served on that of Jewel Tea, but also of others such as Sears, Roebuck, Florsheim Shoe, and American Stores.

Later, in the 1930s, Hancock would go on to play an important part in Lehman Brothers' reaching an accommodation with President Franklin D. Roosevelt's New Deal. Most of Wall Street was hostile to Roosevelt as he took measures that the financial community regarded as antibusiness to alleviate the effects of the Wall Street crash. Roosevelt made Hancock a member of the National Recovery Administration, one of the organizations that dealt with the Depression. He went on in the late thirties to work for Roosevelt on U.S. preparations for World War II, even though many Americans at this stage wished to avoid the conflict raging in Europe. After that war, at the behest of President Harry S. Truman, Hancock in 1946 joined the U.S. delegation to the United Nations Atomic Energy Commission. He helped determine America's first steps toward the international control of atomic power.

But at around the time in the 1920s that Hancock was becoming a Lehman Brothers partner, the United States had endured some strange times. President Harding had died under curious circumstances in 1923. He was on a tour of the West, and food poisoning was thought a likely cause of his demise, but doctors suggested pneumonia. There was no autopsy. The president's wife, Florence, went about the task of burning his papers. Scandal had dogged Harding's presidency, with Albert B. Fall, his secretary of the interior, implicated in the Teapot Dome affair. Private companies had paid bribes for the use of federal oil land, and Fall went to jail. Harry Daugherty was accused of corruption and faced two trials, though eventually he was cleared.

Calvin Coolidge, Harding's vice president, took over after Harding's death. A dapper character, the governor of Massachusetts was famous for his proclamation that the "chief business of the American people is business." Otherwise he did not say a great deal. The Coolidges were one of Boston's ruling families, the city's Brahmins, who were famous for passing comment on very little. The Coolidges were quieter than most and, according to Cleveland Amory in *The Proper Bostonians*, known by the Brahmins as "scions of silence." One famous story told of the dinner hostess who said to Coolidge that she had bet she could get him in the course of the evening to say more than two words: "You lose," he replied.

Like Harding, with his help from Daugherty, Coolidge had influential assistance from behind the scenes. Bruce Barton, part of the emerging industry of advertising and a cofounder of the agency BDO (Barton, Durstine and Osborne), assisted Coolidge in his 1924 election campaign. Barton was a religious character who contrived to find a link between God and mammon. His bestselling book *The Man Nobody Knows*, published in 1925, characterized Jesus as a traveling salesman. Warren Susman, the late cultural historian, described Barton as part of a 1920s new wave that bridged the gap between America's old Calvinist ethic, with its emphasis on hard work, self-denial, and savings, and the increasing demands of a "hedonistic consumer culture: spend, spend, enjoy, use up." As the free market of the 1920s began to race ahead, Barton's message was that it was fine to have and to enjoy your wealth. For Coolidge's election he balanced the rip-roaring economy with the president's quite contrasting character. "Keep Cool with Coolidge" was the campaign slogan and it proved popular.

The economic boom that built through the second half of the 1920s was an uneven affair as far as the nation as a whole was concerned, and particularly when focused on the antics of Wall Street and New York. Socialites organized radio parties, where they gathered around their sets to discuss who was behind the latest raid on the stock market. Newspapers and magazines avidly followed the careers of so-called stock market plungers like Joseph Kennedy. The father of future president John F. Kennedy organized "pools" of wealthy investors who drove up the price of stocks by hefty buying and then dumped them, selling them quickly to gain their profits. Other investors scrambled to sell and get their money back, while companies whose fortunes the pools had played with faced collapse when their share price slumped. Pools were perfectly legal at the time. Among those participating in them, sometimes in partnership with Kennedy, was Lehman Brothers.

Textiles was one area of the economy untouched by the gathering boom, and in the summer of 1924, Al Smith, the governor of New York State, asked Herbert Lehman to intervene in a lengthy strike in the New York garment industry. Smith was a friend of Lillian Wald of the Henry Street community project, where Herbert, in his youth, had volunteered. New York's garment workshops were on the Lower East Side, a short distance from Wall Street and at the same time a world away. The conflict pitted the members of the International Ladies Garment Workers Union against their employers in an argument over generally awful wages and working conditions. Many of the women were Jewish and of Russian and Polish origin, while the company owners were often of German Jewish background like Herbert. He spent two years involved in the deliberations that helped bring a settlement. During this period the union went bankrupt and Herbert loaned it fifty thousand dollars to reorganize itself. Eventually, to Herbert's surprise, the union found the money to pay him back.

Herbert began to spend more time on such political work and less at Lehman Brothers. As he joined the talks over the garment strike, so Governor Al Smith also commandeered his help at the disastrous 1924 Democratic convention in New York. Smith was among those competing for the nomination as the party's presidential candidate for the fall elections. Choosing a candidate took 104 ballots. John W. Davis, a constitutional lawyer from West Virginia and solicitor general under Woodrow Wilson, emerged as the winner, but the Democrats were so divided that Davis had, in effect, lost the election campaign before it started.

Unfortunately for the Democrats, the New York convention was the first one broadcast on radio. To most people radio was still a magic box that made alluring sounds. They emanated from a large piece of furniture full of big batteries and tubes that sometimes weighed hundreds of pounds. Compared with the audiences of later years, very few people were listening, but most of those who comprised the radio audience were garrulous opinion formers guaranteed to spread the word of Democratic disarray.

Hoover, the commerce secretary, helped further the Republicans' electoral cause. While the Coolidge administration proclaimed the virtues of the free market, Hoover again tinkered in the background. In 1924 the Federal Reserve adopted an "easy money" policy: Lower interest rates left more money in people's pockets and, as they then spent that money, boosted business. The Democrats' campaign pointed to the corruption of the Republican administration, but the worst of that appeared to have been in the times of the late and now largely forgotten President Harding. The Republicans pointed to the apparent success of the economy and easily retained the presidency by sixteen million votes to eight million.

|||||||||

In 1925 Philip Lehman announced his semiretirement. He would be available for consultation but, at sixty-five, wanted to spend more time seeing the world and buying antiques and paintings in Europe. He passed over most of his share of Lehman Brothers to his son Bobbie, leaving him in control.

Things had not happened like this before. When Henry died in 1855, control passed seamlessly to his brothers, Mayer and Emanuel. When

Mayer died, Emanuel took over and gradually ceded control to the new generation of Philip, his son, and nephews Sigmund, Arthur, and Herbert. Now that Sigmund had long since sailed away and Herbert was more and more off on his political activities, this left Arthur as the most senior of the full-time partners but now suddenly junior to Bobbie.

A Centennial phrased the matter in gentle tones: "From 1925 Robert Lehman took over control assisted by Philip and Arthur." But it was more like a coup d'état by the old pushy New York side of the family than a gentle transition. In training for his job, Arthur had been apprenticed to cotton in New Orleans and banking in New York. Bobbie had in a leisurely vein wandered Europe learning a lot about art. He had since mastered a good deal of the operations of the firm, but strained relations were likely the order of the day as he stepped over Arthur. Lawrence Buttenweiser, Arthur's grandson, later recalled of Arthur, whom he had not really known since he worked a great deal: "[I]t would be hard for me to believe that he was not the top dog of any enterprise in which he was involved. . . . [H]e could not have breathed in an organization where he was not at the very top." Now Arthur would have to learn to.

It was a case of out with the old and in with the new. These were the Roaring Twenties and the Jazz Age. George Gershwin, the composer, had just scored a big hit with *Rhapsody in Blue*. Al Capone led one of the Chicago gangs that made millions from bootlegged liquor during Prohibition, and socialites swigged cocktails at parties organized around their radio sets. Joseph Kennedy was among those reputedly making big money from smuggling whiskey from Canada; apart from this and his escapades as a stock market plunger with Lehman Brothers, he had big interests in Hollywood moviemaking. His fortune would go on to fund the political careers of John F. Kennedy and his other sons.

President Coolidge appeared a strange counterpoint to all of this. He was Mr. Straight, a front man for forces—both market and black market—manipulating from behind. At the same time, he personified an era of America's absorption with itself. He had little interest in "the foreign field," as he called it. One large international dilemma was Europe's debts to America from World War I; as France and others repaid money to the United States, they pressured Germany to pay its war reparations in order for them to rebuild their battered economies. In turn, Germany's tottering democratic regime faced daily pressures from the extremes of left and right, with Communists and Hitler's emergent Fascists fighting it out on the streets. It was put to Coolidge that the United States could ease demands for European debt repayments. Ron Chernow notes that the idea mystified the president: "They hired the money, didn't they?" Coolidge's reaction was to reduce the complexities of international politics to the simple matter of a financial transaction.

In the mid-1920s Bobbie Lehman was avidly looking for deals, and Lehman Brothers began raising money for a new client, Sam Zemurray, head of the Cuyamel Fruit Company, based in New Orleans. Sam "the Banana Man," as he was known, had begun his business around the turn of the century in partnership with the United Fruit Company. In 1907 the two companies had rigged out a gunboat and a crew of mercenaries to sail to the Central American republic of Honduras and overthrow its government. The Honduran regime had opposed their earlier efforts to set up business in the country because United Fruit had a well-developed habit in Central America of taking complete power once allowed in.

Zemurray and United Fruit had since fallen out and were battling for control of land on the frontiers of Honduras and Guatemala. He was Bobbie's type of character—a maverick and never quite part of whatever environment he was in. Rather than in New Orleans, Zemurray lived in Honduras, where he mixed with mercenaries: Two such characters who had helped his Honduran coup were self-styled "General" Lee Christmas and Guy "Machine Gun" Molony.

When Zemurray later took over the United Fruit Company itself, he continued its adventures in the Central American "banana republics," by now a disparaging term and a byword for corruption and big-country domination over small-country affairs. He invited Bobbie Lehman onto United Fruit's board of directors, where they played roles in such events as the overthrow of Guatemala's democratically elected government in 1954 and the less successful effort to eject Fidel Castro from power in Cuba with the Bay of Pigs invasion of 1961.

In the latter part of the twenties, meanwhile, Lehman Brothers took on new outside partners. Monroe C. Gutman and William J. Hammerslough were "securities experts"; in other words, they knew a lot about shares, bonds, and other paper devices, which might just as well have been called "riskies" if it were not for the financial world's regular use of misleading euphemisms. Their expertise in getting share prices right was important.

With the growth of business between 1925 and 1929, Lehman Brothers took sixty companies to the stock market; most of the work was done by Goldman Sachs, but now Lehman Brothers was better placed to do it itself.

A third outsider now brought in was Paul Mazur, the retail specialist. He had just written *Principles of Organization Applied to Modern Retailing*, a weighty treatise commissioned by the National Retail Dry Goods Association. In 1929 Mazur would be a main mover in setting up Federated Department Stores, a body that brought into alliance such stores as Filene's of Boston and Bloomingdale's of New York. In 1939, Federated, with Mazur on the board, successfully lobbied President Franklin D. Roosevelt to bring the Thanksgiving Day holiday forward by one Thursday in the month to extend the Christmas shopping season. Much thanks to Mazur's work, by 1950 *A Centennial* reported that "of the 20 largest U.S. retailing enterprises, Lehman Brothers has been or is investment banker of more than half."

In Bobbie's book, Mazur had additional virtues. He was a cousin of Bernard Berenson, the art expert and long-standing associate of Bobbie's side of the family. He was one of the best friends in Wall Street of David Sarnoff, the chief of the Radio Corporation of America. RCA was the stock of the moment on the 1920s market, or as some have called it, the "Google of its times." Mazur would serve for many years on Lehman Brothers' behalf on the RCA board.

At this time, Lehman Brothers was developing another fashionable line—the investment trust. The term "trust" had already been used in the past to denote large companies, the "trusts" that were apt to operate in an abusive fashion, and also the "trust companies" that had tired of dealing with wills and estates and contributed to the crash of 1907. In the 1920s banks and companies set up investment trusts ostensibly to make expert investments on behalf of others. People bought shares in the trusts, which then invested the money. Lehman Brothers, as reputable a firm as could be found on Wall Street, was early into this market. Its General American Investors Company made a modest $1 million in 1927, its first year, but soon it had created a new trust and merged it with the first. In two years General American had a face value—that is, the value of its shares on the stock market—of $40 million.

Many others, however, raced to get involved. By 1929 banks and brokerages were opening investment trusts at a rate of one a day. This created another thing to invest in: There were all the companies on the stock market that people could put money into, and then there were the investment trusts, which in turn put money invested in them into the companies on the stock market. Very soon the cocktail set gathered at their radios had varied their excited chatter on how Joe Kennedy and other plungers were fixing the market to include which was the latest and best investment trust. Celebrities joined in; characters such as Groucho Marx, along with his fellow Marx Brothers, and other entertainers, like Eddie Cantor, poured their life savings into investment trusts.

One problem was that they became very confusing. Investment trusts spawned investment trusts. They merged with others to form trusts of trusts. Some trusts would not tell their investors what they were investing in; this was confidential information, they said, and better kept from the attentions of the market chatterers who would use it only to profit themselves.

Another device of the day was the "holding company," which existed only to own other companies. Holding companies were set up by grouping companies together in specialized areas: retail, railroads, insurance. Again, this gave share buyers something new to invest in. Then holding companies took over other holding companies, or they took over investment trusts, or investment companies took over holding companies. Who owned what became impossible for many people to know. Even some holding company owners did not know what they owned. People poured their money in anyway, assured that they could trust the experts who virtually without exception said this was the right thing to do.

Plenty of cheap money assisted the process. Interest rates were low, hence people borrowed to the extent of their means and beyond. The drive for profit threw old-fashioned values like thrift out the window. Banks and brokers encouraged people to invest "on margin"—that is, they put down a marginal amount of 10 percent of the price of the shares as they bought them. It was a never-never land in which very soon those share prices had risen high enough to—on the face of things—make so much profit as to cancel out the money that people owed on them. Many people began to believe that debts never needed to be repaid.

With the market booming, Goldman Sachs decided it had had enough of its partnership with Lehman Brothers. The original arrangement had been born of adversity, when neither firm felt it could alone claim its rightful place in the market. Now there was enough business for everyone.

Goldman Sachs also had a new leader, Waddill Catchings, who was someone, it seemed, who had finally filled Henry Goldman's shoes. (Goldman, incidentally, was thinking of following up on his passion for German organization during World War I by actually moving to Germany. He would do so at precisely the wrong time—in the 1930s, when Hitler was coming to power. Goldman suffered much abuse at the Nazis' hands and returned to America a disillusioned man.) Catchings, a lawyer formerly of the Wall Street law firm of Sullivan & Cromwell, was widely regarded as thrusting and charismatic. Under his leadership, his firm felt quite capable of going it alone. Furthermore, Sidney Weinberg, his number two, had dragged himself up from the streets of Brooklyn during the crash of 1907, and he was not going to tolerate a bunch of well-heeled lightweights like the Lehmans having Goldman Sachs do their work for them.

The relationship between the two firms had deteriorated into one dominated by petty bickering. The partners met each week for lunch at Delmonico's, ostensibly to discuss mutual problems, but the occasion made for a series of dyspeptic encounters in which the sides snipped and sniped at each other. On one occasion a Goldman partner suddenly got up from the table, saying he had to get back to the office because he had left the safe open. A Lehman partner, doing a quick scan of his own firm's colleagues, queried why the Goldman man was worrying: "We are all here."

One bone of contention concerned the advertisements that appeared in the financial press when the firms organized a share issue for this or that company. The ads amounted to little more than a list of banks involved: "tombstones" was the term used to describe the ads in the banking business and aptly summed up their dull nature. The ill-tempered partners were regularly arguing with each other over whose name should be mentioned first. (Investment bankers today continue this tradition and it may be that, with their crumbling alliance back in the late 1920s, Goldman Sachs and Lehman Brothers established the precedent for it.)

"They were both too ambitious to stay married," one insider said later. In their divorce settlement, the two sides drew up a list of their mutual clients; it was as Goldman Sachs had claimed: Of the sixty or so in total, forty were Goldman Sachs contacts. Each side agreed as it went its own way that they would not attempt to steal the other's clients.

The odds at the time were on Goldman Sachs' doing better independently. But that did not account for the zeal of Bobbie Lehman. Reliant on its own contacts now, Lehman Brothers found reserves of strength that few on Wall Street realized were there, and the firm took off. "Lehman Brothers always had a lot of money," said a Goldman Sachs partner, "but that's different from being aggressive to get business. After the dispute they became real go-getters."

|||||||||

Juan Terry Trippe was one man that Bobbie Lehman bet on. Of Irish and Venezuelan background, and from a family that had made a fortune from growing sugar in Cuba, Trippe could have followed his father, Juan Pedro Terry, into banking. But after graduating from Yale in 1920, he shunned the opportunity. Trippe was fascinated by planes and wanted to fly them to Cuba and beyond to set up America's first international airline. Lehman Brothers backed him.

Charles Lindbergh and the promise of air travel had captured the imagination of the world in April 1927, when he became the first person to fly solo across the Atlantic in his small twin-engine airplane, the *Spirit of St. Louis*. Lindbergh, hitherto a midwestern mail pilot, completed the journey in 33.5 hours. Some twenty-four years earlier Orville Wright had been the first person to get a plane off the ground when, in Kitty Hawk, North Carolina, he flew 120 feet in 11 seconds. Trippe had hung around airfields as a youth talking to mail pilots making their routes across the country and claimed to have met Lindbergh. Lindbergh said he could not remember this, but from an early stage came in as an adviser to Pan American Airways, Trippe's new airline; Bobbie Lehman was on the board of directors. The three became lifelong friends.

Trippe had launched his first venture, Long Island Airways, with five thousand dollars in 1922. His first client was the United Fruit Company. As United Fruit's banana boats arrived at the coast of Honduras, Trippe flew their customs documents up to Tegucigalpa, the capital, in the distant central highlands. By road and donkey the journey took days; by air, two hours. Trippe turned his mind to Cuba and bigger prizes at a time when people—reluctant to fly at all—were especially nervous about crossing the sea. Without modern radio contact and other navigational aids, planes easily got lost over water.

Bobbie Lehman was all for the gamble, as was his friend Averell Harriman. The two had become active players in the stock market boom of the late twenties at the same time that the young aviation industry was attracting a lot of speculation. Share prices jumped as they bought up a collection of small airlines and formed them into Aviation Corporation; their intention was to create a "General Motors of the skies," according to Lehman Brothers' correspondence. AVCO, as it was known, eventually turned into American Airlines.

But it was the emergent Pan Am and its creator that prompted a particular fascination for Lehman and Harriman. Trippe was a free spirit doing things they would rather have been doing themselves. Bobbie, for example, had earned a pilot's license. Trippe appealed to young men, wrote Matthew Josephson in *Empire of the Air*, a history of Pan Am, "who relished the chance at a sporting enterprise that took them out of doors, far from the humdrum trades of banking or railroads they were supposed to follow in the trail of their distinguished ancestors."

Trippe won the landing rights for a mail and passenger route to Cuba by flying one of his twin-engine Fokkers to Havana, the capital, unannounced and putting on an impromptu flying demonstration for the Cuban president, Gerardo Machado. Pan Am's advertisements aimed to attract passengers by urging them to take a plane rather than a boat across the choppy waters of the Straits of Florida. One ad for the ninety-mile trip encouraged people to "Fly with us to Havana and you can bathe in Bacardi rum four hours from now," an enticing prospect during Prohibition. Al Capone and his henchmen turned up for the journey one day at the small shack that passed for a terminal building in Key West, Florida. "If anything happens to us, remember, it won't be good for you fellers," Capone advised the ground crew and dropped a thousand-dollar bill in a plate on the counter. The round-trip ticket cost one hundred dollars.

Lehman Brothers stayed with Trippe, even though one of his Fokkers lost its way back from Cuba and crashed in the sea in August 1928, killing one of the two passengers onboard. Beyond Cuba, Pan Am won the mail routes to elsewhere in the Caribbean and into South America. With finance for bigger planes, by the late thirties Trippe had mapped routes to China and planned flights across the Atlantic to Europe. Pan Am continued to operate through and beyond World War II, and was established for many decades as the flagship carrier of America and the world's main airline. In backing Pan Am from its earliest days, Lehman Brothers sponsored much of the modern age of international air travel.

In 1928, Paul Mazur proclaimed that the sky was the limit. He'd written another book, *American Prosperity: Its Causes and Consequences*, which argued the case for an increased role for advertising. In spite of Bruce Barton's efforts to enliven President Coolidge's election campaign, advertising was still a primitive medium. Mazur described it as an educational force and necessary to raise Americans' urge to buy. "[D]esires increase, standards of living are raised, purchases are made," he declared.

He believed Americans had to be dissuaded from buying things solely on the basis of their utility: "[W]e must shift America from a needs culture. . . . [P]eople must be trained to . . . want new things even before the old having been entirely consumed." There were "no limits to the needs and desires of American consumers," he claimed. Though a pioneer of what is known today as the throwaway society, Mazur had not foreseen the limits applied to the desires of Americans by health factors—for example, obesity—or by others such as environmental concerns.

There was a more sinister element. Some records indicate that Mazur was a close associate of Edward Bernays, who also had a book published in 1928. Bernays was a nephew of Sigmund Freud and in the process of introducing his uncle's new discipline of psychoanalysis into advertising. As an emerging force, advertising was taking some interesting directions. Bruce Barton's thrust was to find a meeting point between religious humility and the burgeoning wealth of America. Bernays was unashamedly manipulative and did not beat about the bush in titling his book *Propaganda*. He spoke of the "intelligent minority" of society whose function was the "conscious and intelligent manipulation of the organized habits and opinions of the masses." All this should be done, said Bernays, for the "progress and development of America." He went on to be called the "father of public relations" and would figure again in Lehman Brothers' work.

By 1928 Lehman Brothers had grown to the extent that it was able to move to a new address, One William Street, an eleven-story building that would be the firm's home for more than a half century. Although staff numbers had probably not grown to this point, it was large enough to accommodate several hundred people. Just a short distance from its prior location, Lehman Brothers had taken a smart step up the social ladder. One William Street was described as "baroquely ornamented," in terms of its architecture, by *Fortune* magazine and situated "a discreet distance from a formal Wall Street address." The Seligmans had constructed the building some decades before for their own business use, but the former leading family among *Our Crowd* had fallen from grace. Shoddy dealings with such characters as Jay Gould, badly managed railroad investments, and an inability to rear sons interested in running the business had brought the Seligmans' decline.

Lehman Brothers made a peculiar next move. It had developed several areas of expertise—textiles, retail, railroads, and aviation—but moved into the unknown territory of women's cosmetics—unknown, at least, to a group of middle-aged men of finance. Helena Rubinstein wanted to sell her business, Helena Rubinstein, Inc., and move to Paris. Her husband had removed himself there with their children, saying he was fed up with the amount of time she spent on her work. She was in vigorous competition with Elizabeth Arden, her Fifth Avenue rival, and doing very well, but she was desperate to sell quickly. Curiously, Lehman Brothers did not take advantage of her poor bargaining position and paid a premium price of $7 million. Did Bobbie have motives beyond simply wanting to buy a company? He was mixing with a smart set of people in and around Meadowbrook and at thirty-four may have been looking to marry. His own cosmetics company would have made a fine trophy to parade before a prospective bride.

In the fall, the firm lost a pillar of its stability when Herbert Lehman abruptly departed. His political activities, while consuming more time, had appeared to receive scant reward. The presidential election campaign of 1928 had gone no better for the Democrats than that of 1924. Al Smith, Herbert's friend and governor of New York, was the candidate this time and up against the Republicans' choice of Herbert Hoover, the commerce secretary. Matters had not looked good at the summer convention in Houston, Texas. Delegates arrived in style—not in Democratic tradition. "[M]ultimillionaire oil barons unleashed droves of foreign automobiles," wrote Allan Nevins. "[S]ome moneyed men put on a display of affluence that startled people who thought Democrats were by definition poor."

The Democrats failed to find a case to put to the electorate. As an East Coast man, Smith was a stranger to most of the country. He was also Catholic. During one speech he made in Oklahoma City, Ku Klux Klan members were burning crosses. The speech was broadcast on the radio and Smith's normally fluent speaking style was greatly inhibited. The electorate also suspected that the Democrats would abolish Prohibition, a possibility that infuriated ultrareligious regions of the West and South. With the economy now booming, Herbert Lehman, who was the treasurer of Smith's campaign, saw financial as well as electoral disaster looming for the party. Few big businessmen donated to the Democrats, most preferring the safe bet of backing the Republicans under Hoover.

With a month to go until Election Day, New York's Democrats called Herbert away. They figured that with Smith running for the presidency, the only way they would hold New York State would be if Roosevelt ran for governor. Roosevelt was reluctant, having since 1921 suffered the effects of polio, which had left him permanently crippled. He had opened a therapy center in Warm Springs, Georgia, where he spent a lot of time. He only agreed to run if Lehman ran with him, for lieutenant governor and as his right-hand man. The move worked. Smith lost to Hoover by a wide margin in the presidential race, but the New York Democrats held the governorship. Roosevelt, of old Hudson Valley rural stock, enjoyed an affinity with the state's farmers, and Lehman did especially well among the ethnic and working-class communities of New York City.

Herbert told his brother Arthur, Bobbie, and the other partners that he would be back, having served one normal term as lieutenant governor, in two years' time. For one so set on return, it was peculiar that he asked to take his money out of the firm. Arthur saw no objection, and no one else raised any. Money was no object at the time and, for his share of the partnership, Herbert received a substantial, though undisclosed, sum.

The following spring Bobbie rushed off too, in his case to marry. The bride was Ruth Lamar Rumsey, daughter of Mr. and Mrs. J. Spencer Lamar of Evanston, Illinois, who was well known around New York's social circles. She had been married before, to a Jack Rumsey, which in contemporary terms made the union risqué. A small report in the *New York Times* on May 18, 1929, said Ruth and Bobbie had married in Montreal, Canada, and would live at 7 West Fifty-fourth Street. For the moment, they were already bound for a European honeymoon and had "sailed on the Olympia to see Mr. and Mrs. Philip Lehman abroad."

Bobbie was not so distracted to have missed the latest developments with Lehman Brothers' old partners at Goldman Sachs, where Waddill Catchings had belatedly spotted the promise of investment trusts. Where Lehman Brothers had conservatively viewed investment trusts as a new and useful means of making money, Catchings, saw them as a vehicle bound along a road to ceaseless prosperity. The firm's main investment trust was the Goldman Sachs Trading Corporation, which in 1929 had doubled its worth to $244 million in three months. Catchings promptly followed up by launching two others: One was called Shenandoah, after the long and meandering river of the same name, and the other, Blue Ridge, as if to mark a point on the beckoning horizon. The share prices of both boomed, although in the summer of 1929 one of the Goldman Sachs partners, Walter Sachs, suggested that Catchings now tread more cautiously. As Ellis writes in *The Partnership*, the idea was dismissed out of hand: "The trouble with you, Walter," Catchings said, "is that you've no imagination."

Philip Lehman, watching from the wings of semiretirement, found himself less than overawed by Catchings; he was "too optimistic" and "lacked balance," he said. But apparently Bobbie was more impressed, and in September, Lehman Brothers set up the Lehman Corporation, another investment trust of its own. It issued one million shares at $100 each, and such was the demand for them that their price surged to $136 each on the first day.

At about the same time Lehman Brothers fixed a deal with great significance for the future. It helped set up and launch the National Union Radio Corporation, the initial aim of which was to bring together a number of companies that made radio tubes. The nine million radios in use in the country came with anything from three to twelve tubes, of varying shapes and sizes, made by many different companies. National Union Radio would bring more tube production under one roof, standardize the size of the tubes, and therefore make radios more amenable to mass production. This would mean cheaper and less cumbersome radios and more sales. But National Union Radio was also making tubes for television, the commercial production of which was still a decade away. Lehman Brothers had involved itself very early in this endeavor and with a huge partner: The company behind the deal was the Radio Corporation of America.

Over the previous two years, Lehman Brothers had been developing a close relationship with RCA, whose immediate sights were set on
supplying Hollywood. In March 1927 *The Jazz Singer*, made by Warner
Bros. and starring Al Jolson, became the first talking film. Warner Bros.
was not one of the big five studios—Metro-Goldwyn-Mayer, United Artists, Paramount, Universal, and First National Pictures—but produced
an enormous hit that sounded the death knell of the silent movies. At
the same time, its technology remained primitive, and only a few scenes
came with sound. Very soon RCA produced a far better system, more
like that used today.

The implications were enormous. With radio, audiences made their
own mental pictures. The silent movies had provided vision while their
limited subtitles and piano accompaniments still allowed imaginations
to have relatively free range. The talkies hardly made it necessary for an
audience to think at all. Exciting times lay ahead, especially with a new
wave of advertisers and propagandists making their presence felt.

RCA, however, could not interest none of the big studios in its new
system. They had sunk big investments in fitting their theaters with the
Warner Bros. system. So with Lehman Brothers as advisers, RCA made
its own way to Hollywood. Bobbie's firm organized a national chain of
movie theaters by merging the properties of the Orpheum Circuit and
entertainment entrepreneurs such as Benjamin Keith. According to the
new company's documents, this provided "a chain of vaudeville theaters, both in the United States and Canada extending from the Atlantic to
Pacific coasts—and containing over one million seats." Vaudeville was a
form of entertainment bound for obsolescence.

In on the plan was Joe Kennedy, who in Film Booking Offices of America had his own prospering moviemaking company. The theater chain and
Kennedy's company merged, and RCA took them over as Radio-Keith-
Orpheum, the new and revolutionary Hollywood studio better known
as RKO. It would launch careers such as those of Ginger Rogers and
Fred Astaire, David O. Selznick, and King Kong, movie monster. More
discreetly, it announced the arrival of Bobbie Lehman as a leading Hollywood financier, who would also later advise the studios of Paramount
and Twentieth Century-Fox.

The talkies quickly displaced silent film, and from 1927 to 1930 the number of people attending movie theaters went up by more than half, from 57 million to 90 million. The price of shares in RCA, which had been two dollars apiece in 1920, rose to five hundred dollars by the fall of 1929. Few people questioned that this could go on forever, taken as they were by all the new sounds and flickering images. When the crash came, America was out at the movies.

5

Crash

Herbert Lehman came to work with Franklin D. Roosevelt because he wanted to return to public service. His years in Washington during World War I had given him a taste for it, and his time back at Lehman Brothers had confirmed his belief that his talents were better suited in government. He had done well in private business and had plenty of money. He saw no point in making more.

His wife, Edith, and he had adopted three children: Peter, who was now eleven, John, eight, and Hilda, seven. They hoped that moving to Albany, the New York State capital, would allow for a more normal family life. At Lehman Brothers, Herbert had hated the days, sometimes weeks, on the road. He had been a director of a large number of companies, including Pierce Oil, the Coal & Iron National Bank, and Empire Fuel & Gas, and he had tired of the mundaneness of poring over balance sheets, reading industrial journals, and enduring interminable meetings with economists.

One unnamed Lehman Brothers partner later suggested to Lehman's biographer that he had seen Herbert's departure coming. They had once spent months arranging the launch of shares of a client's company on the stock market, a deal that promised a big fee for Lehman Brothers. At the last moment the client was overcome by "irrational doubt" and begged for a drastic modification. The potential cost to the firm notwithstanding, "Herbert did not even expostulate. Despite his months of toil he instantly assented: 'Certainly,' he said." Herbert, the partner confided, "was not heart and soul a businessman."

But Lehman embraced his role as lieutenant governor, and upon taking office, changed the largely ceremonial post into one of action. Roosevelt remained partly crippled by his attack of polio seven years earlier in

August 1921 and took regular trips for therapy at his spa in Warm Springs, Georgia. He also frequently traveled out of state for political business and as a first-class delegator found plenty of important, and often awkward, tasks for his old friend Herbie to do.

Roosevelt was away in Chicago when Lehman was called from his bed one morning before dawn in December 1928 with news of a riot at the state prison in Auburn. Conditions in New York's overcrowded and ancient prisons were poor, and the Auburn inmates had taken members of the staff hostage. Lehman refused to negotiate and sent in the National Guard armed with tear gas, and the prisoners were back in their cells by the end of the day.

FDR put Lehman in charge of settling another strike in New York City the following May, again involving the International Ladies Garment Workers Union. Sweatshop conditions remained in the multitude of factories in the garment district, and Herbert resumed the role of mediator in the lengthy process needed to reach a settlement.

Herbie's financial experience proved important in January 1929 when he dealt with a bank crisis. City Trust Company, a New York bank used mainly by the Italian community, faced collapse after Francesco M. Ferrari, its chief, had suddenly died under unknown circumstances. Ferrari had a reputation for excess, and rumors circulated that he had funded his extravagant lifestyle using his depositors' money. Account holders, rushing to retrieve their money, created a run on the bank. Suspicions aroused by the matter also fell on Frank Warder, the New York State banking department superintendent, who the governor's office discovered had applied for a passport and planned to leave the country. Lehman stopped him and ordered an investigation, which revealed Warder had taken bribes to overlook irregular goings-on at the bank. The banking superintendent went to jail.

Lehman summoned a group of banks to take over the City Trust's operations. As part of the exercise, a fund was created to guarantee depositors' money, and Herbert put in $1 million of his own. He never received any of it back because of the Wall Street crash later in the year.

President Hoover took office in March, having declared that "we shall soon, with the help of God, be in sight of the day when poverty will be banished from this nation." But he worried that the boom was getting out of hand. In an effort to make speculation with borrowed money more difficult, the Federal Reserve raised interest rates, the upshot of which, as John Kenneth Galbraith wrote in his book *The Great Crash 1929*, was that Wall Street responded with fury. "We feel that we have an obligation which is paramount to any Federal Reserve warning," said Charles E. Mitchell, head of National City, one of the largest banks, "to avert any dangerous crisis in the money market." He implied that the central bank was risking causing a crisis by intervening. National City, he pledged, would lend any money people needed to counter the Federal Reserve's restraints.

Irving Fisher, an eminent Yale economics professor, pronounced in mid-October that "stock prices have reached what looks like a permanently high plateau." The market crashed less than a fortnight later. The twenty-fourth and twenty-ninth of October became known as Black Thursday and Black Tuesday respectively, and the collapse cut the value of shares by many billions of dollars.

Winston Churchill, the British politician who by this stage of his career had held a number of cabinet posts without huge success, stood on Black Thursday in the visitors' gallery of the stock market witnessing the mayhem on the floor below. Churchill had an American mother and many friends in the United States, including Bernard Baruch, a leading investor of the time. One of the purposes of Churchill's visit to America was to check on his substantial stock market investments, which at this moment he was in the process of losing. The effects of the crash and the ensuing Great Depression would spread to Europe and exacerbate the problems left after World War I. Germany had moved from one crisis to another, and in 1933 Adolf Hitler came to power, declaring an end to its humiliation. In Britain, Churchill received his call to leadership in 1940, a few months after the start of World War II.

As the stock market was crashing in 1929, the rest of New York carried on as best it could. Bobbie Lehman and Averell Harriman were flying a large balloon: They had widened their partnership in aviation to include airships. Germany's Zeppelin airship had completed a world tour in the summer, and many people thought that balloons might be a safer and quicker form of transport than airplanes. Juan Trippe's Pan Am planes took four hours to travel the ninety miles to Cuba, while the latest Zeppelin soared at seventy miles per hour. *Flight* magazine reported on November 1 that Zeppelin and Goodyear, the U.S. rubber company, had set up the Goodyear-Zeppelin Corporation of America to make airships, and that Lehman and Harriman had ordered two of them. They planned a "trans-Pacific airship service," first with a route from California to Hawaii, then later to the Philippines and Japan. Nothing came of Lehman and Harriman's balloon venture. Capital for such investments was in short supply after the crash, but airships in general lost their attraction when the *Hindenburg*, a German Zeppelin arriving in May 1937 from across the Atlantic, burst into flames at the Lakehurst Naval Air Station in New Jersey, killing thirty-six people.

Of other New York events, the Museum of Modern Art opened its doors to the public for the first time in the first week of November. Located on the twelfth floor of the Heckscher Building at Fifth Avenue and Fifty-seventh Street, the new gallery showed works by Cézanne, Gauguin, Van Gogh, and others. MoMA's arrival on the scene lifted the spirits of the city's cultural community, but the restorative powers of art had their limits in the exceptional circumstances of this time.

The grave nature of events downtown took a new turn on Friday, November 9. J. J. Riordan, president of the County Trust Company, committed suicide by shooting himself with a handgun he took from one of his cash tellers' drawers. Word of the tragedy was kept from the press until noon on Saturday, after the bank closed its doors for the weekend, thus preventing a run on the bank by worried account holders. Herbert Lehman, a friend of the deceased, may have been a party to this conspiracy and acted as an honorary pallbearer at the large funeral that took place on Sunday.

The reason behind the crash was simple: People had bet all they had, and more besides. Assured that nothing could go wrong, they invested their savings and borrowed more. As such, they had "leveraged" their assets; namely, they had borrowed against their assets and put that money in the stock market too. Unfortunately, the assets that investors had often borrowed against were shares; hence they had nothing of worth to sell in order to settle their debts when the markets crashed.

The crash soon changed the image of the banker from protector of the public's money to greedy shyster out to profit at public expense. More simply, bankers had failed another history test. Galbraith noted, this time in his book *A Short History of Financial Euphoria*, that it usually required twenty years for the financial memory to forget the last slump: "[T]his is normally the time it takes for the recollection of one disaster to be erased and for some variant on previous dementia to come forward to capture the financial mind." Galbraith's assessment was spot-on if the panic of 1907 was the last point of reference. But the United States had only recently had the sharp recession of 1920–21. In 1920s America, dementia had taken hold in less than a decade.

In the wake of the crash, great pyramids of holding companies and investment trusts—the same new investment tools that had become so popular in preceding years—collapsed, since they had no real assets to support them. People had trusted the experts, and as a result, many of them lost everything. Eddie Cantor, one of several celebrities who had hopped on the gravy train while it was still hot, lost his life savings. He thereafter devoted much of his act to bitter humor attacking Goldman Sachs, the firm in which he had put his money.

Of the $173 million lost by investment trusts, Goldman Sachs lost by far the most—$121 million. Waddill Catchings, its senior partner, left the firm under a cloud, but soon shrugged off its effects as he departed for the sun of California, where he became a radio producer. Goldman Sachs had thought it had recovered from the aftereffects of the episode with its old senior partner Henry Goldman, and from the years of being called "the German firm." It would now be associated for years to come with the ignominious collapse of the Goldman Sachs Trading Corporation.

Lehman Brothers was second in the list of losers. Its investment trusts lost $8 million, a far cry from Goldman's losses, but it had been lucky. The firm had launched the Lehman Corporation just a month before the crash and had not had time to invest back in the market the $100 million it had received from its shareholders. It used some of the money to resuscitate the trust by buying back its shares at the far lower price they had slumped to.

But while Lehman fared comparatively well in the investment trust trade, it suffered under the fate of Helena Rubinstein's cosmetics company. Part of the problem was that the firm had struggled to manage products—women's cosmetics—it did not understand. "There is no denying," Rubinstein wrote in her autobiography, "that the beauty business is made up of part theater and part glamour." Lehman Brothers failed to grasp the company's snob appeal. Though Rubinstein catered to members of the upper class who shopped along Fifth Avenue, Lehman Brothers had lowered prices and tried to attract those of the middle class who, before the crash, had joined the ranks of the well-heeled. Many rich customers responded by going to shop at Elizabeth Arden nearby.

In Paris, alas, Rubinstein's marriage collapsed, and she returned to New York. "Ahead of me once more was the lonely treadmill of work," she wrote. "Never had I felt so utterly alone." Lehman Brothers was content, however, to sell her business back to her for a postcrash price of $1 million. Compared with the $7 million she had sold it for less than two years earlier, at least this provided her with six million small causes for cheer after the loss of her marriage.

The crash also caused a split within the Lehman family. Bobbie suddenly became enraged over Herbert's taking his share of the money from the firm when he left for Albany. Bobbie did not turn his ire on Herbert, possibly being mindful of his cousin's nascent influence in high places. Instead he directed it at Arthur, Herbert's older brother. "What Bobbie Lehman did was to blame Arthur for risking the firm to pay off his brother," explained Robert Bernhard, Arthur's grandson and a Lehman Brothers partner in the 1960s. This was in spite of the fact that neither Arthur, Bobbie, nor anyone else saw a risk in paying Herbert off, given that none of them predicted the 1929 crash. Besides, had Bobbie or his father raised any objection, alternative sources of cash were available. "[T]hey could have paid [Herbert] off with shares they owned in private companies—Helena Rubinstein, for example" Bernhard added. The crux may have been that Bobbie was not coping with what for him was an unfamiliar problem: financial hardship. The effect was lasting, however, and even as times improved for Lehman Brothers, the rift between Bobbie and Arthur did not heal.

Meanwhile, some of those in the high echelons of the banking community began to see the crash as a good thing. "The remedy is for people to stop . . . listening to the radio, drinking bootleg gin and dancing to jazz," said Russell C. Leffingwell, leading partner at the banking house of J. P. Morgan. After a "healthy purge," people would "return to the old economics and prosperity based upon saving and working." Like a disapproving deity, the Hoover administration joined the spirit of the purge and cut the money supply. It seemed to say that, with less money in their pockets, people would have to return to a frugal and better life.

The view from the statehouse in Albany was less sanguine. Roosevelt and Lehman had come to office with reforms in mind, such as improving the decrepit state of New York's mental hospitals. Since the Auburn riot, Herbert had added prison reform to the list. Now, with the closure of banks, factories, and other businesses, more money was needed for unemployed people and destitute families. The city of New York tried to levy a tax on transactions in the stock exchange. The exchange threatened to decamp to New Jersey and the idea was dropped.

With state elections due in the fall, in spring 1930 Lehman told Roosevelt that he might not run again for lieutenant governor. After one two-year term, he said, he felt he should get back to Lehman Brothers, which had its own troubles. Herbert may have needed little persuasion to change his mind, however, and Roosevelt quite possibly sealed the matter in a letter: "[N]evertheless you and I both have the same kind of sense of obligation about going through with a task once undertaken, and frankly, the only reason either of us would run again is that sense of obligation to a great many million people." Lehman sensed that obligation too, and decided to run for reelection.

The pair won a comfortable victory at the polls, with Roosevelt's majority 725,000 and Lehman's 607,000. Now they just had to figure out what to do. Classical economic theory provided no adequate guidelines. It dictated that people should be left to their own ingenuity to pull out of a slump, with recovery coming in uncertain due course. This was no comfort when a solution was needed quickly across America's most industrial state. As John Maynard Keynes, the British economist who later updated ancient economic theory, would famously write: "[I]n the long run we are all dead."

Roosevelt and Lehman had to improvise, with a lot of the work falling to Lehman. His contribution was vital over the coming years, in which Roosevelt, both as governor of New York State and then president of the nation, faced attack from economic and political conservatives for policies that they claimed were unduly radical. There was always one fault with the critics' argument: Behind Roosevelt, and often at his side, stood Herbert Lehman, who no matter the claims and criticisms exuded the air, as one observer put it, of the "cautious banker."

Exhausted after the state election campaign of 1930, Roosevelt took a vacation in Warm Springs, leaving Herbert in charge of a "committee of one," as the governor described it. Lehman pushed ahead with job-creation schemes in highway building, improvements to canals, and the development of parks. He called the heads of the private railroad companies together and cajoled them to bring forward the works that they planned to carry out on their lines.

December 1930 saw a turning point, however, both for Lehman and the economy, and it involved another bank crisis. The bank in trouble was the Bank of United States, which was private, although its name sounded like the old central bank from before the days of Andrew Jackson and suggested federal backing. Other banks believed that this was its owners' deceitful intention. Chernow records, for example, that it had an oil portrait of the U.S. Capitol hanging in its lobby. It was Jewish owned, and most of its 450,000 depositors were Jews, many of them poor immigrants who worked in the garment industry and associated trades. Rivals disparaged it as the "Pantspressers bank." J. P. Morgan's Leffingwell observed that it had "a large clientele among our Jewish population of small merchants, and persons of small means and small education, from whom all its management was drawn."

The Bank of United States affair would prove important for a number of reasons. It had engaged in some shoddy shares issues, for example; in so doing it had used its depositors' money to sponsor the kind of deals that the Roosevelt administration would crack down on with the Glass-Steagall Act of 1933, which made it illegal for banks that took the public's deposits to engage in such gambling activities.

The Bank of United States was also the fourth-largest bank in New York City. More than one thousand U.S. banks had failed in 1930, and, if this one collapsed, it would be the biggest so far. Lehman and Joseph A. Broderick, his state banking superintendent, devised a plan to merge it with three other banks, supported by a loan of $30 million from Wall Street. As a precedent, earlier in the year J. P. Morgan had bailed out the bank of Kidder, Peabody with a loan of $10 million.

Broderick summoned a meeting of the leading Wall Street banks for the evening of December 10. Lehman came from Albany for the meeting, but when he arrived at his city apartment, Broderick phoned him to say that Lehman did not need to be at the meeting, and that, actually, it was inadvisable that he attend. Nevins relates this exchange without clarifying why Lehman's attendance was inadvisable. As with the Kidder, Peabody case, however, the bankers were handling the matter themselves and the presence of a high-ranking government official might have caused undue alarm, whether among the bankers or, if the word seeped out, the public.

Broderick phoned Lehman several times during the evening to say discussions were going well. After midnight, however, he called with the news that the bankers had withdrawn their $30 million commitment. They had found irregularities in the Bank of United States' accounts. Indeed, the bank was known to have engaged in suspect share dealings and two of its heads would eventually go to jail. Broderick urged those at the meeting, however, to think of the bank's depositors: "I asked them if their decision to drop the plan was still final. They told me it was."

Imploring Broderick to keep the group together, Lehman caught a cab downtown. Some of the bankers had gone by the time he arrived. "I made the strongest possible plea," Lehman said, "not to let the bank fail. I pointed out the effect its closing, with very large deposits mainly from small people, would have on the entire business situation."

The bankers would not change their minds. The disappearance of the Bank of United States, after all, meant one less rival for them. Others had different interpretations. Roy Cohn was one person who did. Cohn in the 1950s would be the legal counsel for Senator Joseph McCarthy during the campaign led by McCarthy to root out alleged Communists in U.S. government positions. At that time, Cohn, who incidentally was a friend of Bobbie Lehman, would come into conflict with Herbert. In the case of the Bank of United States, however, the bank's president, Bernard K. Marcus, was Cohn's uncle and one of the owners who went to jail. According to Chernow, Cohn always blamed the bank's failure on an anti-Semitic plot.

Whatever truth there was to that, Broderick had his own views. He later said that he told those gathered at the meeting that they were making "the most colossal mistake in the banking history of New York."

Herbert Lehman was of a similar mind. "He always believed," wrote Nevins, that the collapse of the Bank of United States "had a marked effect in sapping general confidence in the banking system." In short, it was a key moment in transforming the crash on Wall Street in 1929 into the Great Depression of the 1930s.

Ironically, Lehman's old family bank would find itself in a similar position to that of the Bank of United States some seventy-eight years later.

Herbert Lehman was a banker who had inherently trusted the members of his own profession to do the right thing. After this he would not leave bankers in charge of any decisions whose importance stretched beyond the confines of Wall Street. He had other beliefs that had taken a knock too. As with the City Trust bank in early 1929, he had had faith in his personal philanthropy as a means of easing the path to recovery. Now Bank of United States depositors came to him and asked that, since he had given $1 million to help City Trust and its mainly Italian depositors, could he not do the same for them? But the sum involved—$30 million—was beyond his means. The crash of 1929 showed that it was primarily government action, not personal charity, that was required to sort it out.

As the Depression applied its grip, unemployed people staged marches in leading American cities. The Communist Party organized a hunger march in Albany, and protesters occupied the State Assembly chamber. In 1932, thousands of veterans of World War I gathered in Washington demanding an early payment of a bonus they had been promised for their part in the war. Major General Smedley D. Butler gave a speech to them at a rally. Butler, a retired Marine, had a distinguished service record of thirty-three years in Central America and the Caribbean, and he backed their cause. President Hoover said the early bonus idea made no financial sense and had federal troops eject the veterans from the city.

In Herbert Lehman's youth, people of his Midtown upbringing had had to take the train down to the Bowery if they wanted to witness poverty. Now the poor came to them. Homeless people in American cities built ramshackle slums called "Hoovervilles" on available green spaces. New York's Central Park housed one of them, in clear view of Fifth Avenue.

In 1931, Paul Mazur lamented in his book *New Roads to Prosperity* that he had not seen the crash coming when he wrote *American Prosperity* in 1928. The Lehman Brothers partner had the foresight, however, to predict one important outcome. Many millions of unemployed people meant society would turn its thoughts to sharing work, even after a recovery. Americans worked six days a week, but Mazur foresaw that "all labor in America would be limited to five out of the seven days of the week. . . . [T]o the forty million adult workers of the United States there would be suddenly given one added day of leisure per week."

Mazur, with his retail hat on, could see past the Depression to a time when Americans would do a lot more shopping. Mazur also reflected on the causes of the Depression. He spoke of "the tragic lack of planning that characterizes the capitalist system." It was incumbent on all those who believed in it, he argued, to correct this deficiency. There had, in short, to be a plan. And by the summer of 1932 there were two people who had a plan. Roosevelt had decided to run for the White House and Lehman for the governorship of New York. With few doubts this time, Lehman regarded it as "almost a necessity" to run. In an article for *Atlantic* magazine, he wrote of the need to "emphasize the value of experienced businessmen in government in a time of economic crisis."

Lehman ran the affairs of New York State from early 1932 on, enabling Roosevelt to be away on his national campaign. Roosevelt called him "the other governor." Meanwhile, Lehman had his own campaign for the governorship to conduct. One of his policies was to back the repeal of Prohibition. By some estimates, wrote Allan Nevins, "the reopening of breweries and distilleries, the reappearance of bars, the increased patronage of restaurants and hotels, and the larger trucking business" would create a hundred thousand jobs in New York State.

William Donovan, the Republican candidate, said Lehman's welfare policies were "ruinous." Lehman countered that Donovan lacked "social imagination." Known as "Wild Bill," Donovan was a decorated war veteran who went on to head the Office of Strategic Services, the forerunner of the Central Intelligence Agency. In the 1932 election, Herbert Lehman won by an unprecedented margin of 2.7 million votes to 1.8 million. Louis Waldman, a Socialist candidate, polled 103,000 votes.

In his inauguration speech in Albany on January 2, 1933, Lehman pledged to work for those in need. About 1.5 million people in New York State had no jobs, and nearly the same number worked only part-time. Roosevelt spoke too, and said Lehman would provide leadership "of definite action founded on liberal thought."

Herbert did not attend Roosevelt's inauguration on March 4 in Washington, DC. This was the occasion when the band played "Happy Days Are Here Again," and in his famous speech, the new president said, "The only thing we have to fear is fear itself." Lehman had planned to go but faced another bank crisis; he had a meeting scheduled with the state's leading bankers and had no intention of missing it.

The crisis had been brewing in the period leading up to Roosevelt's inauguration. Three weeks before he took office, Roosevelt survived an assassination attempt while visiting Miami. Giuseppe Zangara, a mentally ill bricklayer, fired a number of shots, one of which killed Anton J. Cermak, the mayor of Chicago, a member of Roosevelt's party. A potent mix of political and economic uncertainty in the approach to FDR's swearing-in caused people to rush to withdraw money from the banks, and about five thousand banks—a fifth of America's total—ceased business on the day before the inauguration.

Lehman convened his meeting of New York's bankers at 10:00 P.M. that evening. Among the roomful of people were the state's banking superintendent Broderick, Leffingwell, J. P. Morgan, and others, such as George Harrison of the New York Federal Reserve. The gathering, at times a stormy one, lasted until 3:30 A.M. The bankers wished Lehman to declare a "bank holiday" until the panic passed, although they wanted the move to appear as if it had been the governor's initiative. Lehman insisted that the request be seen to come from them; he did not want them later claiming that the state government had blunderingly forced its way in. At 4:20 A.M., Lehman released an agreed statement to the press. "The spread of hysteria and the restrictions imposed upon banking facilities of the country," he announced, "have placed upon New York banks a burden so great that it has finally rendered drastic action imperative here."

Lehman decreed that New York's banks would close for two days, Saturday March 4 and Monday March 6. One of Roosevelt's first acts on entering the White House was to extend this, and to announce that all of the nation's banks would close until March 9. Both in New York and all over the United States, Roosevelt and Lehman aimed not just to let the crisis pass but to take measures that would send it packing. They planned a thorough review of banks' books to decide which were worth opening again. Most banks did reopen; about five hundred did not. Those that returned to business came with the assurance that the government had checked them for solvency, and deposits flowed back in as public confidence returned.

Lehman and Roosevelt had once stood on the outside of the crisis and reacted to it. Now in New York and Washington, they had taken the offensive.

|||||||||

King Kong, the movie about a monster gorilla running rampant in New York, premiered at Radio City Music Hall on Thursday March 2, 1933, two days before Roosevelt's inauguration. A smash hit, the film proved a godsend for the RKO studios in Hollywood; for David O. Selznick, who ran them and produced the movie; and for Bobbie Lehman, who had helped establish RKO. During the Depression, movie audiences had dwindled and RKO had run out of cash to pay the mortgages on its chain of theaters. *King Kong* brought fear and exhilaration to moviegoers, fame to Selznick, and relief to movie moneymen like Bobbie.

The gorilla served as a kind of metaphor for the American consciousness. In one of the film's most famous scenes, Kong stands holding on to the top of the new Empire State Building, swatting away the kinds of airplanes that Bobbie Lehman financed. Was this a case of capitalism gone mad and the jungle monster within it running out of control, destroying everything in its path? The gorilla had his tender side, though, and in the end he only wanted the white girl, played by the cowering Fay Wray. Perhaps *King Kong* was just a monster movie that allowed Americans to escape the very real problems of the times.

Roosevelt's New Deal planned to take democratic control of the situation, and the prospect filled its opponents with horror. The economic system had long been subject to the forces of mysticism and the control of a privileged few. The New Deal would establish a number of laws to regulate the errant banking system and stock market and others to get the national economy moving again. The measures were similar to those already implemented in New York, and as Herbert Lehman continued to expand his and Roosevelt's work, Lehman's efforts in the state would come to be known as the Little New Deal.

Wall Street was not about to take the issue lying down, and Leffingwell was confident of his ability to sway the new president's thinking. He confided to colleagues that Roosevelt, as an alumnus of such good schools as Groton and Harvard, was no enemy of the system. Roosevelt had also once rented an apartment from Leffingwell and they were friends. At the time Roosevelt came to power he corresponded with the president: "Dear Frank . . . ," he wrote, "nobody gets very far with all this . . . regulation stuff."

Leffingwell, as a confidant of the president, was in line for a high-ranking Treasury job, an idea that the J. P. Morgan banking house fully supported. Leffingwell would have been well placed to temper any bills that attempted to curb the banking system. Nothing came of the idea, however, not least as a result of a testy exchange that followed Leffingwell's letter. Roosevelt rebuffed Leffingwell's suggestion that regulation was wrong, writing back that he wished "we could get from the bankers themselves an admission that . . . there were grave abuses" in the events leading to the crash and the Depression. He added that he would like to see that bankers themselves wholeheartedly support methods to prevent such abuses recurring.

"The bankers were not in fact responsible," Leffingwell replied. "[T]he politicians were." Why, then, he put it to the president, "should the bankers make a false confession?" Perhaps unsurprisingly, FDR vetoed the idea of the Morgan man getting a Treasury job.

After the inauguration weekend's bank closures, Herbert Lehman found himself embroiled for weeks with bankers worried that their banks might not reopen. One bank in particular, which was never identified except as one of the largest half dozen in America, was on the brink of bankruptcy. It had a large mortgage problem, having granted a lot of home loans to people who now could not pay them back. Lehman believed this predicament would ease with time, and that the bank was solvent. He was convinced that the bank had to reopen. "[I]t had a multitude of depositors and hundreds of millions in deposits," wrote Nevins. "[I]f it remained shut people would take fright and the panic might start all over again."

Lehman did some intense lobbying of William H. Woodin, Roosevelt's treasury secretary, and FDR himself to keep the bank in business. "I was on the telephone literally for hours with Woodin," he said, "and arguing with equal fervor to Roosevelt." The president of the bank came to Lehman's house "in intense anguish, begging that every means be exhausted to get a favorable verdict." Eventually Lehman's lobbying, and his access to the very top of the political tree, saw the bank's doors again swing open. Doubtless the bank's president was grateful at the time but, according to Lehman, not for very long. "Within two years this man was one of FDR's main critics, denouncing him venomously," he later recalled. "There were a good many instances of that."

The bankers were particularly angry at the New Deal's 1933 Banking Act, or Glass-Steagall as it became better known, which clamped down on their ability to gamble with depositors' money. Senator Carter Glass of Virginia, Woodrow Wilson's former Treasury secretary, and Congressman Henry Steagall of Alabama, introduced the bill. It split up the two broad functions of banking, basically, the cash box and the casino sides of the business. Banks could no longer use depositors' cash to invest in exotic bonds or risky share launches. If, on the other hand, rich investors wanted to leave sums in the hands of banks specifically for gambling purposes—that is, risky investments with the prospect of high returns— that was fine too. But such banks had to be separate from those that took ordinary deposits.

Glass-Steagall passed through Congress against a background of rising public anger. Hearings convened by Ferdinand Pecora, a shirt-sleeved, cigar-chewing former assistant district attorney of New York, highlighted one dubious practice of the financial community after another. Before the crash, for example, National City Bank had made risky loans to weak governments in Brazil, Cuba, and elsewhere in Latin America. The bank had then repackaged the loans as bonds and sold them to members of the public, with the assurance from its salesmen that these would provide a healthy rate of interest as income. That was as long as the Latin American governments repaid their loans to the banks, which they often did not. National City had had nearly two thousand salesmen on the streets touting its bonds.

The new act made banks declare what they wanted to be—a depositors' or a gamblers' bank. Lehman Brothers chose to be the latter, though this was not the kind of term that financiers preferred to use; with Glass-Steagall, therefore, the investment bank was born. Commercial or retail banks—the kind that were visible on the Main Streets of America rather than tucked away on Wall Street—were the banks that could handle deposits, and make conservative loans to earn modest sums of money.

The investment banks played the big stakes. Michael Lewis, a former investment banker with Salomon Brothers, wrote in his book *Liar's Poker* that when he began his career in the 1980s, one of the first things he learned as a trainee was that Glass-Steagall, a half-century earlier, was a kind of year zero from which a new form of business life had emerged: "An investment banker was a breed apart, a member of a master race of deal makers. He possessed vast, almost unimaginable talent and ambition."

Back in 1933, the government brought banks to heel. Lehman Brothers' partners resigned any directorships they had on the boards of commercial banks and learned to live their new life. Two of its top people played important roles in the New Deal. One was John Hancock, who joined FDR's National Recovery Administration. Alexander Sachs, Lehman Brothers' chief economist and a member of the firm's board of directors, was the other. He helped organize the National Recovery Administration. Sachs was a friend of Roosevelt's, which would prove important later when Lehman Brothers found itself by chance caught up in America's preparations to face Nazi Germany in World War II.

In the meantime, Lehman Brothers was competing with an old rival in showing willingness to join forces with the New Deal. Sidney Weinberg was the new head of Goldman Sachs and one of the few other businessmen who aligned with the New Deal. He became an adviser to Roosevelt and started a Goldman Sachs tradition of keeping close to government. This would serve it well in the future, not least in the collapse of 2008, from which Goldman Sachs emerged remarkably well.

Bobbie Lehman's position on the New Deal changed with the wind of prevailing events. He was a Republican and one of many leading businessmen who had thrown their weight behind the notion that free-range capitalism answered mankind's desires. The crash had been an awful shock to them, and for many it was humiliating when the government had to bail out the economy. Aside from the few who rallied to Roosevelt, the rest either criticized the New Deal or maintained their distance. Bobbie was instinctively someone who distanced himself from tricky situations as he worked out the odds. His grandfather Emanuel had acquired a certain distance from politics as a result of the Civil War, and his father, Philip, had showed no obvious interest. For the time being, Bobbie remained aloof from the politics of the 1930s. He had enough to deal with as far as the business environment was concerned.

Amid these changing times Lehman Brothers could not resist a last flirtation with the old days. In summer 1933 it joined Joseph Kennedy— its old partner when launching the RKO movie studios—as he organized one of his share pools. Kennedy had spotted a likely prospect in the Libbey-Owens-Ford Glass Company of Toledo, Ohio. If he and his share pool partners made an initial move, others would likely follow, reckoning that with the end of Prohibition and Americans about to return en masse to large-scale alcohol consumption, the shares of a manufacturer in the glass industry were likely to keep on rising.

In fact, Libbey-Owens-Ford was not a bottle-glass maker at all but one of the first manufacturers of laminated safety glass used for car windshields. Less wily investors than Kennedy, however, did not necessarily know that. Kennedy's other partner in setting up the pool was Walter P.

Chrysler, from the family whose main line of business was automobile manufacturing.

In June 1933, and over about four months, the pool bought half a million shares in Libbey-Owens-Ford. Other investors rushed to follow, and they bought another half million. The price of the stock rose, and when the pool dumped its shares back on the market, its members made a profit of four hundred thousand dollars. The profit was reportedly modest by the standards of previous pools, but those who shared it doubtless found the ready cash welcome in those depressive times.

As its share price plunged, Libbey-Owens-Ford nearly went bust. Kennedy, on the other hand, advanced his career. Roosevelt was looking for someone to lead the Securities and Exchange Commission (SEC), his new body to regulate the stock market. In 1934 he appointed Kennedy, since he knew more tricks than most. As one of his first moves Kennedy banned the practice of share pooling that had brought Libbey-Owens-Ford near bankruptcy. Before that the practice had been "unethical but not illegal," commented Timothy Messer-Kruse, a historian at the University of Toledo looking back on the case many years later. If someone were to do the same kind of trading today, he added, that person "would go to jail." At the time, Lehman Brothers stayed within the realms of legality but earned the dubious distinction of being part of Wall Street's last legal share pool.

In the middle of the Depression, Lehman Brothers was quick to spot the nation's need for a drink. The end of Prohibition quickly led to alcohol becoming one of the nation's few growth industries, and Lehman Brothers launched a $3 million share issue on the stock market for Schenley Distillers. Alcohol production had been strictly monitored during Prohibition, yet Schenley had built a chain of companies making whiskey and other alcohol that stretched from its Pennsylvania base to California's Napa Valley. Lehman Brothers priced the shares at sixteen dollars each, but behind the scenes they were selling for forty dollars before the public got sight of them. From 1934 to 1935, Schenley's sales grew by well over half.

Nonetheless, Lehman Brothers, like many other businesses, was still enduring the stressful circumstances in the Depression of being short of capital. Bobbie helped rectify this by selling a share of the firm to John D. Hertz of Chicago. Hertz had made a fortune in the 1920s when General Motors bought his Yellow Cab Company. Now he came into Lehman

Brothers as a partner when Bobbie sold him an 8 percent share of the firm. Bobbie's father supported the idea, which involved a far larger share of Lehman Brothers going to someone outside the family than before. (Paul Mazur, for example, had only 3 percent.)

The move widened the split between Bobbie and his cousin Arthur. "Over Arthur's objections, Bobbie and Philip brought Hertz in," Robert Bernhard, Arthur's grandson, said much later. "It alienated my grandfather— that I know." Arthur may simply have objected to so large a share in the firm going to an individual outside the family. His objections stood little chance of swaying Bobbie's mind on the matter, though, because not only did Hertz have capital to invest, he was also a member of the board of General Motors, and Bobbie would have seen potential advantage in having a connection with America's biggest company.

Hertz and Bobbie shared a passion for horses and became good friends. Bobbie followed Hertz's lead in becoming a successful owner and breeder. In one gesture of their friendship, Hertz signed over to Bobbie the use of his private box at Churchill Downs racetrack in Louisville, Kentucky.

Robert Bernhard noted that when he worked at Lehman Brothers as a partner in the 1960s, he rarely if ever heard Arthur's name mentioned. Admittedly, this was some good few years after Arthur's day—he died in 1936—but there were plenty of old partners around who would have remembered him. Arthur was just not a topic discussed in Bobbie's company.

During the 1930s, stress from the office was hardly alleviated by the circumstances of Bobbie's personal life. On May 1, 1934, his wife, Ruth, sued him for divorce. A small notice in the *New York Times* said she filed her suit in Reno, Nevada, and alleged "cruelty." This was a standard charge used at the time by divorcing couples, and there was no other indication of Bobbie having been violent. He managed to get his own parting shot in a day earlier in a gossip item in the New York *American*. The article said that it could not see what Ruth would gain from divorce after the "devoted attention" that Bobbie had showered on her. She had "hob-nobbed with the smart polo set" and "presided over a country house out on the exclusive Sand Points Sector." The *New York Times* reported that "an agreement was reached as to property" but without further details.

Possibly on the rebound, Bobbie married again a month later. His second bride was another Ruth, and the daughter of Ruth Bryan Owen, former representative for Florida in Congress and the first woman to be a U.S. ambassador. Roosevelt had appointed her to the embassy in Denmark the year before. The grandfather of Bobbie's new bride was William Jennings Bryan, the late Democratic eminence. Was Bobbie warming to the Democrats? A small wedding announcement in the press made clear who the most distinguished Lehman in New York was these days: Bobbie, it said, was "a cousin of the governor."

But the pleasantries of being a newlywed again did not change the difficulties of the time. In 1934 Bobbie and Averell Harriman suffered a blow dealt by the airline industry. Their most prized part of the Aviation Corporation was American Airways, later known as American Airlines. It ran services to many of the United States' main cities and also to Canada and Mexico. But Errett Lobban Cord, an aircraft manufacturer and stock speculator, gradually bought an interest in the airline and now wrested control from Lehman and Harriman. In the propaganda battle to win the affections of shareholders, Lehman and Harriman hired Edward Bernays to help them. The effort failed, with Bernays giving the impression that Bobbie was not at his best. "I seldom saw Lehman," he said. "He seemed a shadowy character who slipped in and out of rooms."

For a while Bobbie may well have been a shadow of his normal self. His personal files indicate that he went to see his doctor, Harold T. Hyman, on December 14, 1934, complaining of ailments that may have been caused by stress. "Stick to straight whiskey or sherry," advised Hyman. "[Y]ou are bound to get into difficulties if you take the noxious cocktail combinations and the irritating wines which include red wine, claret and champagne." Bobbie was only a light drinker and a nonsmoker: "[Y]our sensitivity to cigar smoke is understandable and could be corrected by a smoke absorber which may be purchased at any of the shops." One problem with this was that in a throwback to United Cigar days, silver cigar boxes dotted the corridors of One William Street, with free Havanas available to partners and clients. "Your practice of taking fruit juices during the day is commendable," added Hyman, who advised finally that he should "continue with your exercise . . . so long as it is not the violence of competitive sport such as you have indulged in in the past." Bobbie was likely ahead of his medical adviser on this one; a bill of sale showed he had sold some polo ponies the year before.

Herbert provided Bobbie with a pick-me-up in the New Year. After a comfortable reelection in the fall polls, he invited Bobbie to attend his inauguration in Albany on January 1 and a celebratory dinner a few days later. In spite of Bobbie's arguments with Arthur, he had at least reached a relatively amicable arrangement with Herbert. There was no telling when you might need a politician on your side.

Lehman Brothers' business was picking up. In 1935, the firm raised finance for Studebaker, which in the early part of the Depression had gone into receivership. People were buying cars again. Lehman Brothers also launched a share issue for Black & Decker, the toolmaking company. If toolmakers were optimistic about future demand for their products, then more Americans were getting back to work. The unemployment rate, which had been 25 percent in 1933, when 12.5 million people were without jobs, fell to about 20 percent in 1935. Nonetheless, that still left 9.5 million people hunting for gainful employment.

In a more glamorous arena, Hollywood producer David O. Selznick started his own Selznick International Pictures. The *New York Times* reported in October that Bobbie Lehman and Cornelius Vanderbilt Whitney, a former polo-playing comrade of Bobbie's, were among the *King Kong* man's chief backers. Six months later Selznick had the chance to buy the film rights to *Gone with the Wind*, a new novel about the American Civil War by Margaret Mitchell. She was a literary unknown, her book was very long at over one thousand pages, and Selznick wondered whether the Civil War had any interest for the U.S. public. He pondered the question and eventually decided to buy the rights for fifty thousand dollars.

Herbert Lehman, for his part, had a bumper year. He pushed measures through the Albany legislature raising the minimum age at which children could leave school from fourteen to sixteen, providing free milk for children who needed it, and creating an unemployment insurance fund. "The people of the State of New York," he said, "should feel proud that it is . . . leading the nation in legislation which will increase the economic and moral security of its working people." His Republican opposition did not see it this way. State troopers had to be called to maintain the Assembly's order on one occasion. A session in April 1935 lasted twenty-nine hours.

Yet Lehman was getting his message through to the electorate regardless of their party loyalties. Robert P. Ingalls in his book *Herbert H. Lehman and New York's Little New Deal* records that after going to the polls in the 1934 election, Maurice C. Burritt, a public service commissioner from a small town in upstate New York, wrote in his diary: "Vote Republican ticket generally, to hold 'new deal' in check, but make exception to vote for Governor Lehman because of his honesty, sincerity [and] business [administration]."

Where Roosevelt's New Deal in Washington led the way with such measures as the Works Progress Administration (WPA), which was set up to provide work for people without jobs, Ingalls argues that Lehman's reforms in New York on, for example, public housing, unemployment relief, child labor, and minimum wages went beyond those of Washington's. Herbert banned so-called yellow dog employment contracts that stopped workers from joining unions, and he took other steps, such as permitting women to serve on juries. All this had much to do with the character of the governor himself. In an address in October 1935, he declared that he saw no inconsistency "between being a business man, and a liberal."

In February the following year, economic theory finally followed practice. John Maynard Keynes published his *General Theory of Employment, Interest, and Money*, which argued that it was government's responsibility to supervise the money supply in order to keep businesses functioning and people in work. Keynes, a patron of the arts and member of the British intellectual collective known as the Bloomsbury group, had a large body of counter opinion to contend with in his own profession. Standard economics had its long-established article of faith that it was not the role of man to interfere with the economy.

Despite initial criticisms, Keynes's theories went on to serve as the basis for running an economy for the next forty years, though not everyone followed them consistently. Even the Roosevelt administration changed course. In 1936, with the economy in recovery, Henry Morgenthau, Jr., FDR's treasury secretary (who was married to Herbert Lehman's niece Elinor), persuaded the president that, in spite of the fact that unemployment remained high, it was time to tighten the money supply again. Both were nervous about inflation, and Morgenthau duly raised taxes and cut back the amount of money in circulation.

Herbert Lehman and Morgenthau had been good friends. In *Lots of Lehmans*, Morgenthau's son Henry Morgenthau III points out that as a child, his mother had been close to Herbert, and that Herbert and his wife,

Edith, had actually first arranged for Henry III's parents to meet (with an invitation to Kildare lodge in the Adirondacks). The politics of the Depression appear to have come between the New York governor and Roosevelt's treasury secretary. "[A]s they all got involved in politics," said Henry III, "there was considerable rivalry between my father . . . and Herbert. . . . They tended to distance themselves from each other." Whether this was specifically about if and when to put money into the economy is uncertain, but Morgenthau's measures were a step back into the old economics. Very soon, the sharp recession of 1937–38 halted America's climb out of the Depression.

In May 1936, Arthur Lehman died suddenly at the age of sixty-three. Previously in good health, he had suffered a pulmonary embolism. An obituary in the *New York Times* called him an "ardent optimist" who during the worst of the Depression "persistently held out hope." He died tacitly defending his brother. The *Times* quoted a recent statement of Arthur's on "[t]he enlarged participation on the part of the government in the affairs of business." This, he agreed, had probably unsettled businesspeople, but "on the whole the constructive acts of the government have overbalanced [the] adverse factors."

Herbert was so upset at Arthur's death that he considered retiring from politics, but it did not take long before he was back in the fray. In the summer at the Democrats' convention in Philadelphia, he gave the speech renominating Roosevelt to run for a second presidential term, and there was a note of anger in his choice of words to describe the New Deal's opponents. The convention could not allow social reforms, he proclaimed, to be "killed by the forces of merciless reaction."

He appeared more committed to politics than ever. In the fall, he ran for a third term as governor, and in an address on October 24, 1936, stated his beliefs. "I believe in the profit motive, individual opportunity, reward for individual effort," he said, "but not through uncontrolled exploitation of the under-privileged." He believed in "the rights of capital" but "with equal ardor in the rights of labor and the consumer." Liberty meant, he declared, "the freedom to live fully and prosper greatly—not the freedom to be exploited by circumstances or starved by want."

These may have sounded like radical terms, but Lehman was not alone in his views. He won his 1936 election comfortably, with a majority of half a million votes. This was down from previous elections, but circumstances had changed and Herbert's opponents had come around. A lot of old Republicans had retired from politics, and a new wave came in who represented a different approach. William Bleakley, Lehman's electoral challenger and a state supreme court judge, had carried out a campaign that accepted the principle of social security.

The last few years had redefined the ground rules of American society, which were now far and away from those when Herbert's late uncle Henry Lehman had arrived in 1844. Henry had understood the stark terms of the deal he was making in coming to America: If you did not make it by your own efforts, you failed. Now that was considered inappropriate and, quite possibly, inhumane. Efforts to curb poverty and promote greater equality, once considered socialist or un-American, were widely supported as normal, and as the government's responsibility.

Even Bobbie Lehman, the staunch Republican, had moderated his stance. In November 1936, he accepted an invitation to appear before the SEC, which was still looking into the causes of the crash seven years before. Bobbie warmed to the opportunity to give his views, which appeared decidedly in favor of regulating the financial community. Any individual "will, through the very fact of control of a substantial amount of money, be in a position to obtain benefits improperly for himself, directly or indirectly," he stated. Such types of abuse "can be controlled by appropriate legislation."

The *New York Times* summed up the speech with these words: "Banking House Advises SEC That Wider Curbs Are Desirable."

|||||||||

Lehman Brothers had long been involved in motion pictures, but it soon embraced a new medium. In the late 1930s the firm backed Allen B. Du Mont, otherwise known as the "father of television." Du Mont was a brilliant engineer who began his career at the Westinghouse Lamp Company and then decided in 1931 to set up business in the garage of his home in Cedar Grove, New Jersey. He developed the modern oscilloscope, which is used in laboratories to study electrical waves. As noted in the Lehman Collection at the Harvard Business School, he also perfected "the use of the cathode ray tube as TV screens."

Perhaps Bobbie Lehman, the fine-art connoisseur, appreciated Du

Mont's eye for perfection. His TV sets were of the highest quality and were known for having the finest picture. Du Mont did not worry that this made them more expensive than others. He set up his own television network, which lasted into the mid-1950s and, alongside NBC, ABC, and CBS, was America's fourth TV network.

Lehman Brothers gave its support to Du Mont by organizing and financing the first-ever stock market launch for shares of a television company. Bobbie, however, was being somewhat promiscuous in handing out his favors. His firm had been the banker to the Radio Corporation of America for a decade by this time, and Paul Mazur had his seat on the RCA board.

In 1937 Du Mont had beaten RCA by producing the first commercial television, but RCA was the corporate power in the TV world. RCA had a full room given over to its sets at the New York World's Fair, which was staged across expansive grounds in Flushing Meadows, Queens, and opened in April 1939. One of RCA's models had the TV screen set horizontally in the top of a large cabinet with the picture projected to viewers by an adjacent mirror. It was so ahead of its time that it never caught on.

As for Bobbie Lehman's support for Du Mont, his move may have had less to do with his betting "on the man" than hedging his bets and keeping an eye on a loose-cannon rival. For the moment, however, the development of television had to cede ground to the approach of World War II and would not emerge as a social phenomenon until after it.

Bobbie still seemed to be the victim of stress. His personal files show that a medical check by his doctor in March 1938 reported that he suffered from "insomnia and easy fatigability in early afternoon." Within a "multiplicity of symptoms," wrote his medical adviser, Bobbie had problems "in the gastro-intestinal tract." In today's terms, he probably had irritable bowel syndrome.

Bobbie's mother, Caroline, had died a year earlier, which was no doubt stressful for him, his father, Philip, and other members of the family. Business health, however, was fine, in part thanks to a deal with Philip Morris, the cigarette maker—"the PM was a great success," he wrote on June 28, in a zestful letter to Philip, who was on an antiques-buying trip to Europe. "[A]ll preferred stock sold." Lehman Brothers had just completed a successful share sale for the company. The negative health effects of tobacco were not discovered until decades later and so posed no threat to Americans' cigarette consumption. "PM" would remain an important client for years to come.

In the same letter Bobbie reported more good news from other quarters: "I was at the Pan American meeting this morning and it looks as if we might have the possibility of doing some finance for them." The possibility, in fact, was a very good one. With Charles Lindbergh advising Pan Am, the airline had steadily increased its routes. Lindbergh had often acted as the company's diplomat, using his celebrity to visit countries, call on their leaders, and ease the way to new destinations. In 1932, Lindbergh's life had suffered a tragedy when his young son had been kidnapped and murdered. Lindbergh escaped some of the unwanted publicity by moving to Europe, and in the late 1930s Pan Am was raising the funds to buy larger planes and extend its services to Europe.

Political tensions in Europe grew. Bobbie, for example, referred to "these troubled times" in his letter to his father. To Herbert Lehman, meanwhile, it was clear that his principles of freedom and liberty were going to require defending. In Germany, Jews were under attack from the Nazis, and Hitler had just taken over Austria. If America was to confront the danger that Herbert perceived, he would have to impress his views of the matter on more than just the electorate in New York.

In October 1938, Hitler marched into the Sudetenland, the German-speaking area of Czechoslovakia. This followed the ill-fated pact in Munich in September, when the British and French governments had agreed to Hitler's demands that he be allowed to take control of the area. Six months later the rest of Czechoslovakia would fall. Curiously, Charles Lindbergh had played a diplomatic part of sorts in the crisis. In 1936 and 1938 he visited Germany at the invitation of Hermann Goering, head of the German air force. As well as an aviator, Lindbergh was a German American. He pronounced himself highly impressed with the efficiency of the German air force, and Goering gave him the service cross of the Order of the German Eagle with star, Germany's highest honor for foreigners. The award caused an outcry in the United States among critics of Nazism.

Herbert Lehman had been receiving urgent requests for help from Jews in Germany since Hitler came to power in early 1933. About two hundred thousand were stateless after Hitler's takeover in Austria, and a similar number were in the same position following the fall of Czechoslovakia. As the Nazi government's attacks on Germany's Jewish population increased, it seemed that U.S. immigration regulations had merely tightened. Immigrants needed pledges of support from American relatives or friends and to undergo other time-consuming procedures. In times of post-Depression hardship, calls for looser immigration laws were not widely welcomed. Even after the atrocities of Kristallnacht, or the Night of Broken Glass, in November 1938 in Germany—when thousands of Jewish-owned storefronts were shattered and after which tens of thousands of people were sent to concentration camps—attempts failed to put a law through the U.S. Congress increasing the number of German Jewish children allowed into America.

The Lehman family set up the Mayer Lehman Charity Fund, named after Herbert's father, to help members of the Lehman family in Germany to get out. At first the fund also helped nonrelatives, providing pledges of financial aid and other visa requirements, travel arrangements, someone to meet arrivals at Ellis Island, lodgings, finance, hospital treatment, and work in the United States. In the late summer of 1939 the family had to stop assisting nonrelatives because their number was impossible to handle.

U.S. politics took an ominous turn in September after Charles Lindbergh returned to America with his family. War had begun in Europe at the beginning of the month when, following Hitler's invasion of Poland, Britain and France declared war on Germany. Lindbergh's father had been a Minnesota congressman, and it seemed that he also harbored political ambitions. On September 15, 1939, Lindbergh made what appeared to be a challenge to Roosevelt's authority; FDR was sympathetic to British and French opposition to the Nazis. A huge audience listened as Lindbergh took to the air, this time in a radio broadcast from the Carlton Hotel in Washington, DC. "These wars in Europe are not wars in which our civilization is defending itself against some Asiatic intruder," he said. "[O]ur sentiment, our history, our personal feelings of sympathy" were in danger of obscuring "the issue," Lindbergh continued. As far as he was concerned that issue was to "carry on Western civilization" by staying out of the war. With German troops storming across Europe, the odds at this stage were firmly on Germany winning.

One person who found himself listening closely to Lindbergh's broadcast was Leo Szilard, a Hungarian scientist exiled and living in New York. In the 1920s in Berlin he had worked with Albert Einstein, the physicist who at the age of only twenty-six in 1905 had first outlined the theory of relativity. In Germany, Szilard and Einstein had developed their own patented model of a refrigerator, a household good that was becoming steadily more popular, but in the absence of anyone like Lehman Brothers willing to back them, they had abandoned the idea.

Szilard and Einstein left Europe after the Nazis took control in Germany and made their separate ways to America. Szilard worked at Columbia University in New York researching ways to create a nuclear chain reaction, the process with which the United States, six years later, would make the atomic bomb. Szilard was particularly worried about circumstances in Czechoslovakia, which, since the Nazis had seized control, had stopped its exports of uranium. His research had showed that uranium could be a vital element in the nuclear process, and Czechoslovakia was one of the few places in the world known to produce it. Szilard felt sure the Germans were sending the uranium back to their laboratories for their own nuclear research. He wanted to take his worries to President Roosevelt, whom he did not know, so he had to look for an important person to act as an intermediary.

Szilard turned to Einstein, whose research into the theory of relativity had made him the most famous scientist in the world, and with his help drafted a letter to Roosevelt warning of the dangers of the Nazis having uranium. They wrote that large supplies of it meant a chain reaction "could be achieved in the immediate future" and that "extremely powerful bombs may thus be constituted." The signature "A. Einstein" added further weight to the letter's importance, yet Szilard and Einstein felt they needed another famous person to get the letter to FDR. Alas, they had not kept close tabs on some European developments during the 1930s because, upon Einstein's recommendation, Szilard sent the letter to Lindbergh, unaware of his Nazi sympathies.

"Lindbergh," Szilard quickly wrote to Einstein on hearing Lindbergh's radio address, "is not our man." Someone else was needed to deliver the letter, and fast. At this point Lehman Brothers made an early entry into the story of uranium and atomic power when by chance a friend of Szilard's gave him Alexander Sachs's name. The chief economist of Lehman Brothers, and part of Roosevelt's administration since the early 1930s, was on first-name terms with the president. When Szilard contacted and went to see him, Sachs agreed that FDR had to see the letter.

It took over a month for Sachs to get an appointment to see Roosevelt, whose mind was fully engaged with the war in Europe. When he did see FDR, he insisted on reading the letter to him, fearing that if he just left it with the president, it might be swept aside by other business. Sachs successfully conveyed the point. "Alex, what you are after is to see that the Nazis don't blow us up," said FDR, who promptly set up a board of experts with Sachs as one of his representatives. Roosevelt also wrote back to Einstein politely thanking him for his missive. Einstein's letter, cowritten with Szilard and delivered in a haphazard way through, eventually, the good offices of Lehman Brothers, marked the first stage of the Manhattan Project, which would go on to develop the atomic bomb.

Gone with the Wind premiered on December 15, 1939, in Atlanta, Georgia. Shooting had begun early the previous year, and the movie cost $4.25 million to make, the most expensive ever at that point. Selznick had trimmed the budget by setting fire to an old RKO studio lot rather than build another set to represent the burning of Atlanta. Rich backers of Selznick like Bobbie Lehman were no doubt gratified by such cost-cutting measures.

"'[I]t' has arrived at last," wrote Frank S. Nugent in the *New York Times* on December 20, the morning after the film's debut in New York. Such was the anticipated demand among the movie-going public that "Mr. Gallup's American Institute of Public Opinion has reported a palpitatingly waiting audience of 56,500,000 persons" to see the film, which premiered at two theaters on opposite sides of Times Square. Selznick's film had "absorbingly recreated Miss Mitchell's mural of the South in that bitter decade when secession, civil war and reconstruction ripped wide the graceful fabric of the plantation age," expounded Nugent, "and confronted the men and women who had adorned it with the stern alternative of meeting the new era or dying with the old."

Herbert Lehman, whose father had been part of the fabric to which the *Times*'s critic referred, was worried at the way the wind was blowing. In his opinion, the United States had arrived late into the conflict against Germany in the previous world war and was in danger of doing so again.

Many Americans believed they should not get involved. Few German Americans instinctively had any wish to make war on their old country, and Irish Americans were skeptical about a cause that might only serve the British empire. Fringe organizations such as the America First Committee argued vociferously for the United States to keep out of the war. The German American Bund, an American Nazi organization, staged marches and rallies in New York and other U.S. cities.

When Herbert compiled a budget to increase New York's defense spending, Republican opponents accused him of "emotional alarm" and exaggerating the threat. Lehman carried on regardless, and the state drew up plans for the evacuation of schoolchildren from New York City along the lines of those being used in the London blitz. If the Germans found some way of blitzing New York, the city would be ready. Such an event seemed improbable at the time, as Lehman's political opponents had indicated. The same could have been said of the Japanese finding the wherewithal to attack Pearl Harbor, something they would achieve in about two years' time. Lehman ordered classes to be organized to prepare people for how to react under air attack, and air-raid observation posts were built across the state.

Herbert was not alone in facing resistance to such plans. With the defeat in June 1940 of the British army in continental Europe, a German invasion of Britain seemed inevitable. Lehman and Roosevelt feared that with large areas of Europe under Nazi control, Germany could direct its attack and all the resources of the countries it occupied toward the United States. Roosevelt prepared a bill that would allow for the call-up of nine hundred thousand men between twenty-one and thirty-six for military training; the bill, however, was making only slow progress through Congress.

Here Herbert's links with the American political left proved important. He was due to speak at the annual convention of the American Federation of Labor, the nation's main trade union body. The AFL had many isolationists and pacifists as members and was traditionally hostile to compulsory military service. The White House worried that a negative reaction by the AFL would cause the defeat of Roosevelt's bill. The convention, furthermore, was debating whether it would support Roosevelt for the forthcoming presidential election. FDR was running for a third term, which was allowed under the Constitution but, as his critics loudly argued, was against American tradition.

Lehman regularly spoke at the AFL's convention, which this year was in Niagara Falls, New York. He had usually spoken on employment, welfare, and similar issues. "Contrary to his practice on previous occasions," said the *New York Times*, "Governor Lehman devoted his entire speech to problems of national defense." In a forum where different unions often took the opportunity to fight their own private wars, Lehman called for unity and "peace within the ranks of the labor movement" at this crucial time. The *Times* summed up the result with "State A.F.L. Comes Out for Roosevelt."

In the cause of unity, Lehman felt FDR needed to be worked on as well. The 1940 election campaign was a fractious affair, with isolationists joining virulent anti–New Dealers in their opposition to Roosevelt. There was talk that Charles Lindbergh would offer himself as the Republican candidate and, after sweeping Roosevelt aside at the polls, keep the United States neutral in the battle against Nazism. Wendell Willkie, however, emerged as the Republicans' candidate. He was a businessman by background, and a professed opponent of fascism, yet in his campaign Willkie's supporters pulled him into denouncing Roosevelt as a warmonger.

On the face of it, Roosevelt easily won the election by twenty-seven million votes to twenty-two million, but Lehman was concerned about how, after the election, vocal elements of the Republican media continued to attack Roosevelt. As Nevins wrote, they denounced "Roosevelt's third term as a grave breach of national tradition, the New Deal as a surrender to Socialism, and Roosevelt as a reckless despot intent on war." In the event that the United States came to the brink of war, Lehman feared that such groups as the America First Committee, of which Lindbergh was a leading spokesman, and the German American Bund might maneuver Willkie into leading a movement that threatened national solidarity.

Herbert Lehman told Roosevelt that unity could be achieved if Americans were shown, "as I know you can show them, that you are the chief protector of our capitalist system, that you have not wanted and do not want autocratic powers, and that you are determined to bring all classes together in harmony." Lehman suggested Roosevelt approach Willkie to create an informal pact. The president took his advice and established a cordial relationship with Willkie that they maintained up to and during World War II (though both died before the end of it, Willkie of a heart attack at age sixty-two in October 1944 and Roosevelt at age seventy-two in April 1945).

The vast majority of Americans saw the conflict as a just war, a view long promoted by Herbert Lehman and exonerated by history. After the Japanese attack on Pearl Harbor on December 7, 1941, Charles Lindbergh also had an enemy that he recognized. He served in the Pacific, where he trained American fighter pilots and flew about fifty combat missions.

6

A Little News and a Little Noise

On October 28, 1942, Bobbie Lehman applied for a new passport. Presumably because Pearl Harbor had occurred less than a year before and it was unusual for anyone to be traveling abroad other than for military reasons, Bobbie appended an explanation to the passport office. He planned a journey, he wrote, "to inspect banana lands in Guatemala for my firm."

The war was to the east in Europe and to the west in the Pacific. Old empires like those of the British and the French were under threat from the viciously aspirant ones of Germany and Japan. Bobbie was heading south to the warm and secure lands of Central America, where it was possible to forget there was a war at all. Now fifty-one, he had served his time on the front line in Europe in World War I and would not be going into battle again. Nonetheless, he was walking into a disaster.

Bobbie was the banker for the United Fruit Company, whose boss, Sam Zemurray, had first come to Lehman Brothers for help in 1925. Zemurray had taken over United Fruit in 1933. The company's empire stretched down and through the republics of Central America and into Colombia, in South America. It ranged across the Caribbean, from Jamaica in the north to the tiny island of Grenada in the southern Windward Islands. While United Fruit's main business was bananas, in Cuba it had huge sugar estates. It maintained its control through alliances with various dictators, who kept the peace and intervened with their armies to sort out, for example, any nasty instances of labor unrest on the plantations. In return the company looked after them with bribes and other inducements.

United Fruit was well versed in what would later be called regime change. It replaced one dictator with a more pliant one if he did not do what the company wanted. Within a couple of years of Bobbie's making his

1942 inspection trip, however, a wave of popular opposition in Guatemala professing the political principles of President Roosevelt would eject Jorge Ubico, a dictator long friendly to United Fruit, from office. It spelled the beginning of the end for the company's political power.

Had Bobbie looked closely, he might have learned that in the quiet, tropical climes of Central America, United Fruit's product was also rotting. Tropical diseases had assailed the banana since the beginning of the century, and Zemurray had kept the fruit alive by pumping increasing quantities of pesticide onto his plantations.

United Fruit also engaged in the dangerous enterprise of monoculture. It produced only one type of banana out of the many varieties available, ostensibly in the name of economic efficiency: Using one type of banana meant the company could grow it on a large scale, which kept prices down and created a mass market of consumers. This sole variety, known as the Gros Michel, or "Big Mike," was far from efficient otherwise. Had United Fruit grown more varieties, the tropical diseases would have had to adapt to them, rather than face the relatively easy task of attacking one. The hapless Big Mike was fighting a losing battle against its assailants, and United Fruit depended on a product that could die out at any moment.

The company attempted to manage the threat by rolling on relentlessly. Bananas cost more to produce as the company used more pesticides and the land they were grown on became diseased, but United Fruit just produced more bananas to maintain its profits. It also kept on the move from one huge plantation and region to another. By producing across vast areas, the company hoped to dissipate the risk. It trusted that it could stay ahead of the diseases and not be hit everywhere at once. United Fruit had large reserves of unused land and hung on to old lands it had abandoned in case they proved usable again.

Bobbie Lehman failed to spot United Fruit's problems when he went to Guatemala in 1942. At Zemurray's invitation he was enjoying a pleasant escape from Wall Street for a few days in an attractive Central American country. Bobbie was impressed enough to join United Fruit's board of directors at about this time, and he remained on it until he died.

Meanwhile, the relentless march of economic theory continued. Joseph Schumpeter, a naturalized American born in Czechoslovakia and an academic from Harvard, published his *Capitalism, Socialism, and Democracy* in 1942. After years of Roosevelt and Herbert Lehman intervening in the economy, Schumpeter gave free marketers something to cheer.

He said that the kind of state intervention that Keynes argued for quashed entrepreneurial initiative, whereas boom, bust, and social inequalities kept people on their toes and inventing things. The booms came with major developments like the rush in the nineteenth century to build railroads, while the ensuing busts pushed people on to new projects. The old projects like the railroads remained in place, so that society, in spite of its ups and downs, made a net gain. Schumpeter called this "creative destruction" and, thereby, provided a rationale for mad speculation. Looked at in a Schumpeterian way, speculation that might seem crazy was actually socially useful. As with Adam Smith's theories of the free market, this conjured a view of the world in which people scampered around following their impulses, not necessarily knowing they were part of some grander scheme. Schumpeter's theories won wide acceptance and amounted to "let it rip" economics.

Herbert Lehman sought a new challenge in life when he told Franklin Roosevelt at the end of 1942 that he would not run for governor of New York again. He wanted another job—one that allowed him the service overseas that he had not had in World War I. He had served ten years (twelve if his time as lieutenant governor were included) and left a substantial legacy. The New York budget was in surplus by $80 million, his "ruinous" policies having in fact turned out to be those of the cautious banker. Social security measures in his later years in Albany included aid for crippled children, blind people, and mothers with young families. He had pushed ahead with slum clearance programs. Lehman also left New York with a network of improved highways.

Roosevelt put Herbert in charge of foreign-relief operations. As the Americans, British, and other allies advanced in the war in Europe, Africa, the Middle East, and elsewhere, large numbers of people had to be cared for. Many were in war-torn areas, injured or in a state of shock, hungry or starving. The United Nations was set up in Washington at the beginning of 1942, and its Relief and Rehabilitation Administration, or UNRRA, followed in 1943 with Lehman as its first director general. He started the organization from scratch, amid a shortage of labor, supplies, and transport. At a time of full military action he had to beg for shipping space. During the period Lehman was in the job, UNRRA sent many millions of tons of food, clothing, medical supplies, and farm equipment to almost every country in Europe and Asia hit by the war, along what was called "the longest supply line in the world."

On a typical trip in April 1943, Herbert Lehman was met in London by Averell Harriman. Bobbie's old friend and business partner was now Roosevelt's representative organizing U.S. war supplies to Britain. Lehman had talks with Winston Churchill, by then the British leader, and at Buckingham Palace, an audience with King George VI and Queen Elizabeth. He flew back from London via Lisbon, since airplanes could not yet make the trip straight back across the Atlantic. From Lisbon he flew south to Portuguese Guinea and Liberia on the coast of West Africa. Planes flew the relatively short Atlantic hop from there to Brazil; Pan Am had the contract for this wartime route. Onward and north via Trinidad in the Caribbean and Bermuda, Lehman's return journey to New York from London took three days.

At the UK embassy in Algiers in April 1944, Lehman slipped, broke his leg, and carried on his meetings in a plaster cast from his hospital bed. Charles de Gaulle, future president of France and at the time leader of the Free French forces (France being occupied by the Germans), was among those outlining his needs for supplies from UNRRA. Lehman flew on to Cairo and slept as his plane lost the use of three engines and plunged from eleven thousand to four thousand feet before they burst into life again. In Cairo, Lehman met Captain Richard Weil, whom the U.S. Army had lent to Marshal Josip Tito, whose guerrillas were fighting the Germans in the mountains of Yugoslavia. Tito would come to power after the war thanks to such outside help, and he would maintain a stubborn resistance against the Soviet Union in the cold war that split Europe between East and West. Captain Weil was an old Lehman family friend and the grandson of Isidor Straus of Macy's of New York, who had died on the *Titanic*. He arrived with his list of requirements for food and medical supplies and, after his meeting with Herbert, flew off to be dropped back into Yugoslavia by parachute.

On his return from Cairo to New York, Herbert learned that his son Peter, a U.S. airman, had been killed in an air training accident near his base in Cambridge, in the east of England. Before his military service, in which he had flown many missions over Germany, he had become a partner at Lehman Brothers. Nine of the firm's fourteen partners went off to the war; two were killed. Thomas Hitchcock, Jr., was the other fatality; like his father, Hitchcock had been an avid polo player at the Meadowbrook Country Club, and like Peter Lehman, he died in an air training accident over England, though in his case near Salisbury in the west of the country. All told, Lehman Brothers would have had a staff at this time of a few hundred, and some seventy-five served in the war.

Collectively, Lehman Brothers served as an investment banker to the war. Several of its clients did very well, and Lehman Brothers reaped a healthy harvest of fees, percentage commissions, and all-around profits as a result. Halliburton, the oil services company, had been a client since the wildcat oil boom of the 1930s, when wells sprang up across Texas, Oklahoma, and Louisiana. Oil had gushed forth in out-of-the-way areas, and Halliburton's trucks made toward them under its slogan "We will get there, somehow." In much later years it similarly turned up in war-afflicted zones such as Iraq.

Halliburton always got paid, whether oil was found or not. It was not a drilling company that relied on oil being struck for its profits; it had patented techniques for concreting the sides of wells to prevent their collapse. As oil was discovered in the Gulf of Mexico in the 1930s, so Halliburton turned to mounting drilling equipment on boats and barges. After Japan's attack on Pearl Harbor, the company became a military contractor by mounting guns on U.S. Navy ships.

Kerr-McGee, the oil drilling company, had also been a client since the 1930s. In 1943, it discovered oil northwest of Oklahoma City, which set off a local boom at a time of high military demand for oil. Other Lehman Brothers clients included Black & Decker, which adapted to supply the military with shells and fuses; Fairchild Aviation, run by Sherman Fairchild, an associate of Bobbie Lehman and Averell Harriman from the days of the Aviation Corporation, which made aerial photography equipment for spy planes; and Pan Am, the only international airline at the time, which ran the service across the Atlantic from Brazil to West Africa, among other lucrative contracts.

On April 13, 1945, President Roosevelt died, just a few hours before Vienna, the Austrian capital, fell to the Allies. Harry Truman, his vice president and successor, had no obvious interest in international affairs, and as the war approached its end, a battle was brewing over whether America would turn in on itself as it had after World War I or look outward to take a lead in world politics. Herbert Lehman was convinced that the United States had to maintain its effort overseas. Much of Europe had suffered far more extensive ruin than in the last war, thanks to the new tactic of mass aerial bombardment. Many areas of central London and other British cities were destroyed; ports in France, Belgium, Holland, and elsewhere were flattened. On the defeated side, Italian towns and cities, Vienna, and Germany's main cities, including Berlin, had been laid to waste and needed reviving.

Herbert Lehman spoke to a large rally in New York's Central Park on May 20 for what was called "I Am an American Day." He said true Americanism embraced internationalism. "Are we going to allow starvation in Europe or prevent it?" he asked. "If necessary, are we willing to make a small sacrifice at home in order that millions abroad can regain their health and dignity?" His appeal had an added urgency, because from early on in the war the "tormenting cant of criticism," as he called it, from isolationists toward UNRRA had troubled him.

Newspapers like the *Washington Times-Herald* had led the attack under its publisher, Mrs. Garvin Tankersley. She was the niece of Colonel Robert R. McCormick, the publisher of the *Chicago Tribune*, who was a noted Anglophobe. Ancient hostilities toward the British empire translated into opposition to virtually any American project overseas. Such critics furthermore did not like UNRRA any more than they had New Deal projects like the WPA. The *Times-Herald* had denounced relief efforts such as those carried out by Herbert Lehman as "world planning, world WPA-ing and world spending of U.S. money." The *Chicago Tribune* complained after the war that the United States was expected to make "nearly all" of the relief effort.

Substantial support for Herbert came from abroad. "What sort of Europe we should have had without UNRRA I really do not know," Ernest Bevin, a member of Churchill's war cabinet and the UK foreign secretary after the war, told the House of Commons. "It is too horrible to contemplate. I think it would have been swept by epidemics." In a freezing European winter, UNRRA shipped four million tons of U.S. coal to Europe. For the long term, it revived shattered industries like that of France's winemakers, who needed claret for their processes but had none. UNRRA transported it to them from Portugal. It sent over two million tons of grain to China as the war closed, since the Japanese had devastated large areas of the country. UNRRA engineers helped Chinese farmers by rebuilding destroyed dikes on the Yellow River, vital work, especially given that China was mainly a rural society.

Herbert Lehman was dejected, however, as he watched the world's postwar politics deteriorate. The Russian army continued its occupation of Eastern Europe and brought Czechoslovakia, Poland, and Hungary under Soviet control. After the war's end in 1945, the world moved into the cold war, the state of frozen relations between the bastions of communism and capitalism. Lehman was not sure whether Truman would throw up his hands in disgust and retreat into isolation or stay involved. The administration was winding down UNRRA's work. In March 1946, the month when Churchill's speech at Westminster College in Fulton, Missouri, declared that the Russians were lowering an "iron curtain" to split Europe between East and West, Lehman resigned from his post as the head of UNRRA "completely exhausted."

Lehman made a brief comeback in the fall to run for a New York seat in the U.S. Senate. He campaigned for an American national health program, an idea that was apparently ahead of its time. "We shall vote for you but our wives won't," acquaintances told him. "They are tired of finding nothing in the markets." Price controls, imposed during the war, on items in the shops had now come off, and the cost of buying the goods had shot up. Butchers and their customers endured meatless days. Lehman and many other Democrats lost at the polls and a clutch of new Republicans entered the Senate. One was Joseph McCarthy of Wisconsin, whose anti-Communist efforts in the 1950s would develop into a significant and noisy career. The odds appeared that Herbert Lehman, by contrast, would withdraw into quiet retirement.

On the other side of the family, Philip Lehman, Bobbie's father, died in March 1947. He left an estate of $4.4 million. Tributes noted his role in the development of Sears, Roebuck and Woolworth's. He had remained on the board of directors of both until he died.

Philip's death may have prompted Bobbie to worry again about his own health. Drs. Will Cook Spain and Francis A. Pflum of 116 East Fifty-third Street, whom he consulted in early October 1947, put him on a diet low in cholesterol and caffeine that was radical for the day. Dairy products, including eggs, were forbidden. Avoid tea, they insisted, and he was to limit himself to one cup of coffee a day ("preferably drip coffee. Allow Sanka"). Bobbie's records indicate that they also came and monitored the air in his home. "[P]ositive test reactions were obtained to ragweed pollens, house dust, feathers and down," they reported. He was to remove any large carpets and throw out pillows and mattresses packed with feathers, cotton, or kapok. Such stuffing materials "should be replaced by horsehair." If allergies were Bobbie's problem, his doctors were on a safe bet here, since their client was a well-known horse owner and breeder.

Bobbie had cause to perk up two weeks later as he helped launch the career of Marlon Brando. Frank J. Manheim, a partner at Lehman Brothers and a former professor of French literature and history, had dropped Bobbie a note saying that an "extremely moving—in fact exciting play" sought sponsors and a launch fund of one hundred thousand dollars. Why didn't Bobbie put in five thousand dollars? Cary Grant was among those who had done so. Elia Kazan, a top young stage director, had been attracted to the project by an unusually high cut of the profits—20 percent—with the rest to be divided between Irene Selznick, the producer (ex-wife of David O.), and "the money," namely, those people willing to take a gamble like Cary Grant and Bobbie Lehman.

A Streetcar Named Desire looked "an awfully good bet for success," said Manheim. Written by Tennessee Williams, who had had a hit on Broadway two years before with *The Glass Menagerie* and was still only thirty-six, it was "strictly a one-woman play." Blanche DuBois, an aging Southern belle from Mississippi, lives in a world of illusion; she visits Stella, her sister in New Orleans, is raped by Stanley Kowalski, Stella's husband, and goes insane. Not that Manheim said so, but with Blanche as the Old South and Stanley as the North, this was a picture of America that, historically, Lehman Brothers knew.

Jessica Tandy, the British actress, would take the role of Blanche. Manheim did not mention who would play Stanley. The play opened on December 3, 1947, at the Ethel Barrymore Theatre on Forty-seventh Street west of Broadway. Critics hailed the "practical poetry" of Williams, the "dynamic staging" of Kazan, and how Tandy epitomized the "rare perfection" of the cast in general. *Variety*, the stage business's own publication, found space to write that Brando, the future star of movies like *On the*

Waterfront, *The Godfather*, and *Apocalypse Now*, "pulls no punches" as "hardboiled husband" Kowalski.

Manheim reported back in a memorandum to Bobbie the following August, in case his senior partner was not aware of the fact, that he had recouped his capital. Bobbie had received regular checks of $120 a week as further royalties, though that had fallen in one recent week to $93.52—"due entirely to the extra expenses occasioned by advertising the Pulitzer Prize" that *Streetcar* had just won. The grandeur of the award notwithstanding, Lehman Brothers' partners minded their dollars and cents.

Americans themselves had been transported into a new land called desire, a state prematurely predicted by Paul Mazur twenty years before. As the world's only functioning major economy, America was booming. This was great news for such prime Lehman Brothers clients as RCA, with its televisions (and advertisers encouraging people to fulfill their dreams by buying one), Philip Morris (its customers stylishly puffing away), and Pan Am (with its promise of exotic places just a short plane ride away).

While Bobbie reaped his reward, Herbert did, too, as political circumstances became more to his liking. The national mood had picked up with more money in people's pockets, and Truman won a surprise reelection in the 1948 presidential contest against Thomas Dewey, the Republican governor of New York. The president saw that he had to confront the Soviet threat. After World War I all enemies had seemed to disappear, but this one was obvious and Truman accepted the challenge. He did not run down Herbert Lehman's work at UNRRA so much as extend it into the Marshall Plan, the huge program to pump $13 billion of relief into shattered Europe. With the Marshall Plan, the Democrats in effect exported the New Deal across the Atlantic. This was bound to raise isolationist ire in the United States, but there was postwar money available now for such an adventurous scheme.

General George C. Marshall was in charge of it, the man who had been Bobbie's commander on the European front in World War I and commander of all American forces in World War II. Marshall was Truman's secretary of state, but the Marshall Plan was a bipartisan project; that is to say, it had Republican backing. Allen Dulles, the head of the Council on Foreign Relations—the influential New York think tank on overseas affairs whose membership included secretaries of state, diplomats, journalists, and others—supported it. A character comfortable in the social and political scenes of New York and Washington, Dulles would head the CIA under the future Republican government of Dwight D. Eisenhower, which took office in 1953.

Eisenhower supported the Marshall Plan. The retired army general had led American forces in Europe in the recent war and regarded Marshall as his mentor. Eisenhower believed that postwar America needed to revive Europe lest Soviet-style communism fill the vacuum. The Russians had occupied Eastern Europe with brute force; by contrast, the Marshall Plan would prove a brilliant way of winning friends and otherwise influencing people. Western Europe, too, could be tuned in to the economics of desire that Lehman Brothers had helped create.

At age seventy-one, Herbert found himself called out of retirement. New York senator Robert F. Wagner resigned because of ill health, and the Democrats nominated Lehman to run for his seat. The contest pitched him against John Foster Dulles, brother of Allen, though a far less personable character. Churchill later called him a "bull that carried his china shop around with him." Successful lawyers, both he and Allen had been partners at Sullivan & Cromwell, a New York law firm, where, among other clients, they had been advisers to the United Fruit Company. John Foster Dulles, if anything, was the more successful; in the mid-1930s, during the Depression, his salary was $377,000. This did not necessarily give him the common touch.

A rising star of the Republican Party, Dulles was a strong favorite to win the election, but he made several mistakes. He accused Lehman of favoring the "welfare state." Herbert responded that if this meant supporting humane legislation in favor of "the whole people as distinguished from special interests" then yes, he supported welfare. At a meeting in Geneseo, New York, Dulles said his audience would only have to look at the faces of a typical metropolitan crowd of Lehman's supporters to be confirmed in their loyalty to the Republican Party. Nevins commented that this was widely interpreted as a slur against foreign-born New Yorkers, or people whose families were of fairly recent immigrant background. David Halberstam in his book *The Fifties* writes that Dulles also said of Lehman: "I know he is no Communist, but I also know that the Communists are in his corner." Millions of people who had voted for Lehman as governor over the years did not regard him or themselves as in the Communist corner.

Herbert Lehman triumphed at the polls and took up his Senate seat in January 1950. "I hope to make a little news," he told the *Washington Post* when it asked what his plans were, "but as little noise as possible." He proved wrong on both counts.

|||||||||

Under General Lucius Clay, the U.S. forces in Europe scored a vital cold war success in 1949. The battle centered on Berlin, the old capital of defeated Germany. The victorious Allies of World War II had divided control of the city among themselves, though not equally. The United States, Britain, and France administered the western half of the city, the Russians the eastern half. Soviet forces had the upper hand because Berlin was surrounded by East Germany, which the Russians controlled. In 1948, they had cut off road links and water supplies to West Berlin in the hope that the United States, Britain, and France would cede control of the whole city to them. Instead, the Western powers staged the Berlin airlift. They flew in the supplies that the two million people in the western half of the city needed until the Russians lifted the siege. From the summer of 1948 to May 1949, planes landed in West Berlin at a rate of one every forty-five seconds in a formidable logistical effort organized by General Clay. After Clay retired from the armed forces, he went on to become a Lehman Brothers partner.

From an American and Western perspective, 1949 was otherwise a tough year. Mao Tse-tung, the Chinese Communist Party leader, seized power in China. The Russians developed an atomic bomb, thus rivaling the nuclear strength of the United States. Britain also had the bomb but found that a spy ring in the country had passed nuclear secrets to the Russians.

This animated the deliberations of the U.S. House of Representatives' Committee on Un-American Activities, often known as HUAC, which had for some time been investigating Communist influences in America. Alger Hiss, a State Department official, came before HUAC accused of spying for the Russians. Richard Nixon, a California lawyer recently elected to the House of Representatives, was his chief inquisitor. Hiss had been a junior official at the 1945 Yalta conference in the USSR, at which the Western allies agreed with Joseph Stalin, the Soviet leader, that postwar Europe would be divided into zones of influence between East and West. The West had not quite expected that the Russians would seize control of the Eastern zone. American Republicans suspected that Hiss, despite his minor role at Yalta, had influenced the conference to cede Eastern Europe to the USSR. In January 1950, Hiss was found guilty not of spying, but of having perjured himself in evidence he had given to the House committee.

Two weeks later, on February 2, Joseph McCarthy entered the debate. He shocked a group of Republican women he was addressing at a meeting in Wheeling, West Virginia, by saying that, while he could not take time to name all the Communists in the State Department, he did have "here in my hand a list of 205 that were made known to the Secretary of State . . . and who nevertheless are still working and shaping policy in the State Department." The Democratic secretary of state was Dean Acheson, whom the Republicans accused of being "soft on communism" in Eastern Europe and China. McCarthy, as a senator, was assumed by many people to be telling the truth. The press picked up the story and set McCarthy off for four years, during which his accusations gripped the public and had many believing that the external crisis of the cold war was in large part the product of an enemy within.

McCarthy had an Irish American father, a German American mother, and came from a poor farming background. He had studied hard while working at a grocery store to pass his bar exam. During the recent war he had served in the Marines in the Pacific, and at thirty-eight, in 1947, became the youngest member of the U.S. Senate. He won early publicity by taking up the cause of a group of German army officers found guilty of war crimes at the trials in Nuremberg organized by the United States and its wartime allies to investigate such matters. The German officers said their American captors had tortured them into giving false confessions. McCarthy was bold in defending high-ranking Germans at this time, but his move played well to Wisconsin's considerable population of German background. He convened hearings, clashed with his Senate colleagues, and gained a taste for such political theater.

McCarthy was a gambler (he liked the horses) and a heavy drinker. He enjoyed lengthy sessions at a bar with journalists, and many members of the press reciprocated their appreciation: "McCarthy was a dream story," said Willard Edwards of the *Chicago Tribune*, whose byline was in great evidence thanks to the senator. "I wasn't off page one for four years." Isolationists backed McCarthy. Republican thinking on foreign matters alternated between wanting nothing to do with the crisis overseas and the so-called rollback theory. Under Truman, the Democrats introduced their policy of containment, namely, keeping the Russians contained in Eastern Europe and gradually wearing communism down. John Foster Dulles and many other Republicans said, in contrast, that the Russians should be "rolled back" and given a sharp lesson in U.S. power. Defeated by Herbert Lehman in 1949, Dulles was now earmarked by the Republicans as a future secretary of state.

McCarthy was a friend of Joseph Kennedy, former business associate on Wall Street and in Hollywood of Lehman Brothers. McCarthy dated two of Kennedy's daughters; as a fellow bachelor and senator he caroused around Washington with Jack Kennedy, Joseph's son, a congressman and future president. McCarthy attracted money from oilmen in Texas and the backing of press barons like those who ran the *Washington Times-Herald* and the *Chicago Tribune*. Some Republicans found his methods crude, yet the New Deal had by 1950 been in the White House for seventeen years, and many Republicans concluded that there was no longer any respectable way of unseating the Democrats. McCarthy also struck a chord with a lot of aggrieved people. The world had not shaped up the way Americans had hoped, and to many, McCarthy sounded like a patriot saying that the fault for that lay in a failure of the national will.

In general, Herbert Lehman found himself unimpressed by the Senate and its "abundance of mediocrity and perversity." He thought many members were less than devoted to their duties. James Eastland of Mississippi, a conservative Southern Democrat and white supremacist with whom Lehman had civil rights battles over the years, for example, missed a lot of votes. Herbert formed a staff, first of eight, then of twenty to thirty full-timers; he paid half of the cost himself. His team won the reputation of being the most efficient in Congress and with an expert line on many things, "whether it be barge traffic on [the] Long Island Sound or the Chinese minority in Indonesia."

In particular, Herbert was not disposed to like McCarthy. The Wisconsin senator made his allegations of numbers and names in the Senate knowing he could not be charged with slander. Often his claims that he was about to identify "Moscow's top spy" or people in other such positions evaporated, or they resulted in a name of someone whom few had heard of or who occupied no position of great importance. Lehman was especially disappointed in the way his own Democratic colleagues failed to challenge McCarthy. He expected nothing of the Southern Democrats, who saw communism behind every attempt to extend civil rights among the black population. But many Democrats were either passive, sometimes claiming that to stand up to McCarthy was to get down in the gutter with him, or frightened, imagining that he might turn his attentions on them. "Nearly all the senators," commented Lehman, "did not lift a finger for two or three years."

Lehman was the first to stride down the warpath. Just a few weeks after he had taken his seat in the Senate, he was part of a debate in which McCarthy waved a photostat of a letter that he said proved subversives were at work within the government on behalf of the Communist Party in China. McCarthy resisted requests to put the letter on the Senate record, claiming that it had to stay secret. Lehman insisted that McCarthy show the letter.

Various accounts exist of the ensuing exchange between the two, but according to that of Nevins, McCarthy shouted at Lehman, "Does the senator care to step over?" Amid a burst of laughter from the galleries and a bustle of excitement on the floor, Lehman crossed the Senate aisle to face McCarthy at arm's length. "May I see the letter?" he asked, and held out his hand to receive it.

Further words followed between the two, the upshot of which was that Lehman did not get to see the letter. Finally McCarthy "smote his desk," said Nevins, and boomed, "Will the senator sit down?"; then, to the president of the chamber, "I do not yield further at this time." Stephen Birmingham, commenting in *Our Crowd*, wrote that the letter, when it was eventually published, "turned out to be harmless, as Lehman had suspected."

Herbert had to stand for election again in the midterm elections of 1950, when many Democrats did not fare well. The Korean War had begun in the summer, with Communist forces from North Korea, supported by China and Russia, attacking and nearly overwhelming the south of the country. America entered the war on South Korea's side, along with forces from the United Nations, which President Truman's opponents portrayed as U.S. subservience to the international body.

Joseph Hanley, Herbert's Republican opponent in the elections, tried a domestic gambit. He visited Wall Street during his campaign to stand outside the Lehman Brothers offices at One William Street. "I was just curious to come down and see where the $50,000,000 is coming from that I am running against," he told journalists. The idea that Bobbie Lehman was financing his cousin's campaign at all, let alone with such a sum of money, was an unlikely one. Herbert still won comfortably. "[H]e is easily the quietest candidate in the country, making an election campaign almost an exercise in understatement," the *New York Post* commented. "Yet he gets the votes!"

United States and UN forces turned the tide in Korea, though only to the extent of leaving the country split between the Communist North and the democratic South. With international communism on the attack, McCarthy inspired a campaign during the 1950 elections that saw several Democrats lose their seats amid allegations of pro-Communist sympathies. Richard Nixon elevated his status from the House of Representatives when he won a Senate seat with such a Red-baiting campaign.

The trial of Ethel and Julius Rosenberg preoccupied the nation in 1951, when the Rosenbergs were found guilty of passing atomic secrets to the USSR and sentenced to death. McCarthy chose that time to attack General George C. Marshall. In a Senate speech in June, and making generalized references to Marshall's career in World War II and after, McCarthy accused him of a "conspiracy of infamy" that had led to the Communist takeovers in China and Eastern Europe. Marshall publicly ignored McCarthy, but Herbert Lehman maintained his offensive, telling a CBS radio broadcast that McCarthy's tactics were "character assassination" and "indictments by smear."

During the following year's presidential campaign, in which Eisenhower was running for the Republicans and Adlai Stevenson, governor of Illinois, for the Democrats, Lehman gave a speech to the American Federation of Labor expressing his contempt for politicians, many of them fellow members of the Senate, who excused McCarthy: "[T]hese political cynics are not much better than the McCarthyites themselves."

Eisenhower hated McCarthy, especially for his attacks on Marshall, Eisenhower's army mentor. But he was initially restrained in his responses to the senator. Eisenhower planned a speech during his campaign praising Marshall, but his public relations people discouraged it. It would, they said, antagonize McCarthy, who was appearing before rapturous audiences on the electoral stump. The PR people's view prevailed over a reluctant Eisenhower, and they also persuaded him to accept the personal indignity of allowing McCarthy on his campaign train as it toured areas of the country.

Bobbie Lehman, meanwhile, was embroiled in personal tussles, and in June 1951 divorced again. A lawyer's statement on behalf of Ruth Owen Lehman, Bobbie's now second former wife, said that for many years he had been "far more engrossed with his business activities and business friends" and had shown "coolness and indifference toward her." Bobbie agreed to pay an undisclosed "lump sum property settlement" and took full custody of Robert Owen Lehman, their son, age thirteen.

Just over a year later, Bobbie was married again, to a Mrs. Lee Anz Lynn. The *New York Times* on July 12, 1952, reported that she was a divorcée and an alumna of John B. Stetson University in DeLand, Florida. Mindful of putting her and Bobbie more clearly on the social map, the newspaper again gave the all-illuminating family detail: "She Becomes Bride of Cousin of Senator."

The *Times* also informed readers that the couple was married in the chambers of Judge Albert Cohn, a friend of Bobbie's. The judge was a long-standing associate of Herbert, who had appointed him to the New York Supreme Court in 1937. Roy Cohn, Judge Cohn's son, furthermore had recently made a name for himself as prosecution counsel in the case of the Rosenbergs, the condemned spies. McCarthy subsequently hired Roy Cohn as his legal counsel.

Bobbie soon became the victim of one effect of McCarthyism. With the senator's popularity so high, the State Department needed to be on its toes and on the lookout for suspicious acts and people. In March 1953, and in zealous fashion, its passport office wrote to Bobbie saying it had noticed a discrepancy in his passport. Apparently, his date of birth, as recorded in the document, was wrong. Furthermore, the office had checked back to his previous passport and discovered that this "was mutilated in the same manner." Politely apologizing, Bobbie reached for his guns. His secretary wrote to the passport office, saying, "[I]f you desire to check on Mr. Lehman's veracity, I refer you to the Honorable John Foster Dulles, who has known Mr. Robert Lehman for many years."

Eisenhower had taken office early in 1953, having easily won the presidential election by thirty-four million votes to Adlai Stevenson's twenty-seven million. Dulles, Bobbie's potential referee in the argument about the passport, was the new head of the State Department. Over the coming months, however, Dulles's veracity would also be questioned by the forces of McCarthyism.

Early in his tenure, Dulles nominated Charles Bohlen as ambassador to the Soviet Union. Bohlen was a Russia expert and had been a translator for Roosevelt at wartime conferences. McCarthy challenged the appointment, alleging that Bohlen was a security risk. This prompted an angry response from Herbert Lehman—once again he advanced toward McCarthy in the Senate, this time waving his finger under his adversary's nose. The Bohlen issue, he told McCarthy and the gathering, was part of the "same pattern that has been followed against many loyal, devoted, honest Americans." It looked as if the two might come to blows.

As an attempted sop to McCarthy, when the Republican administration came to power, it gave him his own committee. McCarthy, with Roy Cohn in support, grilled employees of Voice of America, the U.S. mouthpiece abroad, in a bid to prove Communist infiltration. McCarthy also widened his offensive overseas, sending Cohn to search for subversive books in the libraries of the U.S. Information Service, run by the State Department. In a tour of seven Western European nations and their U.S. embassies, Cohn claimed to have discovered over thirty thousand books in the libraries by "pro-Communist" writers. These included works by John Steinbeck, author of such tales of the Depression as *The Grapes of Wrath*. Herman Melville's *Moby-Dick* from the mid-nineteenth century was also among the books that came under suspicion, though it was not clear how a white whale from the deep might be the mouthpiece of an undercover Red. The State Department withdrew many of them amid some reports of book burning.

Given that only two decades earlier the Nazis in Germany had destroyed reading material not to their liking, Herbert made public statements attacking Cohn, saying he had turned U.S. embassies "upside down" and done the cause of anti-communism great harm. The result was an angry exchange of letters in summer 1953 between Herbert and Judge Albert Cohn. The judge wrote, pointing out that he was a constituent of Herbert's, complaining of the attacks on his son and that he, and indeed Mrs. Cohn, had "great admiration and respect" for McCarthy's efforts to fight communism. Herbert wrote back saying that McCarthyism had done such harm to the "moral authority of America" that it probably outstripped "the ambitions of the Kremlin's most ambitious propagandists."

A mark of their different worldviews, and conceivably of the grip that McCarthyism gained on the feelings of America, was that while Herbert was battling McCarthy throughout this period, Bobbie Lehman had no difficulty staying good friends with the Cohns. He continued to do so in the years ahead.

Herbert had another clash with McCarthy in the Senate that summer. McCarthy claimed Lehman had abused privilege by using the free postal system available to senators for business mail to send out copies of a speech he had made entitled "Creeping McCarthyism." Lehman retorted that McCarthy used the system to send out copies of newspaper articles that the Wisconsin senator had put his name on. Lehman, short and in his seventies, stood face-to-face with the far younger and taller ex-Marine, whereupon Paul Douglas, an Illinois senator, stepped between them. Douglas was a friend of Herbert's and, by the way, much taller.

In speeches at the meetings and dinners of scores of organizations, and in the many interviews he gave to newspapers and on radio and television, Lehman maintained an "incessant drumfire," as Nevins described it, on McCarthy and his followers. This required bravery. June 19, 1953, for example, saw the execution of the Rosenbergs, a moment when anti-Communist fervor was high. The next evening Lehman spoke at a Jefferson-Jackson Day dinner in Milwaukee warning of the hysteria being whipped up "into a panic on whose wings McCarthy and his followers hope to ride to national power."

In Herbert's favor was that Eisenhower spoke up. "Don't join the book burners," the president said in a speech at Dartmouth College in July. "Don't be afraid to go into your library and read every book." For a while McCarthy continued undaunted. From the State Department he widened his claims of Communist infiltration to the CIA, thus making enemies of both the Dulles brothers. He went further and questioned the loyalty of the army, which was surely too much for Eisenhower. Whether the president intervened is not known, but the army did accuse McCarthy of abusive behavior and called hearings to question him.

The Army-McCarthy hearings are often cited as the factor that brought about McCarthy's end. They started on April 22, 1954, and lasted thirty-six days. They were televised and later regarded as one of the first illustrations of, to quote the *New York Times*, "the immense power of the new medium of television to shape opinion." With audiences reaching twenty million a day, many people saw McCarthy in action for the first time. He came across as a hectoring and bullying figure to some viewers. Some saw his manner as disrespectful, especially to Joseph Welch, an old-fashioned Boston lawyer representing the army. "Have you no sense of decency?" asked Welch on one occasion. Only two of the four networks covered the hearings; NBC and CBS chose not to. ABC broadcast them, as did Du Mont. Allen Du Mont's network prided itself on having the best pictures and, if that was the case, Du Mont—and Bobbie Lehman, who first financed him—might claim their part in this aspect of McCarthy's downfall.

Yet the hearings were inconclusive. They censured Cohn but did not find McCarthy guilty of anything, although soon he faded away. What finished him was his quite sudden irrelevance. His appeal had been to those who had doubted the national will to face threats from whichever quarter they might come. By now, the Dulles brothers and Eisenhower were royally fed up with McCarthy and would have been grateful for a way to have done with him. By chance they found one.

The United Fruit Company—with Bobbie Lehman a member of its board of directors—had complained to Washington for years about its treatment in Guatemala. The country had rid itself in 1944 of Jorge Ubico, the old dictator, and elected democratic governments since the early 1950s. The latest had said it would take away some of United Fruit's large reserves of unused land and give it to poor and landless farmers, of which Guatemala had many. The Guatemalan government paid for the land with bonds, but the company declared these useless, loudly adding that it was the victim of communism.

With the Dulles brothers kindly disposed toward the company since their lawyer days, the administration's particular concern was to send out a signal to an audience at home and abroad. Whether to the USSR and the wider world, to McCarthy and his supporters, or to the U.S. public in general, the Republicans aimed to show that America meant business in the cold war.

The CIA arranged a coup d'état by finding a dissident Guatemalan colonel who wanted power and a group of disaffected exiles to act as a liberating army; the intelligence agency provided military support. John Foster Dulles barnstormed diplomatic channels to inform the world that Guatemala was becoming a Soviet base in the Americas. United Fruit had hired the services of Edward Bernays, and he fed stories to those many

U.S. newspapers ready to believe them amid the mood of the McCarthy times. One of the impressions that the public relations offensive managed to convey was that the enemy was virtually on the doorstep of the United States itself and about to grab vital American interests. Guatemalan Communists were but a short step, ran one line of argument, from seizing the Panama Canal. The groundwork laid, the coup went ahead, and Guatemala's democratic government fell in the summer of 1954.

The Eisenhower administration had proved it could remove a Communist enemy, real or imagined. It needed no further lectures from McCarthy on the subject and he dropped out of the national picture. He died three years later from an alcohol-damaged liver. He did not so much disappear, however, as recede from view. His spirit remained available for resuscitation in times of fear of a foreign threat and suspicion of an enemy within.

Herbert Lehman played a key role in seeing off McCarthy by being the first to spot what he stood for, and he stayed with the cause to its end. While others found the voice to join him en route, Herbert starred in this peculiarly American drama. Stephen Birmingham suggested in *Our Crowd* that his old family firm had its own perspective on the affair: "And in the meantime his brothers and partners back home in South William Street must have realized that Herbert, 'dirty Democrat' though he might be, 'wild-eyed friends' like Roosevelt . . . though he might have, was nonetheless showering even further glory upon the House of Lehman."

|||||||||

Then again, Bobbie Lehman had been furious with his cousin Herbert after the Republicans came to power in early 1953. President Eisenhower chose Charles Wilson, the head of General Motors, to be his defense secretary, and Herbert Lehman was among a few senators who protested. At hearings on his nomination, Wilson could not see anything wrong with having shares worth $2.5 million in his old company. Nor did he understand when asked whether he could imagine making a decision as defense secretary that went against the interests of General Motors. As well as vehicles, GM made arms and planes for the military, but what if another company was competing with GM for a contract? A conflict of interest, Wilson said, had not occurred to him, because for years, "I thought that what was good for our country was good for General Motors, and vice versa." Garbled reports over the years had Wilson more famously saying "What's good for General Motors is good for the country."

In spite of Herbert's resistance, the Senate confirmed Wilson in his post, though he had to sell his shares. Bobbie took Wilson's side and wrote to Wilson on behalf of Lehman Brothers: "[W]e are all shocked and disturbed by the stand [Herbert] took and, without exception, we all violently disagree with his views and actions.... [Y]our appointment made us all feel proud that we have supported the Republican party for the past 25 years." (Given that this was 1953, Bobbie dated his and Lehman Brothers' support for the Republican camp back to 1928, when the pre-crash stock market was near its height and, overall, it was rather easy to be a Republican.)

"I have not had the pleasure of meeting you," Bobbie added, conceivably fishing for the opportunity. Since Lehman Brothers had its partner John Hertz on the GM board, having a GM man also in the Defense Department gave Lehman Brothers a potentially useful link to Washington. Bobbie wrote again to Wilson to disassociate himself from Herbert. He was aware "that confusion may exist as a result of varying opinion expressed by those carrying the same name." Wilson's appointment assured "fine service on your part to our country." On a copy of this communication, he penned a note about Herbert to Paul Mazur: "Mr. Mazur. This was a 'toughie' but this treats the subject of 'HL' gingerly."

Herbert had been losing battles on all sides, and Bobbie was winning them. During the Korean War in 1950–51, Herbert complained, companies had made bloated profits and yet had been given generous tax concessions. The government's health and welfare budgets came under attack from business interests that wanted their taxes lower still. Lehman Brothers' clients had done well in the war. Military contracts saw Halliburton's earnings of $26 million at the end of World War II more than triple to $93 million by the time Korean hostilities ceased. Halliburton had expanded to new markets like Saudi Arabia, Peru, and Sumatra in Indonesia. Lehman Brothers had launched Halliburton's first issue of shares onto the stock market in 1948. It did the same for Kerr-McGee, which a year earlier had begun operating the world's first offshore oil well in the tidelands of Louisiana. Lehman Brothers had accumulated a large stock of oil shares of its own. *Forbes* magazine calculated that such shares, which had cost Lehman Brothers a mere $17 million, were worth $72 million by 1955.

Herbert Lehman had regular battles in the Senate with Robert Kerr, an Oklahoma senator and Kerr-McGee's cofounder. Kerr wanted control of the United States' offshore oil reserves in the hands of the states that had a coastline nearest the reserves. Herbert said this put oil reserves worth $40 billion—which belonged to all of the forty-eight states of the nation—under the supervision of just a handful. Those individual states had limited bargaining power against the large oil companies and the federal government would have been a far more equal match in regulating them. Kerr and his supporters in Congress outnumbered those of Herbert Lehman, and responsibility for the oil reserves went to the states.

Kerr-McGee had become the first oil company to move into uranium mining. In 1952 it acquired former Navajo lands in New Mexico for the purpose, and its business tripled in the period to 1956 as the nuclear arms race between the United States and the Soviet Union increased demand for uranium. Kerr-McGee opened its first uranium-processing mill in 1954. Herbert Lehman argued that the federal government had spent many billions of dollars in helping build the nuclear industry, which had brought little return to the taxpayer and large profits to the companies. All this was to the benefit of Lehman Brothers as Kerr-McGee's financial adviser.

In 1953 Bobbie Lehman was among those who triumphed in the so-called battle of Wall Street. Three years earlier the Truman administration had taken seventeen investment banks to court, accusing them of operating a cartel to divide business among themselves. Those that had a particular specialty would accept business in that line and refer other customers to banks that had other specialties they required. One bank might prefer to sell government bonds, another to arrange company mergers, and so on. The Truman lawyers alleged, therefore, that banks were acting like monopolies in their specialist fields and fixing inordinately high prices.

Lehman Brothers protested from the outset that it should not be facing such charges. It was a prestigious bank of tradition that did not pick and choose; it did everything in the investment banking line, and did it expertly. Its "special attitudes form a continuity of character that it is impossible to confuse with the modes of business of the other sixteen defendant firms," argued its lawyers, not exactly endearing Lehman Brothers to its fellow accused.

Judge Harold Medina threw out the case in 1953, but did seem to be confused about Lehman Brothers and one of its codefendants. He said that all the banks competed vigorously enough, yet, as an example, he cited the historic rivalry between Lehman Brothers and Goldman Sachs. He was surely thinking of another time; since the great crash, Goldman Sachs had struggled to compete on Wall Street and took it as a compliment that it was among the seventeen defendants at all. "At this point, Goldman Sachs can only be described as an also-ran, a firm with a few good clients and many dreams," wrote Lisa Endlich in her book *Goldman Sachs: The Culture of Success*. Goldman Sachs came out of the war of Wall Street both on the winning side and with a boost to its prestige. As for Lehman Brothers, the judge had publically likened the firm to an old rival that these days it regarded as its inferior.

In the new Republican era, Lehman Brothers went *On the Road*. Jack Kerouac wrote his book of the same name in 1951, but it did not appear until 1957. The book spoke for a rising beat generation, with its experiments in drugs and love of poetry and jazz. In its own way, Lehman Brothers sensed the feeling in the air. Frank Manheim, who had told Bobbie to board *A Streetcar Named Desire*, also said Lehman Brothers must hitch a ride with the rental-car business. People loved their cars, but they also flew more now and wanted their own transport at distant airports. Lehman Brothers had John Hertz in its midst. Manheim had noticed that GM did not think much of the car-hire component of the business and had been selling it off to individual franchises. Lehman Brothers moved in to correct this process. It proposed and helped organize the Hertz Corporation to buy up the individual franchises and create a national network. The value of Hertz Corporation rose from $7 million in 1953 to $100 million by the midsixties. "I get tired of people who think that banking is accounting," Manheim told Joseph Wechsberg, author of *The Merchant Bankers*. "Banking is imagination."

Keen to display that side of his own character, Bobbie staged an exhibition of ninety of the paintings and drawings from his collection in January 1954 at the Metropolitan Museum of Art. He normally kept his art in various locations: in his offices at One William Street; at his eighteen-room apartment in 625 Park Avenue; and in the mansion on West Fifty-fourth Street that he had turned into a private museum. Georges Salles, the director of French museums, visited the exhibit and declared himself "overwhelmed by what he saw," reported *Time* magazine. He may also have been overwhelmed by Bobbie. Here was a banker who, to the French mind, was steeped in the rough tradition of American money-making, yet who spoke (and wrote) fluent French. He also had a lot more in his collection, and Salles suggested that in the future he come to Paris and exhibit.

At about this time in 1954, Bobbie put up the financing that pioneered the electronics industry. Charles Thornton, "Tex" to his friends, had worked under Henry Ford and Henry's son Edsel, helping to sort out the considerable mess that had existed at Ford after World War II. Henry had hung on at the top too long, and Ford had fallen behind its competitors. Others working alongside Thornton at Ford included Robert McNamara, who went on to be John F. Kennedy's defense secretary. Thornton had moved from Ford to work with Howard Hughes, the reclusive owner of Hughes Aircraft Company and Trans World Airlines (TWA), and lately set up his own business as head of Litton Industries.

Thornton later described himself as "confident but not assured" that he would get backing from Wall Street and took his plans and financial statements to Lehman Brothers. Bobbie told him that he could not get very interested in balance sheets. "'I bet on people,' Bobbie Lehman told me," said Thornton. "I blinked my eyes when I heard that." Lehman Brothers raised $1.5 million for his business, part of the deal being that Lehman Brothers bought seventy-five thousand shares in Litton for itself at prices between $.10 and $1.00 each. By 1965, Litton Industries' shares stood at $150 as the company led the electronics market in products from calculators to missile guidance systems.

From the political wing of the family, Herbert Lehman was aiming his attack at the Lehmans' political legacy in the Old South. His regular battles with Senator Eastland of Mississippi and other hard-line opponents of civil rights bore fruit in 1954, when the Supreme Court ordered that all states end segregation between black and white children in their schools. Lehman "rejoiced as loudly" at the decision as Eastland lamented it, said Nevins. The next year, Rosa Parks, a member of the National Association for the Advancement of Colored People in Alabama, led her protest in Lehman Brothers' old city base of Montgomery when she refused to sit at the back of a bus, the area designated for black people under segregation laws. Her action began a yearlong boycott of the Montgomery bus system led by Martin Luther King, Jr.

Bobbie made a contribution of his own to the affairs of the South when he backed *Cat on a Hot Tin Roof*, another play by Tennessee Williams. This tale of lies, hypocrisy, and repressed sexuality opened on March 24, 1955, at the Morosco Theatre on Broadway and ran for 694 performances. Ben Gazzara, Barbara Bel Geddes, and Burl Ives, the folksinger, took the lead roles. In recognition of an emerging taste among white people for black music, Sonny Terry and Brownie McGhee, the blues duo, joined the cast. Elia Kazan again directed, though life had changed for him since *Streetcar* in 1947. HUAC had summoned him in 1952 during its investigations into communism in Hollywood, and Kazan had named names. Among those he had said had Communist sympathies was Zero Mostel, an actor who was blacklisted as a result and unable to find work in the movies for the rest of the 1950s. HUAC forgave Kazan his earlier membership in the party, and he had since resumed his career, directing Brando in the movie *On the Waterfront*.

In June, Bobbie sent the president an ice-packed box with a product of one of his expeditions to Canada. It was not the first. Thank you, Eisenhower wrote back, "for, again, sending me a salmon from the Restigouche." In September the president had a heart attack—moderate, said his doctors—and he was back working from his hospital bed by October. Bobbie was only a year younger than Eisenhower and may have sensed his own mortality. *Fortune* magazine asked him to contribute his thoughts on the art of collecting as part of a series it was running on great American art collectors; among the others were John D. Rockefeller III, Walter P. Chrysler, and Edward G. Robinson, star of gangster movies about the 1920s. Bobbie wrote that he had begun very young collecting stamps and postcards of the countries and monuments he had visited with his parents and moved on to collecting works of art with them. "It can become a consuming interest in early childhood," he wrote, "and is the last to possess one in old age."

Various forces killed off Allen B. Du Mont's television network in the mid-1950s, Bobbie Lehman being one of them. Paradoxically, this happened soon after it had reached a peak of popularity with coverage of the Army-McCarthy hearings. Quality viewing was Allen Du Mont's goal, and in that sense money was no object. He would not lower his prices to make cheaper sets for an industry that was increasingly appealing to a mass market. His company had produced *Mary Kay and Johnny*, television's first situation comedy, and the first soap opera televised by a TV network, *Faraway Hill*. Du Mont was destined to disappear beyond it, however, and to become America's forgotten television network.

Allen Du Mont may have tested how far Bobbie Lehman was prepared to tolerate a maverick. His network was always short of money, yet Du Mont argued with advertisers. In fact, his views revolutionized television's business model, specifically the way it made its money, which is still in use today. Most shows depended on one sponsor, but Du Mont realized that this might lead companies to tell his producers how to make their programs. So he sold slots to many advertisers; as well as being called the father of television, Du Mont would have fair claim to the title of father of the TV commercial.

After Bobbie Lehman's early help, Du Mont had raised capital by selling a share of his network to Paramount Pictures, for which Bobbie was also the banker. Paramount was a movie company that—with reason—never overcame the view that TV was a rival, and Du Mont did not get the money he needed. At some stage, it is not clear when, Bobbie concentrated his financing on RCA and contributed to the downfall of the pathbreaking TV network he had helped create. In the beginning he bet on the man; in the end, on the corporation.

For its part, RCA had a new toy to play with. Paul Mazur, for Lehman Brothers, and others on the RCA board, could only have had an inkling of what they were getting into, but the company they ran took the conscious step. In 1955, rhythm and blues, known as "black" music, first stormed the "white" charts with Chuck Berry and his song "Maybellene." White music was the realm of crooners like Bing Crosby, Frank Sinatra, and Perry Como, along with clean-cut youngsters like Pat Boone. The view went around that a white boy was needed who could sing in a crossover style that would overcome whites' resistance to buying black music. Boone recorded Little Richard's "Tutti Frutti" with chart success, though he admitted the song's lyrics made little sense to him. Sam Phillips, a recording studio expert and producer from Memphis, had Elvis Presley, from Tupelo, Mississippi, on his books. Ahmet Ertegun, owner of the Atlantic label, bid to buy his contract for twenty-five thousand dollars, later saying that this was the value of everything Atlantic had, including his office desk. RCA paid thirty-five thousand dollars. Presley justified the price by recording such hits as "Jailhouse Rock" and "Hound Dog." He also made more than thirty movies, and in the view of such diverse commentators as Leonard Bernstein and John Lennon, laid the basis of a social revolution that became, in a few years' time, "the sixties."

Lehman Brothers was more excited—though with mixed feelings—by the big business event of early 1956. A syndicate of 720 banks came together to underwrite the public share issue of the Ford Motor Company. So many banks were needed because the sum involved, $650 million, was so large. Letters of congratulation for being one of the main banks concerned with the issue arrived at One William Street, along with solicitous requests for Bobbie to put some shares aside. "[W]hile I realize the issue will be very much oversubscribed . . . ," wrote Judge Albert Cohn. Roy Cohn, writing from his home at 29 Broadway, asked Bobbie to put aside two hundred shares for him. He would have been lucky; such was the demand that many investors were getting only five to ten, some only one.

The shares—initially priced at $64.50 each and soon trading at $70—sold quickly. None of the banks need have worried about any being left on their hands. Merrill Lynch, First Boston, and Kuhn, Loeb must have been happy to be among the main banks involved. On the other hand, Bobbie Lehman may have been less than gleeful. That was because one bank had good reason to feel overjoyed at the occasion: Goldman Sachs had more or less orchestrated the whole thing.

When old Henry Ford died in 1947 (son Edsel had died before him), Henry Ford II, the founder's grandson, contacted Goldman Sachs' head, Sidney Weinberg. The elder Ford had been fiercely anti-Semitic, but Weinberg, who had a way of getting along with potential enemies, as he had shown with Roosevelt and the New Deal, had became a Ford family confidant. The family had kept shares in the company to itself, but Henry II realized that Ford needed to raise money in the public share market in order to modernize. Over nine years Weinberg had valued the company's assets and worked out future plans for Ford's vast organization. He and Henry II had managed to keep this secret. Word had only come out when they needed to organize the banking syndicate. With the successful share sale, another fact became public knowledge: Goldman Sachs was back in contention with the leaders on Wall Street.

Herbert Lehman suffered his own setbacks. In 1956, in the Senate, he failed again to stop a bill removing federal regulation of large companies involved in vital resources, this time in the natural gas industry. "Grabbing and greed can go on for just so long," he complained, "but the breaking point is bound to come sometime."

Maybe others from different parts of the political spectrum began to see this. Eisenhower favored moves for deregulation but had not liked some of the techniques used by the gas industry to win the argument; one lobbyist was found to have contributed to a senator's election campaign fund. Such "arrogant" methods risked, said the president, "creating doubt among the American people concerning the integrity of governmental processes."

Herbert was not easily consoled. He observed that seventy-seven corporations in the United States had assets of over $1 billion. It was not big business he objected to, he said, but giant business. Corporations like General Electric and DuPont, the chemical company based in Delaware, dominated their markets and could dictate to customers what they would get and at what price.

In the approach to the fall election for the presidency, Herbert failed to get the Democrats to adopt a radical stance on civil rights in the South. Black people wanted greater participation in elections, he said, yet faced intimidation at the polls. America demanded that the USSR allow free elections in such countries as East Germany and Hungary—but what about South Carolina?

He decided not to run for reelection to the Senate and to retire in early 1957. He felt thwarted. There remained much to do in civil rights, and big business bent capitalism to its own ends. But he had cause to take heart. Overseas, Eisenhower's administration had chosen neither rollback nor isolation but taken the Democrats' stance of containment of the USSR and support for alliance with Western Europe. In the fall of 1957, federal troops would also be sent to Little Rock, Arkansas, to enforce desegregation in the schools.

Eisenhower indicated that it would be madness for the Republicans to abandon the New Deal's social programs. Should any party attempt to abolish Social Security and unemployment insurance, he said, "you would not hear of that party again in our political history." The president had also followed a New Deal line on public works when in 1956 he announced plans for an interstate highway system. As governor of New York, Herbert Lehman had left the state with improved highways; Eisenhower envisioned thousands of miles of highways from coast to coast.

The president, nicknamed "Ike," called his approach "modern Republicanism." His electoral slogan "I Like Ike" resonated in America and overseas as the United States embarked on a period of unequaled prosperity. Eleanor Roosevelt wrote to Herbert after he announced his retirement: "No one can look back with greater satisfaction than you can on a life of public service. . . . [Y]ou have won the admiration of all of us."

7

"Aristocrat of the Autocrats"

Bobbie Lehman was among the VIPs invited by President Eisenhower to the inauguration of his second term in January 1957. The Eisenhower administration was pro-business, and in his election campaign the president had emphasized the "peace and prosperity" of his first four years in office. Eisenhower liked to convey a relaxed air and gave informal stag parties for businessmen. He was also a great fan of golf, the modern businessman's game. He had a green installed on the White House lawn and on warmer days passersby could see him practicing his putts.

Cold war events, however, disrupted the mood of calm. At around the time of the election in November 1956, the USSR had invaded Hungary after that country had tried to secede from the bloc of Eastern European countries under Communist rule and its military organization, the Warsaw Pact. With Hungarian refugees fleeing across the border into Austria, Bobbie Lehman responded to a request in December from First Aid for Hungary, which was based in Manhattan, with a donation of $250. He apologized for the "modest check," pointing out that he had already donated to the Hungarian cause, although it is not known how much he gave.

In early December 1956, Fidel Castro had invaded Cuba in an attempt to overthrow the regime of Fulgencio Batista, who enjoyed the backing of Washington. Castro came from a quite wealthy Cuban background, his father having been a sugar planter on land leased from the United Fruit Company. He had trained a small rebel force in Mexico City of about eighty, many of whom were killed in the invasion. The survivors fled to the Sierra Maestra mountains in the southeast of the island, far from Havana in the northwest but from where they continued fighting. Cuban affairs were not yet part of the cold war and were viewed as of real relevance only to the Americas.

Che Guevara was a member of Castro's rebels and had hastened to join them after the United Fruit coup in Guatemala in 1954. An Argentine doctor, he had been in Guatemala over a period leading up to the coup, and had even tried to get work in one of United Fruit's plantation hospitals. He had fought on the defeated Guatemalan government's side, sought asylum in the Argentine embassy, then fled to join Castro in Mexico, declaring that the only way to fight the company and *yanqui* "imperialism" was through the "armed struggle."

The coup in Guatemala had wider implications for the Eisenhower administration. Encouraged by the ease with which the Guatemalan government had been overthrown, Allen Dulles's CIA started to slip its military advisers into Southeast Asia. The French empire in that region had ended in 1954 with the Vietnamese army's defeat of French forces at Dien Bien Phu. Washington had moved to fill the vacuum left by the French, and within a decade the Vietnam War would grab the attention of the American public.

The Guatemalan affair had also led to an extraordinary about-face by the Eisenhower administration. The coup prompted protests and demonstrations in many parts of Latin America against U.S. involvement in the region's politics, after which the administration appeared to grasp that the United Fruit Company was a source of discontent. The Department of Justice, therefore, accused United Fruit of acting like a monopoly in the banana market, and started proceedings to take away some of its Guatemalan land. The case, which United Fruit finally lost in 1958, appears to get no mention in Bobbie Lehman's files, though it can be safely assumed that for any member of United Fruit's board of directors the affair was a serious or even traumatic one. The loss of an important part of its assets, and the fact that Washington had turned on it in such a way, dealt a blow to United Fruit's business and morale from which it never recovered.

From early in his second term President Eisenhower faced enemies in his own party. Barry Goldwater, a Republican senator from Arizona, attacked Eisenhower and "modern Republicanism" in a speech in April 1957, calling it "the siren song of socialism." That same year, Ayn Rand published her most famous work, *Atlas Shrugged*, in which she conjured a world where creative people rebelled against an oppressive government similar to the type her many readers believed existed in the United States. Rand advocated money as a true measure of worth, and fierce individualism and rational self-interest—or even rational selfishness—as proper bases for society. She decried "moochers," people and governments who lived off welfare and foreign aid.

Lehman Brothers itself engaged in an intriguing exercise in foreign aid at the time. It moved into Europe and raised $35 million for the European Coal and Steel Community. The following year saw the formation of the European Common Market, or as it was more formally known, the European Economic Community. The United States gave the organization a lot of important assistance. As the Marshall Plan had been an expansion of the New Deal to Europe, so the EEC was a logical extension of the Marshall Plan—pulled up by its postwar bootstraps, Europe could now take hold of them itself.

For the Europeans, the formation of the EEC was a gamble, and the chances of the idea working were limited. Europe was a group of diverse states with no common language or currency, each with its own separate cultural identity. Britain, unable to see any need for a united Europe, would not join the organization, given that in the 1950s large parts of the British empire remained intact. Initially, the EEC was an alliance of Germany and France, with the smaller states of Belgium, Italy, Luxembourg, and the Netherlands participating in an attempt to heal the wounds of World Wars I and II.

From an American perspective it was risky having a "United States of Europe" as a rival in the world, but Bobbie Lehman and some of his influential friends did not think so. Averell Harriman backed the idea. He had risen to the positions of U.S. ambassador to Britain and the Soviet Union during World War II and after, and from 1948 to 1953 also administered the Marshall Plan.

John Foster Dulles supported a united Western Europe as a bulwark against the USSR. Dulles was a friend of Jean Monnet, who in the early 1950s drafted the French proposal for Europe to pool its coal and steel resources, the base on which the EEC was founded. Monnet became known as the architect of a unified Europe. He and Dulles had each served their respective national delegations at the Versailles peace talks in Paris in 1919 after World War I. When Dulles died in 1959, Monnet was an honorary pallbearer at his funeral.

Bobbie had also joined the Council on Foreign Relations, through which he had many other acquaintances well connected to the European discussions. Lehman Brothers raised much more money for the EEC over the following years, and the organization eventually evolved into today's European Union. Britain eventually joined in 1972, and today the EU has twenty-seven states as members.

The summer of 1957 saw another of Bobbie's forays into Europe and one that he may well have considered his greatest triumph. The Orangerie art gallery in Paris staged a show of the best of Bobbie's collection. This was the idea that Georges Salles, the French director of museums, had put to Bobbie three years earlier. The Orangerie stood in the gardens of the Tuileries, the royal palace from the days when France was ruled by the house of Bourbon. Now it succumbed to the house of Lehman.

The Orangerie showed 293 of the 1,000 pieces in Bobbie's collection. One estimate of the value of the pieces he sent was $14 million. Works by Rembrandt, Goya, the Impressionists, and other masters went on exhibit. Bobbie was nervous, and just before the opening he was flicking the last specks of dust off canvases with his handkerchief. He need not have been concerned. French art critics acclaimed him, one writing that he had provided "dazzling evidence" of his artistic taste. About seventeen thousand people came in the first two weeks alone, and the public lined up to see the exhibit for the rest of the summer.

His partners back at One William Street had become less impressed with Bobbie's Francophile side. From the late 1940s he had struck up a close friendship with André Meyer, the head of the New York office of Lazard Frères, the French investment bank. Bobbie and Meyer shared a love of art and got along well personally and in business. During the war, Meyer had fled from the Nazi occupation of Paris, where he had been an important financier for Citroën, the French car company. On Wall Street, he joined Lazard, which Charles R. Geisst in *The Last Partnerships* says was a "sleepy backwater," and through one machination or another displaced its chief, Frank Altschul, the brother of Herbert Lehman's wife, Edith. Meyer had a dominant personality and was an adept trader, with a mind that could put large deals together quickly. "He acquired a reputation for being the most loathed man on the Street by his employees and competitors," wrote Geisst.

Not by Bobbie, however. He brought Meyer into Lehman Brothers' deals with such important clients as RCA and Chase Manhattan Bank. Lehman Brothers did appear to gain some benefit; one of Meyer's chief clients was International Telephone & Telegraph Corporation (ITT), which he would lead on a takeover spree in the 1960s as it acquired such businesses as the Sheraton Hotel chain and Avis car rentals. From the late 1950s Lehman Brothers did regular business with ITT, but Bobbie's partners felt the share of the arrangement was disproportionate. "It was considered a terrible blow when Lazard got half the RCA business," one told Geisst.

After his success in France, Bobbie enjoyed further public acclaim with a lengthy article in the December 1957 issue of *Fortune* magazine entitled "The House of Lehman: A Banker's Art." It had an artist's depiction of the firm's headquarters at One William Street with the walls stripped away to show activity inside. On the top, or eleventh, floor was the gymnasium, where the firm's masseur was "kneading" a partner into condition. Lehman Brothers' restaurant, with its French chef and nine staff members, was on the eighth floor. The sixth-floor library was "one of the best in the Street." Bobbie's office on the third floor was empty ("Lehman was in Paris"), while on the second floor salesmen called clients to test interest in a Kerr-McGee stock offering.

Oil was the great success story. Lehman Brothers had fixed $1 billion of financing for oil companies since World War II ended twelve years earlier. From such deals, the magazine added, Lehman Brothers took its "bite." Every firm charged fees; Lehman's were high. The firm did not contest the point but boasted that it offered a premium service for which clients expected to pay a premium fee. They gained prestige by having Lehman Brothers as their banker.

Fortune called the firm's seventeen partners "merchants of money." They had their weekly meeting at 1:00 P.M. on Mondays, when over lunch they discussed share issues and bond offerings, and merger possibilities, another profitable line. Lehman Brothers had arranged for Philip Morris to buy a packaging company and was presently working on a "worldwide tie-up" between Hertz and American Express.

Singling out Lehman Brothers characters, the article focused on Paul Mazur, an "energetic and distinguished-looking man in his early 60s." He was the "intellectual hair shirt" of the firm and of the investment banking community. The magazine recalled that Mazur had foreseen the five-day workweek as "a device to spur consumption and lift the standard of living." He went against the grain of conventional thinking; sometimes, noted *Fortune*, he argued with his partners, or even clients, just for the exercise.

After the article was published, Bobbie had copies made and sent to his many clients and friends. Among those writing back was King Umberto of Italy. His family, the house of Savoy, had survived Benito Mussolini, fascism, and World War II only for the Italian people to dethrone him in an election in 1946. Umberto sent a letter saying thank you for the article and invited Bobbie to meet him when next he came to Europe.

Bobbie Lehman himself was sometimes called the "aristocrat of the autocrats." Another of his titles, writes Stephen Birmingham, was "the last of the imperiously rich men." As Birmingham added, "the phrase 'Bobby [*sic*] wants to speak to you' strikes terror in the breast of all at One William Street." Then again, Bobbie was not one given to the Wall Street tantrums of later years, so this sounds like a possible exaggeration. Those who did go to see him may have felt at a disadvantage in his rather oppressively small office. Only nine feet wide and not quite fifteen feet long, and with a small air conditioner sticking in the window, it was far more humble than the offices of many junior partners. Yet it helped Bobbie—small in stature— fill the space. Many who came to it felt crowded out by him.

He rose early to meet the demands of his day, rarely sleeping past 6:00 A.M. But that did not mean he was crossing the threshold of One William Street before dawn. "He'd talk to his horse trainer first thing," a friend said. "He'd call his partners between 7.30 and 9:00 A.M." That was the time his partners had to be alive to Bobbie's demands. "If you weren't in on the early morning telephone circuit, you weren't on the in team."

He was eminently chivalrous. "'No matter who you were, he would always hold your coat for you,'" reported the *New York Times,* quoting "one lower echelon worker." The first time he did this "you felt sort of funny." Some also found it difficult to comply with his invitation to "call me Bobbie."

Nonetheless, he was very much in charge. "When Bobbie said, 'Fellows, I think . . . ,'" said a former executive of the firm, it was not a wish but an order. He kept partners on their toes. Anyone who came to him rejoicing at a deal he had just made was likely to receive the answer, softly delivered: "Fine. What else are you doing?" Bobbie Lehman was not from the high-fives school of later years.

According to Joseph Wechsberg, Lehman called himself a "nontechnical banker." He was "a people-oriented individual, rather than fact-oriented," said one partner. He dealt by instinct, and in spite of his aristocratic background, he had the common touch.

In general, under Bobbie's leadership, Lehman Brothers did solid business based on the shared memory of the Depression. It marked and tempered the actions of everyone who had been alive at the time. From the 1930s, for example, Lehman Brothers had pioneered the practice known as "private placement" for companies issuing shares. After the disenchantment caused by the crash of 1929, the firm often avoided the market by putting its clients directly in touch with big insurance companies and pension funds that were among the few bodies with large sums of available money. A note in Bobbie's files to Bank of America on January 20, 1956, offered to underwrite a share issue on Bank of America's behalf, pointing out that Lehman Brothers had the "best relationship" of any Wall Street firm with insurance companies and pension funds. "[I]t would be our purpose to place the Bank of America stock," said the note, "where it would most likely stay 'put' and not among traders." Handing the shares over to traders, it seemed to suggest, was to invite a return to mayhem.

Lehman Brothers made sure to keep plenty of money in reserve. In 1958, it launched the One William Street Fund, a mutual fund; the public sent money and the firm promised to invest it wisely. Lehman Brothers expected the fund to be $40 million, but investors sent $200 million (about $2 billion in today's dollars). The fund pledged to invest three quarters of the money and keep a quarter as a reserve so that people knew cash was available should they suddenly want it back. Such precautions were natural to those who remembered the Depression but would be abandoned by Wall Street in later years.

Discreet recommendation among trusted contacts was a key means of doing business. Bobbie wrote a short note in February 1959 to Leonard Florsheim at Florsheim Shoe in Chicago, a long-standing business acquaintance, referring to a Mrs. Edna Williams, a new client. Lehman Brothers liked dealing with the Mrs. Williamses of this world. Her account was $2 million and its investment advisory service would not handle accounts of less than $500,000. Nor did it advertise its service, and Bobbie thanked Florsheim for having recently put her in touch.

Lehman Brothers was, nonetheless, making efforts to break into the new era. It helped launch the computer age in 1957 when it funded Digital Equipment. Computers were rare in the late 1950s; they occupied enormous air-conditioned rooms and required skilled operators. RCA and General Electric had had no great success in making them, and the word "computer" had created a good deal of skepticism. Ken Olsen and Harlan Anderson founded Digital with the aim of making computers without calling them that. Instead, Digital manufactured "printed circuit modules." Some banks thought Olsen and Anderson, at thirty-one and twenty-eight, too young to finance, but Lehman Brothers took the chance and acted as underwriters for the company's first public issue of shares. Digital went on to produce the smaller computers that did not need air-conditioned rooms and could be used by individuals who had never used one before. That said, Lehman Brothers itself would not get a computer for another ten years or so.

Beyond his work, Bobbie kept up his active social life. Mrs. (Millicent) Randolph Hearst sent him an invitation in November 1957 to buy tickets for the Metropolitan Opera in aid of the Free Milk Fund for Babies. The wife of William Randolph Hearst, Mrs. Hearst had founded the charity in the 1920s. "The opera will be *La Traviata* with Madame Maria Callas," she informed him. Bobbie scribbled "2 at $25" on the invitation. He made sure to pass on such notes to his accountant for tax purposes. Mrs. Hearst's husband had been dead since 1951, though long before then she had tired of his affairs and of living with him at Hearst Castle, overlooking the coast of California at San Simeon. The owner of such newspapers as the *San Francisco Examiner* and the *New York Journal*, Hearst was an early master of sensationalist journalism. "[Y]ou provide the pictures, we'll provide the war," he had famously said at the time of the Spanish-American War, when the United States ejected Spain from the Caribbean.

Sixty years later, war returned to that part of the world. The fighting in Cuba increased throughout 1958, and in the first days of 1959 Castro seized power in Havana. From the outset of his rule, he made the United Fruit Company a target, which augured badly for Bobbie and the board. Ironically, United Fruit money had reared and educated Fidel and his brother Raul Castro, who knew all about its affairs. Well looked after by previous regimes, the company had paid minimal taxes and taken far more out of the island than it had put in. Soon after he took power, Fidel Castro made a speech near the American military base at Guantánamo and called the company a "grave social problem." Before long the new government seized United Fruit's lands and threw it out of Cuba.

Howard Hughes summoned Bobbie Lehman and André Meyer at the end of the decade to meet him in Los Angeles. Few people summoned them anywhere, but they made an exception for Hughes, a multimillionaire whose behavior was known to be unusual. During the 1930s, and as part of his early involvement in aviation, Bobbie had owned an interest in TWA. Hughes, the reclusive aviator who lived much of his life on the verge of nervous collapse, now owned this aspirant rival to the power of Pan Am. But TWA was in financial trouble and Hughes needed help. Lehman and Meyer had instructions to meet him at the Beverly Hills Hotel, where Hughes lived in a bungalow. Having rented bungalows themselves, they were to await his call. They waited and waited until advised to go to a banquet room for the meeting. Hughes still failed to show, and his would-be rescuers finally tired of the exercise and returned to the East Coast. Hughes never did get the help he needed and lost control of TWA in 1960.

Bobbie Lehman, however, had further dreams of Europe to occupy him. In February 1960 Lehman Brothers opened an office in Paris, its first overseas branch, although France was not the most obvious center of European business. Badly damaged in World War II, it had struggled to modernize and remained a quite rural society. On some French farms horses still pulled the plows. Yet Bobbie saw Paris at the center of a large Lehman Brothers European network. To mark its presence there, six hundred guests attended a reception as again Bobbie Lehman seized the attention of the Parisian well-to-do. Guy de Rothschild of the banking family was among those present, as was Georges Pompidou, managing director of Rothschild's bank and future president of France.

|||||||||||

Lehman Brothers' partners served on the boards of directors of over one hundred companies. With a strategic role in such concerns as Pan American, United Fruit, American Express, Getty Oil, and General Motors, the firm guided the direction of much of corporate America.

In spring 1961 the Supreme Court had named Lehman Brothers as one of several firms under review in an investigation into the illegal use of insider information. Such circumstances arose when a company director, for example, who knew that his organization was on course for some good news that the market was not yet aware of, tipped off contacts to buy shares. Their price would rise when other people in the market heard the news, and those who had bought early would profit accordingly. Nothing came of the case, but the publicity around it affirmed that Lehman Brothers was at the top of the business world.

President Eisenhower had left power on a disturbing note. As he handed over control to John F. Kennedy, Ike spoke of something he called the "military-industrial complex" and its possible "unwarranted influence" in government. It was as if he was just catching up with the thoughts of Herbert Lehman, who had protested against Eisenhower's appointment seven years earlier of General Motors' boss as defense secretary and had made many complaints about big business in general. The departing president referred to a potentially "disastrous rise of misplaced power."

On April 12, 1961, the USSR launched Yuri Gagarin as the first man in space and provided an indication of how history was moving on. Less than a week later, however, on April 17, Lehman Brothers was linked to a botched effort to turn the clock back: the Bay of Pigs invasion of Cuba, an attempt to oust Fidel Castro from power. The CIA had organized it and hoped to repeat the easy success it had had when removing the government of Guatemala in 1954. The United Fruit Company was again involved. Two of the seven ships used in the invasion came from its large fleet of banana boats. Presumably the decision to lend the boats was taken at the highest level of the company and with the backing of the board, including Bobbie Lehman.

Exiles from Castro's Cuba based in the United States made up the invasion force, the organization of which had begun under the Eisenhower administration. Former vice president Nixon had been particularly in favor of the invasion, seeing it as a potential vote winner for him as he ran for president in 1960. But delays had pushed the time of the assault until after Kennedy, not Nixon, acceded to the presidency. Having inherited the plan from the outgoing administration, the new president was cool to the idea. But the invasion was in an advanced state of preparation, and Kennedy allowed it to go ahead while giving it only halfhearted support.

Some of the training of the invasion force had taken place around United Fruit's old Southern capital of New Orleans. Its two banana ships were loaded with arms and munitions at the Newport News naval base in Virginia, after which they headed south. The invasion force, composed of about fifteen hundred Cubans, went down to a heavy defeat at the Bay of Pigs in the southwest of the island. About thirteen hundred landed, approximately one hundred were killed, and most of the rest were captured.

The planning of the invasion had long since leaked out, and Castro's forces were sufficiently well prepared to defeat it.

Allen Dulles resigned as head of the CIA, but some people never forgave Kennedy for the humiliating failure. The invasion had had insufficient aerial cover. Castro set about building his aerial defenses against the possibility of further U.S. attacks, and the Soviet Union agreed to help him do so. During the subsequent year or so, the Soviets began shipping missiles to the island, although this would not become apparent to the United States until late in 1962, whereupon the safety of the world came under threat during the Cuban missile crisis. The decision to invade Cuba at the Bay of Pigs precipitated what many people consider to have been the worst incident of the cold war.

Bobbie Lehman's files appear to contain no mention of the Bay of Pigs, though on May 4, just some three weeks after the debacle, Thomas Sunderland, the president of United Fruit, wrote to Bobbie asking him to endorse his application to become a member of the Council on Foreign Relations. In asking for Bobbie's recommendation for membership, Sunderland wrote whimsically, "I have to date been not guilty of too many high crimes and misdemeanors." Neither he nor Bobbie saw the Bay of Pigs as worthy of such damning description, and with Bobbie's backing, Sunderland joined the Council on Foreign Relations.

In his private life Bobbie shifted the emphasis from the manly pursuits of old to those more centered on his wife, Lee. In March 1961 he had written to a friend saying that he was not up to duck shooting anymore. He went fishing in July in Canada only to report that he caught no fish. In November, he was enjoying the twist, the dance craze made famous by Chubby Checker. Bobbie had attended parties over the years: a gathering for Frank Sinatra in Miami, a stag party for the president of El Salvador, a reception for a California gossip columnist passing through town at which Ethel Merman sang her most popular songs, and so on. But here perhaps was a new Bobbie Lehman, belatedly letting himself go, thanks to Lee's having unleashed a joie de vivre that he had not found in his earlier marriages. Fernando Eleta, the Panamanian finance minister and a friend of Bobbie's, wrote thanking him for a party that the Lehmans had just thrown and to say that before he and Graciela, his wife, flew home, they had bought every twist record they could find in New York, "for we intend to introduce the new rhythm in Panama."

In early 1962 Bobbie allowed a photographer from Time-Life to take a picture of the Monday partners' luncheon. In the photo, Bobbie sits at the head of the table, Paul Mazur to his left, and on the wall behind them hangs one of Bobbie's Impressionist paintings. Crystal glassware and elegant pepper and salt shakers stand at each place setting on the highly polished walnut table. Around it sit men in their fifties and beyond in dark suits, bald, and graying or with comb-over hairstyles.

These were obviously not the people who would be able to cope with the transformation of life that, from about this time, the 1960s would bring. What would Bobbie have made, for example, of Andy Warhol's first painting in the series of his Campbell's soup cans that appeared in July? Campbell Soup was an old client that made a mundane staple of the household diet and not an obvious cultural icon. Bobbie surely would have asked himself, Is this art? Then maybe he would have wished that Warhol had come to him and asked for finance.

Sixties life at One William Street proceeded in gentlemanly style. Lehman Brothers detected in January 1962 a possibly useful merger of Coca-Cola and the Folgers Coffee Company. A tie-up would benefit both and bring a good fee for Lehman Brothers. The firm had noticed Folgers was not keeping pace with the latest developments; it "doesn't have a decaf," noted an internal memorandum. Decaffeinated coffee was catching on, possibly as more people adopted the low-caffeine regimen recommended to Bobbie by his doctors years earlier. If Folgers and Coca-Cola merged, Folgers could develop its own decaffeinated brand, said the memo, and give Coke the caffeine by-product for mixing in its drinks. At present Coke bought its caffeine from Sanka, the decaffeinated division of General Foods, which no doubt extracted a good price from Coke.

One possible hurdle to this neat scheme's progress was that Folgers, a family company, enjoyed a good market in the West, Southwest, and Pacific coast regions, and it might resist selling. Lehman Brothers hoped to tempt it. Pepperidge Farm, the cookie maker, had agreed to give up its independence a few years earlier and sell itself to Campbell Soup. "[T]he Pepperidge Farm people got $40 million out of it," noted the memorandum. In the end, however, Coke cut short Lehman Brothers' musings. R. W. Woodruff, Coca-Cola's chief executive, wrote to say the company was busy on other matters, but perhaps Bobbie and he, Woodruff added, could "have a cocktail together some afternoon or possibly lunch."

The *New York Times* announced on October 15 that as a charity measure Bobbie would open his house to "1,000 artistically and socially prominent New Yorkers" prepared to pay $50 each for the privilege. But thoughts abruptly turned to other matters. Robert McNamara, Kennedy's defense secretary, was learning that the USSR had secretly installed its missiles in Cuba. The crisis steadily built to the end of the month. Kennedy, McNamara, and the rest of the administration came under pressure from the top brass of the U.S. military to launch a nuclear strike, but they stuck firm to their favored option of putting Cuba in "quarantine." No more Soviet ships would be allowed to pass through a ring of American warships, and the USSR would have to withdraw its missiles. The world faced the prospect of nuclear ruin, but Nikita Khrushchev, the Soviet leader, agreed to the American terms on October 28.

When General Lucius Clay came to join Lehman Brothers as a partner early the following year, risk management was the order of the day in both finance and international politics. Washington and Moscow had agreed to set up a "hot line" between them so that their leaders could get on the phone to each other in a crisis. This led the way for Averell Harriman to negotiate the Test Ban Treaty, whereby the United States, the UK, and the USSR agreed to ban nuclear tests.

In finance, deals were getting bigger and put the partners' own wealth at greater risk. Members of partnerships stood to lose everything; in the case of a catastrophic loss, Bobbie Lehman could have lost his art collection. Geisst writes in *The Last Partnerships* that from the early 1960s "loose management and a lack of attention to detail began to take their toll" at Lehman Brothers. It seemed that Bobbie might have been aware of this, and it was Clay's job to employ some of his logistical cold war talents to sort it out.

The partners did not like his proposed solution. He decreed that "management by committee is expected to minimize the risk." Lehman Brothers' partners were entrepreneurs who pursued their own ideas and were not the classic military material that Clay needed if Lehman Brothers was to go forward like an army on the march. The nearest thing they had to a committee was the Monday luncheon, and ultimately Bobbie called the shots.

Clay did have a more effective sales line in scaring people. His most recent posting had been as Kennedy's personal representative in Berlin, and he would brief guests over lunch in the eighth-floor restaurant about the cold war. "Found General Clay's comments on our nuclear strength versus the Soviet Union's most interesting and somewhat frightening," Joseph Eckhouse, executive head of Grand Way Stores of New York, wrote in a thank-you note to Bobbie. It had the desired effect, at least as far as Bobbie was concerned. He had wanted Grand Way as a client should it ever want to raise money, and Eckhouse had sufficiently shown himself to be amenable. He said in his letter that his company had previously used Goldman Sachs for financing, but in the future Bobbie and Grand Way "might wish to talk."

As the general was trying to set Lehman Brothers on the straight and narrow, so Bobbie was distracted by all sorts of diversions from his business life. He was abroad at least twice a year, usually in Europe or taking the Caribbean sun. With his free first-class travel pass from Pan Am, a privilege Juan Trippe afforded to board members, he could travel when and where he liked with ease. Since 1958, the introduction of the Boeing 707, which could fly nonstop from North America to Europe, made it all the easier.

His passion for horseracing and bloodstock continued unabated. In 1961, Ambiopoise, one of Bobbie's big winners, had won the New Jersey Derby. He had horses in training in Britain, Ireland, and, stateside, in New Jersey and Kentucky. At the beginning of 1964, he had interests in fifteen racehorses and had sixteen stallions and twenty-three brood mares at stud.

He attended lunches and dinners. In early 1963, he was at a dinner for leading businesspeople given by the president and Mrs. Jacqueline Kennedy at the White House. In September, he had lunch with Richard Nixon at the stock exchange. The former vice president had officially retired from politics to join the law firm of Mudge, Stern, Baldwin & Todd. It was said that Nixon should be able to make two hundred thousand dollars a year as a lawyer, which was more lucrative than remaining a politician. Nonetheless, he had not given up on that and had lately toured Europe meeting its leaders.

Bobbie had his eye on his legacy and donated half a million dollars to Yale, his alma mater, to endow a chair in art history. He had recently given away a prized artwork. "I am making a donation," he wrote to the Metropolitan Museum of Art in New York, "of my Tintoretto (Jacopo

Robusti) painting of St. Francis in Ecstasy." Bobbie would continue to make more such gifts, some with detailed notes from him of their place in art history. "I believe that you agree with me that this is an extraordinary example of the very large Madonnas which were originally painted for Church altarpieces," he wrote of one work by an anonymous artist "of the Umbrian School, XIVth century." The museum wrote back one of its regular letters of thanks to him for "your generous contribution." James Bean, the associate curator of the Met, came at Bobbie's invitation to see his collection and wrote to Bobbie how much he appreciated seeing the paintings and drawings "so handsomely installed in W54St." The Metropolitan may have guessed, and certainly would have hoped, that Bobbie was planning to give it all of his collection.

In the office, Bobbie was a prolific letter writer. This was in keeping with the custom of the time but was time-consuming. When not dropping people polite notes, he wrote letters ordering caramels from Fouquet in Paris and flashlights from AEG in Germany. He had broken his, he told the German manufacturer, and would like a replacement. AEG sent one back to him without charge. Bobbie apparently preferred German flashlights to those by General Electric. He wrote letters of greeting and thanks at Christmas, each one a little different from the other. At such times, firms went about the lengthy business of giving presents—a silver-top malacca cane from Lehman Brothers to its clients and friends one year; a silver box from Lazard Frères another. Bobbie wrote to André Meyer thanking him for the gift, "in which I expect to keep my pills."

Bobbie had been a worrier about his health in the past. If it was not the dust in the air of his home or tobacco smoke around the corridors of One William Street that was troubling him, then he was off to the Presbyterian Hospital in New York for a barium enema or an X-ray on his gallbladder. Lately, however, he had been having fun. Bobbie, Lee, and *Bobbilee*, their forty-four-foot cabin cruiser, made news in July 1963 when he tried to outrun a hydrofoil in the Long Island Sound. The cruiser's engine overheated, and the hydrofoil had to take Bobbie and his guests to shore. It was making its first run on a new route to Wall Street, and with journalists onboard, Ira Dowd, the hydrofoil's owner, got so excited that he fell overboard. The *Wall Street Journal* photographed him, bedraggled but delighted, alongside Bobbie, his wife, and their guests—Mr. and Mrs. Samuel Goldwyn from the MGM studios in Hollywood.

Bobbie seemed to be onto a certain sixties winner when theatrical producer Frederick Brisson wrote to him in the summer of 1964 saying he had bought *Alfie*, a new British comedy. Terence Stamp was to star; *The Collector*, his first motion picture, had "catapulted him to fame," and in London, he was a face of the "Swinging Sixties." David Bailey, the leading young photographer, featured Stamp in his work, and he was regularly in the company of Jean "the Shrimp" Shrimpton, the top model of the times. "The play sets off at a brisk clip and never slows down for two rich, funny, and heartbreaking acts," said Brisson. His description of the main character, Alfie, might have summarized the sixties itself: "bright, breezy, amoral." He didn't mention that one of Alfie's string of girlfriends had an abortion, a taboo subject rarely broached before this time. Bobbie put in twenty-four hundred dollars for a one percent share of the investment.

Alfie opened in mid-December 1964 at the Morosco Theatre in New York, ran for two previews and twenty-one performances, and closed on January 2, 1965. Its net losses were $174,000, which Bobbie would have had to share with his fellow investors. Such was Stamp's stardom that he had an offer to take the movie role, but he turned it down. Richard Harris, Laurence Harvey, and Anthony Newley, among others, declined the role before Michael Caine, far less well known than Stamp, said he would take it. The two were good friends and shared a London apartment. Caine later said he tried to persuade Stamp to take the role, and for years had nightmares that his pal had taken the advice. Bobbie Lehman lost money, but the character he invested in made Caine's Hollywood career.

In August 1963, when his mind may well have been on other things far more to his pleasure, Bobbie made a business decision that would prove key to his firm's future. He decided to set up a trading department at Lehman Brothers. Interest rates were low and companies keen to raise money by way of issuing bonds or "commercial paper" in the old Marcus Goldman mold. In fact, Goldman Sachs was doing very well from this line of business and Bobbie copied their idea. He also stole the people to put it into practice. An aggressive trader named Lewis Glucksman worked for the firm A. G. Becker, and Bobbie enticed him away, along with his entire trading team.

Lehman Brothers, as bankers, thought and, if need be, deliberated at length; theirs was a gradualist business geared to long-term investment and growth, not to trading for quick profits or, for that matter, losses. By instinct Bobbie was a believer in relationships with clients built over a good length of time rather than in the fast and impersonal world of trading. But Goldman Sachs' success tempted him.

Lew Glucksman was delighted to be working for Lehman Brothers. Ken Auletta spoke to him for his book *Greed and Glory on Wall Street: The Fall of the House of Lehman*, published in 1986: "They were the pillars," Glucksman said. "You looked upon Lehman as the furthest you could go."

Yet Lehman Brothers and Bobbie should have represented everything Glucksman hated. He came from a Hungarian Jewish background and a generation of migrants who had arrived to find German Jews established at the top end of society. Glucksman detested the *Our Crowd* set for its complacency and assumption that it enjoyed its privilege by right. Glucksman had had to work for his, and had studied at night school to get his master's degree in business. Around the office he was sharp-elbowed and loud, in the trader's pushy style. He had no time for the manners of bankers: They were out for themselves as much as anyone else in business. But Glucksman loved Bobbie, who gave him a good deal and a better share of the profits than other partners.

Most of the partners at Lehman Brothers reciprocated Glucksman's disdain for them and did not understand why Bobbie had hired him. Perhaps as a result, Bobbie did not find room for Glucksman in the One William Street headquarters. The trading department—a few blocks away on Water Street—was located in keeping with the preference of most partners: out of sight, out of mind.

One of Glucksman's early moves was to join a small group of trading firms in an informal partnership. They were Merrill Lynch, Salomon Brothers, and another called Blyth & Co. Merrill Lynch employed a large and aggressive group of brokers, the "thundering herd." Salomon Brothers was thought by traditionalists to be a very low-grade firm. In their offices, its partners did not have the kind of sedate surroundings of One William Street but worked alongside junior employees in a dirty and disheveled place called "the room." They snatched take-out Chinese meals and spent long hours on the phone frenetically trading bonds and other pieces of financial paper.

The group became known as the "fearsome foursome" and aimed to sell vigorously and undercut the commissions charged by old and established firms like Morgan Stanley. Of course, Lehman Brothers itself was an old, established firm, and the fearsome foursome's other members were delighted to have it involved for the prestige that it brought them. Bobbie's step in going into business with Lew Glucksman meant quite a change in style and image from that cultivated by the Lehman Brothers of legend.

|||||||||

On November 22, 1963, President Kennedy was shot and killed by Lee Harvey Oswald, an ex-Marine and suspected Soviet sympathizer, while visiting Dallas, Texas. The assassination shocked the United States, its allies in Western Europe, and people in many parts of the world. Vice President Lyndon B. Johnson succeeded Kennedy as commander in chief.

Two weeks later, on December 5, Herbert Lehman, age eighty-five, died of a heart attack as he was about to travel to Washington to receive the Presidential Medal of Freedom, the nation's highest peacetime award to a civilian. Kennedy had chosen him for the award, and Johnson was to have presented it to him.

Nelson Rockefeller, the governor of New York, declared a thirty-day period of mourning. Flags on state buildings were already flying at half staff after Kennedy's death, and Rockefeller ordered that they remain so until January 5. In spite of his eight years in the Senate, Herbert had always preferred to be called "Governor Lehman." An obituary in the *New York Times* remembered that FDR, a former governor himself, had referred to Herbert as "that good right arm of mine."

The *New York Times* also quoted President Johnson as saying that the best words he could use to describe Herbert were in the citation that was to have accompanied the award: "[H]e has used wisdom and compassion as the tools of government and has made politics the highest form of public service."

Dore Schary, national chairman of the Anti-Defamation League of B'nai B'rith, the Jewish humanitarian organization, said: "We can never forget . . . when he stood virtually alone in the Senate against the nightmare of McCarthyism, or his eloquent advocacy of human rights all the years of his life."

Many tributes arrived at One William Street, though some mourners were confused as to how Herbert and Bobbie were related. Mr. and Mrs. Antenor Patiño, of the family that made its millions from Bolivia's tin mines, expressed sympathy to Bobbie on the loss of an uncle. The chairman of one American company thought Herbert was Bobbie's brother. A Spanish industrialist wrote of the "great loss you have suffered in the death of your father." Bobbie answered, pointing out that they were cousins.

In one or two replies there was perhaps a hint of Bobbie's wanting to put some distance between himself and Herbert's memory: "I have the finest recollections of activities with him when I was a pretty young fellow." Herbert's partnership at the firm had been "some good while ago." But good grace prevailed, and Bobbie generally contented himself with saying thank you for the kind messages. To some people he mentioned that Lehman Brothers had recently taken on Herbert's son John as a partner.

Bobbie's politics took a sudden lurch in his late cousin's direction in 1964. Johnson faced a presidential election that year, and Barry Goldwater won the Republican nomination. He had had little time for Eisenhower's modern Republicanism, which he considered a revamped New Deal. He wanted lower taxes at home and a tougher stance abroad: rollback was again on the Republican agenda, namely, taking the cold war fight to the USSR. Goldwater mentioned dropping nuclear weapons in the "men's room at the Kremlin." His campaign ran a slogan: "In your heart you know he's right." The Johnson camp responded, "In your guts you know he's nuts."

Bobbie Lehman abandoned the Republicans and joined a group of leading businessmen who formed the National Independent Committee for President Johnson and Senator Humphrey. Hubert Humphrey from Minnesota was Johnson's running mate. Among the groups' organizers was Sidney Weinberg of Goldman Sachs, and Bobbie acted as an occasional spokesman.

Regardless of his views on politics, Bobbie's business was going well under the Democrats. There was a construction boom, and during his election campaign President Johnson reeled out plans that would do no harm to prospects. His Great Society included housing, transport, and urban development schemes, with plenty of federal money to back them. One of Lehman Brothers' clients was the Caterpillar Tractor Company of Peoria, Illinois, a supplier to the road- and house-building industries. Bobbie made sure to keep on the right side of its top management. He gave the company's president, William Blackie, a tour of his art collection at West Fifty-fourth Street at around the date of the election and in summer sent its chairman, Harmon S. Eberhard, one of his salmon from Canada. "When I got home last night, I found the fish you had sent," wrote the grateful Caterpillar man. "I can imagine the pleasure you get from just being in the place where there are fish like this one."

Johnson beat Goldwater by a landslide—forty-three million to twenty-seven million votes—carrying forty-four states and the District of Columbia. Even Vermont, a safe Republican state, swung to the Democrats. In case anyone felt that the vote for Johnson had been inflated by the popularity of the late president Kennedy, Bobbie told the press that LBJ's victory was "a personal one not in any way based on tribute to his predecessor." He added diplomatically that he did not mean by that to detract from Kennedy.

In statesman-banker mode, he opined that in international affairs Johnson had shown "outstanding ability to cope with such issues as communism" and deserved congratulation for his "conservative approach to the nation's economic and racial problems." Johnson was hardly conservative on the latter issue; he widened civil rights in the South in a manner that would have pleased Bobbie's late cousin Herbert. As Johnson himself predicted, it would see Southern whites abandon the Democratic Party for the Republicans.

Bobbie wrote to Johnson the following May: "Our economy is reaching unprecedented heights due in large part to the confidence which you have engendered." Johnson had sent U.S. Marines into the Dominican Republic, one of the countries in the Caribbean where the United Fruit Company had long played an important role, amid claims that Communists were about to seize power in Santo Domingo, its capital. "I earnestly believe that you have prevented another Cuba by your strong and prompt action in Santo Domingo," Bobbie offered, while complimenting Johnson on his "courage and wisdom" over Vietnam. "What is most important to the welfare of our country is your well-being for which all of us pray."

His viewpoint was not universally shared. The U.S. presence in Vietnam of sixteen thousand military advisers increased to troop numbers of half a million over the next three years and caused antiwar protests across the country.

Foreign affairs featured in the conversation when Joseph Wechsberg visited One William Street as part of the research for *The Merchant Bankers*. "When will Red China become an important industrial power?" asked one of the partners. The prospect seemed a long way off, although it would only be another five years or so before, in the early 1970s, Washington recognized Communist China, rather than Taiwan, as the main Chinese power. Wechsberg's book appeared in 1966 and included an essay on Lehman Brothers. Where *Fortune* had called Lehman Brothers partners "merchants of money," Wechsberg upgraded them to "money-magicians." He mentioned some of the great deals of the past: Hertz's rental cars, Litton's electronics, and others. A sigh went around One William Street at the memories, he said.

Wechsberg spoke to General Clay, still intent on getting organization and risk management right. "Next year we shall make a big step forward," affirmed the military veteran. "We'll be completely computerized."

Bobbie was pensive. "[I]ndividuals now count less than before," he told Wechsberg. He was possibly being modest when he added that respect for a few great names had gone; he only mentioned J. P. Morgan's. But "a few great firms" remained, and he liked to think Lehman Brothers was among them. It still ran like a family, albeit a very large one, consisting now of seven hundred people. On the whole it had "preserved the early spirit of Lehman Brothers," he concluded. *"Plus ça change, plus c'est la même chose"* ("The more things change, the more they stay the same").

Bobbie allowed Wechsberg to view his private art collection at West Fifty-fourth Street, a right still offered only to an exclusive few. Art experts, socialites, and company executives Bobbie wished to woo might get the opportunity. Bobbie sometimes went alone, at night, to prowl the silent rooms. Other members of the family were not guaranteed to get in. Shortly before her death in 1965, Sissie, widow of Arthur, Bobbie's older cousin with whom he argued after the crash of 1929, told Robert Bernhard, her grandson, that she had never been to the mansion to see Bobbie's pictures. Bernhard went to Bobbie, told him that Sissie was ill and would like him to let her see his collection. Bobbie was unmoved. "[H]e wouldn't do it," said Bernhard. "He still bore the grudge."

An armed guard opened the entrance door to Wechsberg, "watching me through a slit." Bobbie employed a curator who switched on batteries of lights and showed the visitor around. Ancient paintings from Tuscany filled two downstairs rooms, the oldest by Duccio di Buoninsegna, who was at work in his studios perched over the narrow streets of Siena in the latter part of the thirteenth and early fourteenth centuries. One second-floor room paneled in sixteenth-century red velvet was as Philip, Bobbie's father, had left it. Wechsberg sat "entranced" looking at works by such artists as Botticelli and Bellini. "I still cherish the memory of these intimate moments. . . . [T]ime stands still in this room."

But it was not standing still for Bobbie. The question of his plans for the collection after he died remained a live one. Inheritance taxes meant that the Lehman family would not be able to maintain the collection intact. "[T]o begin with, Bobbie isn't going to die," said Benjamin Sonnenberg, Bobbie's publicist. "He's firmly convinced he's immortal. And furthermore, if he should turn out to be wrong, being a Lehman he'll figure out some way to take it all with him."

Bobbie started 1967 vigorously enough, and in February, he wrote again to the White House. Early in the year of "flower power," the "summer of love," and the advance of the peace movement, LBJ's morale needed a boost: "I assure you, Mr. President, that in the opinion of the majority of the people you are doing an outstanding job both in domestic and foreign affairs." Notwithstanding Bobbie's reassurances, protests against the war in Southeast Asia intensified.

Worries about his health increased as the year went on. A brief note in his files said that he had had a stroke. In November 1967 the Metropolitan Museum of Art made Bobbie chairman of its board of trustees, a post specially created for him. It was drawing him into its warm embrace, conceivably to ensure he made the right decision about the fate of his collection. André Meyer wrote on November 17 congratulating Bobbie on the appointment, hoping that "it may also be the best cure for your present tiredness."

He recovered sufficiently by the following May to attend Juan Trippe's last board meeting at Pan Am, though Marylin Bender and Selig Altschul's account described him as "76 and feeble." The setting was the Pan Am Building, astride Park Avenue, a symbol of Trippe's achievements. In the early 1960s it was the biggest office building in history. Charles Lindbergh was among other board members present.

As Trippe stood down, the old days of flying gave way to a different age. For a decade now, the Boeing 707 had brought hushed luxury to air travel. People dressed up to fly, the food was worth missing a meal in an airport restaurant for, and the service was unhurried and excellent. The time of the wide-bodied 747 was approaching, meaning space for far more passengers and cheaper flying. Lehman Brothers had just led the issue of shares that raised $175 million to finance the 747, and Trippe had committed Pan Am to spending $1 billion more on the aircraft out of future profits. One income source boosting profits at the time was the Vietnam War. Pan Am had contracts to fly soldiers to and from Asia and on their rest and recuperation trips to Thailand, Hong Kong, and Japan. It also flew those killed in action back home in body bags.

In June, the Lehmans received flowers from President Johnson and Lady Bird, the First Lady. Lee Lehman replied with a "Dear Mr. President and Lady Bird" note of thanks, concluding "Bobbie and I love you both dearly." Johnson himself was exhausted and said that he would not run again for the presidency. He spoke of "division in the American house." The war in Vietnam would continue for some years yet, but peace talks with North Vietnam began in Paris, with Averell Harriman leading the U.S. delegation.

During the presidential election campaign, Bobby Kennedy, brother of the late president and a Democratic candidate, was shot dead in Los Angeles by Sirhan B. Sirhan, a Jordanian-born American. At his trial Sirhan criticized U.S. policy in the Middle East. Kennedy's death opened the way for the Republicans to win the elections with Richard Nixon.

Late November 1968 brought Bobbie a delivery of flowers to One William Street from the United Fruit Company. John Fox, the company's present chairman, sent them, and Bobbie's secretary replied, "[H]e has been much better the last two weeks but tires easily."

The banana company was not in a much better state of health. United Fruit had had to strip its plantations of Big Mike, the diseased banana, and replace it with another one, the Cavendish. The company continued, however, to grow just one type of banana. Within a year, United Fruit succumbed to a hostile takeover by Eli Black, a leading New York investor, and Bobbie was not able to play a part in trying to fend him off. United Fruit's PR man, Thomas McCann, recalled in his book, *An American Company*, that he had spoken to Sonnenberg, who had hinted once at Bobbie's immortality, about the possibility of help from Bobbie, but he had "waved the name aside as though to say I was being absurd." McCann added: "He said Lehman was an old man and that we shouldn't look for anything from him." Black's investment bankers, meanwhile, were Goldman Sachs.

Paul Mazur retired from Lehman Brothers on January 1, 1969. The seventy-six-year-old had been an "unconventional participant" in Wall

Street life, the *New York Times* wrote, remembering some of his achievements. In the 1920s he had been a pioneer of "installment selling," the means by which customers could buy goods and pay for them in stages. It was another idea taken for granted now, but not when Mazur championed it.

Mazur usually had something to say that was worth listening to, and he went into retirement on a critical note. There was a part of the business world that troubled him; he was worried about economics, the subject he had studied at Harvard. It had lately become a far more numerate discipline, with arcane formulae and algebraic symbols to represent the economic functions of society. "Economics is basically sociological," Mazur insisted. People were now being left out of the equation.

Lehman Brothers itself was functioning poorly. In February, the SEC censured General Clay, of all people, for the firm's lack of organization. The year before, the number of shares traded in one day on the New York Stock Exchange hit twenty million for the first time. As a result of the increased business, banks found it difficult to keep their records straight, a problem worsened by the cumbersome shift from manual to computer systems, and Lehman Brothers was among those that could not cope.

Bobbie's records indicate that he was tying up some of his life's loose ends. On April 1 he sold one of his prize-winning horses, Sette Bello, a seven-year-old sired by Ribot, the famous Italian colt of the 1950s. The price was $75,000. Two weeks later, Bobbie probably could have gotten a bigger price, as Godolphin Darley, the French breeders, asked if the horse was for sale; they had "two other Ribots," they said. For Bobbie it hardly mattered. At the beginning of June, he handed back the use of the private box at Churchill Downs to the family of John Hertz, his late friend. "For the past two years my health has not been up to par," he explained in a note to the racetrack. In early July, Lehman Brothers announced to its staff that it was equipping itself for the future and had installed "two of the most sophisticated third-generation computers" to get on top of its office organization, said a monthly internal publication. It failed to mention that no machine could replace Bobbie, and he had left no successor.

He died a few weeks later, but lived to see how the bets that he had placed on the miracle of flight those forty years earlier paid off; in July the United States reached the peak of achievement as it got its astronauts to and from the moon. At the same time, during the course of this exercise, man maintained control over technology. A switch needed to get the lunar module off the moon had broken, but Buzz Aldrin shoved the end of a pen into the socket, got the engines started, and the astronauts made it home.

Coincidentally, Sidney Weinberg, who was the same age as Bobbie, also died. Bobbie might just have put his last bet on himself to outlive his rival. He did so by nearly a month and passed away at his Sands Point home on August 9, 1969, at age seventy-seven.

8

Traders

Pete Peterson joined Lehman Brothers as a partner in June 1973, having previously served as commerce secretary to President Nixon, and less than three months later he was in charge of the firm. In the four years since the death of Bobbie Lehman, it had struggled under the leadership of Frederick Ehrman, who had been at Lehman Brothers since World War II. But he lacked the authority of his predecessor, and the firm's performance had suffered. The partners removed him in a boardroom coup and offered Peterson the job, trusting that he would lead them into a bright, new post-Bobbie era.

Peterson had been a creditable member of President Nixon's administration and part of one of America's most successful governments ever in relations with the outside world. The United States had reopened links with China, which had been cut when the Communists seized power in 1949, by sending a table tennis team in 1971 to play in Beijing, giving rise to the term "ping-pong diplomacy." Henry Kissinger was very much the diplomatic superstar of the day and, first as national security adviser and then as secretary of state, had led the period of détente, the easing of relations with the USSR. Peterson organized talks with Leonid Brezhnev, the Russian leader, to improve trade between the United States and the USSR and won considerable acclaim. As Peterson points out in his autobiography, *The Education of an American Dreamer*, the *New York Times* called him the "economic Kissinger."

Nonetheless, he had endured his share of trouble within the Nixon administration. A number of Cuban exiles involved in the Bay of Pigs invasion in 1961 had remained in the pay of the CIA, and in 1972 some were caught burgling and bugging the Democratic Party's election headquarters at the Watergate complex in Washington. This was during Nixon's successful bid to be elected for a second term. He had not known about the burglary in advance, but several people connected with him had, and Nixon took part in the attempted cover-up of administration involvement. The president became increasingly paranoid about media coverage of the case—which was fast evolving into the "Watergate scandal"—and White House suspicions fell on Peterson. He and his wife at the time, Sally, enjoyed the Washington social scene and mixed with members of the press; Nixon saw him as a "leaker" of damaging information. Thus Peterson left Washington—as far as the press and public opinion were concerned, on the side of the angels—and joined Lehman Brothers.

John Connally, the treasury secretary, had hastened his departure. Former governor of Texas, Connally had been sitting next to President Kennedy when he was assassinated in Dallas in 1963 and had been shot and wounded. He resumed his political career and, having reached the Treasury Department under Nixon, saw Peterson and the Commerce Department as rivals. In some political scuffles, Connally shoved Peterson aside. Peterson's time at Lehman Brothers would again show that he was not adept at dealing with pushy people.

He was an outward-looking Republican in the vein of the modern Republicanism that had become popular since Eisenhower. Peterson had reason to fear the isolationist mentality. His parents were immigrants from Greece and ran a twenty-four-hour diner in Kearney, Nebraska. His father, George, told him of times in the 1920s when the Ku Klux Klan had paraded outside with signs saying DON'T EAT WITH THE GREEK.

George Peterson had already changed his family name from Petropoulos because he found many Americans could not pronounce it, although he regretted doing so; he would not want anyone to think, he said, that he was ashamed of being Greek. Pete, on the other hand, showed a degree of sensitivity on the name issue and was content with the Scandinavian connotations of "Peterson." When he was a student at Northwestern University in Evanston, Illinois, in the 1940s, he said he was happy there in the heart of the Midwest to have people assume that, in spite of his having dark hair, he came from "hearty Nordic stock in someplace like Sweden."

Peterson's education had suffered a setback when the first university that he went to, MIT in Cambridge, Massachusetts, expelled him for plagiarism. One of his fraternity brothers was a friend of Roy Cohn, a student at Columbia in New York at the time whom Peterson had met on a social visit there. Cohn was a sharp intellect clearly destined for big things. Peterson and his friend borrowed a term paper of Cohn's and each handed it in at MIT as if the work was their own. Peterson's friend submitted his paper in the Cohn original, while Peterson made considerable adaptations to his. He was the one who was caught. He said he had no idea what raised his teacher's suspicions that this was not his own work, but he admitted everything under professorial interrogation. He later retrieved his honor and studied business at Northwestern.

He had no banker's training when he came to Lehman Brothers, though he had been a successful head of Bell + Howell, the photographic company famous for its movie cameras. When in Washington, he and Sally used to throw movie parties and hand out popcorn to their guests. At the same time, Peterson had a banker's persona; he was urbane, a contacts man and someone who developed long-term relationships. He liked dropping names: "Henry," for Kissinger, was a favorite. He was a trustee of the Museum of Modern Art, a patron of the arts like Bobbie Lehman.

Peterson had had a great deal of interest in overseas affairs. Nixon had discussed with him the prospect of making him America's first ambassador to Europe—a united Europe, that is, as opposed to the individual states—but in the end nothing came of it. As well as his deals with the USSR, he had negotiated important textile agreements with Japan, a fast-rising economic power. He was a trustee of the Japan Society, which aimed to improve Japan's cultural contacts with the world, and the treasurer of the Council on Foreign Relations. An article in the *New York Times* on Peterson's early time at One William Street called him a "White Knight" who "sheds an international glow on the Lehman image."

Moving to Lehman Brothers meant a large jump in salary: to $300,000 a year from the $42,500 he had earned in Washington. He did have to find $750,000 to buy his share of the partnership, which was difficult, and he reached an agreement to pay the figure over several months. Within a month, however, the firm's struggles after Bobbie Lehman's death reached a peak; its trading department reported heavy losses, as a result of which, for the fiscal year (which in Lehman Brothers' case was to the end of September) the firm recorded a loss of $8 million. The partners viewed it at the time as a disaster. (When, incidentally, Lehman Brothers went bankrupt thirty-five years later, it would have debts of $768 billion.) Lew Glucksman, head of trading, had blundered in buying some bonds that he was unable to sell at a profit. With their dislike of Glucksman and his fellow traders, several bankers among the firm's partners wanted him sacked.

Lehman Brothers had opened two more foreign offices: London in 1972, the year Britain joined the European Economic Community, and Tokyo in 1973. Following its defeat in World War II and under American military occupation until 1952, Japan had rebuilt its economy by adapting and improving Western industrial methods. The West disparaged cheap goods made in Japan as poorly manufactured at first, but by the early 1960s, Japan was competing with the West in quality as well as price, in making such items as Honda and Suzuki motorcycles. Japan won a lot of favorable attention in 1964 when Tokyo staged the Olympics, the first in an Asian country. The well-organized games had been televised live across the world, a rare feat at the time. Through the 1960s and '70s, demand for Japanese products increased, with cars, televisions, and electronic goods leading the way.

Lehman Brothers was apparently spreading its international wings at the right time, but at home it was not keeping up the pace. Computer technology sapped its old mystique in underwriting share issues; these days any company vice president could determine the right price at which to launch shares on the market with a little help from his computer department.

Peterson was shocked by his first meeting with Joseph Thomas, the partner in charge of mergers and acquisitions. "M&A," or the buying and selling of companies, was central to Peterson's plans. He found Thomas, old, bulky, and debilitated by alcohol and emphysema, in the eleventh-floor gymnasium, with cigar in hand and a bottle of bourbon nearby. As Thomas smoked his cigar, tubes in his nostrils led to an oxygen tank. Peterson was not encouraged as to future prospects; indeed, one wrong move at this juncture and the whole place could have exploded.

Running parallel with Lehman Brothers' problems was the fact that the politics and economics of the Western world appeared on the edge of collapse. The Middle East war of October 1973 saw the Arab nations first use oil as a weapon in their fight against Israel. OPEC, the Organization of Petroleum Exporting Countries, raised prices to such an extent that the United States suffered its first major gas crisis and rich and poor economies alike faced ruin. Western European countries ran short of money to finance their welfare states. Western Europe had enjoyed great prosperity dating back to the Marshall Plan, but that was now threatened by spiraling prices. The mid-1970s saw an inflation rate, for example, of 25 percent in Britain.

In the United States, 1973 effectively marked the end of the New Deal. Over the previous quarter century the money earned by most Americans had doubled, and with it their ability to buy homes, college educations, and consumer goods. Taxation had distributed wealth away from the richest 5 percent of the population and toward the majority. But now economic theories revamping the classical economics of old came back into fashion. John Maynard Keynes was dumped in favor of Professor Milton Friedman of the University of Chicago, who proposed "monetarism," the idea that inflation could be curbed by cutting the supply of money. With less cash around, people might lose their jobs but, monetarists argued, the economy would turn in time.

The monetarists produced figures and theorems to prove it. In the second half of the 1970s, mathematical economics, of the type that Paul Mazur of Lehman Brothers had warned against some years before, took hold of teaching in the universities. Professors stood back from their blackboards to admire the formulae that, they argued, described human behavior in the marketplace. Keynes's economics had been more intuitive and required the intervention of human judgment: a decision by a government, for example, to channel money here or there to boost employment. The proponents of this latest economics placed it above all that—they dealt in numbers, not subjective criteria. It was, they said, objective.

President Nixon resigned over the Watergate scandal in 1974. As one by one he sacked his aides, it took awhile for him to realize that he also had to go. Senator Barry Goldwater had been deputed to go to the White House to persuade Nixon that it was time to stand down. Goldwater undertook the task as a senior and highly respected Republican, something that marked a political shift in America. From someone who had denounced the Eisenhower government as practicing socialism and a few years later, in the election of 1964, had been dismissed by much of the electorate as "nuts," Goldwater had become an elder statesman.

Former Lehman Brothers clients featured in the breakdown of the political order. Nixon had solicited contributions to his election campaign from ITT, the telecommunications giant, in return for the government calling off antitrust actions against the company. ITT, which owned a

Chilean telephone company, was also found to have been involved in the military coup there in 1973 that overthrew the government of Salvador Allende. The democratically elected Allende died in the coup and was replaced by the regime of General Augusto Pinochet.

In 1975, United Fruit hit the headlines. In New York, its boss Eli Black threw himself to his death from the window of his office in the Pan Am Building. Not long after he had taken over United Fruit in 1969, the diseases that attacked its bananas had significantly worsened and eaten into profits. Black had also bribed the military leaders of Honduras to win his company favors. The reputation of some old Lehman Brothers friends was going down in disgrace.

Peterson looked beyond Wall Street's problems and adopted an international approach. In 1974, he sold 15 percent of Lehman Brothers to Banca Commerciale Italiana of Milan, the thirty-fifth-largest bank in the world. This brought in capital of $7 million. Three years later the firm took over Kuhn Loeb, the old bank of Jacob Schiff. Ken Auletta in his book *Greed and Glory on Wall Street* points out that in Peterson's decade in control of Lehman Brothers, he increased its capital tenfold.

In the past partners had relied on fees for their services, but now Peterson encouraged them to risk more of their own money—in buying and selling companies, for example. In such a way they would get part of the action, a percentage of the profits made. Peterson was blurring the old distinction between traders and bankers and encouraged the banking partners to move from their dependence on old contacts and painstaking arrangements to become upfront risk takers. He wanted quicker deals, more cut and thrust.

This should have chimed with Lew Glucksman's worldview. The bankers were apparently coming around to his way of doing things, but he watched such developments from his office at 55 Water Street with skepticism. Peterson remained a banker as far as he was concerned, and typical of the *Our Crowd* set, with its contacts and easily opened doors that he loathed.

Glucksman's office was sometimes referred to as "the chart room" because of the pictures of ships and navigational maps that hung on the walls. He had lied about his age during World War II when he enlisted at seventeen in the navy and served on a ship hunting for German submarines in the Atlantic. These days Lehman Brothers was his life. He arrived at the office by 6:00 A.M., stayed late, would often have his driver wait for him as he ate alone in a restaurant on his way home, and did not see much of Inez, his wife, an editor at a book publishing company. Peterson recalls that Glucksman took little care of his appearance. He wore light-colored suits in defiance of Wall Street's dress code, and when he wore dark ones there would be dandruff on his shoulders: "Rumpled was the kindest way to describe him."

He was brought up on New York's Upper West Side by parents who had both been born in the city. His father owned a factory that assembled marble table lamps and made decent money. After the war Glucksman got a degree in accounting from the College of William and Mary and took night classes to earn his master's in business at New York University.

He was a Truman Democrat and, in his own mind, a man of the people. Among his staff, wrote Auletta, he might burst into a round of expletives— "fucking-a-well," "dipshit!"—or rush up to a trader and kiss him on the cheeks to show his appreciation. Out of shape and overweight, he had a "face like a Russian general." He had tried to keep fit by joining a swimming club that he passed en route to work, but he could not get a membership and suspected it was because he was Jewish. A partner at the firm said he knew somebody who was a member and, incidentally, Jewish; he would try to help. That person's efforts were to no avail but did lead to his receiving a furious phone call from Glucksman, presumably for being a member of such a club himself. He was "the kind of Jew who should have gone to the gas chambers," Glucksman told him.

Glucksman's judgment of Peterson was wide of the mark. He was neither a banker nor a member of Our Crowd, and although he had an air of hauteur, Peterson came from a family background that was more humble than Lew's. He had also stepped in on Lew's behalf over the money lost on the bonds. Peterson deterred the other partners from dismissing him on grounds that Glucksman had the skills to get the firm out of its financial hole.

Glucksman would have agreed with that: In his view, traders did the work of the firm. Take the case of Dick Fuld, his senior trader. Fuld left the office during his twelve-to-fifteen-hour workday only to play on the Lehman Brothers baseball team or have a high-powered game of squash. Otherwise, he was in front of his computer screen making the quick-fire decisions that made the money. Future descriptions of Fuld often referred to him as being "intense." Andrew Gowers, who was in charge of public relations for Lehman Brothers as it approached its end in 2008, called him "almost unbearably intense." It was becoming a characteristic feature of Wall Street people in the 1970s; Glucksman was like that too. As far as he was concerned, it was the people who had such qualities who made the place function.

Yet Peterson seemed reluctant to invite people like Fuld to lunch. He also rarely appeared on the trading room floor. Peterson gave an interview to the press a year after he arrived at Lehman Brothers, saying the firm's "creative entrepreneurial work" was its core: the companies it had financed, the ideas it had allowed to bloom. It was not its trading in bonds, stocks, and so on; there were a lot of people around who could do that. To Glucksman this was all highly disrespectful. It would have been difficult to imagine Bobbie Lehman acting like that.

The opening of Bobbie's wing at the Metropolitan Museum of Art on May 12, 1975, attracted a rare crowd to its VIP reception. Mrs. Peggy Cronin, Bobbie's former secretary, prepared the list of attendees. The leading members of the Rockefeller, Astor, and Randolph Hearst families came, Henry Ford II and Pan Am's Juan Trippe alongside them. The directors of such companies as Gimbels and United Fruit were there. Several widows of the famous honored Bobbie's memory: Mrs. Herbert Lehman, Mrs. Samuel Goldwyn, Mrs. Charles Lindbergh (Lindbergh himself was on the invitation list but died just before the reception). Paul Matisse, grandson of Henri, the French Fauvist painter, attended. Roy Cohn was there too. Mrs. Cronin had drawn up the list, she said, for people who were genuine friends of Bobbie. Lew Glucksman was included in the gathering, and may have been in touch with Mrs. Cronin just to make sure he was. She wrote against his name: "Lew is the one partner who has repeatedly voiced and shown his appreciation for all RL [Robert Lehman] did for him."

The opening made a media splash. "The last great private collection goes public," wrote Byron Belt in the *Long Island Press*. At least it remained intact. Other American collections, like those once belonging to the Morgans and the Mellons, had been dispersed throughout the land. The museum had carved out an area of Central Park to accommodate this one. To initial opposition from ecologists, the Robert Lehman Wing encroached on "a treasured oasis of green space," but Bobbie's strength of spirit won through from beyond the grave. The critics praised this museum within a museum in which his collection revealed itself in its "awesome entirety." By the time of his death he had acquired some three thousand works of art valued at $100 million. "An extraordinarily fine assembly of rare, precious, glittering objects," wrote Thomas B. Hess for *New York* magazine, that exuded "a sensation of great wealth, of money lavishly poured."

A month earlier, Pan Am had been the last international airline to fly out of Saigon as the United States made a disorderly retreat from Vietnam. On the day of the opening of Bobbie's wing, U.S. forces took part in their last action of the Vietnam War. Cambodian forces, the Khmer Rouge, seized the *Mayaguez*, an American container ship in Southeast Asian waters. Three days later, U.S. Marines seized it back. Government and press alike were triumphant, the tone they struck giving the impression of an America that was already hitting back.

A year later, however, Jimmy Carter ran for the presidency advocating a change of approach and mood: America should combat hostile forces through his policy focus on human rights. He aimed his ideas at the USSR, with its denial of the right of Russian Jews to move to Israel and of Russian intellectuals to freedom of expression. At home he argued that Americans should deal with the oil crisis by limiting their oil consumption. For many Americans his policies failed. Opponents to hard-line allies of the United States, like the shah of Iran and the Somoza family in Nicaragua, took heart from Carter's talk of human rights and overthrew those regimes in 1979. Iranian revolutionaries in November seized the U.S. embassy in Tehran, took its diplomats and staff hostage, and held them for over a year. In December, the USSR invaded Afghanistan, in fear of the forces of radical Islam around its own borders, but it looked as if the Soviet army was exploiting American weakness.

At Lehman Brothers, meanwhile, Glucksman really had no time for some of Pete Peterson's pussyfooting policies. The acquisition of Kuhn Loeb had meant taking on such partners as Mario d'Urso, an Italian banker whose father had been a friend of Bobbie Lehman. D'Urso was lean, suave, and aristocratic, attended the best New York parties, and jogged in Central Park in a designer tracksuit. In spring 1978, the press had him dashing off on a European holiday with Princess Margaret, sister of Queen Elizabeth II of Britain. D'Urso did not believe that Lew Glucksman's trading department should gamble with the firm's money. Glucksman did not believe in employing dandies like D'Urso.

Peterson was truly toughening up one particular side of Lehman Brothers' business. Mergers and acquisitions was a field far more highly charged than in the days when Lehman Brothers wondered whether Coke could help Folgers develop a line in decaffeinated coffee. Modern M&A experts vigorously solicited business, telling chief executives how they should be acquiring this or that company, by hostile takeover if need be. Deals were big. Stephen Schwarzman, Lehman Brothers' own M&A person, in 1979 engineered the takeover by Beatrice Foods Company of Tropicana Products for $500 million. Each bank had one or several such experts who were all fiercely competitive and on the make. By Glucksman's standards you could not get enough of this type of aggression. By the early 1980s, his trading department was no longer the adjunct to banking activities that it once had been but contributed over half the firm's profits. Peterson acknowledged this; the offices at One William Street were old and it made no sense to be separate from the trading division. He had Glucksman organize a move by the whole firm to Water Street. Many of the partners did not want to go and still regarded the traders as a lower breed, but Peterson insisted.

The national mood was in step with Glucksman. America was getting pushed around, and what with Vietnam, the oil crisis, and Iran, it was time to fix some quick deals that would get the world back in its box. Ronald Reagan proposed such a line for the 1980 elections and comfortably defeated Carter. Glucksman, like many former Democrats, switched his vote to the Republicans.

|||||||||

Lew encouraged the idea that there was a kind of class war at Lehman Brothers. This raged between the blue-collar toilers at the lathe such as himself and the elite at the top who hogged the wealth. Dick Fuld went along with what he said: "Those fucking bankers," he was heard to say around the trading department.

There was very little that was blue collar about Fuld. He had grown up in the genteel surrounds of upper Westchester County, New York. His family ran United Merchants & Manufacturers, a clothes-manufacturing company that his grandfather, Jacob Schwab, had founded. In his teens, Dick excelled at athletic pursuits rather than his studies, and his ambition was to be a test pilot. While enrolled at the University of Colorado in the mid-1960s, he joined the Air Force ROTC and began studying aeronauti-cal engineering. Neither suited him.

The ROTC threw him out after an argument with an officer, a senior-year student who was bullying one of the other recruits. Fuld took exception, got into a fistfight with the senior, and was told that the military did not tolerate this kind of behavior.

His engineering studies involved a lot of work with graphics, and Fuld could not master the architectural drawings. He was a numbers man, something that he could put to use when he did a summer internship at Lehman Brothers in 1966. His grandfather was a client and got him the position at the firm's small trading office in Denver. Where aeronautics had not suited him, finance did, and in his senior year Fuld elected to study international business as his major.

He joined Lehman Brothers full-time in 1969, when Bobbie Lehman was dying and One William Street was in a mess as it installed its first computers. Dick was both apart from all this and quite at one with the era. He worked with Glucksman at 55 Water Street and was so good at what he did that the distinction between man and machine blurred. Dick was known as the trader with a "digital mind."

He was not a great talker, especially when put on the spot and required to say something. He tended to communicate in monosyllabic grunts and, at some stage, someone nicknamed him "the Gorilla." Fuld seemed to enjoy this, and in his later career he kept a large stuffed gorilla in his office.

Glucksman promoted him quickly, and in 1978 Peterson made him a partner of the firm. Fuld was thirty-two when awarded this privilege, although he did not appear overly impressed. A phone call late on a Friday afternoon summoned him to Peterson's office, but Fuld was getting mar-ried the next day, and he and Kathy, his wife-to-be, were due at a wedding rehearsal. He said he could not come. A red-faced Glucksman burst into Fuld's office an instant later yelling, "What the fuck are you doing, you idiot?" and dragged him along to Peterson's office. Fuld was so focused on where he should be that he barely mumbled a thank-you when Peter-son gave him the news of his promotion to the firm's top table. He kept thinking, "I'm in big trouble with Kathy."

Peterson's trouble was with Glucksman, though having handled the likes of the Russians in the past, he chose diplomacy as the best approach. He made Lew the Lehman Brothers head of operations; all the departments of the firm, including the bankers, reported to him. The banking partners did not like it, but Peterson insisted on the move, and anyway, it suited him. Peterson had recently undergone brain surgery, from which he had thought he would not recover. He and Sally had broken up; it was Peterson's second marriage and, like his first, it had ended in painful divorce. He had to measure his priorities and was happy to hand the day-to-day running of the firm over to Glucksman while he handled its grander strategy. Pete would be Lehman Brothers' "Mr. Outside," the face it presented to the world. Lew would be its "Mr. Inside."

But Glucksman was acquiring a penchant for dealing with the world outside. He gave an interview to *Euromoney* magazine for its April 1981 edition, and with its foreign perspective, the publication asked for his view of the world. He asserted a stubbornly American one: "I tend to look on international—without being parochial about it—the way I do Indianapolis."

What he meant was that all Lehman Brothers operations had a common headquarters in New York, but Peterson was aghast. He wished to portray Lehman Brothers as part of a new world run by superoperators who glided effortlessly around it satisfying the needs of their clients. The article proved a tremendous embarrassment, with the London office reporting back to New York that its rivals in Europe were endlessly ribbing it for Lehman Brothers' being parochially minded. Among the clocks on the wall in the London office showing the time around the world— London, New York, Tokyo—someone squeezed in another one, marked "Indianapolis."

Under Peterson, the business turned around. His first five years were tough, but during the last five, Lehman Brothers had recorded unequaled profits. In his dealings with Glucksman, he continued to trust the arts of diplomacy. He had after all been part of an administration that had brought the Chinese in from the cold. Perhaps he could do the same for Lew: Keep him close, use his energy, get him under control.

In this regard, Peterson was following what he believed to be the example of Goldman Sachs—and he later regretted it. Banking rivals occasionally dined with each other, and in spring 1983 Peterson and Glucksman had breakfast at 55 Water Street with John Whitehead and John Weinberg, the co-heads of Goldman Sachs. Peterson described the occasion as a "goodwill breakfast" to discuss business trends in a cordial atmosphere.

As a result, it occurred to him that he could adopt the Goldman Sachs leadership model. Why didn't Lehman Brothers have co-leaders too? Wall Street was a notoriously egotistical place, but, thought Peterson, "if the egos could be harnessed, a combination of top talents could produce real benefits."

Glucksman was delighted and gratefully accepted his offer to co-head. Peterson's tenth anniversary at the firm was due, and at a small party, Glucksman gave him a "beautiful Henry Moore drawing," Peterson wrote. "The Moore fit well with the modern art that I by then was collecting with a passion."

His wife Joan—Peterson had married for a third time—had a different view of what was going on and told him he was being naive about Glucksman: "Give him a fingernail and he's going to take an arm." Things in the Lehman Brothers world had changed markedly from when the senior partner simply told people what he thought they should be doing and they did it.

Things had changed in other respects as well—in the way the firm hired people, for example. Once upon a time, a gentlemanly conversation or letter of recommendation would result in a bright young man from a good school being invited to drop in for further assessment, likely as not a favorable one. In the early 1980s, this was not what Michael Lewis found when he underwent what was known as the Lehman Brothers "stress interview." The future author of *Liar's Poker* had lined up for hours in the snow in his final year at Princeton in order to make sure he got his name on the Lehman Brothers interview list posted in the university's career advice office. There was a lot of competition to get on it. Trading rooms had once recruited from high school graduates, but the word on Wall Street was that "no more schleps" need apply. Many people from an Ivy League background wanted a trader's job. Ten to fifteen years earlier they might have protested against Vietnam and studied for a liberal arts degree. Now they had arrived at the conclusion that a career in making money was the one for them.

Lewis both wanted to make money and had a liberal arts degree. He had studied art history, and his interviewer—"a square-shouldered young man of perhaps twenty-two"—brusquely asked him, "[A]ren't you frightened of not getting a job?" Lewis's interrogator was possibly not aware that Bobbie Lehman, the most famous leader of the firm, was a great patron of art history studies; for that matter, he might not have cared. History was a thing of the past, as, in the interview, was Lehmanesque courtesy. Part of the deliberate stress of the interview, Lewis wrote, was that when he walked into the room and offered a hello, his interviewer said nothing. When he did comment, it was to say, "Open the window." Lewis investigated and found that since they were in a room forty-three floors above Water Street, the window was sealed and did not open. The interviewer's intention, he concluded, was to see if interviewees cracked under the pressure and proved themselves incapable of a life in investment banking.

Lewis flunked his interview, not because he lacked the knowledge of the industry but because, when asked why he wanted the job, he replied, honestly enough, that it was for the money. The interviewer, who Lewis estimated had probably worked on Wall Street for only a year, replied that the job required working long hours, and he would need to be motivated by far more than that. Lewis was summarily dismissed: "[T]hat's all."

Back in the bowels of the firm, Peterson kept coming up with ideas to please Lew. He made his bonus for the year less than Glucksman's: Peterson got $1 million and Glucksman, $1.25 million. Fuld topped the bonus charts with $1.6 million. People like him in lowlier positions than Peterson and Glucksman received lower salaries, but Fuld, who was the senior trader in what had been a very good year, got a handsome reward for his efforts.

Peterson's diplomacy, however, did little good and the co-leaders finally had a face-to-face meeting that thrashed the issue out. Glucksman said bluntly that he wanted to run Lehman Brothers. Peterson went away to think about it, came back, and suggested they continue the joint arrangement for a transitional period. Peterson had hoped to stay for two or three more years; maybe they could agree on a time and, after that, he would hand power to Glucksman. Lew said no: He wanted it now—he was fifty-seven.

For that matter, so was Peterson, but he agreed to go. He thought for a while about fighting Glucksman but reasoned that there was little point in doing so. A fight would damage the firm, and if Peterson won, it would only lead to Glucksman's leaving and taking his trading department with him. But it was the personal considerations in Peterson's mind that overrode the petty skirmishes of Wall Street. Joan Peterson had had a cancer scare, and although she had recovered, the question of wider perspective came into play. They decided to enjoy themselves a little more, and getting Glucksman out of their lives would not be a bad start.

Peterson left on September 30, 1983, and Lew was so keen to get rid of him that he gave him a very good deal. Peterson had enough to invest in starting a business of his own. He said he wanted to get into "merchant banking," an old-fashioned term for investing in companies, maybe buying them, building them up, and selling them. It was what Lehman Brothers had done in the past.

As a final detail, Peterson added that he wanted one percent of any profit Lehman Brothers' partners might make should they sell themselves to another company over the next couple of years. This was speculative on Peterson's part, since there seemed no reason why Lehman Brothers should sell. Profits were good; Lehman Brothers also had an excellent level of capital and now—minus Peterson—seventy-six partners to use it sensibly. Lew said yes to Peterson's one-percent notion without hesitation.

Some partners were highly concerned. Glucksman was an operations man, and a Mr. Inside, maybe. But he was never a Mr. Outside who would know how to represent Lehman Brothers to the world. One person happy with Peterson's departure, though, was Dick Fuld. "[I]t didn't bother me," he said.

Glucksman had been offered a fifty-fifty deal and a chance to gradually usher in a new era under his leadership. It did not seem to occur to him that he did not have the skills for the task. He wanted everything now, and in a turn of phrase that gained wide use in the '80s, he wanted to "have it all." What happened next could be summed up by a rather more ancient and largely forgotten English phrase: "Give a beggar a horse and he'll ride himself to death."

Lew put his own people in the firm's important positions. When the time came to decide bonuses for the year, he also embarked on a radical wealth redistribution plan. It remained a game among millionaires, so no one ended up on poverty's doorstep, but banking partners had their bonuses and shares in the firm cut, and traders saw theirs increased. The biggest bonuses went to Glucksman and Fuld, with $1.6 million each.

Glucksman pushed some partners out, while others decided to go. D'Urso soon departed with his tracksuit and list of blue-blooded contacts to become a member of the Italian parliament. One partner in his late fifties decided he had other priorities and left and went to Israel. Another said he had always had a yearning to travel and learn a foreign language.

Those who departed took their capital with them. This was their right, but it was a worry to those who remained. It was a drain on the firm's reserves of capital. If many more went, Lehman Brothers would have little capital to work with. And if it had insufficient capital with which to work and make money, it would experience losses, which could drain its capital away to nothing.

Glucksman had put his star protégé, Dick Fuld, in charge of all trading: bonds, shares, everything. At a meeting called to discuss the key issue of capital, Fuld was asked how he could help boost capital in the future. "How did you make money in your trading operations over the last five years, and how are you planning to make money over the next several years?" asked one partner.

Fuld was out of his element. He was fine in the trading room, but he was not a meetings man. If he had a cogent answer in his head, he did not know how to formulate it in convincing sentences. "I don't know how I made it over the last five years," he replied. He was also unclear about the future. He had "hired some people," he said, to study the matter. The partners were shaken. If Fuld did not know where the capital was going to come from, who did? Glucksman tried to explain it away by pointing out that Dick had a problem communicating.

Partners were also concerned about Glucksman's behavior. He had gone in for a radical change of image, having shed seventy pounds, divorced his wife, and bought a sporty convertible. He purchased a five-room apartment in a block of luxury towers by the Museum of Modern Art, within a stone's throw of Bobbie Lehman's old mansion on West Fifty-fourth Street. Around the financial district, he was boasting that he was the toughest guy on the street. He shocked one visitor to his office by suddenly picking up a small ax and plunging it into his wall. Other marks on the wall suggested this was not the first time.

As partners left the firm, those remaining pressured Glucksman, saying that he should be looking for an outside partner—another firm, but one with money to spare—to put in capital. In March 1984 word got into *Fortune* magazine of the firm's internal divisions, and that Lehman Brothers partners were busy "peddling the firm." Glucksman's hand was forced. If uncertainty about the firm's future continued, an outsider could just step in and buy it for a song.

American Express showed an interest, and in April, Glucksman began negotiations at American Express's offices just across the plaza from 55

Water Street overlooking the harbor. The company, better known for its credit cards, had recently bought Shearson, a large brokerage, and was now called Shearson/American Express. Shearson was big but did not have the pedigree and prestige of Lehman Brothers—precisely what American Express believed its latest operation could use. Shearson Lehman American Express would have that extra insertion of class.

Glucksman soon reported back to his partners that he had made a deal: The sale price was $380 million. All the partners would do very well from the sale of their shares in Lehman Brothers, which would make them multi-millionaires, and many could stay working for the new organization. For some this was not the point. Herman Kahn, who had become a partner at the firm in 1950, told Ken Auletta his reaction: "[T]o me, investment banking was a noble undertaking, whereby capital was used for social purposes as well as personal gain. . . . I wept."

Dick Fuld was distraught. "I loved this place," he said. Fuld had resisted the idea of selling and, until the last, never believed it would happen.

It had, however, and in 1984, after only a few months in control, Glucksman and his followers had thrown Lehman Brothers' independence away. And as he shuttled the short distance from Water Street to American Express's offices while he negotiated the deal, Glucksman was only yards from the point of Manhattan where Henry Lehman approached the shore 140 years earlier.

|||||||||

"Frankly, there is no Lehman anymore," said Jeffrey B. Lane, Shearson Lehman's vice chairman a year after the deal. "The focus is different and our pitch has changed." One newspaper headline heralded the merger of the "The Upstart and the Aristocrat," and away went the partners' dining room and their silver boxes filled with Havana cigars. In the 1980s the big swallowed the small, and the old aristocrats were sacrificed for the sake of progress. It was a shame, perhaps, that there was "no Lehman anymore," but time could not stand still.

President Reagan struck the keynote of the era—and, as it happened, for the next thirty years—when he pronounced that "government is the problem." The government would get out of the way, cut taxes, reduce regulations that hampered business, and restore faith in the free market's "invisible hand." He affirmed the nation's wider foundation in faith, backing, for example, the teaching in schools of the biblical account of creation. If there was an air of the 1920s about this, the president did little to discourage it; he even hung a picture of President Calvin Coolidge in his office.

Margaret Thatcher, prime minister of Britain, ably assisted him from across the Atlantic. "There is no such thing as society," she said. The communal group was composed of individuals going about their daily business. No relationship was required between them, other than that they offered what they had, and sought what they wanted, leaving it to the marketplace to decide the price and quantity. The Thatcher dictum, in essence, was a trader's charter.

As the forces of capitalism grew in confidence, the West sniffed the air and sensed it was winning the cold war. The continuing struggle in Afghanistan had tied up the Soviet army in its own rerun of Vietnam. Three Russian presidents died between 1982 and 1985, furthermore, as the Soviet government gave the impression that it was run by either sick or very old men. Reagan hammered home his advantage with rhetoric he might have borrowed from Goldwater. Speaking on March 8, 1983, to the National Association of Evangelicals in Orlando, Florida, he called the USSR an "evil empire." About a fortnight later he followed up with an address to the American people in which he proposed "Star Wars" —formally known as the Strategic Defense Initiative—a system in which lasers situated in outer space would be positioned to strike down Soviet missiles.

Mikhail Gorbachev, the fourth Soviet president in three years, took over in 1985 and signaled that he wanted to negotiate with the USSR's Western rivals. The Soviet economy, composed wholly of state-run industries trying to meet state-devised five-year plans, could not provide anything like the consumer goods Soviets knew existed in the West, let alone match the United States in an arms race of the Star Wars variety. Gorbachev advocated *perestroika*, a move to run the Soviet economy on free enterprise lines, with companies in some cases able to decide what they produced and to whom they sold their goods. Alongside this he proposed *glasnost,* which envisaged more open government and freedom of information than the Soviet Communist Party had allowed in the past.

Wall Street followed Washington's lead. Communism was apparently in decay, while Western Europe's middle-of-the-road social democracies had been demoralized since the economic crisis of the 1970s; they had had to cut sharply the money they spent on their welfare states. Wall Street people became frontline troops advancing the free market. Strutting guys with suspenders and slicked-back hair populated the financial district and symbolized American success. Sport as well as business became a proxy for war. Banks installed basketball hoops in their offices to help traders maintain their competitive edge.

The men worked all hours. In the feminist seventies, executives who spent long days at the office and afterward went out drinking with the guys typified male neglect of the female. As far back as 1951, Bobbie Lehman's second wife had cited such tendencies of her husband in her divorce case against him. Now long hours were essential if you wanted to get ahead. Obsession suddenly became a good thing, especially with work and success. Other obsessions resulted; the taking of drugs such as cocaine became common around the trading rooms. It showed the lengths to which some people would go to drive themselves toward their goals.

As with the straitlaced Coolidge in the 1920s, President Reagan's character contrasted with the hyperactive second half of the '80s. An actor by background, he was a far better speechmaker than Coolidge; during his first election campaign in 1980, he had portrayed a "shining city upon a hill" as voters looked for something to lift them out of the valleys of 1970s' setback and crisis. Now, with the economy booming, at the end of a normal working day Reagan would go off to catch the evening soaps in his home within the White House, where Nancy, his wife, made sure he kept to a sensible schedule for a seventy-year-old.

Mrs. Thatcher in Britain was more a symbol of the obsessive busyness of the times. She was said to get by on three hours' sleep a night. Women, however, only started coming into the trading rooms in the mid-1980s, and then not in great number. Brash, foulmouthed macho culture dominated, with the "Big Swinging Dick," according to Michael Lewis, the "most revered of all species." He said the phrase brought to his mind an elephant's trunk swaying from side to side, though that was presumably open to interpretation: "Swish. Swash. Nothing in the jungle got in the way of a Big Swinging Dick." Traders, male and female alike, aspired to the title; after a large sale of bonds, a manager would call up to congratulate them: "Hey, you Big Swinging Dick, way to be."

In 1986, Lewis (having failed to join Lehman Brothers, he had found work at Salomon Brothers) visited the London School of Economics to give a talk to the university's Conservative Society, which generally supported the British Conservative Party. His subject of bond trading, he assumed, would guarantee only a small audience, but more than a hundred students came, nearly all keen to learn about his job. One dissident shouted from the back of the hall that Lewis was a "parasite," an impolite suggestion that investment bankers lived off the wealth created by others. The room booed the person down.

Lewis recalled that in 1968 the LSE had been one of Europe's centers of student revolution. Now he detected in Britain that same feeling he had noticed in early 1980s America. Students, who in past generations might have studied for humanities degrees between bouts of protesting against U.S. wars, had their minds set on investment banking, and American investment banking in particular. Jacques Gelardin, head of Shearson Lehman in London, told the *Financial Times* of the large turnouts his company attracted at university presentations. "There is a type of person who is more attracted to our type of business," he said. That type of business was more "performance-oriented" than in Europe, and the person who wished to get involved in it presumably had more "get up and go." The *Financial Times* referred to this cultural trend as "the U.S. paradigm."

Lew Glucksman would surely have relished running Lehman Brothers at this hour. "International" and "Indianapolis" to his mind had been one, and it appeared that the world was coming around to his way of thinking. It was too bad that he had blundered, though he still ended up a wealthy man. Of the $380 million sales tag on Lehman Brothers, Glucksman made $15 million from selling his shares in the firm. He had taken up consultancy work around Wall Street, and had far more time to indulge his passion for looking at ships. He married an Irish American and traveled regularly to the southwest of Ireland, where in 1984 he set up a home in the port city of Cork.

Financially, Pete Peterson left Lehman Brothers better off than anyone else. Thanks largely to his one-percent share of the profits made from the sale, he received more than $20 million. He had more than enough to start his own business and did so by partnering with Stephen Schwarzman, Lehman's former expert on mergers and acquisitions. They set up the Blackstone Group, which in twenty or so years' time would make billionaires of both of them.

After the Glucksman disaster, Dick Fuld had descended into the innards of Shearson Lehman to get on with what he did best: trading. He was put in charge of the division dealing in such things as government and mortgage bonds. Although on the losing side as Lehman Brothers was sold, he made $8 million from the deal.

Peter Cohen, the president of Shearson Lehman, was the grand victor. He was the protégé of Sanford "Sandy" Weill, a temperamental man who had built Shearson from a tiny firm in 1965 into a large network of brokerages that absorbed numerous other companies. He sold it to American Express for $1 billion in 1981 and took a place on the American Express board.

The Lehman Brothers purchase was Cohen's deal. Cohen was about five feet tall and a driven character. A solid C-grade student at Columbia University, he had hung around Midtown brokerage offices concentrating on the market rather than his books. He had joined Shearson at twenty-one, and in the 1970s was an anonymous number-crunching analyst at Shearson Hayden Stone, a small brokerage that sold shares to the public, and that had Weill as its chief executive. As Weill masterminded the deals that turned Shearson from a lowly company into a main player on Wall Street, Cohen became his henchman.

A gruff workaholic of the type who would rise to Wall Street and national prominence in the 1980s, Cohen made millions while in his twenties. Even his enemies, wrote the London *Sunday Times*, "admitted he was a good administrator and cost-cutter." He was sometimes photographed smiling, with a large cigar between his teeth. On the desk in his office in the World Trade Center overlooking Manhattan he had a sculptured chain saw, and next to it a model of a pinstriped character with its legs cut off at the knees. He was given to posturing: Once, during an interview with a journalist, he called in a shoeshine man; the journalist noticed that Cohen was wearing shiny patent-leather shoes.

In March 1984, while at his weekend mansion on Long Island, he had read the *Fortune* article that said Lehman was "peddling itself." Cohen's weekends were reportedly sacred to him, and devoted to his wife and family after a hard week at the office. Nonetheless, on that Friday night he had curled up in bed to read a business magazine. He spent the weekend making arrangements for a deal, knowing American Express would be pleased; it had said it wanted a "blue chip"—top class—company to link with Shearson, namely, a partner with prestige more comparable to its own.

Shearson was a "wire house," traditionally a firm with its own private communications network along which it did a lot of its buying and selling. The wire today was a computer system. Shearson also worked by telephone, selling to old customers or to new ones selected at random from the telephone directory or other lists of potential customers. It came under the category of organization known as "smile and dial."

As circumstances would have it, Lehman Brothers, the junior partner in the new company, would outshine its big brother in the "smile and dial" department. Martin D. Shafiroff, a top Shearson Lehman executive, wrote *Successful Telephone Selling in the 80s*, with cowriter Robert Shook. The book said that after the oil crisis of the 1970s, things would never be the same: "By 1980 the average cost of a personal sales visit to an industrial customer had passed the $100 mark!" In the 1960s a motel room cost less than $10 a night, and the same amount could feed a salesman on the road three meals a day. The price of everything had risen dramatically. Even the cost of dictating a letter to a secretary to set up an appointment with a potential buyer, which had been about $3.05 in 1970, had nearly doubled to $6.07 by 1980. Hence Shafiroff and Shook's book described techniques on how to sell on the phone, and it became a bible in its field.

Shearson Lehman traders comported themselves on the telephone more successfully than those at any other company, leaving others like Merrill Lynch and Bear Stearns in their wake with the volume of sales they made. Unfortunately, telephone selling left a lot to be desired. This was not what the book stipulated, but callers made spurious claims that partners at their brokerage wanted to share their market secrets with those on the other end of the line. Some recipients of this news thought it was their lucky day. Buyers were often sold shares that the broker had had trouble unloading on more knowledgeable people in the market. Unless they slammed the phone down, people who received calls found it very difficult to get their callers off the line, and phone salespeople were trained not to give up until they had received three insistent statements of "no" from a prospective customer. In the meantime, they might just get a sale.

On visiting Shearson Lehman's call office on Madison Avenue, *Fortune* magazine found a "bullpen one-quarter the size of a football field" full of young men in white shirts talking on headsets. What kind of people were they selling to? One broker responded that all that was required of a buyer was "a pulse and money."

Throughout its history, Lehman Brothers had been at the forefront of every major emerging trend in America—from automobiles to movies to aircraft. Today it pioneered the art of telephone selling.

The 1980s was a decade of major scandals in the markets, and Lehman Brothers had links with the main people involved. A measure of the depths the firm had sunk to was seen in 1986, when Litton Industries sued Shearson Lehman for $30 million, alleging insider trading. In 1954 Lehman Brothers had launched Litton, which went on to become one of the giants in the world of electronics and a star in the Lehman Brothers firmament. Now Litton was in effect claiming it had been robbed by its bankers. Litton had used Lehman as its adviser on mergers and acquisitions in 1982, when it set about purchasing Itek Corporation, a smaller electronics company. As it engaged in what were meant to be secret negotiations, however, Litton found that Itek's share price kept rising inexplicably.

Normally, when there are rumors of a merger, there is a rise in the share price of the company that is being taken over. Investors like big companies buying smaller companies; it often means the big company will inject more capital for expansion plans or cut costs by reducing the number of staff. As the price of Itek shares increased, so, too, did the price Litton would have to pay for the company.

The case involved Dennis Levine, a former managing director of Drexel Burnham Lambert, one of the leading investment banks involved in the large buyouts of companies that were very popular on Wall Street at the time. Levine had also worked for Lehman Brothers, and Ira Sokolow, a vice president of Shearson Lehman, had passed Levine information about the pending sale of Itek.

It was only by chance that Levine was caught. He would get his information from people like Sokolow and then buy large quantities of shares in the companies being taken over. Levine would sell the shares when the rest of the trading world discovered a merger was about to happen and the price went up. He did his buying and selling through a branch of Bank Leu International, a Swiss bank in Nassau, in the Bahamas. Bank Leu used a broker at Merrill Lynch to carry out some of Levine's trades. The broker noticed how successful the trades were and copied them for himself, a process known as "piggybacking." He also tipped off some colleagues, one of whom was in the Merrill Lynch office in Caracas, Venezuela. That trader copied the trades, as did another trader in the Caracas office. Then someone else in the Caracas branch saw what they were doing and anonymously informed the Merrill Lynch compliance office back in New York. That office existed, as at other banks and trading institutions, to make sure traders complied with the rules on matters such as insider trading. The Merrill Lynch compliance office passed on the anonymously provided information to the Securities and Exchange Commission, which pried open a whole can of worms.

Sokolow went to jail for a year. Levine received a sentence of only two years because of information he provided that implicated others. One was Ivan Boesky, "the Russian," as he was known, who had made a fortune betting on corporate takeovers. Boesky confessed to various cases of insider trading, paid fines of $100 million, and was given a three-year jail sentence. Information given by him led to Michael Milken, another buyout specialist from Drexel Burnham Lambert, receiving a ten-year sentence. The Boesky and Milken cases made the career of Rudolph Giuliani, the U.S. attorney for the Southern District of New York and future mayor of the city. Gordon Gekko, the main character of *Wall Street*, Oliver Stone's 1987 film, is said to be an amalgam of Boesky and Milken.

In March 1987 reports circulated that American Express might have had enough of its connection with Shearson Lehman and was looking to sell. American Express shareholders were reported as "almost unanimous in their enthusiasm for the idea." Employees of the Lehman wing of the operation were similarly keen not to be associated with Shearson. When they took calls from clients, they identified themselves only as "Lehman Brothers!"

The *Wall Street Journal* speculated that a foreign buyer might be interested, in keeping with the age of "globalization." This was a relatively new word; a world divided between the Communist East and capitalist West was not exactly "global." In the East, however, Japan was an important bastion of capitalism, so the term had relevance. The United States was certainly capitalizing on this element of globalization. With the mass of automobiles, electronics, and other goods it sold to the United States, Japan generated a large trade surplus. It recycled a substantial part of this surplus back into the U.S. economy as the U.S. government borrowed it by, for example, selling its Treasury bonds to Japanese buyers. As the Japanese trade surplus came back to America in monetary form, so there was a large amount of cash for U.S. companies and American people to borrow. Such borrowings soared under the administration of President Reagan, an old-fashioned leader in whose time old-fashioned values like thrift were abandoned.

One area of borrowing was mortgages, and Shearson Lehman had a mortgage department, as did other investment banks. Deal makers like investment banks were traditionally not involved in mortgages; these were unexciting investments handled, for example, by commercial banks that made sensible loans and looked after people's savings. But the investment banks had found that they could bundle up the mortgages and sell them to investors in the form of a bond. The investment banks got a handsome fee for the service, and the investors in the bond received a flow of income over time as people paid their mortgages back, plus a rate of interest.

A lot of these bonds were very complex and devised by young people in the mortgage department with brilliant mathematical minds. As a group they would become known as "quants," given their quantitative skills, or as "rocket scientists." Some of them had advanced training in disciplines such as physics and engineering that may well have qualified them for a career in rocket science, but they were attracted to investment banking by the often superior money that it paid. These people operated in such a rarified world that often even their bosses did not understand them.

The late 1980s provided one example of this during what became known as the savings and loan crisis. Savings and loan associations were "thrifts," organizations based on the old model of building societies in Britain, which held people's savings and provided mortgages to home buyers. As laws that regulated the savings and loan industry were loosened and thrifts lent too much, over seven hundred went bankrupt, and the government had to bail out the industry to the tune of $125 billion.

Merrill Lynch was one of the banks that did a spirited business repacking mortgages into mortgage bonds, until in April 1987 it announced a $250 million loss on a risky bond handled by its mortgage department. Aghast, Merrill Lynch executives blamed their chief mortgage trader for keeping them in the dark about the bonds, alleging that he had hidden them in a drawer. "[W]e didn't know he owned them," they claimed. Whether they would have been any the wiser about the bonds had the trader painstakingly explained the math behind them was debatable.

All these features of 1987 would be repeated some twenty years later in the crash of 2008. That time it would be the money from the Chinese trade surplus that was channeled back into the American economy. This would lead once again to heavy mortgage borrowing in the form of complex bonds devised by Wall Street, and managements would say they had little idea of what was going on within their own banks.

In the spring of 1987, word leaked into the press of further discontent on American Express's part. It had ordered Shearson Lehman to make potential employees undergo drug tests. Here was a conservative corporate giant with an international reputation to protect getting a little tired of current Wall Street practices.

Human failings to one side, in July, Shearson Lehman suffered a technological reverse. The firm's word-processing system broke down, and Lehman Brothers was unable to produce its weekly monitor of government bond prices, a publication much read around the markets. "There isn't a typewriter in the place," complained Eddie Abbott, the monitor's coeditor. This was a sad confession, given that Lehman Brothers had launched Underwood Typewriter on the stock market as long ago as 1910. But mainly it showed how dependent people were on computers.

This point was highlighted when the markets themselves crashed in October. Much to blame was "program trading," trading carried out by computer. When the sale of some shares was made in sufficient quantity, computer programs automatically triggered the sales of others. This had increased the level of panic in October as the markets plunged. Program trading had been a phenomenon almost unheard-of until then. Machines appeared to be taking the place not just of human action, but also of human thought.

The stock market collapse ended the Reagan boom. A heady period recalling the late 1920s ended in disappointment and scandal. The crash set off a search for culprits, and suspicion fell upon those of insufficient faith. Elaine Garzarelli, a Shearson Lehman stock market analyst, had been one of the few who had seen that the markets were overheated and advised her clients to sell. The media publicized her views, and many people blamed her, saying she was a doom monger who had caused the collapse. Some made such hostile verbal attacks on her that she called an ambulance to her apartment one morning after the crash: "I thought I was having a heart attack."

In the postcrash gloom, Peter Cohen decided to leap into the market by buying E. F. Hutton, an old brokerage second in size only to Merrill

Lynch. In early 1988 he paid nearly $1 billion for the prestigious firm, and for a while it became part of the newly named entity of Shearson Lehman Hutton. Some congratulated Cohen for single-handedly attempting to drag Wall Street to its feet. *Euromoney* magazine voted him Banker of the Year.

Observers noticed a change in his behavior. Cohen began "believing his press cuttings," wrote John Cassidy in the London *Sunday Times*. "The gruff bottom-line operator tried to turn himself into a gentleman banker." Cohen and his wife started mixing with New York's high society, and he worked on improving his tennis and golf. But he seemed to sense that he needed something more to fulfill the role assigned to him. He began going to museums, places not known for their moneymaking potential. As he went on business trips abroad, he found an urge to learn more about the world's cities beyond their offices and airports. "Now when in Rome or Madrid, Cohen tried to take half a day to take in the things he had missed," wrote Bryan Burrough and John Helyar in *Barbarians at the Gate*. He also managed an hour or two in Paris: "At forty he discovered the Louvre."

The E. F. Hutton purchase flopped. The 1987 crash had taken such a toll of its business and so many investors had fled the market that it could not recover. Subsequent Cohen moves saw him link up with a British company named Beazer in an attempted hostile takeover of Koppers Company, a Pennsylvania construction company that employed a lot of people in the Pittsburgh area. Its directors appeared in the media cutting up their American Express cards.

He led an effort to buy out RJR Nabisco, a multibillion-dollar deal that he lost to Kohlberg Kravis & Roberts, a New York company that was more expert than he in such large buyouts, and that stepped in to snatch it from his hands. In Wall Street's terms it was highly embarrassing to be beaten like this, but the case also attracted national interest. Shearson Lehman had acted for F. Ross Johnson, RJR Nabisco's chief executive, who, according to *Time* magazine, stood to pocket $100 million from the deal. The magazine featured the issue on its cover with the headline "A Game of Greed." By this stage American Express was tiring of Cohen's rendition of the U.S. paradigm. Dick Fuld, on the other hand, had been doing very well. In 1989 he made a bonus of $1.6 million from his trading department's activities. This was no better than Lehman Brothers had paid him in the past, but it showed that his employers were pleased.

November 1989 brought momentous world events as the Berlin Wall fell in Europe to end the cold war. On Wall Street, meanwhile, Dick Fuld was emerging from the ruins of Shearson Lehman, poised to take on the 1990s.

9

"Call Me Dick"

American Express put Dick Fuld in charge of a business development committee to plan strategy for the nineties. As the decade began, however, American Express largely took matters into its own hands in a situation that deteriorated into near total confusion.

In early January 1990, Jeffrey B. Lane, Peter Cohen's number two, resigned. Cohen went less than a month later. He was "history," wrote John Cassidy of the London *Sunday Times* about the forty-three-year-old, "a walking museum piece from the Roaring Eighties and the most prominent victim of the new decade of austerity on Wall Street." That decade certainly got off to an austere start. Wall Street shed about fifty thousand jobs, one fifth of its total, and further departures were in the cards.

Sixty Lehman Brothers analysts applied themselves to contemplating how the world would look over the next decade. In a 224-page report, they made a number of reasonably accurate predictions. There would be a new world currency, they said; a united Europe would introduce its own. They guessed it would be called the "monnet," after Jean Monnet, the architect of the European Union. They also forecast that the markets would soar for an extended period up to the beginning of the new millennium in 2000. This would give way to a "major bear market," in which prices would be clawed and slashed remorselessly.

To its great embarrassment, American Express had got it wrong with the whole Shearson Lehman experience. "The stately giant was not content with making money every time its 30 million clients used their Amex cards," said Cassidy in the London *Sunday Times*. "It had fallen for the fashionable myth that synergy existed between all forms of financial services." In short, it had discovered that running a travel service and issuing credit cards did not mean you could run a bank.

"It is about time that people started to focus on credit and the responsible management of Wall Street," said American Express's chief executive, James D. Robinson III, the patrician "Jimmy Three Sticks," after Cohen's departure. "I can assure you our direction in the 1990s will be substantially different from the 1980s."

As everyone worked out what to do next in February 1990, Howard L. Clark, American Express's chief financial officer, assumed the Shearson Lehman burden. In early May, it was said that a name change was possible; a new entity would be called either Shearson American Express or Lehman American Express. The press complained that the company had changed its name so often that it was having an "identity problem." In late May, word had it that American Express could split up the company between its stockbrokering side, of twenty-six thousand Shearson people, and its banking and bond trading side, of about seven thousand Lehmanites.

Finally, American Express decided that this was what it would do. Amid rapturous cheers from the trading floor, Clark appeared in June wearing a Lehman Brothers baseball cap. Lehman Brothers was both to get its identity back and to have a change of name. Great minds at the board of directors level had worked hard to come up with the right one. They could think of none better, said Clark, than "Lehman Brothers."

After all the turmoil of the last ten years, Lehman Brothers was going back to where it started. Although, was it? After the name change, what next? Not very much, Clark indicated. There were to be "no changes overnight." The two new entities of Lehman and Shearson were to be separate divisions of American Express but not separate corporations. "We have no intention of selling either part or all of either," he said. "I think the reintroduction of the Lehman name is what everyone is excited about."

Less than ringing endorsements came from outside the company. Lew Glucksman spoke up. "Lehman stood for excellence and we were on the cutting edge of everything that was going on in investment banking for 50 years," he said, recalling the good old days. Between visits to Ireland, he worked as vice chairman at the investment bank Smith Barney. This was part of Primerica Corp., the new empire run by Sandy Weill. He had become fed up working within American Express and set out on his own again.

Glucksman was far from sure that the new organization with an old name could match the Lehman Brothers that he had known; it would have "its work cut out to be able to assume that mantle." Roy Smith, a finance professor at New York University and a partner at Goldman Sachs, also commented. Lehman Brothers "was once a great name to the people of my generation," he said. But "going back to the name is nothing more than a marketing device, and the real success of the firm will depend on what the firm does."

First, a lot of rebuilding of credibility was required. Robinson, American Express's boss, had spoken about the responsible management of Wall Street as it went about its principal business of raising credit. Some strongly expressed the opinion that Wall Street employed the wrong type of person. "Our product is money," said Malcolm Lowenthal, a Shearson stockbroker for eleven years. "And money attracts scum." Shearson promptly fired Lowenthal for airing his views. He had not mentioned Shearson by name, but a company spokesman responded that his opinions "do not conform with the firm's philosophy of quality service."

Quality service had not exactly been the keynote among the real and imagined Wall Street characters that had embodied the 1980s. The Boeskys, Milkens, and Gekkos had seen to that. Then there was Wolfe's Sherman McCoy in *The Bonfire of the Vanities*. McCoy was an educated and WASPish trader on New York's international bond market and one of the self-centered and overly rich characters that were said to be especially numerous in that arena.

In large part this was because of the vast amount of wealth it traded. Until the late sixties, bonds had been a relatively dull field, at which point President Johnson's administration had brought it to life by printing a lot of money to finance American involvement in the Vietnam War. While this had given all markets more dollars to play with, it provided a particular boost to bonds.

Governments and companies placed bonds for sale to raise the large sums of debt they needed for their capital projects—roads, dams, factories, weapon systems, and so on. The oil crisis after the Middle East war of late 1973 saw additional billions recycled onto the U.S. and world markets from Arab oil-producing countries. They had become very rich from the large increase in oil prices and recycled their money to make yet more on the international markets. Bond traders frenetically competed for the enormous profits available and won a reputation for being the wild men of the market.

At Lehman Brothers itself, the clearing-up operations went on. In April 1991 the New York Stock Exchange fined the firm $750,000, the second-largest fine ever imposed by the exchange, to settle charges of abusive sales practices. The exchange had mounted a four-year investigation into aggressive telephone "cold calling." The stock exchange did not reveal the nature of the abuses, but it said that Lehman Brothers had made big profits in the 1980s using "carefully crafted scripts to make unsolicited sales pitches" to investors. The firm agreed to settle the claim without admitting or denying wrongdoing, but added that the issues concerned "took place nearly five years ago." It had since brought in "strict controls" over telephone selling.

It was revealed that American Express was making brokers display a card on their desks spelling out company principles, one of which was to make every client feel "special." American Express was trying to change the "fast-talking nature of the brokers with this card," said one broker. "It's kind of a joke," he added. "But it's important." He was bound to say that, given how keen he would have been to keep his job.

Early in 1992 American Express said it was thinking of selling Lehman Brothers to its management for $1 billion. By now Dick Fuld was jointly in charge of running Lehman Brothers with J. Tomilson Hill, a long-serving Lehmanite. Hill headed the banking division, which mainly took care of mergers and acquisitions, while Fuld ran trading. American Express still was not clear about what to do with Shearson, which continued to drain its finances.

More past murky dealings emerged when in mid-1992 news from London indicated that Lehman Brothers had been involved in the case of Robert Maxwell, the wealthy publisher and former British member of parliament who died in late 1991. Maxwell went missing from his yacht, the *Lady Ghislaine*, while sailing alone off the Canary Islands, and drowned. His body was found in the sea, and whether he committed suicide or fell overboard was not determined.

It was discovered that he had left behind huge debts and stolen $600 million from the pension fund of the *Daily Mirror*, the British newspaper that he owned. Lehman Brothers had lent money to Maxwell, with Maxwell using the pension fund as collateral. The pension fund was obviously not his to offer as a guarantee.

Lehman Brothers eventually agreed to pay $90 million in compensation to *Daily Mirror* pensioners. (Goldman Sachs was similarly involved and paid back nearer $110 million.) Court hearings revealed that Lehman Brothers people had been on the phone to Maxwell on his boat discussing the money he owed the firm just before he died. Whether this played a part in his going over the side did not come under discussion.

The scandal again raised concern about business conduct. During the Reagan and Thatcher booms, regulation by government was considered an unnecessary evil. In the United States, the SEC, in cracking the Levine insider trading case, had had to rely on an anonymous tip-off from Caracas. Business leaders pleaded that they could be left to govern themselves, but post-Maxwell, the mood was changing. The Securities and Futures Authority, the London stock market's body that handled self-regulation, was worried about the involvement of companies such as Lehman Brothers in the case. Christopher Sharples, the head of the SFA, pointed out that if business did not clean up its house, then government would. "[W]e are in the Last Chance Saloon for self-regulation," he said.

In the United States, the 1992 election campaign was in full swing, the result of which had appeared a foregone conclusion. President George H. W. Bush, Reagan's vice president and successor from 1989, had in 1991 led a successful war against Iraq. This was after Saddam Hussein, the Iraqi dictator, had annexed and occupied Kuwait, his neighbor on the Persian Gulf. Live television covered the war, which was observed with great enthusiasm by American correspondents on the ground, or from the roofs of their hotels, as they conveyed their excitement back home. A widespread American view was that the quick U.S. victory had atoned for the defeat in Vietnam. President Bush, however, had kept his objectives limited, another legacy from Vietnam. Having chased Saddam out of Kuwait, the United States did not pursue him to Baghdad, his capital, given American wariness of getting bogged down in a Vietnam-style quagmire.

A former head of the CIA, Bush was a foreign policy devotee. In the 1980s, when the Soviet Union had lost so many heads of state in so few years, Bush, as vice president, seemed to be constantly attending funerals in Moscow. In so doing he was able to refine his excellent contacts among world leaders. When his reelection campaign approached, Bush's Democratic rivals had shown reluctance for the fight. A veritable B-list of candidates offered themselves for the race, the front-runner of which turned out to be Bill Clinton, the governor of Arkansas. The Southern state and its capital, Little Rock, had rarely been in the news, at least internationally, since Eisenhower had sent troops there to desegregate its schools in 1957.

Clinton and Al Gore, his running mate and a senator for Tennessee, presented themselves as members of a new generation, the first of the politicians born after World War II to run for the White House. They advocated a new look for America that used more high technology, had more education, and employed more skills. The danger, they said, was that this generation was being left in a fix by the actions of the old. The economy in the early nineties was in the doldrums and, for the first time since the Depression, a generation of Americans faced not being able to have a better standard of life than the one before. The Bush administration, they argued, threatened the very basis of the American Dream.

As a result, Clinton was able to turn Bush's foreign expertise against him. Bush had a policy for every country in the world except the United States, said the Clinton campaign, and no answer to the nation's predicament. When asked what that predicament was, Clinton's answer became a famous one. It was the "economy, stupid."

Bush had one person in particular to thank, or rather to blame, for losing him the election: his chief monetary adviser and head of the Federal Reserve, Alan Greenspan. The crash of 1987 had left inflation high and Greenspan concerned. He told Bush when he took over the presidency that the solution was to push up the interest rate to curb people's spending. This in turn would peg back the worrying level of price increases.

Greenspan was not generally one to tinker with the market mechanism. In his youth he had been an ardent supporter of Ayn Rand and felt anyone who messed with the market was probably trying to guarantee someone a soft ride. No soft ride resulted for President Bush as his Federal Reserve chief reduced everyone's spending so much that the economy went into recession. Bill Clinton's argument, therefore, resonated with the American public, and he approached the 1992 polls firmly in the lead.

Clinton called his economic program Putting People First. It would invest to improve education, training, and skills, though his plans had another element to them that the Democrats called industrial policy. This was the idea of giving more support to key American industries, like electronics. Such industries needed government help, the Democrats argued, not least to keep up with competition abroad. Japan, for example, was an especially strong competitor in electronics.

Clinton's team had revived the approach proposed by Paul Mazur of Lehman Brothers after the crash of 1929. Free market capitalism stood for anarchy in the marketplace, as individuals dashed hither and thither, often to no rational end; when crashes came it was not enough to reassure those suffering the consequences that they were merely actors in a drama of creative destruction, and that they would see the benefits at some time in the future. Planning would moderate the peaks and troughs of the market.

J. K. Galbraith had been an early advocate of industrial policy. Robert Reich, a Harvard academic who became Clinton's first labor secretary, was another. At the Massachusetts Institute of Technology, Lester Thurow was especially concerned to match the challenges from Japan. The U.S. economy, he argued in his book *The Zero-Sum Society*, if left to its own devices, "will not provide jobs for everyone who wants to work."

Such ideas had their precedent in industries in which the old Lehman Brothers had involved itself. Radio and RCA would never have taken to the airwaves had it not been for the promotion of the industry by Franklin D. Roosevelt, then undersecretary of the navy, after World War I. Pan Am would not have got off the ground for any extended period of flight had the government not awarded it international routes.

In the buildup to the 1992 election the subject prompted wider debate about the nature of capitalism itself. The system had failed in 1929, the Reagan boom had recently ended in tears, and the economy was still in a slump. The early nineties also allowed space to hold the discussion. Capitalism had claimed its political victory at the Berlin Wall three years before, and the threat from communism was dead. A review of capitalism's failings could therefore be held in a relatively relaxed light. The basic system was accepted but needed modification away from the idea that it could manage itself. The fact that any public discussion was taking place was remarkable. Since the McCarthy era, and possibly before, even the mention of the word "capitalism" was taken to infer criticism and invite suspicion that the user of the word was a Communist.

To some, planning was a taboo subject. It interfered with the sanctity of the market and dared suggest that man could assert influence over its celestial forces. Opponents of industrial policy lodged their arguments:

You could not cherry-pick industries worthy of government support; matters were far better left to the impersonal marketplace, which had no favorites and worked according to the invisible hand; in spite of the crashes and disasters, just leave the system as it was destined to be.

What finally confounded Clinton's ideas was Greenspan. After the election, Clinton invited him to Little Rock. They had never had a conversation before and met on the morning of December 3. They had quite different views, and their meeting amounted to Ayn Rand meets John Maynard Keynes. Rand and the Fed chief won; the new administration had to face certain priorities, Greenspan argued, the principal of which was to win the confidence of the markets.

The most pressing problem in this regard was the budget deficit, the difference between what the government spent each year and what it received in taxes. The deficit had reached extraordinary levels, about $200 billion. The Republicans were the reputed party of sound finance, but the finances of the nation were far from that. The savings and loan crisis in the late eighties, the Iraq War, and Star Wars were among the contributors to the deficit. If it continued rising at the present rate, it would be $350 billion by 1997.

That would be a key year for Clinton, when he hoped to begin a second term in office. Government spending had to be brought down, because it was hogging too much of the available money. Therefore, it pushed interest rates too high, which meant that private business could not easily borrow. On the other hand, if Clinton could get the deficit and interest rates down, and win business's confidence, the economy would revive and he would have a good chance at reelection.

Clinton enjoyed this chat. Scheduled for two hours, it lasted far longer and through lunch. "We can do business," Clinton told Gore of his impressions from the meeting, and he may have initially missed the implications of Greenspan's position. Clinton would have to cut his investment plan and industrial policy ideas, because they would cost too much federal money. He was soon made aware of this and learned that if he wanted to be in office longer than four years, he was going to have to pick up the tab for the Reagan and Bush deficits, and cast aside his own plans, in order the win the goodwill of the markets. "You mean to tell me," he said to his advisers, "that the success of the program and my reelection hinges on the Federal Reserve and a bunch of international bond traders?"

He was precisely right. Clinton, therefore, turned his attention to getting the economy moving again in the way that Greenspan had advised, and the idea of addressing the anarchic way in which the market worked went by the board. A chance to change the mentality of those running the markets went with it.

The president soon had other things on his mind. In February 1993, within a month of his taking office, terrorists detonated a car bomb in the parking garage of the north tower of the World Trade Center in New York. The bombers failed in their aim to destroy the building, which they hoped would topple onto the south tower next to it, but the blast left six people dead and more than a thousand injured. Could more such attacks be expected? The culprits were fundamentalist Muslims from Egypt, Pakistan, Kuwait, and the Palestinian West Bank, which was occupied by Israeli troops.

Early 1993, meanwhile, brought big changes at American Express. James Robinson gave up his chief executive's post, having failed to solve the problems left by the Shearson Lehman years. Sandy Weill stepped in to buy Shearson for $1 billion, the price he had sold it to American Express for in the early 1980s.

American Express appointed Dick Fuld in March as Lehman Brothers' president. Tom Hill resigned from running the banking side, leaving Fuld in charge of all operations. Lehman Brothers was about to get full independence, and Fuld's appointment, said American Express, removed any confusion about who was in control.

His rise to the top spot gave Fuld a "full-blown anxiety attack," he later told an audience at the Wharton business school at the University of Pennsylvania. It caused him to stop breathing for forty-five seconds. He had not looked for the job, and the sudden realization that he had it shocked him. But once he had regained his breath and thought about the offer overnight, he said, "I came in the next day with terrific resolve."

Fuld gave a speech shortly after to Lehman Brothers' employees to say how delighted he was to be leading them. A staff video recording was made of the occasion, in what looked like a hotel banquet suite; a shower of green and white balloons was released from the ceiling and rained down on the gathering. Under Fuld, green was the official Lehman Brothers color, with the offices decked out with green walls and carpets and Fuld urging his people to "bleed green" for the company.

Having spoken to the staff on this occasion, he offered a few extra words to the person with the video camera saying how Lehman Brothers was going to "conquer all the people that stand in front us." The Goldman Sachses, the Morgan Stanleys, and the rest had better watch out, because the firm's ambition was "basically to crush our enemies, like this." With that, he bared his teeth like a dog snarling. Was it Dick's attempt at humor or to cover the awkwardness he felt when required to say anything in public? For a moment he looked slightly mad.

The *Financial Times* reported Dick's promotion, or as the newspaper put it, "the ascension of Mr. Fuld, a former bond trader, to the pole position at Lehman." John Mack, from a comparable background, had just taken over at Morgan Stanley, and similar big appointments were happening elsewhere. Fuld's elevation "represents another victory for bond traders on Wall Street."

So much, then, for the post-eighties agonizing about Last Chance Saloons. Along Wall Street the same guys were still drinking at the bar.

||||||||||

Lehman Brothers reemerged in the spring of 1994 not as the partnership of old but as a limited company. This meant that in the event of the company's going bust, the shareholders' losses would be "limited" to the amount of money they had invested. This was a substantial change from the partnership system of Bobbie Lehman's day, when the partners stood to lose everything they had should a disaster occur. By and large, they had tended to be cautious, and knew exactly where they were putting their money. In a limited company, those in charge used the funds provided by the shareholders, and by others like banks and bondholders that lent the company money. Those running the business were playing with other people's cash rather than their own.

Dick Fuld, however, tried a variation on the limited company model by tying Lehman Brothers' people to the firm. He wanted to prevent the kind of problems seen in Lew Glucksman's darker days, when partners were leaving Lehman Brothers at an accelerated speed. Fuld decreed that Lehman employees had to have a substantial amount of their salary and bonuses paid in shares. If they left the company, they could not cash in the shares for some years.

Thereby Fuld strapped himself and others to what he called "the mother ship." Lehman Brothers had been his entire working life and his obsession and, in paying people to such an extent in shares, he may have aimed to make it similarly the obsession of those around him. As the good ship Lehman Brothers floated, all aboard would prosper. If it went down, they would all go with it.

Capital remained a problem, because, relatively speaking, Lehman Brothers did not have a great deal of it. The total of its shareholder capital—the money the firm had to work with—was about $3 billion initially. This did not match the biggest investment banks, the so-called bulge bracket, some of whose members, like Merrill Lynch, had nearer $5 billion. Although Lehman Brothers had regained its independence, there was a good chance that it would be quickly swallowed up again by a larger rival.

What Lehman Brothers particularly lacked was a broad range of things to do. After the 1987 stock market crash it had run down its share trading work. It also did not have a wealth department that calmly advised rich people where to put their money, as in the days of Bobbie Lehman. The new Lehman Brothers was what critics disparaged as a "bond house." Its income, for example, from banking came mainly through fixing company takeovers and was $800 million a year. Its trading department, which traded bonds and other financial instruments, brought in double that. But within the trading category, the firm did have one dominant feature that would be significant in the future: Lehman Brothers stood second only to Morgan Stanley in selling mortgage bonds.

Fuld set out to cut expenses. Some one thousand people lost their jobs in the first year, roughly an eighth of the workforce. He made a target of the company's taxi bill of $12 million a year. Cabs "lined up in droves" outside Lehman Brothers' offices, said one report, well before 8:00 P.M., when employees were allowed to begin using them on the firm's tab. Some $3 million had to come off that. He cut the free meals Lehman Brothers personnel had in the staff restaurant. In line with the old dictum, under Fuld there would be "no free lunch."

The rumors persisted of Lehman Brothers' being taken over again, and it was against such a background that Dick devised his pièce de résistance. Fending off the external threat would involve a lot of bluff to convince people that Lehman Brothers was far stronger than it was. It would have to ooze confidence if it was to make its way. At some stage, Fuld seemed to have decided that the best way to do this was by completely revamping his own image, even, if possible, his personality.

In May 1995 *Business Week* magazine published an interview with Fuld, just a year after he had led Lehman Brothers into its renewed status as an independent firm. "Free at Last" read the headline, mimicking the cry from the 1960s of the late civil rights leader, Martin Luther King, Jr.

Fuld reported that he had just returned from Israel, where Lehman Brothers had opened an office. Though Fuld was Jewish, this was his "first major trip" there. The Israelis' spirit impressed him, their sense of "we are all in it together," by which he may have meant being surrounded by a collection of hostile neighbors. This was also "the guts" of Lehman Brothers' culture, he said. On the other hand, company togetherness no longer included the one thousand people that Fuld had laid off in the previous year.

An accompanying photograph captured the key theme of the article. It showed a sideways-on shot of a dark-suited Fuld reclining in a Victorianesque armchair. With his head turned straight to the camera and arm bent at the elbow, it looked as if he was about to make a thoughtful, even philosophical contribution to a conversation. In his trader days Fuld would not have been caught at work posing pensively in an old armchair. Rare pictures of him from past times usually had him sitting at a trading desk and computer screens, his tie tightly tied and his collar fiercely buttoned up, jacket off. Such old snapshots give the impression of a man pausing just long enough for the photographer to get his picture before getting back to work.

But evidently, Dick was no longer a trader. "For the clients we're targeting," he said of Lehman Brothers' ambitions, "we want to be their top 1 or 2 banker." This was a radical departure by a man who had once spoken of those "fucking bankers." Fuld, it appeared, had discovered business was not simply a matter of deals and transactions but of clients and relationships. On his recent trip to Israel, he had apparently also taken the road to Damascus.

He was not alone in his itinerant ways. In a 1996 piece for the *New York Times* entitled "The Death of Sherman McCoy," Michael Lewis said others were en route from the raucous '80s: "[T]hey read the books, saw the movies, studied the lawsuits and decided on balance that it paid them to clean up their acts and pretend to be modest like everyone else." Some big-time traders left their jobs at investment banks to join new institutions such as hedge funds. Hedge funds were pools of unregulated capital, a term for rich people's money invested in lucrative places where the government would not interfere. They were sometimes back-street operations, albeit in quite exclusive back streets. London's posh Mayfair district, nestled between Piccadilly and Park Lane, became a hedge fund haven. Some traders-turned-hedge-fund types had changed their style: "The very same people who seemed unable to function without cigars, suspenders and thousand-dollar suits were suddenly turning up for work in sneakers." Not all, of course, because by and large, Wall Street firms encouraged formal wear, but the indications were that the transformation was more one of image than substance.

As far as Dick was concerned, some people guffawed: The idea of his turning into a client-relationship man was tantamount to Jack Welch, the hard-nosed head of General Electric, discovering his touchy-feely side. Was this a ruse on Dick's part or did he believe it? Would the slam-bang mentality of the modern market even allow such a thing? But in the can-do trader's mind, to wish for something was as good as to have it done. And after all, Dick was, at his heart, a trader, albeit one who had willed himself to become a banker.

He seemed to have decided that it would give him some stick to lean on as he led Lehman Brothers into a difficult future. To an extent it meant looking back to the past; the ghost of Bobbie Lehman still seemed to hover above.

"Call me Dick," he would tell visitors and others whose instinct was to be more formal. As in the old days of "call me Bobbie," this made many people of lower rank feel uncomfortable. Graciousness was not the norm in modern-day banking, but Fuld, in his often stilted way, attempted to instill a semblance of old-fashioned politeness. Any woman, however junior, standing by the elevators would be ushered in first.

Teamwork was a mantra of Fuld's, and here he was critical of the past. Bobbie had not been a team player, he claimed. In those days, "it was about me. My job. My people. Pay me." Dick still sometimes spoke in a staccato fashion like this. Lehman Brothers under him, he was saying, would not be like that. Bobbie had not encouraged an atmosphere that shared ideas or "helped build relationships." Here Fuld was setting himself some stiff targets. The relationships that Bobbie Lehman had those many years ago had generated some very good ideas.

On firmer ground, he was critical of Lew Glucksman. He had made errors that led to the firm's fall in 1984, but "I was just as guilty as anyone.

I couldn't reach over to embrace the bankers." Dick's aim was to unite the sides. Everybody, traders and bankers alike, would be on the same profit-and-loss account and work together in the common cause. Lehman Brothers' maxim, he proclaimed, would be "One Firm."

He liked to hire people who were good at sports, because he believed this showed they were team types. His leadership style, said Gary Silverman of the *Financial Times*, was that of the "football coach." A keen sportsman himself, Fuld did not put on weight in spite of his voracious appetite. He often sent out for a large order of ribs during the day and worked it off with his driven approach, or by playing squash. At his expansive home in Connecticut, one of several he owned, Fuld had his own courts. A photo from 2002 shows him in playing gear alongside America's leading squash players, who were taking part in national team trials staged on his courts. An accompanying article on the Web site squashtalk.com refers to Fuld as the team's primary sponsor.

Second in command to Dick after Lehman Brothers regained independence was Christopher Pettit. He was a trading room protégé of Fuld's and a veteran of the war in Vietnam, where he had been an army captain. Fuld as chief executive and chairman was the strategist, and Pettit, the company president, his chief of day-to-day operations. Dick was Mr. Outside, Pettit, Mr. Inside. Pettit possessed a comfortable manner and an open smile, and may have imagined he was destined for the big job, an impression he gave when interviewed in his office by Shawn Tully of *Fortune* magazine. Pettit had arranged a collection of different Lehman Brothers baseball caps on his shelves, plus a couple of books turned to display their titles. *Never Work for a Jerk* by Patricia King was one, and *The Death of Common Sense* by Philip K. Howard the other. He had such ambition, he said, that one day "I want my name etched in granite in the corridors of Lehman."

Speaking at Wharton, Fuld had stated more of his business secrets. "Read" was one of them. Given the length of Dick's workday, it was a wonder he found any time to read. Weekends were surely the only time he held out any hope of seeing his family. "Try to limit the surprises" was another piece of his advice. "Surprises kill you." Otherwise, he said, "[n]etwork. Connect the dots."

To connect the dots, Fuld became a disciple of the new age of globalization. Maybe he had some leaning toward it from studying international business in his Colorado school days. Lehman Brothers was at a disadvantage when it emerged from the mess of Shearson American Express because other banks had leaped ahead in developing their international sides. The Lehman Brothers foreign base built by Bobbie Lehman had grown little farther. Dick would change that: He would travel the world.

Capitalism had that world to play with. With the Soviet Union and the old East/West divisions gone, globalization could proceed at full force, and America, as the strongest economy, was its natural leader. Communications and capital reached across frontiers, and countries like Brazil, Russia, India, and China, once inhibited by communism or poverty, burst onto the capitalist scene. These became known as the BRIC nations and the fast new movers on the international stage. The old phrase "Third World" disappeared; since the split between first and second worlds—capitalism and communism—did not exist anymore, the idea of a third was redundant. The terms "developed" and "underdeveloped" were also less used than before. Under the new order, those nations that showed some chance of making it became known as "emerging markets."

Fuld was not the most natural traveler. Bobbie Lehman went to Europe twice a year to look around and absorb the atmosphere. Dick probably went a lot more, but the demands of an investment banker meant that you did not stick around. There was limited chance, therefore, of knowing any culture but your own. Dick proclaimed "One Firm" and might also have added "One World": that as seen from the office in New York. In November 2008 *New York* magazine recalled a family holiday that he took on one occasion in Africa. At night he would hike to a spot where he could get a signal for his cell phone and call in: "I'm out in the bush," he said. Dick the gorilla was presumably unabashed by any prowling lions likely to be in the bush at that time of day. He wanted to catch up on business, he told his executives. "Little business transpired," one recalled. "It was more like he missed us."

Lehman Brothers under his leadership made a poor start in China. When it went independent, the company opened an office in Beijing but was soon embroiled in Oriental problems. Eleven leading traders among the firm's local staff in Hong Kong resigned over what Leah Nathans Spiro and Pete Engardio of *Business Week* called "culture clashes" between them and their "hard-charging" managers from New York. The magazine did not clarify, but the unnuanced style of the average New York trader was alien to Chinese culture, in which such concepts as loss of face had to be taken into account.

In November 1994 Lehman Brothers had also filed lawsuits against some companies it did business with in China, blaming them for losses it suffered on foreign exchange deals. The Chinese filed lawsuits in retaliation, and the conflict escalated. An initial personal approach might have worked better, suggested the magazine. Fuld told the magazine that "we want to be the premier investment bank serving our clients globally," but *Business Week* sounded skeptical. In China, "where relationships are paramount," Lehman Brothers might have irreparably harmed its business.

At home, the picture was more cheerful, as Alan Greenspan's forecast to President Clinton of better things had come true. The World Wide Web turned into a feature of daily life for an increasing number of people in the midnineties, and the new Internet age made household names of companies like Microsoft, Google, and Amazon. The "new economy" came into use as a phrase to describe such modern enterprises. "Old economy" features like oil and manufacturing began to sound ancient.

Toward the end of November 1996 Lehman Brothers abandoned one of the elements of its old economy, in fact, the one in which it had made its beginnings. A month earlier it had stopped buying and selling precious metals and natural gas and would soon cease trading in all commodities, it said. Much of its business now was in mortgage bonds and abstruse investments related to them, like "collateralized debt obligations." This was a long way from the days when it had begun trading in cotton, exchanging one material good for another with Alabama farmers who came to Henry Lehman's Montgomery store.

Lehman Brothers also in November abruptly truncated the career of Christopher Pettit. He had promoted traders like himself into top positions at the expense of bankers, and Fuld may have spotted divisive shades of Lew Glucksman at work, with himself cast in the role of Pete Peterson. But reports suggest other issues were in play. Lehman Brothers under Fuld had a corporate culture akin to that of a monastic order: a tightly grouped collection of people with a rigid set of values. Vicky Ward, in an extract from her book *Devil's Casino* in the April 2010 edition of *Vanity Fair*, wrote of Fuld's "family first philosophy." Pettit had left his wife of many years, with whom he had four children, and had an affair with a woman at the company. A Roman Catholic, Pettit had once made grand statements about how the leading people at Lehman Brothers had durable marriages and families and that this was the essence of its success.

Pettit left the firm after falling out with several of his colleagues, among them Joseph Gregory, a senior executive and friend of Fuld's at the firm since the Glucksman days. Contrary to Pettit's hopes, there would be no granite plaque bearing his name in Lehman Brothers' corridors. Those who sought his memorial had to look elsewhere. He died a few months later in a snowmobile accident on a frozen lake in Maine. Reports said that Fuld never spoke of him again.

According to Ward, Fuld worried about the state of people's marriages and asked about them if he detected tensions. He was also anxious about Scott Freidheim, who became one of his leading directors in 1996 but remained unmarried. Fuld did not know what to make of this. Freidheim eventually put him out of his misery by getting married at the age of forty-three.

Work dominated the top employees' lives for a long period each day, but the firm's ethos did not stop there. When Karin, the wife of Bradley Jack, another executive, was pregnant and went into labor, Bradley had to attend to business guests visiting from Hong Kong and could not be with her. Another time, when one of their children was seriously ill, Karin and Bradley were still expected to accompany Gregory, who was flying his helicopter for the occasion, on a management outing to see a new house Gregory was having built on Long Island. This kind of appointment outweighed family sickness in the list of Lehman Brothers' priorities.

In December 1996, meanwhile, Greenspan tried to calm everyone down about the economy as a whole. The Internet age was turning into the Internet boom and generally driving up prices on the stock market. From about this time, big enterprises began to report their results and takeovers in billions of dollars, not millions anymore. In a speech to the American Enterprise Institute, the head of the Fed referred to the "irrational exuberance" of the markets, suggesting that prices of shares, houses, and other assets might be too high. It was like the word of God, as the financial community took the cue and the markets fell quite sharply. Then everyone forgot the message Greenspan gently conveyed and carried on as before.

By 1997 Lehman Brothers had added a new string to its business bow that extended its range beyond bonds. This was in commercial property. Mark A. Walsh was Fuld's head of global real estate and considered Wall

Street's most brilliant property financier. He shared some of Dick's personal traits: He was both socially awkward and enjoyed the outdoor attractions of Colorado. He took clients fishing there, and his tactics worked well.

Walsh fixed some very big deals in 1997, and one in particular gave Fuld a chance to indulge his client relationships side. ITT, a Lehman Brothers client in former times, was for sale. It had a lot of hotels and casinos, and Barry Sternlicht, head of Starwood Hotels and Resorts, intended to buy it. He needed $7 billion, a sum that Goldman Sachs undertook to raise, but it did not do it quickly enough for Sternlicht, who was at risk of losing the deal. When Walsh said that he would get the money, Sternlicht still needed reassuring. Lehman Brothers' chief arrived to soothe his brow with some old-style armchair banking. "Dick Fuld sat there in my living room," recalled Sternlicht in admiration, "and said, 'You have our word. We'll get this done.'"

Lehman Brothers beat Goldman Sachs to the ITT deal and made a $20 million fee. Walsh was involved in other big deals, including the sale of both the Chrysler Building and the Woolworth Building in Manhattan. The sums required were large for a firm the size of Lehman Brothers to handle, and the bank took out large loans to finance them. But the market was healthy, and as commercial property prices rose, Walsh's success enabled Fuld to fulfill his role as Dick the banker. Fuld approved pay and bonuses in 1997 for his bankers that far outweighed those of his bond traders. Walsh, therefore, helped Lehman Brothers widen its business and, or so it appeared, place it on more solid ground. He enabled Lehman Brothers' "swanlike transformation," wrote the New York Times, "from a second-tier bond trading shop into a full-service investment bank."

A collection of black swans, however, chose the late nineties to pass ominously across the millennial horizon. The bomb attacks on August 7, 1998, that killed more than two hundred people and destroyed the American embassies in Nairobi, the capital of Kenya, and Dar es Salaam, the capital of Tanzania, in East Africa were carried out by Islamic fundamentalists and orchestrated by Osama bin Laden, a dissident member of a wealthy Saudi Arabian family. He led an organization calling itself Al Qaeda. The attacks involved people trained in, or otherwise connected to, such countries as Afghanistan, Sudan, and Somalia, places that were largely remote from the Western mind. While the United States, Europe, and elsewhere tuned in to globalization and the new universe of the Internet boom, their attentions had seemed so focused on the computer screens in front of them that they had missed how some parts of the world were dangerously going their own way.

Later in August 1998 it became clear that Dick's old trading instincts had pulled Lehman Brothers into a crisis a little nearer to home—in Russia, to be precise, where financially catastrophic events threatened to take Wall Street with them. To an extent, Russia had been an exemplary exponent of the new capitalism, having changed to the free enterprise system as soon as communism had been ejected from power. At the same time, it was suspected that many leading members of the old Communist Party had just changed their appearance and, rather like late 1980s Wall Street people, gone into other lines of business.

The problem stemmed from Long-Term Capital Management, a hedge fund whose business dramatically slumped in 1998. Lehman Brothers and all the major banks had invested in the fund because it was said to have an infallible way of making money. John Meriwether, a former bond trader with Salomon Brothers, and Myron Scholes and Robert Merton, two American economists, had set up LTCM. Scholes and Merton had won the Nobel Prize for their mathematical theories about managing risk, and the hedge fund employed those ideas as it made enormous bets on minuscule movements in the price of bonds issued by governments. In theory, all bond values gravitated toward being the same. Unfortunately, the theory failed to allow for the unlikely event of a sovereign country's defaulting on its bond repayments.

Bobbie Lehman had "bet on the man"; Dick Fuld and others bet on the formula. Russia, alas, turned out to be its misbehaving variable. Dramatic falls in the prices of oil, natural gas, and metals, which were commodities that Russia depended on for its income from overseas sales, meant that the country ran out of money to meet its bond commitments. Investors panicked and rushed for the safety of U.S. bonds, creating a great divergence between them and others. It was not meant to happen, nor was LTCM supposed to lose nearly $5 billion in four months.

On September 11, 1998—the 154th anniversary of Henry Lehman's arrival in America—Lehman Brothers had to take a rare step for a bank, namely, denying that it was bankrupt. Rumors of the amount of money it had lost by investing with LTCM ranged as high as $1 billion. With all the main banks in danger of suffering heavily if LTCM collapsed, the Federal Reserve Bank of New York organized a rescue for the hedge fund. Twelve banks put in $300 million each, while Lehman Brothers would go no higher than $100 million. Fuld postured, saying that his bank did not have as much money tied up in LTCM as the others.

The banks could have drawn various conclusions from the LTCM case: The "impossible" could happen; mathematical models that suggest otherwise make no sense; and all banks' operations were so interlinked that one nasty instance posed a threat to them all. They failed to grasp these points to any extent that might have helped them, particularly Lehman Brothers, in future years. One message they might have detected, on the other hand, was that the U.S. banking authorities seemed quite willing to organize a bailout in the event of a threat to the economic system.

Some years later, in 2003, a court case involving Lehman Brothers in London shed more light on the LTCM question. Kerim Derhalli, a British citizen, had been head of Lehman Brothers' Russian office at the time of the crisis. Derhalli had endured this difficult time in Moscow, only for Lehman Brothers to sack him soon after. He demanded damages from the bank of about $15 million for breach of contract.

Derhalli painted a picture of panic within Lehman Brothers as the 1998 bond crisis hit, which had put him under pressure to collect money owed to the bank. The company had hired former employees of the KGB, the old Soviet Union's intelligence service, to physically get the money, and Derhalli feared for his life. People who owed money in Russia, he said, often killed the people they owed it to. It made Lehman Brothers appear all the more ungrateful in its treatment of him.

The case introduced to the public gaze some aspects of the life of investment bankers, not least their pay. Dick Fuld was reported to have received $8 million in 1998. Derhalli's income had been $3 million a year. People he worked with who specialized in Scandinavian, Central European, and Turkish bonds made over $1 million. At one point in the proceedings, Lehman Brothers claimed that Derhalli was "extremely motivated" by money. He did not deny it, adding that he was "no different from any other investment banker."

Derhalli's statements also touched on the extent to which Lehman Brothers had been financially vulnerable to the Russian crisis. It had provided figures to the markets and the other banks about its exposure, but the methods it used to calculate them "did not correspond to any normal measure of risk assessment used internally." Also, in presenting some of the details of the Russian affair, the bank, he alleged, had engaged in "misleading accounting practices."

The case ended abruptly as it was about to begin its ninth day. Lehman Brothers agreed to a payment to Derhalli that the *Independent* newspaper indicated was about $8 million. A short statement released by the sides said that both parties had "expressed a desire to get back to work."

|||||||||

As the millennium approached, Dick Fuld had acquired the image of a plucky character who battled against the odds and survived. "Cats with their nine lives have nothing on Lehman Brothers," wrote the *Financial Times* in December 1998, recalling the travails of the Long-Term Capital Management crisis. The bank had "kept its franchise intact during the worst of times." A year on from LTCM and Fuld's admirers were proclaiming him the comeback kid, with his firm on course for its first billion-dollar year.

Just before Lehman Brothers announced that its net income for 1999 had reached that mark, Fuld gave an interview to *Investment Dealers' Digest*, a specialist observer of Wall Street affairs. "We're just scratching at the surface of what this firm is going to do," Dick told Christopher O'Leary, the *IDD* correspondent. O'Leary was impressed by his visit to 3 Financial Center, Lehman Brothers' headquarters adjoining the World Trade Center. The atmosphere in the investment banking division on the eighteenth floor was quiet and in sharp contrast to the "rough and tumble" trading floor. "But the hushed, almost placid office suites belie the frenzied activity of dealmakers on the make."

Lehman Brothers was punching above its weight among its larger Wall Street rivals. In May 1999, it had orchestrated the $65 billion takeover of Telecom Italia, the fourth-largest telephone company in Europe, by Olivetti, a successful cell phone company. Olivetti was much smaller than Telecom Italia, but Lehman proposed and organized the takeover. Chase Manhattan, a far larger bank, put up most of the money and tried to muscle Lehman out of the deal, but Lehman Brothers' "soldiers in Europe" resisted this challenge and claimed their firm's share of the spoils.

IDD indicated that not everyone had welcomed the bid. A lot of Italians opposed this intervention in their country by American capitalism. But the deal inspired by Lehman Brothers had "opened up Europe to hostile takeovers." The implication was that the old continent was ripe for this more aggressive way of doing business.

With his hostile moves and soldiers in the field, Fuld was clearly worth his mention in dispatches by financial America. The warlike mood was palpable, yet, suggested *IDD*, Fuld was under pressure to do more. He was showing a diminished "appetite for risk," according to market analysts and some of his rival banks. The article commented that Lehman Brothers was possibly cautious as a result of so recently enduring the crisis of Long-Term Capital Management.

This touched on the role of risk in an investment banker's life. In a predominantly male world, virility was measured by it. Lawrence G. McDonald, a former vice president of Lehman Brothers, in his 2009 book *A Colossal Failure of Common Sense* refers to some of the people he knew at the firm as "the most brilliant of Lehman's traders and risk takers." One danger was that the willingness to take risks could become prized above all else. Fuld had survived his risky Russian exercise and, apparently, his response had been to show restraint. Now the word was that he had to show more spirit.

Lehman Brothers' mortgage department was not doing as much as it could. It had enjoyed a large part of the market—about one sixth of the total—for most of the 1990s but had toned down its efforts. Lehman Brothers was going in for too much "plain vanilla" activity, the easy stuff, when it could get more mileage from B- and C-rated mortgages, that is to say, those made to poorer people or others with a high credit risk. By reducing its activities in such areas, chided its competitors, the firm could be cutting itself off from the growth sectors of the market.

The area of particularly strong growth was that of the so-called subprime mortgage. In spite of its name, it was very lucrative, because people who fell in the subprime category had lower credit ratings and hence paid a higher rate of interest than the average. This meant that when the mortgages were bundled together and sold to investors, those investors received more money than they would for similar investments.

One factor that inhibited mortgage activity was the interest rate on borrowed money. Alan Greenspan had begun raising the interest rate in 1999 to calm down the markets, which had been racing ahead with all the new Internet company activity. It dictated how many people took out mortgages and also how much money Lehman Brothers borrowed for its mortgage business. Lehman Brothers issued its own mortgages, as well as bought mortgages issued by other companies; all of these it bundled into bonds.

The recent repeal of the 1933 Banking Act, better known as Glass-Steagall, was a key reason for the apparent urgent demand for Dick to take more risks. The repeal had abolished the separation of commercial banks and investment banks, which left commercial banks equally at liberty to gamble with their depositors' money; they had a wealth of cash to do so.

The banking industry had poured $300 million into lobbying for the act's repeal, the main sponsor of which was Senator Phil Gramm of Texas. President Clinton stood with him as he made his speech on the occasion. The senator adapted Ronald Reagan's words—"government is the problem"—when he said, "Government is not the answer." Competition and freedom, he added, were the best things to promote economic growth.

Clinton had not liked the idea of abandoning Glass-Steagall, which for sixty-six years had done a good job protecting the popular purse. Its abolition represented a remarkable turnaround by his administration. He had come to office arguing for a review of capitalism and left it handing power to the free market. Clinton was a much weakened president. Opponents had long assailed him over lying about his sexual affair with Monica Lewinsky, a former White House intern, which had damaged his credibility.

Alan Greenspan's influence was also crucial in ending Glass-Steagall. Since 1987 he had undermined the old act by allowing commercial savings banks to devote 5 percent of their business to casino-style investment activity. By 1996, he allowed that to rise to 25 percent of the commercial banks' business, making them, in many ways, just like investment banks.

Glass-Steagall's death knell sounded with the planned formation of Citigroup, the bank that resulted from an $85 billion merger between Citicorp and Travelers Group. Citicorp was a commercial bank, and Travelers owned Salomon Brothers, the investment bank. Hence commercial bank and investment bank were to join and the merger required Glass-Steagall's repeal.

Sandy Weill was the head of Citigroup, and as a memento of a land-mark time, he kept one of the pens Clinton used to sign the bill revoking Glass-Steagall and hung it on his office wall. However, in less than ten years, Citigroup became one of the banks most badly hit by the subprime mortgage crisis of 2008, and it turned to the government for many billions of dollars in bailout money.

But in 1999, the Internet boom seemed to promise mounting prosperity. Lehman Brothers. joined in the fun with such moves as a first public launch of shares, worth $84 million, for China.com, the English-language portal in Hong Kong. At home, Lehman Brothers helped AT&T, the telecommunications giant, buy MediaOne Group for more than $60 billion.

Technology euphoria took hold with companies like Pets.com, which raised $100 million to sell cat litter online. Its sock puppet mascot was featured in an advertisement during the 1999 Super Bowl. Webvan spent $1 billion on its grocery delivery business. They and many other Internet companies would collapse very soon.

Near the end of the century, euphoria was mixed with a sense of impending disaster. Computers ran the world, and experts agonized that the system would crash at the stroke of midnight on December 31, 1999. The machines, it was claimed, could not make the transition to the new millennium and a century beginning with the numeral 2. Y2K—or the millennium bug, as it was also called—threatened to bring the apocalypse. Computer specialists ran around looking for a solution—without firm reports of their finding one.

The end of 1999 passed without catastrophic incident, and people forgot about Y2K almost as soon as they abandoned their New Year's resolutions. Yet a few weeks later, a collapse did happen: that of the Internet boom. Beginning on March 10, 2000, a stock market crash removed 80 percent of the value of technology shares, restyling many dot-com boom companies as "dot bombs." Talk of the new economy faded almost as quickly as that of Y2K.

In keeping with the forecast by Lehman Brothers analysts ten years earlier, a bear market clawed and slashed at the economy and the question was what to do about it. The visible hand of Fed chief Greenspan came into play. To alleviate the effects of the collapse, he began to cut interest rates. People, companies, and banks could borrow more cheaply and spend more freely—on mortgages, for example. Greenspan continued his interest rate reductions for several years; it was the very thing Lehman Brothers needed to rediscover its risk appetite.

The fall of 2000, meanwhile, saw the approach of America's presidential elections and more hitherto distant places dragged into the Middle East conflict. On October 12, suicide bombers linked to Osama bin Laden attacked the USS *Cole*, a destroyer that was refueling in the port of Aden in South Yemen, killing seventeen American sailors. Aden was an old coaling station abandoned by the British in 1967.

George W. Bush, the son of former president George H. W. Bush, ran for the Republicans. He had served two terms as governor of Texas. But most of the actual governing of Texas was traditionally performed by the lieutenant governor. The new president also did not have his father's feel for foreign affairs and his foreign policy had traits of old Republican roll-back theory. In his campaign, Bush called China a "strategic competitor." China had a large trade surplus with the United States, brought about by America buying a lot of Chinese goods and China not reciprocating.

Bush won a controversially close election against Clinton's vice president Al Gore. The result turned on Florida, where there were lengthy delays in completing the count. Gore was an economic interventionist, with firm ideas, for example, on the need to combat climate change. Irrespective of the closeness of the electoral result, however, the Republicans were not to be deterred from pushing government even further out of the economy than before.

The last days of the Clinton administration did little to discourage them. Congress passed more legislation freeing up the markets. The Commodity Futures Modernization Act of 2000 was again sponsored by Senator Gramm of Texas. Lawyers from Enron, the large energy company based in Houston, helped draft it. Enron chief Kenneth Lay was a friend of the Bushes and an important financial contributor to the Bush campaign. Enron traded energy and did a lot of its work on the energy futures market. One part of the new legislation, which freed this market from the strictures of regulation, became known as the "Enron loophole."

The modernization act also removed the type of market controls that had been in place since Teddy Roosevelt's time in 1908, when bucket shops were banned. The side bets on the market that bucket shops handled had played their role in the panic of 1907. The new act cleared the way for widespread use of the market side bet known as the credit default swap, which would go on to play its part in the crash of 2008.

The new president Bush was a disciplined early-to-bed early-to-rise character. A born-again Christian, he was the most avowedly religious U.S. president in many years and had passionate faith in the free market to match. He would occupy the White House during America's most unrestrained exercise in market forces since the 1920s. Both Bush and President Harding in the '20s—followed by President Coolidge after Harding's death—came to office when the United States had no visible enemies and was by far the world's strongest power. Capitalism was in charge and America's future there for the making; conversely, it was there for capitalism and the administration to ruin.

Lehman Brothers envisioned good economic prospects under Bush, particularly because of Alan Greenspan. Following the collapse of the Internet boom, some skeptics predicted a possibly serious recession in 2001, but Lehman Brothers disagreed. The Federal Reserve chief was "well aware of what's happening and he's going to do whatever it takes to make sure the economy gets back on track," said Lehman's chief U.S. economist, Stephen Slifer. More interest rate cuts by Greenspan were anticipated.

The *Financial Times* in London interviewed Jeremy Isaacs, the head of Lehman Brothers in Europe and Asia. He was expanding the bank's European operation to take advantage of the continent's new unified currency—the euro, as it turned out, rather than the monnet. In his midthirties, Isaacs was said to be the youngest person to hold such a senior position in a major bank. "The Young Turks are in command," wrote *FT* correspondent Charles Pretzlik. Isaacs's elevation meant that old-style "relationship banking" was a thing of the past. Banks' products these days were very complex and made the "execution" of them more critical than the cozy relations of yore between banks and clients.

The execution of business was indeed critical, as shown when in May 2001 the market collapsed after Gontran de Quillacq, a young Lehman Brothers trader based in London, punched the wrong figure into his computer. He typed £300 million—about $500 million—when he had intended £3 million. A rash of selling followed and removed, in seconds, many billions from the value of shares of leading British companies. The *Guardian* newspaper ascribed the mistake to "fat finger syndrome," whereby fingers strayed onto the wrong key. The advanced computer technology that Lehman Brothers had spent billions of dollars on installing had failed to detect the error.

Closer investigation showed that "program trading" was in play, as it had been in the crash of 1987. Such large sales as the mistaken £300 million were programmed to trigger automatic sales of other shares. The latter sales, therefore, were not determined by human thought and a rational assessment of a company's performance or prospects, but by numbers. The urge for fast transactions meant that technology and the occult science of numerology governed much of what the market did. In New York, reports said, program trading had grown to such an extent that it executed between a third and almost a half of all market transactions.

Dick Fuld was in a reflective mood when *FT* journalists Silverman and Pretzlik interviewed him for an article in summer 2001. They asked him about rival banks that had more capital than Lehman Brothers. His bank could count on capital of $7 billion when giants like Citigroup had ten times as much.

It was and would be forever thus, Fuld suggested. He recalled a formative moment during his early days as a trader when he had been on vacation and playing blackjack for a few dollars a hand in Las Vegas. A high roller came to the table, and every time he lost, he doubled up his bets. At first it worked, but the attaché cases of cash that he brought with him emptied through the course of the night, and he approached dawn a broken man. Witnessing the occasion turned Fuld's stomach. "I don't care who you are," he said, "you don't have enough capital."

There was no doubt that Lehman Brothers had a certain esprit de corps, said the article. Fuld's top executives shared a fraternity house familiarity, and several of them met at 6:00 A.M. each Friday morning to play basketball. A common pedigree bound them. Like Dick Fuld, many had cut their teeth as bond traders and had used their traders' instincts for being quick on their feet to assume new roles as investment bankers. "We thought a lot of this was common sense," said one of Fuld's chief market men, a matter of "knowing right from wrong."

The article sounded uncertain about the bank's future. Lehman Brothers' rate of profit was good compared with that of its rivals, which suggested it employed its capital well. But there remained "some measure of mystery in how the company does this."

Much of its income came from bets, large and small, that it made with the firm's or customers' money. As to the outcome of those bets: "[I]ts results may reflect outsized risk taking," as the article noted, "or good luck."

10

"Sad in Some Respects"

The first plane, an American Airlines Boeing 767, hit the north tower between the ninety-third and ninety-ninth floors on September 11, 2001, at 8:46 A.M. Ira Zaslow, a technical expert and assistant vice president of Lehman Brothers, had arrived at his desk at the World Trade Center headquarters at 8:00 A.M. He was a creature of habit, and at a little after eight-thirty each morning would take the elevator from his thirty-eighth-floor office to the cafeteria on the fortieth to return a few minutes later with some coffee and a muffin. Ira was trapped in the elevator when the plane hit the tower. "They did recover his body," said his son Bryan. "He died from what they called head trauma."

The one person among Lehman Brothers' employees to die on 9/11, Zaslow was fifty-five and had worked for the bank for fifteen years. He had been brought up in his early years in the Manor Avenue area of the Bronx, near Yankee Stadium, and when he was about six his family moved to Elmhurst, Queens. At the time of his death, he and Felicia, his wife of thirty-one years, lived in North Woodmere, Long Island. They had two children, Bryan and his younger brother, Adam. On the weekends Ira was an avid paddleball player, rising early to play with friends. "An argument over a foul ball? Play it over, he would say. Anything," Bryan recalled, "to play more." At other times he would stay listening to the car radio while Felicia shopped at the mall.

"My father was nothing but modesty in what he did, and one of those rare guys you learn a lot about when they're gone," said Bryan. "I've had people come up and say, 'He helped me get my first job,' or 'I didn't have the means to go to school and he helped me get a scholarship.' His was not a big, boisterous voice." The Zaslow family set up the Ira Zaslow Foundation, which helps in community works, such as providing playgrounds for local children or trips for them to places such as Walt Disney World.

The sense of shock from 9/11 was profound. The cold war had ended over ten years earlier, but here was a new madness in the world to succeed it. Al Qaeda, led by Osama bin Laden, had organized the attack, the most intricate of his plans so far. More than three thousand people had died as the attack hit the heart of America's major city and the heart of capitalism, of which the World Trade Center was a symbol. The attackers were religious fundamentalists and anti-consumerist. Some people also argued that 9/11 was an attack on the kind of world unity that globalization had brought about. The victims in the towers, for example, were of many nationalities, and they were not only bankers and stock market analysts but restaurant staff and other manual workers from places like Mexico and the countries of Central America.

Principally, it was an assault on America, and here lay the main grounds for shock. This kind of thing did not happen in the United States; it did maybe in Europe, with its wars. But the United States was a haven of peace, with a protective ring thrown around it since the Monroe Doctrine of the 1820s. It was why so many immigrants had come to America.

Lehman Brothers was the worst affected of the main banks. It lost its offices in the World Trade Center, and the collapse of the towers damaged its headquarters nearby at the World Financial Center beyond any rapid repair. Company people were on the move immediately to keep the operation going. The company had a backup technical facility in Jersey City, New Jersey, and some employees were being rushed to it by ferry only fifteen minutes after the first plane hit the trade center. Windows of the building had the doleful prospect of directly facing Ground Zero, as the ruins of the World Trade Center came to be known.

Three of the Jersey City building's five stories were rapidly transformed into emergency trading floors: two for the firm's principal business of bonds and one for shares. Lehman Brothers had its systems ready for when the bond markets resumed working again two days later. Its share traders were ready by that time too, but the New York Stock Exchange did not reopen until a day later.

As for Lehman Brothers' lack of main offices, Dick Fuld's client contacts came into use. Barry Sternlicht, in whose living room Fuld had sat in 1997 while assuring him that his ITT deal would go ahead, owned the Sheraton Manhattan Hotel on Seventh Avenue in Midtown. Lehman Brothers moved in, ripped out the beds from its 650 rooms, put in makeshift tables, and accommodated two bankers per room. One, Joseph Tibman, who later wrote *The Murder of Lehman Brothers*, said the Sheraton was a dingy place in need of a makeover anyway. Bankers putting together stock offerings and underwriting debt on their cell phones and laptop computers also occupied the cocktail lounge, the lobby, and other areas of the hotel.

During the early period after 9/11 Dick Fuld was in his element. He was all movement and action, and his performance outshone that of his banking rivals. His company had suffered bad damage, while for the other banks it was soon business as usual. Lehman's hardship was their gain, and it did not take long before they were phoning up Lehman clients and saying that Dick's firm was once again finished. Joseph Tibman records in his book that he had never really liked Fuld. Tibman was a banker, and he remembered Dick as one of the traders who had been among Lew Glucksman's people in the early 1980s who nearly ruined the firm. When you met Fuld in his office, he said, he could not maintain his gaze on the person speaking to him for longer than a few seconds before it was flitting back to the screen on his desk to catch the latest numbers.

Fuld was now a man transformed. He came to address employees from the stage in the Sheraton ballroom. Tibman said that when he had seen Fuld in the past, his face looked pale, but now he was fired up. Tibman could not recall much of what he said, such was the emotion of the moment. But he did remember his saying that "[T]hose bastards got one of us." It was that embattled "we're surrounded by enemies" sense again. Not only had Al Qaeda attacked New York, but Lehman Brothers' competitors were saying it could not survive. Somehow Fuld managed to align Lehman Brothers' cause with that of the nation. His audience came away from the speech full of admiration and convinced, said Tibman, that "Lehman's survival was now a patriotic imperative."

In the city, Mayor Rudolph Giuliani was the champion performer. He warned fraudsters collecting for bogus charities for 9/11 victims that he would catch them and they would go to jail. In spite of thousands dead and the city in mourning, unrestrained enterprise knew no bounds. On the other hand, recent events must not be allowed to stop legitimate activities, said the mayor. With the economy in shock after the outrage, people should beat the terrorists by going shopping and getting the stores moving again.

When President Bush came to speak near the rubble at Ground Zero, he had the unified spirit of the American people on his side as they willed him to provide a lead. He embraced one of the rescue workers and with the crowd chanting "USA!" he addressed them through a bull-horn: "The people who knocked these buildings down will hear all of us soon."

Two weeks later Lehman Brothers had a proper headquarters. It could not wait for its old premises to be repaired, and Morgan Stanley had a new building ready that, apparently, it could spare. Fuld bought it for $680 million, on a high-rise block on Seventh Avenue. Lehman Brothers took some criticism for moving into new headquarters and abandoning down-town Manhattan. The critics implied that the bank was fleeing Ground Zero and conceding victory to the terrorists. It refuted this. These days technology meant you could work anywhere. Midtown, any town, Wall Street "can be anyplace," said Jonathan Beyman, Lehman Brothers' chief information officer. "Wall Street is virtual."

The building was a far cry from the old days of Lehman Brothers. Where the firm had once worked from the mock classical surrounds of One William Street, this new home was hardly investment banking at all. It had LCD—liquid crystal display—screens that covered the first several floors of the building. They displayed electronic information of text, images, and moving pictures in bright colors to the passing crowds. People stopped to look up at artistic video montages, for example, of the light on a field of yellow wheat as a thunderstorm rolled in. This was Midtown eye candy, not the columns and somber facades of Wall Street.

It was a little garish by Dick's standards, but he soon had the interior decorated to his taste. The carpets and walls were painted green, the Lehman Brothers color. In some cultures green was the color of hope, in others that of envy, and in Dick's America the color of money. His employees knew he wanted them to "bleed green" for the company, and such determination was the more appropriate in these difficult times.

President Bush declared his "war on terror," and it had some unforeseen results. China became a new friend and a fan of Bush throughout his time in office. The Communist government in Beijing gained Washington's moral support in efforts to clamp down on Muslim separatists in East Turkestan in northwest China.

Within a month of 9/11, the United States hit back by bombing remote mountain regions of Afghanistan where Osama bin Laden was thought to be. By mid-November U.S. Special Forces backed by British troops had driven the ruling Taliban regime out of the capital, Kabul. In December, fighting concentrated around the Tora Bora cave complex in the White Mountains but failed to find bin Laden. He had slipped away into Pakistan to the south, or so it was believed.

As with Dick Fuld, the period after 9/11 was Bush's finest hour. The president had a 90 percent approval rating at home, while abroad there was widespread sympathy for the United States. At European soccer grounds, for example, when a minute's silence was called as a mark of respect, that silence was sometimes broken by crowds again chanting, "USA!"

Yet even at the height of his popularity, the president suffered a setback. Early December saw the collapse of Enron, a centerpiece of life in the city of Houston. Enron was meant to exemplify free market capitalism at its best. Kenneth Lay was a deeply religious man who saw the workings of economics and the heavens as moving hand in hand. The Enron case revived memories of the Teapot Dome scandal under Harding in the 1920s, when bribes had changed hands to win private companies oil concessions on federal land. No bribes appeared to be involved here, but Enron had benefited greatly from the relaxing of laws governing the supply of electricity to California.

Enron was found to have cooked the books. Much of the profit it claimed to have made was bogus and entailed illicit accountancy maneuvers with shady subsidiary companies that gave a false picture of Enron's figures. Arthur Andersen, its accountant and one of the Big Four accountancy companies in the world, went out of business as a result. Lay was found guilty of fraud and faced some twenty years in prison but died of heart disease before the court passed sentence.

With a warlike mood alive in the nation, early in 2002 Dick Fuld put his staff on a military footing. He told employees to smarten up, and banished the casual clothing codes that had slipped into practice during the Internet age. He had not been one for ROTC discipline, but these were exceptional times. "Casual Friday" became a thing of the past. "Dear Colleague," read a memo to staff, "We have decided to return to a 'formal' business dress policy . . . Business dress for men is a suit and tie, and for a woman, a suit with either a skirt or trousers, a dress, or other equivalent attire."

Dick had never liked the free and easy style, and, wrote Vicky Ward in *Vanity Fair*, Lehman Brothers had been the last of the Wall Street firms to go casual in the late 1990s. Only Joe Gregory had persuaded him, saying that he did not like it either but that "we have to do this for the younger people." Even as he agreed to it, Fuld had said, "It is a dark day for the firm." He saw the renewed dress discipline as all part of getting Lehman Brothers properly shipshape. Even some staff agreed it was a good idea, if only "to look busy." If you had a suit on, you probably had a client to visit, said one. If you did not, someone in authority might think you were underemployed and, at a tough economic time, fire you.

As for keeping everyone busy, Alan Greenspan endeavored to help. The shock of 9/11 had depressed the stock market, the Enron scandal rocked business confidence, and the country was at war. Greenspan determined that it was necessary to keep reducing interest rates in order to guarantee businesses and people at large the chance to borrow cheap money. He had started doing so after the crash of the tech boom and would continue to do so.

With more money for people to spend on things like mortgages, Dick and Lehman Brothers seized the hour. Lehman Brothers' quarterly results announced in March 2002 showed revenue from mergers and acquisitions down as companies sat out the downturn rather than engage in spending sprees to buy others, but Lehman Brothers' income from bonds backed by mortgages had jumped by 30 percent, to $681 million. Reports attributed the results to record refinancings of mortgages as people renewed or took out larger mortgages to take advantage of the lower interest rates. There was no better time than a crisis to set store by the comforts of home.

June saw the next set of figures. American businesses announce their results quarterly, a practice sometimes criticized for encouraging short-term thinking on Wall Street, but for Lehman Brothers the latest data suggested the development of a long-term trend. Earnings for investment banks in general remained down; share traders had been hit by the stock market's problems, and mergers and acquisitions experts continued to suffer a lean time. But Lehman Brothers' bond trading figures rose by 2 percent.

Dick Fuld made a statement attributing his company's good showing to the "diversity of the bank's franchise." His suggestion appeared to be that Lehman Brothers was vibrantly involved in more areas of activity than other banks. As one area suffered, therefore, another was there to take the strain—in Lehman Brothers' case, bond trading. Actually, the opposite argument was as likely to be the case. Lehman Brothers had a particular strength in mortgages and mortgage bonds, and it was these, along with Greenspan's low interest rates, that were carrying it through.

Bryan Zaslow recalled that he met Dick Fuld in the summer of 2002. It was in Fuld's office on the thirty-first floor of the company's Seventh Avenue headquarters, where with other senior members of management Fuld kept himself tucked away for most of the working day. Ordinary members of staff referred to it as "Club 31." Zaslow was invited into its exclusive surrounds, with its antiques and fine furnishings, having sought backing for the foundation his family had set up in his father's name. Lehman Brothers initially showed interest. "We sat in that room, and Dick Fuld acted as if he would do something," said Zaslow. An attorney by background, with his own business, Zaslow said he did not want handouts but support; a contribution to a fund, for example, that might see some kids through college. He made several requests and "gave several options," but after that meeting "Lehman Brothers did nothing for us. . . . I gave up." The Ira Zaslow Foundation carried on nonetheless, and among its latest projects provides scholarships for young people to attend fashion college.

Lehman Brothers' profits continued to rise dramatically during the rest of the year. December's quarterly figures showed them up by 87 percent. The financial press saw the reason: "booming bond trading."

In late 2002, Lehman Brothers won the title of "Bank of the Year," an award much valued in the investment banking world and presented by Thomson Financial, the large wealth adviser based in London and publisher of *International Financing Review* magazine. The bank had made "outstanding" progress over the year "amid extremely challenging market conditions," said Thomson Financial. Lehman Brothers was the provider of "creative, tailored solutions," had proved it could compete with the world's largest financial conglomerates, and "demonstrated that size is not everything."

Dick Fuld agreed, and in accepting the award, released a statement. "[I]t's not about playing basketball where the other banks are 7 foot and we are 5 foot," he said. "It's about brains." In little over a year Lehman

Brothers had pulled itself up and out of the rubble of 9/11, and Dick Fuld was top of the heap.

|||||||||

The debate raged throughout a good deal of 2002 and early 2003 about the Bush government's plans to invade Iraq. The administration had shifted emphasis from attempting to capture Osama bin Laden in or around the wild frontiers of Afghanistan and homed in on a longer-standing enemy of the United States: Saddam Hussein, the tyrannical leader of Iraq, whom President Bush's father had fought and beaten a decade before.

Members of George W. Bush's administration, not least Vice President Dick Cheney, made claims that Saddam had links with Al Qaeda. Beyond the fact that Saddam and bin Laden were Muslim, this was debatable. Saddam in the past had been branded as a follower of socialism, a materialist creed that in bin Laden's fundamentalist book was as devilish as American capitalism. But the Bush administration both stuck to its guns and resolved to use them.

There were other views as to what the Iraq war was about. Was it simply a matter of "regime change" and wanting to remove Saddam's ruthless dictatorship? Was it about unfinished business? President Bush's father had failed to remove Saddam, and here was his son's chance to come out of his father's shadow. Or was it just about business? Companies such as Halliburton, the Lehman Brothers protégé from the old days, which until recently had been run by Cheney, was among several companies that stood to make good money from the war. Iraq was an oil-rich Middle Eastern country.

The principal argument revolved around weapons of mass destruction, or WMD. These were anything from chemical to nuclear weaponry, and the United States and Britain both claimed that Iraq had them. Iraq had had chemical weapons in the past, but pressure from the United States and other allies since the first Iraq war had seen them dismantled. At least, that was what the weapons inspectors sent in by the United Nations said. The United States and the UK nonetheless prepared to launch their war.

An unexpected entrant into the WMD debate was Warren Buffett, one of America's leading financiers, head of the Berkshire Hathaway investment firm, and known, from his background in Nebraska, as the "Oracle of Omaha." When Buffett spoke up, the American business world listened. In his annual letter to Berkshire Hathaway shareholders, Buffett affirmed that WMD did exist, except in an unlikely location. They were, he suggested, in the U.S. economy. Buffett was speaking in metaphorical terms and in relation to derivatives, the financial instrument that had become very fashionable in recent years on Wall Street. Derivatives were the "financial weapons of mass destruction," he wrote, and carried "dangers that while now latent, are potentially lethal."

The credit default swap was one derivative that was very popular, not least because the Commodity Futures Modernization Act in 2000 had removed any risk of its being thought an illicit gamble. Mathematical experts at J. P. Morgan had invented the credit default swap a few years before, and it did have a practical use. Principally, it was an insurance policy. A bank might use it, for example, when making a loan to a company; it could insure that loan by buying a credit default swap through an insurance company, like AIG, the largest in America, or another bank, or any institution that might wish to insure the risk. The credit default swap got its name because the risk a bank took on making a loan—that is, the risk of a creditor's defaulting—could be swapped, as it were, to whatever third party wished to insure the risk.

Insurance made sense, but with another of its uses, the credit default swap idea began to go haywire. Others, too, could take out an "insurance policy" on the loan: If they thought the company taking the loan might fail to repay it, they could also pay the fee to buy a credit default swap on the loan. This was in spite of the fact that they had not made the loan themselves.

The credit default swap in such cases was not an insurance policy but a bet on the loan's failing. If a bank, or anyone else, had made a $1 billion loan and covered itself by taking out a credit default swap, and then, say, nine other people had bought credit default swaps on the possibility of the loan's failing, a situation had arisen whereby if the loan did fail, the payouts would amount to not just the $1 billion of the loan itself, but a total of $10 billion. The difference, furthermore, between the party making the loan and the nine, or however many others, making a bet on the loan was that the one that had made the loan had no interest in the loan's failing—all the others, on the other hand, wanted it to fail. These people could then take measures to try and get the loan to fail. They could simply walk around the stock market talking down the reputation of the company that had taken the loan, in the hope that confidence in the company might be damaged. Its fortunes might deteriorate to the point that it could no longer do business and repay its loans.

Another measure they could employ was that of "short selling." Short selling was gambling against a stock. Hedge funds were institutions that made a lot of their money this way. If short sellers thought a company's share price was too high—that the company, for example, might have some underlying weakness which meant that before long its share price would fall—then they set about making money from the situation. They borrowed shares of that company from institutions that were willing to lend them. Pension funds, for instance, hold large investments in company shares that they are willing to lend to short sellers for a fee. The short seller would then sell the shares on the market at the present high price and get the money. Then, when the price of the shares had fallen, he would buy them back at the new cheap price and return them to the pension fund he had borrowed them from. His profit would be the difference between the high price he first sold them for, and the low price he bought them back for—minus the fee paid to the pension fund, or whoever he had borrowed them from.

If a short seller could, by selling the shares of a company in this fashion, get others to think there was something wrong with that company, they might flock to sell the shares of the company themselves, and before long that company could be in trouble. The short seller, having bought credit default swaps as a gamble on that company's failing, could be in for making some big money.

As with the case of bucket shops before they were banned in Teddy Roosevelt's day, a lot of people were betting on the market without having a direct interest in it themselves; they were not investing in shares and providing some benefit to American industry. Their best-served interest was if the market failed.

Many buyers of credit default swaps were like vultures and hyenas on the lookout for rotting carcasses, and Buffett was perplexed. This market was unregulated and huge numbers of bets were out there waiting for an adverse event to happen. No one knew how many, but the very knowledge that they were lying in wait might be sufficient to cause that event to happen. Credit default swap enthusiasts could gamble, for example, on a bank's going bankrupt. Enough people doing this could see confidence in the bank collapse and bring about its failure. Hence these derivatives were a WMD just waiting to explode in the American economy's face. Many billions of dollars rode on the outcome. Buffett said it straight: "[T]he range of derivatives contracts is limited only by the imagination of man (or sometimes, so it seems, madmen)."

On March 20, 2003, Lehman Brothers issued details of another bravura performance, with profits for the previous quarter up by 61 percent. On the same day the Bush administration went to war in Iraq with an offensive named Operation Iraqi Freedom.

The U.S. military advanced quickly to Baghdad, leaving the British behind to occupy the port of Basra on the Shatt al-Arab. On May 1, President Bush gave the impression that the job was done. He made a speech on the deck of the warship USS *Abraham Lincoln*, reporting rapid progress in the war, while a large banner behind said "Mission Accomplished." How could this be? Saddam himself was still on the run. Jubilant Iraqis had three weeks earlier toppled his statue in the center of Baghdad, but there was presumably more to the war than that. No sign had emerged of weapons of mass destruction. Was the message possibly premature? Bush appeared to be seeing the conflict as a kind of trader's war—quick in, quick out, and you claim your bonus.

Whether in Iraq, Afghanistan, or the remote regions of Pakistan, there was also no firsthand sighting of bin Laden. Some suggested he might already be dead or holed up in a cave on a dialysis machine. He was said to have serious problems with his kidneys. He could not have gone far, so where was he?

Alan Greenspan gave the answer the following month, in a comparable fashion to Warren Buffett's identification of the whereabouts of WMD. Greenspan had lowered interest rates again, and in June 2003 they stood at one percent, their lowest in over forty years. Interest rates at one percent, allowing for a little bit of inflation, amounted to giving money away. Greenspan's efforts to keep the economy moving in such a way had taken on yet greater urgency following the trauma of 9/11. Thus, bin Laden had insinuated his way into the American economy. Nowhere yet everywhere, his influence was all around.

In the mortgage market, Lehman Brothers had been burrowing away in ways unbecoming a respectable bank. In June 2003, a jury in California found Lehman Brothers guilty of being linked to mortgage fraud.

First Alliance Mortgage Company had used high-pressure sales techniques on thousands of people to take out mortgages. Many of them were senior citizens. First Alliance had concealed high fees and charges it later demanded from them.

Lehman Brothers provided finance to First Alliance and bought the mortgages for bundling into bonds. Some seventy-five hundred aggrieved people provided testimony in the case, which had only made its way to court thanks to a concerted investigation by the *New York Times* and the ABC news program *20/20*.

An internal memorandum from the mid-1990s showed that Lehman Brothers had known for years about First Alliance's methods. It described the company as the "used car salesman" of subprime mortgages and a place where you left "your ethics at the door." The court fined Lehman Brothers $6 million.

In September a report in the London *Times* said several leading investment banks might be taking too much risk. Goldman Sachs in particular was mentioned, because its revenues in the third quarter of the year had fallen quite sharply. Each bank set a daily target of how much, in total, its traders were allowed to lose. Goldman allowed $64 million and Morgan Stanley $54 million. Lehman Brothers, their smaller rival, permitted $23 million. Shareholders had not liked the Goldman figure and sold enough of their shares to knock about $3 off the share price, to $89.57.

Goldman Sachs blamed its performance on a sharp fall of mortgage bond prices over the summer. This suggested that there were too many such bonds around and they were no longer such an attractive business line. Goldman Sachs was picking up the message that its risk activities might be better directed elsewhere, but Lehman Brothers continued unabashedly. Its bond trading revenues had leaped by 128 percent in the previous quarter. For Lehman Brothers, it was still full speed ahead in the mortgage market.

Such spirit enabled Greenspan to deliver his own mission-accomplished speech to mark New Year 2004. On the balmy West Coast, the Federal Reserve chief spoke to the American Economic Association, which was meeting in San Diego, California. "Despite the stock market plunge, terrorist attacks, corporate scandal, and wars in Afghanistan and Iraq," he said, the United States had "experienced an exceptionally mild recession." Thanks to interest rate cuts, consumer spending was rising and house prices going up quickly.

Greenspan indicated, however, that his approach during this new boom would be the same as that during the Internet boom of the 1990s: He would not intervene to hinder free enterprise while things were going nicely, but move in to alleviate problems if they were to happen. His sense was that this had all worked well so far, so why change the approach. There was one potential problem, in that businesspeople might take his words as permission to tear ahead: The central bank appeared willing to pick up the pieces afterward.

Spring saw Lehman Brothers move into new offices in Tokyo and London. Its new home in the Japanese capital was in Roppongi Hills, a development carved out of the urban heart of Tokyo with high-rise towers of offices, apartments, movie theaters and restaurants, a museum, and even—precious features in Tokyo—parks. The bank's new offices in London were amid a similarly grand design: the Canary Wharf complex in the east of London, the old renovated Docklands area that had symbolized Margaret Thatcher's dream of a free enterprise Britain rising from the remnants of empire and the years of muddling through on Western European–style socialism.

Gordon Brown, Britain's treasury secretary and future prime minister, gave a speech at the Canary Wharf occasion, which Dick Fuld had flown over to attend. "Lehman Brothers is a great company today that can both look backwards with pride and look forwards with hope," said Brown. A correspondent for the British satirical political magazine *Private Eye* filed a report and referred to Brown having droned on and on. Amid his praise for Lehman Brothers, Brown, the correspondent pointed out, made no mention of its more embarrassing business ventures, like that with Robert Maxwell.

Private Eye also reported that Lehman Brothers had been closely engaged with Enron. The subsidiary companies that Enron had set up in order to hide some of its activities and give a false view of its profits came with mysterious names like LJM2. Apparently Lehman Brothers helped Enron set up LJM2. Bethany McLean and Peter Elkind's book *The Smartest Guys in the Room* confirmed the story. Various banks, such as J. P. Morgan, Merrill Lynch, and Citigroup, provided sums of between $5 million and $15 million for the venture, keen as they were to get business from Enron. Lehman Brothers contributed $10 million.

Wall Street's leading banks came to the Securities and Exchange

Commission in August for permission to use more money. Their delegation was led by Henry Paulson, the head of Goldman Sachs, seeking a change in the rules made by the SEC on how much money the banks could borrow in order to then lend out again. Presently they had to hold $1 in reserve for every $12 they borrowed. This was in case anyone who had lent them money wanted it back—it was felt that $1 in $12 would cover that eventuality. Yet the banks complained that, when multiplied, this meant for every $12 billion they had borrowed they had to have $1 billion in their vaults that was doing nothing. They wanted a dramatic amendment in the ratio: from 12 to 1 to 40 to 1.

Paul Mason, economics correspondent of the BBC, points out that this important change in banking rules was agreed at a forty-five-minute public hearing that was neither attended nor reported by any main news outlet. The SEC approved the change. Mason adds that had it not been made, Lehman Brothers and others were unlikely to have built up the kind of debts that sank them four years later, in 2008.

Many critics have highlighted the woeful state of regulation of the banks at this time. On the one hand, Alan Greenspan was pushing ahead, making money so cheap that it was bound to fuel the mortgage market and a housing boom, which eventually could only crash. On the other, the SEC gave in to whatever the bankers wanted. These were times, however, when regulation was very much out of fashion. Greenspan, for his part, was a hands-off regulator, content to believe that participants in the marketplace would act rationally and do the right thing. The SEC, meanwhile, had only a handful of regulators—the BBC's Mason says seven—to keep watch on Wall Street's combined assets of $4 trillion.

Regulation was an undervalued vocation. An SEC regulator might earn $120,000 a year, far less than many people in the industry that he or she was there to keep a watch on. Even several years earlier, a Lehman Brothers specialist in Turkish or Scandinavian bonds could make over $1 million. A brilliant and clued-in regulator could probably find much more lucrative work by joining an investment bank. Anyone dedicated enough to public service to accept a relatively modestly paid SEC job would not only have to contend with sharp and supremely paid bankers but also their lawyers. The latter would be told to spare no expense in winning whatever issue was under discussion. Keeping tabs on the banks was nearly impossible. A regulator had to know every trick in the bankers' books, plus the new ones they invented to get around the rules. The situation in the new millennium was how the financial community had wanted it—faithfully left in their hands to regulate themselves.

In the buildup to the presidential elections of 2004, the Iraq War dragged on, with still no sign of WMD. Bush beat Senator John Kerry of Massachusetts at the polls, with strong support from a large turnout of evangelical Christians. The economy was also doing well and in this the Republicans had an unlikely ally: Communist China, already a political friend, had become an economic one too. The Chinese people were savers rather than spenders, and their country was making a lot of money in its unequal trade with the United States. But the government in Beijing was investing much of it in U.S. Treasury bonds, a low-interest but secure investment. With this money making its way back into the economy, American banks and consumers had more to borrow and spend.

After his win at the polls, the president's popularity rating began a marked decline. In January 2005 the defense department's Iraq Survey Group finally confirmed that Iraq had no WMD. It had disposed of them as long ago as the early '90s when the United Nations put sanctions on Saddam Hussein after the first Iraq war. The president's rating fell below 50 percent and then, following his handling of Hurricane Katrina in August, to 37 percent in 2006. This was as low as Harry Truman's in 1951 when the Communist scares of the McCarthy era took their toll on government popularity.

But house buyers appeared quite happy, and in spite of some rises in interest rates from their low level in mid-2003, house prices kept going up. Lehman Brothers was doing well, and Justin Schack, a writer for Institutional Investor.com, interviewed Dick Fuld for an article published in May 2005. Lehman Brothers' performance was making its competitors sit up, wrote Schack. Market experts had described some recently healthy profits declared by Goldman Sachs as "very Lehman like." Was the erstwhile chief rival of Goldman Sachs getting back on equal terms?

It had certainly made some profitable moves in mergers and acquisitions. Lehman Brothers had recently advised Kmart, the retail chain, on its $11 billion purchase of Sears, Roebuck, a famous name from Lehman Brothers' history. The Hertz Corporation also changed hands in 2005 in an operation known as a "leveraged buyout." The LBO was a technique that dated back to the 1980s and the roaring days of Milken and Boesky.

A buyer raised a large amount of debt—leverage, or borrowings—bought another company with it, and loaded the debt onto the purchased company's books. The purchased company then paid off the debt out of its future earnings; it effectively bought itself, though it had a new owner who had paid little if any of his own money to buy it. It was a smart Wall Street trick. The Hertz deal was worth $15 billion, with Lehman Brothers pocketing a substantial fee. Once upon a time, Lehman Brothers created such companies as the Hertz Corporation. Nowadays it merely traded them.

Words of praise for Dick Fuld came from Henry Kravis, one of the heads of Kohlberg Kravis & Roberts and a legend in the world of company buyouts. Once "nobody gave this guy any hope of making it," said Kravis, but Dick had "proved everybody wrong." Pete Peterson also paid his compliments. Dick had built "a new culture" at Lehman Brothers and had been "wise" in doing so, he told *Institutional Investor*.

Peterson was not one to harbor a grudge, or at least not one to air it publicly, since Fuld had been a key figure in his departure from Lehman Brothers over twenty years earlier. The Blackstone Group had done well under his and Stephen Schwarzman's leadership. Peterson had used his international connections well, especially with Japan. He had helped Sony buy Columbia Pictures, and then Bridgestone, the Japanese tire manufacturer, acquire Firestone, its American counterpart. Blackstone had built from there.

Institutional Investor's reporter threw an awkward topic into his conversation with Fuld. He recalled an incident from the early 1990s when Dick was hiking in Bryce Canyon National Park in southern Utah with a friend, James Tisch, chief executive of Loews, a corporation with interests including hotels and broadcasting. Tisch's young son Ben came along, though he suffered from asthma and had breathing difficulties on the trip. Fuld was helping to encourage the boy back up to the top of the canyon when they met a hiker on the trail. The guy commented to the effect that the boy was wheezing quite badly, which was possibly an attempt at sympathy. Dick didn't get it: "Eat shit and die!" he roared. He strode on and shouted again: "Eat shit and die!"

The young boy had seen Dick as a hero ever since, but, said *Institutional Investor*, Fuld was "uncomfortable talking about the episode." It recalled a time when he was a "younger, more impetuous man." It reminded him, in other words, of his trader days.

Euromoney heaped praise on Lehman Brothers by making it its investment bank of 2005. The magazine ran a picture of Fuld apparently debating life alongside Rudolph Giuliani. *Euromoney* mentioned that although the weight of Lehman Brothers' business was toward mortgages and bonds, it had a "conservative approach to risk management." The market had begun to suffer lately, but Lehman Brothers "hedged its exposures effectively." True to form, Dick also made sure to talk about his beliefs in the old values of banking: He wanted relationships with clients "over a long period of time," he said. "I do not want our bankers simply being in the soup sniffing around for a trade."

This was not how things were on the ground, where sales of mortgages proceeded at a rigorous pace. As in the 1840s, when Henry Lehman arrived in America, hundreds of thousands of peddlers were out on the road—some estimates said half a million in California alone. Rather than the horses and carts of Henry's day, flashy sports cars were now their chosen mode of transport. Twenty-first-century mortgage salesmen worked eighty-hour weeks and made six-figure incomes. They also had far more snazzy products than Henry's pots and pans.

No-deposit loans gave people the full price of their house. "Ninja" loans stood for "no income, no job, and no assets"; they went to people with particularly restricted means and little chance of repaying. The Hispanic community had "*fecha y firma*" loans, so named because to get one they required only a "date and signature." Some loans came with a premium: If someone wanted a mortgage for a house costing three hundred thousand dollars, he might get thirty thousand dollars added to the loan for other spending.

Subprime mortgages came with "teaser rates," very low rates of interest for the first two to three years to tempt people to take them. The rates and repayments were scheduled to jump very sharply after that time. No doubt the small print mentioned that; conceivably, the salesmen glossed over the point.

Lehman Brothers had two companies, BNC and Aurora, with branches across the country, that issued mortgages. These plus the mortgages it bought from other companies comprised the bundled bonds sold as "collateralized debt obligations," or CDOs. These might be valued at several hundred millions of dollars, or even a couple of billion, and were sliced up and sold to investors in America and the world. Banks and pension funds were keen buyers; the rates of interest on the CDOs were far higher than those of U.S. Treasury bonds and a lot of other investments. Lehman Brothers added a nice percentage fee to each slice sold.

The assumption was that the CDOs could not fail. Inevitably some people would be unable to repay their mortgages, but the probability of many people doing so at the same time was extremely low, and the risk to investors, therefore, would be dissipated. The analysts and rocket scientists within the issuing banks devised some high-technology mathematics to prove this. In some cases, their explanations spread to hundreds of pages of formulae.

Business had become so good that more and more complex investments were invented: CDOs of CDOs, or CDO squareds, as they were known, came into existence. It was similar to the period building up to the crash of 1929, when investment trusts of investment trusts, and holding companies of holding companies, provided people with new things to put their money into without their having much understanding of where they were putting it.

Lehman Brothers profited as sales of subprime mortgages doubled in 2004 and doubled again in 2005. At the turn of the millennium, the apparent value of CDO investments made of subprime mortgages had been $80 billion, which on the face of it was a substantial sum. By 2005 the figure was $800 billion.

Lew Glucksman, meanwhile, was well away from all such frenetic business activity. Dick Fuld's old mentor had found solace on the southwest coast of Ireland and he, too, had tapped into his latent Bobbie Lehman. In mid-2005 he set up the Lewis Glucksman Gallery, at University College, Cork. He also established a foundation for modern art studies. His gallery did not have the grand opening and guest list of Bobbie's wing at the Metropolitan Museum in New York thirty years earlier but did attract Mary McAleese, the Irish president, who came to open it. Next to the gallery was a gathering place for pleasant chat and banter, the Café Glucksman. On balance, it sounded more Paris than New York, and not a lot like Indianapolis. Glucksman died, presumably at peace, about a year after the opening of his gallery.

There was also some hint that Dick Fuld might be seeking his redemption in art, although it was probably a false alarm. Just across the road from Bobbie's old West Fifty-fourth Street mansion, Dick sponsored a new room at the Museum of Modern Art—the Kathy and Richard S. Fuld Gallery. Once again, it did not compare to Bobbie's wing at the Metropolitan

Museum, but it was a start. A few more years of Lehman-style success, and it would doubtless grow a lot larger. The works on show included some by the late American artist Mark Rothko. Yet was this quite Dick, or rather, Richard S. Fuld? He gave a bashful speech when MoMA held a reception marking his "advocacy of cultural and civic endeavors." His wife, to whom he was devoted, should take the credit. "Kathy loves modern art," he said, "and I love Kathy."

The housing market peaked four months later, in June, and spelled the end of any more grand artistic dreams that the Fulds might have had. House prices had more than doubled in just a few years, but interest rates had climbed to 5.25 percent. Fewer new mortgages were being taken up, and there were no easy rates to refinance old ones. Construction companies cut back house building, and mortgage companies began missing their profit targets.

Alan Greenspan sounded the alarms on derivatives, which confirmed that Warren Buffett had had a point when he had done so two years earlier. The credit default swap market was an unseemly mess of criss-crossing gambles that no one kept track of. Lots of the swaps were taken over the phone and scrawled on pieces of paper, with many written down incorrectly. Such conditions were unacceptable, complained Greenspan. Surely technology could be used to bring some discipline to the swap market. Furthermore, "the rapid proliferation of derivative products inevitably means that some will not have been adequately tested by market stress," he told a conference convened by the Federal Reserve Bank of Chicago. He meant no one knew how much money would be involved in payouts if the markets suffered a nasty jolt.

Particular worry had gathered around the prospects for the big mortgage-backed CDOs produced by Lehman Brothers and others. Experts were now putting their bets on their failing to sell to investors. Nonetheless, companies like AIG continued to sell credit default swaps at a great rate and maintain their faith in the mathematical guarantees behind the mortgage market. AIG's London office, in the posh district of Mayfair, kept up a roaring business with the hedge funds gathered in the area.

Newspapers in California and elsewhere in the United States were reporting that a large number of people were defaulting on their mortgages. After two to three years, interest rates on their mortgages had reset sharply upward and repayments doubled, tripled, or worse. People once paying fifteen hundred dollars a month might even have to find six thousand dollars. Those with no jobs had no hope of repaying. Many with jobs found their repayments were more than their monthly salaries. Some homeowners gave up, turned in their keys, and left in the dead of night.

The word soon got around. American investors began to lose interest in buying stakes in the mortgage-backed CDOs. Lehman Brothers had spent billions funding them and needed to keep selling them to stay alive. Matters reached a critical point at the time it announced its results for the year in December 2006. On the face of it, the results were good—in fact, another record. Bear Stearns, the fifth largest of the U.S. investment banks and the next one down in size from Lehman Brothers, also announced its results. Both reported increased income from bonds, with, as the *Financial Times* noted, "continued growth in Europe and Asia."

The results announcement was accompanied by a conference call, during which investors and other interested parties, such as analysts from rival banks, called in to ask questions. Lehman Brothers' conference call on December 14 saw Chris O'Meara in the chair and fielding questions. O'Meara was the firm's chief financial officer and, formerly of the accountants Ernst & Young, a hot man with numbers.

On this occasion political and diplomatic answers were more the required order of the day. The telling question came from one of the analysts employed by ancient rival Goldman Sachs. U. S. investors were surely shying away from the mortgage bond market, so what percentage of that line of Lehman Brothers' business, asked the Goldman Sachs person, was "now derived from outside the U.S. versus in the U.S.?"

O'Meara could not avoid the answer. "[I]t is an increasing percentage," he admitted, though he added, in an effort at defiance, that it was one "we intend to keep growing."

There'd be little chance of that. Lehman Brothers' mortgage business had over the last few years taken advantage of senior citizens, people with low incomes, and now unsuspecting foreigners. Give a little time for them to wise up, and the mainstay of Lehman Brothers' living would be dead.

||||||||||

Dick Fuld prophesied the crash that led to Lehman Brothers' demise. He did this well over a year before on a mountaintop in Switzerland, in Davos, the exclusive skiing resort where in January each year Masters of the Universe meet at the World Economic Forum. In between raucous parties, they hold conferences and seminars to give the occasion an air of serious purpose.

The forum in 2007 had been especially lively, as the champagne flowed in celebration of the booming markets. Dick Fuld arrived in a brooding mood, however, his brow tightly knit. Andrew Gowers, his chief communications officer and former editor of the *Financial Times*, had organized a private lunch for him with newspaper editors. It was a background briefing, an exchange of views among opinion makers rather than one designed to evoke sensational headlines, and Dick chose as his theme risk in the modern world of finance.

"This could be the year," he said, "when the markets crack." Fuld did not speak in his customary staccato or barking tones, but softly. There might be trouble from the American housing market. There was an excess of leveraged finance—everyone was borrowing too much. Oil prices were rapidly rising. Any one of these things could cause a major problem and, indeed, all three could combine.

Lehman Brothers would stick to its tradition of strong risk management. It had "taken a bit of money off the table," Fuld said, a phrase taken to mean that he was reining back and gauging each step. His audience departed, said Gowers, "visibly impressed at the apparent prescience of Wall Street's senior statesman."

The reason for Fuld's mood became clearer next month when HSBC declared losses of $11 billion on its mortgage business. HSBC, formerly known as the Hongkong and Shanghai Banking Corporation, was one of the largest banks in the world, its roots in the wealth of the old British families that prospered after the opium wars of the 1840s, when Britain seized Hong Kong from China. For many years before the territory passed back to China in 1997, HSBC acted as the central bank of Hong Kong, where it was known as "The Bank." It had been caught in the subprime mortgage crisis after it bought a housing finance company in Chicago. HSBC now recognized that it was time to come clean about its mistake and get back to serious banking.

The stock exchange in China reminded HSBC of its wider responsibilities when, on hearing the news of its losses, the market plunged dramatically for a day. Furthermore, if a global bank like HSBC knew about the subprime crisis, it was clear that the word was out to the world.

As for Dick Fuld taking money off the table, he certainly did so in a personal sense. An announcement said he had been paid $40 million for his 2006 performance. Joe Gregory received $35 million. In investment bankers' terms, Fuld may have felt that he was tightening his belt. Lloyd Blankfein, head of Goldman Sachs, received $54 million.

Otherwise he showed no obvious sign of restraint. Dr. Henry Kaufman, a Lehman Brothers board member, later told the U.S. Bankruptcy Court investigating the causes of Lehman Brothers' demise that at a board meeting in March 2007, the bank's management told the board that in spite of trouble in the subprime market, "the current distressed environment provides substantial opportunities." As a result, Lehman Brothers decided to embark on a "countercyclical strategy"; in other words, with the market turning down, to plunge into it in the expectation of rich pickings. Dr. Kaufman had had a lengthy career on Wall Street, where he had been a managing director of Salomon Brothers and earned a reputation for caution. Such qualities at this time, however, did not seem to have much influence.

Fuld did face considerable unrest in the ranks. Mike Gelband, one of his chief bond experts, had been twenty-six years at the firm and, according to Lawrence McDonald's *A Colossal Failure of Common Sense*, had urged Fuld for some time to cut back on big spending projects. One obstacle, said McDonald, was Gregory, Dick's chief henchman, who wanted "risk, more risk." Gelband felt Gregory and Fuld were out of touch and out of their depth: "Mike Gelband thought Dick Fuld was thick. And he believed Joe Gregory was, if anything, thicker."

Fuld chided Gelband for his caution. "You don't want to take a risk," Fuld told him, which in a trader's world was one of the worst things anyone could say. Gelband left the company in May.

Fuld was soon on his travels again, this time to the sands of Dubai in the Persian Gulf, where in June, Lehman Brothers opened a new office. His mood was quite different from that of a few months earlier. Where he had been so down in the Alps, he was now up in the desert: Oil riches gushed hundreds of billions of dollars into the Middle East, and emerging nations like Dubai had plenty to spare. It all pointed to plentiful cash available on the financial markets and scope for yet more huge borrowings. Fuld's vision, said communications chief Gowers, was of an "almost limitless pool for investment banks like Lehman to swim and prosper in."

What also accounted for his mood was that Dick had just embarked on a major deal that was going to transform the fortunes of Lehman Brothers. With subprime doomed, he had looked to his commercial property guru Mark Walsh to rescue the situation. Walsh had duly delivered a deal to buy the Archstone-Smith Trust, a property company. It owned a large portfolio of apartments in some of the most desirable neighborhoods of America's major cities. Archstone cost $15 billion. Lehman Brothers' capital base, meanwhile, was only $20 billion. This was Dick Fuld engaged in his countercyclical strategy.

Archstone was going to put him back on a level with his old adversary, Pete Peterson. Fuld may have treated Peterson's exit from Lehman Brothers over twenty years earlier with indifference, but he watched him closely now. Peterson was eighty years old and flourishing. Blackstone was due later in the month to be floated on the stock market, and Peterson about to make substantial wealth from his share of the company—about $1 billion after tax.

Peterson and Stephen Schwarzman were enjoying themselves, and in February, Schwarzman's sixtieth birthday party had made the press. He had hired Rod Stewart to entertain the gathering, along with the singer Patti LaBelle and the Abyssinian Baptist Choir. True to name-dropping form, Peterson recorded in his memoir that he had sat at the same table as Jack Welch, head of General Electric.

A few days before the party, Blackstone had sealed its own major property deal. It had bought Equity Office Properties, which owned large and high-class office towers. The contract was worth $36 billion, one of the biggest of its time, and led *Fortune* magazine to call Schwarzman the "new king of Wall Street." In April, Peterson and Schwarzman had rapidly followed up and "stunned Wall Street," noted the *Financial Times*, with a string of lucrative deals to sell several of the Equity office towers.

This was the kind of fast, highly profitable arrangement that Dick Fuld wanted. Lehman Brothers had lately been involved in a veritable hodgepodge of moves: Eagle Energy of Houston, International House of Pancakes, the Home Depot chain. Oil, pancakes, home improvement— Lehman Brothers snapped up deals. It bought hedge funds. At the end of 2006 Lehman Brothers' borrowings amounted to some $480 billion, about thirty-two times its capital.

Such free-spending practices would have been unheard-of in the old days; when Lehman Brothers launched its One William Street Fund in 1958, for example, it had assured shareholders that one third of the fund would remain untouched in the firm's coffers to act as a reserve.

Now, that would have been regarded as absurd. All money should be out making more money, which, in theory, was a highly efficient formula for exploiting what you had. In practice, it was fine-tuned to the point of disaster. Bobbie Lehman would have known this as an owner of pedigree racehorses: They achieved top performance but were so highly bred that if something upset them at the starting gate, they'd buck and lose every bit of money you put on them. They were skittish, temperamental, and had scant resilience to shocks. As Dick Fuld once said of his own world, surprises can kill you. At thirty-two dollars borrowed for every one dollar of its own, Lehman Brothers was very delicately poised if anything went wrong.

Dick thought he should do better than Pete Peterson. And with the fall of subprime, Mark Walsh was about the last card he had left to play. With prices on the commercial property market running very high, Walsh had done some other big deals of late. Lehman Brothers had made a splash abroad and bought Coeur Défense, the glass tower complex of modern offices in La Défense, the prestigious area near the heart of Paris. A subsidiary of Goldman Sachs sold it to Lehman Brothers for nearly $3 billion, thus making a profit of $1 billion over the three years it had owned the property.

Fuld wanted yet more deals, hence Walsh found him Archstone, and everyone agreed that it was a good move at the time. There was, however, only one problem. It turned out that Fuld had bought at the top of the market, where Peterson had sold at exactly the right time. Soon commercial property prices also took a nosedive. In the period to come, the bank would need all the cash it could muster, but Archstone stayed stuck on its books, dragging it toward bankruptcy. It was, said one executive later, the "worst deal Lehman Brothers ever made."

In the summer Lehman Brothers helped spark the panic known as the "credit crunch" when it shut down BNC, its subprime mortgage company, which was heavily in the red. People began to take full account of the gravity of the mortgage crisis. Credit dried up as the banking system seemed to run out of money. All banks need to lend to each other—short-term loans that get them through the night or the weekend and enable them to do their hour-by-hour business. None would lend now except at high rates. The toxic mortgages were out in the world in the poisonously bundled CDOs. Rather than dissipate the risk, the CDOs had sent it to investors all over the world. The magic formula had not predicted that so many bad mortgages could happen all at once. Since all the banks were involved in the business, each feared it might be lending money to a fellow bank that was about to go bust.

In Britain such a bankruptcy nearly happened. Northern Rock, the UK's fifth-largest mortgage lender, faced collapse. Once an aggressive lender, it ran out of cash and had to go to the Bank of England for salvation. Lines formed outside its offices as depositors rushed to get their money, conjuring images of the 1929 Wall Street crash. Eventually the British government took it over. Like Lehman Brothers, Northern Rock traced its roots to the mid-nineteenth century, when it was formed as a savings institution for working-class families. It had also lately lapsed into subprime, though in a more discriminating way than Lehman Brothers. Northern Rock would not deal with the riskiest subprime mortgages—it would give them, but then, under an agreement between the two companies and for a fee, sell them to Lehman Brothers, which was willing to take them.

Somehow, in spite of its problems, Lehman Brothers kept declaring good quarterly results. How did it do this when others—Bear Stearns, Morgan Stanley, Citigroup—were taking huge losses? Chris O'Meara spoke up again to say it was all because of good "risk management." In December he became the bank's global head of risk management, his place as chief financial officer taken by Erin Callan, one of the few women on Wall Street in such a high position.

In January 2008, Lehman Brothers announced more excellent results. Its earnings for the year just ended had reached a record of more than $4 billion with the bank's capital at $30 billion. Its share price stood at over $65. Yet just eight months later Lehman Brothers' share price would be down to $4, as the bank filed for bankruptcy with debts of over $700 billion.

Andrew Haldane, the director for financial stability at the Bank of England, later pointed out that Wall Street banks, in effect, had no risk management at all. They had become dangerously dependent on one form of business—their mortgage bond business. If anything went wrong with it they risked not only individual bankruptcy but also blowing up the entire system. "In just about every non-financial discipline—from ecologists to engineers, from geneticists to geologists—this evolution would have set alarm bells ringing," said Haldane. In banking, it did not.

Paul J. Davies, capital markets correspondent for the *Financial Times,* pursued Haldane's ecological point. In an article entitled "Banking's Banana Skin" in April 2009, Davies compared the subprime crisis to the days of the old United Fruit Company, one of Lehman Brothers' most famous clients in Bobbie Lehman's time. Like the United Fruit of yore, investment bankers claimed to be superefficient; in their case, they regularly culled their staff to keep expenses down, and had every last borrowed dollar out earning more money. Yet, as with the the fruit company, which had efficiently produced only one type of banana that then fell victim to a killer disease, they had developed into a monoculture vulnerable to the ultimate inefficiency of collapse. Bankers, in short, were bananas.

Bear Stearns marked the beginning of the end. The fifth-largest of the investment banks collapsed in March 2008, though the U.S. government saved it with a bailout package and a hasty merger with J. P. Morgan. Bear Stearns, which had survived the crash of 1929, was grossly overexposed on subprime mortgages, and the cry went around Wall Street: "Who's next?" Lehman Brothers, the fourth-largest investment bank, was the prime candidate.

Fuld was in India on a business trip and aboard one of Lehman Brothers' aircraft preparing to return when a phone call from Henry Paulson, by now George Bush's treasury secretary, informed him of the emergency. Fuld asked Paulson if he could expedite his journey by getting the plane clearance to fly over restricted Russian airspace. The treasury secretary said even he would be unable to do that.

In the Canary Wharf office in London, Andrew Gowers was phoning investors, journalists, and "anyone who would listen" to reassure them that Lehman Brothers was all right. Jeremy Isaacs, his boss, however, came through on the internal speakerphone. "I don't think we're going bust this afternoon, but I can't be one hundred percent sure. . . . A lot of strange things are happening." Gowers sensed the temperature in the room drop by several degrees.

In New York, the authorities rallied to help. The Federal Reserve said it would lend money to firms engaged in such things as bond selling. This facility was open to all, but some referred to it as the "Save Lehman Act of 2008." The Fed telephoned around to Lehman Brothers' rival banks telling them not to say or do anything in the market that could damage the firm. Its competitors saw the sense of the warning. "[W]e don't want another run on a bank," said one.

Paulson offered informal advice to Dick Fuld. A little after the Bear Stearns collapse the two had dinner together, at which Paulson suggested Lehman Brothers needed a partner to put in capital, or to even buy the bank outright. Paulson, who during his Goldman Sachs career had developed good contacts in China, said Dick might find interest in Asia. Reports of the meeting say Fuld was not inclined to accept Paulson's counsel: "Don't tell me how to run my bank." Maybe this was how Lehman Brothers' partners in the old days of lunch at Delmonico's routinely got along with their Goldman Sachs counterparts. For Dick's part, it was an undiplomatic way to deal with a treasury secretary, especially one who was trying to help.

Over the next few months Fuld failed to grasp that his options for survival were steadily narrowing. He seemed to grab the wrong end of the stick on several occasions in his dealings with Paulson. After the dinner he e-mailed Lehman Brothers' legal director, Thomas Russo, giving the impression that Paulson was fully behind Lehman Brothers. "We have a huge brand at Treasury," as Dick put it. Paulson said later that he had told Fuld that Lehman Brothers' existence would be in jeopardy if he did not have a buyer and a definitive survival plan. Fuld said he did not recall the warning.

Fuld wasted a lot of time railing against short sellers. They began to sell Lehman Brothers' shares at a quick pace after the collapse of Bear Stearns. Fuld was not alone in his anger. John Mack of Morgan Stanley, deeply affected by subprime, also attacked the short sellers. Fuld's rhetoric, however, was unparalleled: "When I find a short seller," Fuld said, "I want to reach down, tear his heart out, and eat it before his eyes." Bobbie Lehman would never have spoken like this. Banker Dick had reverted to Trader Dick again. The point he overlooked was that the short sellers were acting entirely within the rules of the free market game. Fuld seemed to have developed a view that he was exempt from them.

The short sellers soon came out into the open. David Einhorn, who had his own hedge fund, Greenlight Capital, was the most prominent.

Einhorn homed in on the Lehman purchase of Archstone, a much over-valued asset, he pointed out, now that very few people were buying in the commercial property market. It gave a false picture of Lehman Brothers' real worth.

As Einhorn said further, there were "a lot of concerns" about Lehman Brothers and its uncanny ability to provide endlessly good results. Speaking to the Ira W. Sohn Investment Research Conference in New York in May 2008, he described the bank's figures as "incredible," in the derogatory sense of the word. When he had asked for clarification on points of detail, he had not received plausible explanations.

Those who doubted Lehman Brothers' figures would eventually feel justified by the report of Anton Valukas, the official examiner appointed to investigate the bankruptcy of Lehman Brothers. Stretching to over two thousand pages and released in March 2010, the report stated that the bank had used mysterious accountancy methods to shift awkward figures off its books. One such was known within the company as Repo 105 and enabled Lehman Brothers to move amounts of up to $50 billion off its accounts for just enough days to get through the end of a quarter and appear healthier than it really was. Valukas concluded that the manipulation was "intentional" and for "deceptive appearances."

The question arose as to how much Dick Fuld knew about it. Bart McDade, a leading executive, said he had e-mailed details of Repo 105 to Fuld and later shown him how it was used. The Valukas report's findings brought back memories of Enron. Was this normal tinkering with accounts or worse? "I don't think it's just financial engineering, I think it's cooking the books," said Lynn Turner, the former chief accountant of the SEC. "It is amazing to me that we're back here again."

As the *Financial Times* said of the Valukas report, the Lehman Brothers it portrayed was not the "successful upstart presided over by an aggressive but inspirational Mr. Fuld that has become part of industry lore." On the contrary, it showed an organization "prepared to take short cuts and huge risks" and where control was "sorely lacking."

Matters had become so bad for Lehman Brothers that nothing was able to paint a cheery picture of its figures in June. It reported a loss for the quarter of $2.8 billion, its first-ever deficit since it had reemerged as an independent firm in 1994. Joe Gregory resigned. Erin Callan quit after only six months in her job as the firm's chief of finance. Given that she could hardly have been responsible for Lehman Brothers' subprime problems, her departure suggested that Wall Street had not adjusted to the idea of women in leading jobs. Bart McDade took over from Gregory. Some of Fuld's top bankers insisted that he should not resign, apparently still convinced that without Dick there was no Lehman Brothers.

By now press comment was almost entirely negative. "It's hard to see where Lehman Brothers fits in," said one analyst. "When you have a pack of dinosaurs, the slowest gets picked off," said another. The London *Sunday Times* ran a picture of a snarling King Kong superimposed over a backdrop of the New York skyline. This was not a reference to the old Lehman Brothers role in the iconic film of 1933 but to Dick Fuld's "Gorilla" tag.

On September 11, another anniversary of Henry Lehman's arrival in America, J. P. Morgan, the bank that lent Lehman Brothers the money to manage its day-to-day affairs, demanded $5 billion as extra collateral. Fuld was barely able to find it and the view took hold that his bank was doomed. Jeffrey Sonnenfeld, of the Yale School of Management, contrasted Fuld's lingering on in his job with that of the late talk show host Johnny Carson, who fronted the *Tonight* show between 1962 and 1992. "Johnny Carson knew how to walk out at the top," said Sonnenfeld. "Guys in finance don't seem to know that."

Hopes for a foreign buyer had disappeared. The Korea Development Bank had shown interest until early September, but then, having taken full account of Lehman Brothers' books, cooled to the idea of a deal. There was always some doubt about how hard Fuld was looking for a buyer. He had been against the idea of selling the firm in Glucksman's day and, according to some sources, had recently said, "I will never sell this firm." When in the summer a Korean delegation visited, Dick was reported to have bargained hard, as if all the cards were in his hand. Investors from China had discussions, but nothing came of them. The *Financial Times* was pessimistic: "[I]f you cannot cut a deal with Asia's government-backed investors, alternatives look scarce."

The *New York Times* had reported on September 10 that even the government might not be able to help. After the Bear Stearns collapse in March, the general feeling around Wall Street was that Washington would not let a bank fail. That assumption came under review as a result of events involving the large mortgage companies Fannie Mae and Freddie Mac. Chartered by the government, they had been left in an awful state by the subprime crisis; Paulson ordered that the government would assume more control over them and removed their bosses. By now, said the *New York Times*, Washington might have just too much on its plate to get involved with anyone else.

Paulson convened a meeting of the leading banks for the weekend of September 13 and 14 at the New York Federal Reserve to sort out the Lehman Brothers crisis. Among those present were Mack of Morgan Stanley and Blankfein of Goldman Sachs. Others included Citigroup's chief Vikram Pandit and J. P. Morgan's Jamie Dimon. The uncertainty over the future of Lehman Brothers had to be brought to an end. Its shares had nearly been wiped out in heavy selling, and when the markets opened again on Monday, there was every chance it would just be driven out of business.

Some seventy-five years earlier, in 1933, Lehman Brothers almost certainly would have won a favorable deal. Herbert Lehman understood from the failure of the Bank of United States in 1930 the draining effect of a bank collapse on confidence in the economy as a whole. He had fought to reopen as many banks as possible after his and President Roosevelt's enforced "bank holiday" in 1933, and the system had revived.

Now, ironically, it was Herbert Lehman's family bank that was up for judgment, but the situation was quite different from that in 1933. The Bush administration was the most committed to the free market since Ronald Reagan. At the same time, a line was forming of banks or other financial companies that were in trouble. Principal among them was AIG. Thanks to the bets it had taken on the fate of the large mortgage-backed bonds—now failing at a rapid rate—AIG already faced payouts of $20 billion. There was no telling where this crisis might stop.

Paulson arrived in New York in a mood to draw the line. The presidential election campaign between Senators Barack Obama and John McCain was in full swing, and Congress members up for election were facing questions from their constituents about banks being bailed out while other companies and people had been led to believe over the past thirty years that free enterprise principles should prevail. As Paulson recorded in his memoir, *On the Brink*, President Bush himself at the time of the Bear Stearns crisis had said to him, "We're not going to do a bailout, are we?"

There was no Dick Fuld at the meeting. "Dick is in no condition to make any decisions," the treasury secretary informed the heads of the banks. Fuld, he said, was "in denial," and "dysfunctional." Paulson had let it be known that Fuld was not wanted there, and McDade attended in his place. Various reports suggest that Fuld by now had lost his authority at Lehman Brothers. The argument, however, was academic—Lehman Brothers itself had no authority and was beholden to what happened at the meeting.

Paulson said there would be no deals involving further government money. The bankers would have to sort things out themselves on that score. Two deals to which they could lend their financial assistance had initially seemed possible. Fuld, *in absentia*, held out late hopes of a sale of Lehman Brothers to Bank of America, which was one of the possibilities in the cards. Barclays, the British bank, was also interested, and had sent representatives to the meeting.

Shortly before the meeting started, however, Paulson had spoken on the phone to Bank of America's chief, Ken Lewis, and learned that he was not interested in taking over Lehman Brothers. John Thain, the head of Merrill Lynch, had already excused himself from the gathering and offered Lewis and Bank of America a deal to buy Merrill Lynch. Thain later said he realized that whatever happened to Lehman Brothers, Merrill Lynch, which was also in a parlous state as far as subprime mortgages were concerned, was probably the next in line to fail.

Fuld peppered the meeting with phone calls from his thirty-first-floor redoubt at Lehman Brothers headquarters, with a mix of suggestions and pleas for help, all of which were ignored. He made several despairing calls to the home of Ken Lewis in Atlanta, unaware that Bank of America had a merger in the making with Merrill Lynch. Donna, Lewis's wife, finally told Fuld to stop calling, saying if her husband wanted to speak to him, then he would do so.

The possibility of a Barclays deal lingered on for much of the weekend but disappeared when the bank said it would need to get confirmation of support from its shareholders in London. This would not be possible until the following week, by which time Lehman Brothers would have already died at the hands of the stock market. The UK government, fur-thermore, would make no guarantees of financial support for the deal. Paulson aired his views on the subject in the meeting. "[T]he British," he said, "screwed us."

There were, and remain, alternative views, some particularly with regard to the attitude of the other banks. None made any decisive move to devise a rescue plan for Lehman Brothers, along the lines, for example, of the deal that had bailed out Long-Term Capital Management ten years earlier. Resentful memories may have lingered of Fuld's refusal to join that rescue to the extent of its fellow banks. There is also the point that the disappearance of Lehman Brothers offered the prospect of more business for everyone else. One of its senior overseas executives, who preferred to remain unnamed, later offered this straightforward view: "They were happy to get rid of a competitor."

Harvey Miller of Lehman Brothers' bankruptcy lawyers, Weil Gotshal & Manges, was called to the Federal Reserve's offices on the Sun-day afternoon. Miller, in his midseventies, born in the week in March 1933 when Roosevelt came to office and one of the most experienced bankruptcy lawyers in New York, assumed it was a "fire drill." Like almost everyone else, he imagined that Lehman Brothers would not be allowed to die.

For its failures, however, it was to be banished from the fold. About twenty-five officials from the Federal Reserve, the Treasury, and the SEC were present, and in the evening Miller and a colleague from his firm were instructed to leave and prepare the bank's bankruptcy petition. Miller protested, unable to believe what he was hearing: "This will cause finan-cial Armageddon," he said. Nonetheless, they were ordered to go: "They basically threw us out." On his way down in the elevator, he said, "I think they don't like us."

Back at the Lehman Brothers offices, at street level all was pandemon-ium, with crowds of media people in the streets and Lehman Brothers employees removing personal belongings from their offices. On the thirty-first floor Fuld was distraught: "I guess this is good-bye."

It was in the early hours of Monday, September 15, by the time Miller had prepared the petition, and, as he recalled, very dark out-side. The final act required sending an e-mail. "[I]t was the end of an institution which was one of the originators of Wall Street," Miller observed, "and here it was all coming to an end by pressing a button on a computer."

It was, as he said, "sad in some respects."

|||||||||

A few days later the *Jewish Daily Forward* ran a piece about present-day members of the Lehman family and their reactions to the collapse of the bank. "The Lehmans?" asked the headline. "They've Moved On. Sad? A Little."

The writer of the story, Marissa Brostoff, had spoken to various members of the clan, most of whom seemed to be living very well, in part from their own efforts but also to a great extent because of the legacy of their wealthy ancestors. They felt no great affinity with the company that had just gone under. The subhead of the article read "Troubled Bank Is No Longer the Family's Business."

Mayer Lehman, who had fled as a political exile from Europe in the 1850s, alone had six hundred descendants. They held periodic get-togethers, one of which had been in Bobbie Lehman's wing of the Metropolitan Museum of Art. The *New York Times* could be guaranteed to show up to take the pictures.

They led an aristocratic life: John Loeb, for example, seventy-eight, and a great-grandson of Mayer, had been an American ambassador to Denmark and celebrated a recent birthday at Winston Churchill's ancestral home of Blenheim Palace in England. His children, like Russia's last czar and czarina, were named Nicholas and Alexandra. The Lehmans had intermarried with other great New York Jewish families, such as the Guggenheims and the Schiffs. (Although giving the children the same names as the Russian royal family might not have pleased the late Jacob Schiff.) They had also crossed the WASP divide and married into such families as the Vanderbilts.

Loeb said that as far as he knew, only one family member had remained working for the bank until the end, and that was his son, Nicholas, now thirty-three, who had been at its office in Palm Beach, Florida. Robert Bernhard, the last Lehman to be a partner, had retired in 1973. He kept in touch with clan members and their friends by way of occasional attendance at Temple Emanu-El and the Harmonie Club in

Manhattan. The Harmonie was one of the clubs founded by German Jews as alternatives to the WASPs' country clubs from which they were excluded.

Stephen Birmingham, not a family member but a good friend, did wax lyrical about the old days. He remembered the restaurant at One William Street, "the waiters with white gloves," the choice of steak or lobster, a fabulous view of the river, and the elevator operator who when you walked in the door would say, "Welcome to Lehman Brothers."

His sentiments were supported at least by one member of the family. Wendy Lehman Lash was the granddaughter of Herbert Lehman and daughter of Peter Lehman, who had been killed in World War II when she was only a baby. "It's very sad," she said, "to see the family name go down the drain."

Lehman Brothers was like a Zelig of modern American history. It had been present at almost all of the momentous occasions. It was indeed sad that it should be present at this one. Lehman Brothers in the end had turned out to be less like Dick Fuld's "mother ship" than Herman Melville's *Moby-Dick*, the white whale of legend. Mortally wounded, it turned and rammed the American ship of state. In the whirlpool that it created it took almost everything with it. President Bush, who by this time enjoyed about as much popularity as Dick Fuld, found the words for the moment. They could have come straight from Melville himself: "[T]his sucker could go down."

Predictably, with Lehman Brothers' summary passing, the confidence drained from the system. AIG, plus several banks riddled with the consequences of toxic mortgage debt, had to be saved. Lehman Brothers' ancient ally and rival Goldman Sachs came out of it best, and from the huge bailout package rapidly thrown together by the government, received a healthy amount of billions to cover the bets it had made with AIG on the collapse of the mortgage market, and that AIG itself was unable to pay.

With all banks clinging to whatever cash they had, companies around America and the world could not borrow the money they needed to live on a daily basis. Stock markets collapsed. Whole countries threatened to follow: Ireland, Iceland, Hungary, Ukraine—the crisis even reached out to the Central Asian republics. Huge bailouts and economic "stimulus" programs had to be put in place to keep the system alive. The eventual bill remains incalculable, although at present estimates it will dwarf the cost of many New Deals and Marshall Plans.

In the financial press the phrase "since the collapse of Lehman Brothers . . ." still turns up in articles on a daily basis. It marks a key point in history, the end of a spectrum that began with the fall of the Berlin Wall nearly twenty years earlier and during which the free-market experiment was handed every chance to succeed. The bank's end marked the restart of the debate on how much the system needed regulating, a discussion that will continue, and possibly rage, for several years yet.

As the family indicated, there were really two quite different Lehman Brothers histories. The Lehman Brothers of the early days built and invested and developed the wealth that it had enjoyed. It dealt in solid things, materials that could be seen and touched. You could not fault it as far as risk taking was concerned; its founders crossed half the world under treacherous conditions to get where they were. Lehman Brothers was built with consistency and flair. Its imagination rarely wandered, however, from a calm assessment of the realities and the people it was dealing with. Lehman Brothers of this era spent its own money, not that of other people. It developed a high reputation for public service and was at the forefront of America's growing prosperity and reputation around the world.

From around one of the high points of American history—the moon landing of 1969—Lehman Brothers entered its second phase, and one of decline. Short-term thinkers seized control. It moved away from productive enterprises and businesses of substance and did not much care who it exploited as it developed a talent for fast talk and deceit. Lehman Brothers took excessive risks and betrayed all principles of financial good sense. Fatefully, it moved into bogus products like toxic mortgage bonds.

This was all far away from how it started. Henry Lehman came on a boat from Europe with his experience of the world and to help build America. He dealt and peddled on the byways of the South with honesty and the things that people wanted. Much later, the business he founded strayed from these first principles. Lehman Brothers died when, over 150 years on, a once proud institution was caught peddling junk to the world.

ACKNOWLEDGMENTS

Special thanks to: Sally (Holloway) for the idea and her encouragement, to Zoe (Pagnamenta) for her great support, and to Felicity, Michele, and all in the Felicity Bryan office; to Brooke (Carey) at Portfolio for her much valued advice and patient editing; to Bhavna (Patel) and Peter (Cheek) in the *Financial Times* Library for their invaluable help; to Marie for listening, advising, and keeping me going, and to Alex and Pepito for always being there; to my mother and Maria for their help throughout the years and Marie I for her concern and contribution to the editing; to Bill, Sue, and the boys for their enthusiasm; to Gary (Basralian) for his wise counsel and hospitality; to Stephen Glass for his assistance and Mateja Osonjački for her willingness to help. Among colleagues at the *Financial Times,* special thanks go to Paul J. Davies, Gary Silverman, Francesco Guerrera, and John Plender, but also to all those others on both the editing and writing staffs whose work I am fortunate to be closely in touch with and who steadfastly monitor the follies of the financial community.

NOTES

A Note on Sources

A number of sources were invaluable in preparing this book. Principal among them were the following: *Lehman Brothers: A Centennial*, a short history produced by Lehman Brothers in 1950; the late Allan Nevins's biography of Herbert Lehman, *Herbert H. Lehman and His Era*, published in 1963; the late Joseph Wechsberg's *The Merchant Bankers*, from 1966; Stephen Birmingham's *Our Crowd*, first published in 1967; Robert P. Ingalls's *Herbert H. Lehman and New York's Little New Deal*, published in 1975; *Greed and Glory on Wall Street: The Fall of the House of Lehman* by Ken Auletta, which appeared in 1986; *The Lehmans: From Rimpar to the New World: A Family History* by the German writer Roland Flade, published in 1996; *Lots of Lehmans: The Family of Mayer Lehman of Lehman Brothers Remembered by His Descendants*, edited by Kenneth Libo, published in 2007; the archives of Lehman Brothers held by the Baker Library at the Harvard Business School; the newspaper archives of the *Financial Times*.

Chapter 1: Alabama Fever

1   **"Delicious was the sight of the land"**: Roland Flade, *The Lehmans: From Rimpar to the New World: A Family History* (Würzburg, Germany: Konigshausen and Neumann, 1996), p. 43.

5   **"generally defective in size, arrangement"**: See "The Tenement as History and Housing," by Ruth Limmer and Andrew S. Dolkart, Tenement Museum, Thirteen/WNET New York, www.thirteen.org/tenement/eagle.html.

5   **"Lehman Sisters"**: Letter, *Financial Times*, May 21, 2009.

7   **In 1829 Gottfried Duden**: Flade, p. 38.

7   **a new Jewish periodical**: Ibid.

8   **Leopold Sonnemann**: *Frankfurter Zeitung*, Ibid.

10 **"[S]tarting on foot showed a certain physical stamina"**: Stephen Birmingham, *Our Crowd: The Great Jewish Families of New York* (London: Futura, 1985), p. 51.

10 **"the Harvard Business School of that day"**: Kenneth Libo, ed., *Lots of Lehmans: The Family of Mayer Lehman of Lehman Brothers Remembered by His Descendants* (New York: Center for Jewish History, 2007), p. 4.

11 **"white visitor [had] a status of equality"**: Oscar Straus, quoted in Flade, p. 45.

12 **"crowded, hub to hub"**: *Lehman Brothers: A Centennial* (New York: Lehman Brothers, 1950), p. 2.

15   **"our little monk":** Birmingham, p. 52.

15   **"There is money to be made here":** Ibid.

15   **"[n]o Jewish community was there":** Flade, p. 47.

17   **"the *Neue Fränkische Zeitung*, the local newspaper":** Flade, p. 51.

20   **they even enjoyed the state's passion for pork:** Birmingham, p. 78.

21   **"they marry cotton wives":** Robert N. Rosen, *The Jewish Confederates* (Columbia: University of South Carolina Press, 2000), p. 22.

21   **"Agents for the Sale of Leading Southern Domestics":** Birmingham, pp. 52–53.

21   **"persistence his ancestors had applied to the Talmud":** Libo, p. 6.

Chapter 2: *"It's All Over"*

23   **a "slave for life":** Ken Auletta, *Greed and Glory on Wall Street: The Fall of the House of Lehman* (New York: Overlook Press, 2001), p. 28.

23   **W. H. Russell:** *Harper's Weekly*, July 13, 1861.

24   **"Jews wanted to acclimate themselves":** Bertram Wallace Korn, *Jews and Negro Slavery in the Old South, 1789–1865* (Elkins Park, PA: Reform Congregation Keneseth Israel, 1961).

25   **According to family tradition:** Kenneth Libo, ed., *Lots of Lehmans: The Family of Mayer Lehman of Lehman Brothers Remembered by His Descendants* (New York: Center for Jewish History, 2007), p. 6.

25   **"[S]he advised him constantly":** Allan Nevins, *Herbert H. Lehman and His Era* (New York: Charles Scribner's Son, 1963), p. 19.

26   **"they entered into the social life very well":** Nevins, p. 8.

28   **Davis was to be found:** *Lehman Brothers: A Centennial* (New York: Lehman Brothers, 1950), p. 9.

28   **"to accept the wild acclaim of throngs in Court Square":** Ibid.

28   **He scrawled on a notepad:** Stephen Birmingham, *Our Crowd: The Great Jewish Families of New York* (London: Futura, 1985), p. 79.

30   **Mayer strengthened the firm's position when in 1863 he went into partnership with John Wesley Durr:** Roland Flade, *The Lehmans: From Rimpar to the New World: A Family History* (Würzburg, Germany: Konigshausen and Neumann, 1996), p. 63.

30   **"I have appointed Mr. Mayer Lehman":** Flade, p. 64.

31   **"flags flying, bands playing, spurs and swords jingling":** Nevins, p. 11.

31   **This story was told years later:** Libo , p. 12.

32   **Lehman Brothers provided:** Flade, p. 68.

33   **Mayer against a Victorian backdrop:** Ibid., p. 67.

33   **"No woman was safe on the streets":** Nevins, p. 12.

33   **Mayer wanted to get away:** Flade, p. 68.

35   **"a universe parallel":** Libo, p. 15.

38   **"The American invents as the Greek sculpted":** http://libwww.library.phila.gov/CenCol/tours-machineryhall.htm.

40   **Emanuel became a director:** *A Centennial*, pp. 21–22.

42   **"Now, Mayer":** Nevins, p. 3.

43   **Kildare in the Adirondacks:** Libo, p. 64.

44   **Hilary Herbert and Edward Douglass White, Jr.:** Nevins, p. 20.

46 **"the cause of the Common Man":** Simon Schama, "America's phobia of banks," *Financial Times*, May 15, 2009.

46 **"A noble, manly, wide-beloved man!":** Flade, p. 75.

46 **Fellow investors in the idea included P. A. B. Widener:** Charles R. Geisst, *The Last Partnerships: Inside the Great Wall Street Money Dynasties* (New York: McGraw-Hill, 2001), p. 52.

46 **Of the 4,192 cars produced:** "Timeline: History of the Electric Car," broadcast on PBS, October 30, 2009, www.pbs.org.

46 **a fleet of 2,000 on the streets of:** From paper by John B. Rae, associate professor of history, Massachusetts Institute of Technology. See "Early EV History" at www.econogics.com/ev/rae.htm.

Chapter 3: Stuff of Dreams

53 **Philip's large summer home:** Charles D. Ellis, *The Partnership: A History of Goldman Sachs* (London: Allen Lane , 2008), p. 10.

53 **"intense, high-strung, didactic man":** Stephen Birmingham, *Our Crowd: The Great Jewish Families of New York* (London: Futura, 1985), p. 382.

53 **The agreement was scrawled:** Ibid., p. 5.

54 **Emanuel wrote to his partners:** *Lehman Brothers: A Centennial* (New York: Lehman Brothers, 1950), p. 24.

55 **Henry Goldman knew Jake Wertheim:** Ellis, p. 9.

56 **The product's image suffered:** "Cigars and Cuba," *Cigars* magazine, www.cigarsmag .com.

56 **Julius Rosenwald:** Ellis, pp. 10–11.

57 **the most influential American propaganda in the Soviet Union:** See Sears, Roebuck in Lehman Brothers Collection, Harvard Business School, www .library.hbs.edu/hc/lehman.

60 **"an extremely shaky base for the system":** Ron Chernow, *The House of Morgan: An American Banking Dynasty and the Rise of Modern Finance* (London: Atlantic Books, 2003), p. 122.

63 **"strong anti-Semitic undercurrent":** Charles Geisst, *The Last Partnerships: Inside the Great Wall Street Money Dynasties* (New York: McGraw-Hill, 2001), pp. 7, 58.

63 **"Whatever knowledge I have had of business":** Allan Nevins, *Herbert H. Lehman and His Era* (New York: Charles Scribner's Sons, 1963), p. 42.

65 **"I was shocked":** Ibid., pp. 30–31.

66 **"spasmodic alternation of inattention and frenzied interest":** Ibid., p. 44.

66 **Studebaker earned the distinction:** See Studebaker in Lehman Brothers Collection, Harvard Business School, www.library.hbs.edu/hc/lehman.

66 **Arthur had married Adele Lewisohn:** Birmingham, p. 380.

67 **"rich Beaux-Arts style":** Christopher Gray, "Interior Details Come Home Again to Millionaires' Row," *New York Times*, June 18, 2006.

68 **"lots of nice pictures to be seen":** Postcard from Bobbie to Philip Lehman, November 23, 1915. See Robert Lehman/Lehman Brothers Collection, Baker Library, Harvard Business School, www.library.hbs.edu/hc/lehman.

69   **"Laurence Binyon of the British Museum told me":** Postcard from Bobbie to Philip Lehman, February 12, 1915. See Robert Lehman/Lehman Brothers Collection.

70   **"Kuhn Loeb, German Bankers, Refuse to Aid Allies":** Geisst, p. 60.

70   **one dinnertime conversation on foreign affairs:** Ellis, p. 14.

71   **Herbert nonetheless maintained his support:** Nevins, p. 56.

73   **William "Billy" Wood:** Nevins, p. 58.

73   **With war under way:** Bobbie and Herbert Lehman exchange of communication, May/June 1917. See Robert Lehman/Lehman Brothers Collection.

Chapter 4: Flying

76   **"To you and me this may be a mysterious realm":** Obituary of Robert Lehman, *New York Times*, August 10, 1969.

77   **"If I see something I like, I buy it":** Stephen Birmingham, *Our Crowd: The Great Jewish Families of New York* (London: Futura, 1985), p. 436.

78   **"costs more than the whole account is now worth":** Roland Flade, *The Lehmans: From Rimpar to the New World: A Family History* (Würzburg, Germany: Konigshausen and Neumann, 1996), p. 76.

79   **"shipping a lot of water":** Internal memorandum, June 17, 1960. See Robert Lehman/Lehman Brothers Collection, Baker Library, Harvard Business School, www.library.hbs.edu/hc/lehman.

82   **"He was just a man with a moustache":** Kenneth Libo, ed., *Lots of Lehmans: The Family of Mayer Lehman of Lehman Brothers Remembered by His Descendants* (New York: Center for Jewish History, 2007), p. 151.

82   **"tall, burly, restless":** Allan Nevins, *Herbert H. Lehman and His Era* (New York: Charles Scribner's Sons, 1963), p. 65.

83   **"scions of silence":** Cleveland Amory, *The Proper Bostonians* (New York: E. P. Dutton, 1947), p. 19.

84   **Warren Susman, the late cultural historian:** Cited in "The Forgotten Imagemeister: Adman Bruce Barton was the most formidable operative in American politics—until he took on FDR," by David Greenberg, www.thefreelibary.com.

84   **Al Smith . . . Herbert Lehman:** Nevins, p. 85.

86   **"From 1925 Robert Lehman took over control":** *Lehman Brothers: A Centennial* (New York: Lehman Brothers, 1950), p. 40.

86   **"[I]t would be hard for me to believe":** Libo, p. 154.

87   **"They hired the money, didn't they?":** Ron Chernow, *The House of Morgan: An American Banking Dynasty and the Rise of Modern Finance* (London: Atlantic Books, 2003), p. 251.

87   **Cuyamel Fruit Company:** Peter Chapman, *Bananas: How the United Fruit Company Shaped the World* (New York: Canongate, 2007), pp. 59–74. Also see Cuyamel Fruit Company in Lehman Brothers Collection, Harvard Business School, www.library.hbs.edu/hc/lehman.

88   **"of the 20 largest U.S. retailing enterprises":** *A Centennial*, p. 46.

88   **"He was one of the best friends":** "Did RCA Have to Be Sold?," *New York Times*, September 20, 1987.

90   **"We are all here"**: Charles D. Ellis, *The Partnership: A History of Goldman Sachs* (Allen Lane/Penguin, London, 2008), p. 17.

91   **"After the dispute they became real go-getters"**: Ibid., p. 18.

91   **Juan Terry Trippe was one man**: Marylin Bender and Selig Altschul, *The Chosen Instrument: Pan Am, Juan Trippe, and the Rise and Fall of an American Entrepreneur* (New York: Simon & Schuster, 1982), p. 22.

91   **first venture, Long Island Airways**: Robert Daley, *An American Saga: Juan Trippe and His Pan Am Empire* (New York: Random House, 1980), pp. 9–12.

92   **"General Motors of the skies"**: Letter from Sherman Fairchild, November 23, 1964. See Robert Lehman/Lehman Brothers Collection.

92   **"who relished the chance at a sporting enterprise"**: Matthew Josephson, *Empire of the Air* (New York: Harcourt Brace & Co., 1944), p. 36.

92   **"Fly with us to Havana"**: Pan-American World Airways in Lehman Brothers Collection.

92   **"remember, it won't be good for you fellers"**: Josephson, p. 34.

93   **"[D]esires increase, standards of living are raised"**: Paul Mazur, *American Prosperity: Its Causes and Consequences* (London: Jonathan Cape, 1928), p. 215.

93   **"[W]e must shift America from a needs culture"**: Al Gore, *The Assault on Reason* (London: Bloomsbury, 2007), p. 94.

93   **"no limits to the needs and desires of American consumers"**: Mazur, p. 217.

93   **"conscious and intelligent manipulation"**: Chapman, p. 116.

93   **"baroquely ornamented"**: T. A. Wise, "The House of Lehman: A Banker's Art," *Fortune*, December 1957.

94   **"[M]ultimillionaire oil barons"**: Nevins, p. 97.

96   **"The trouble with you, Walter"**: Ellis, p. 25.

96   **he was "too optimistic" and "lacked balance"**: Birmingham, p. 383.

96   **The company behind the deal was the Radio Corporation of America**: See National Union Radio Corporation in Lehman Brothers Collection.

97   **"a chain of vaudeville theaters"**: See Keith-Albee-Orpheum in Lehman Brothers Collection, Harvard Business School.

98   **people attending movie theaters . . . from 57 million to 90 million**: www .shmoop.com/great-depression/statistics.html.

Chapter 5: Crash

99   **"irrational doubt"**: Allan Nevins, *Herbert H. Lehman and His Era* (New York: Charles Scribner's Sons, 1963), p. 67.

99   **"Herbert did not even expostulate"**: Ibid.

100   **in January 1929**: Ibid., p. 117.

101   **"We feel that we have an obligation"**: John Kenneth Galbraith, *The Great Crash 1929* (London: Penguin, 1992), p. 63.

101   **Winston Churchill . . . Black Thursday**: Galbraith, p. 122.

102   **"[T]his is normally the time it takes"**: John Kenneth Galbraith, *A Short History of Financial Euphoria* (London: Penguin, 1994), p. 87.

103   **Eddie Cantor**: Eddie Cantor, *Caught Short! A Saga of Wailing Wall Street* (Toronto: Musson Book Company, 1929).

103   **Lehman Brothers was second in the list:** Charles D. Ellis, *The Partnership: A History of Goldman Sachs* (London: Allen Lane/Penguin, 2008), p. 28.

103   **"There is no denying":** See Helena Rubinstein Inc in Lehman Brothers Collection, Harvard Business School,. www.library.hbs.edu/hc/lehman.

104   **"Ahead of me once more was the lonely treadmill of work":** Helena Rubinstein, *My Life for Beauty*, (New York: Simon & Schuster, 1964), p. 74.

104   **"What Bobbie Lehman did was to blame Arthur":** Kenneth Libo, ed., *Lots of Lehmans: The Family of Mayer Lehman of Lehman Brothers Remembered by His Descendants* (New York: Center for Jewish History, 2007), p. 157.

104   **"[T]hey could have paid [Herbert] off with shares":** Libo, p. 156.

104   **"The remedy is for people to stop":** Ron Chernow, *The House of Morgan: An American Banking Dynasty and the Rise of Modern Finance* (London: Atlantic Books, 2003), pp. 321–22.

105   **The exchange threatened to decamp:** Nevins, p. 143.

105   **"[N]evertheless you and I both":** Nevins, p. 123.

105   **"cautious banker":** Robert P. Ingalls, *Herbert H. Lehman and New York's Little New Deal* (New York: New York University Press, 1975), p. 24.

106   **"pantspressers bank":** Nevins, p. 119.

106   **Leffingwell . . . "a large clientele among our Jewish population":** Chernow, pp. 326–27.

106   **Lehman came from Albany for the meeting:** Nevins, pp. 118–19.

107   **"I asked them if their decision to drop the plan":** Chernow, p. 326.

107   **Cohn always blamed the bank's failure on an anti-Semitic plot:** Ibid, p. 327.

107   **"most colossal mistake in the banking history of New York":** Ibid.

108   **Mazur foresaw:** Joseph Wechsberg, *The Merchant Bankers* (New York: Pocket Books, 1966), p. 242.

108   **"the tragic lack of planning":** "1931 The Tragic Year," Ludwig von Mises Institute, www.mises.org.

109   **"emphasize the value of experienced businessmen":** Nevins, p. 128.

109   **William Donovan, the Republican candidate:** Ibid., p. 131.

109   **"of definite action founded on liberal thought":** Ibid., p. 132.

110   **"The spread of hysteria":** Ibid., p. 137.

111   **"Dear Frank":** Chernow, pp. 354–55.

112   **He was convinced:** Nevins, p. 137.

113   **National City had:** Chernow, p. 356.

113   **"An investment banker was a breed apart":** Michael Lewis, *Liar's Poker* (London: Hodder & Stoughton, 1989), p. 26.

115   **Lehman Brothers launched:** Wechsberg, p. 248.

116   **"Over Arthur's objections":** Libo, p. 158.

116   **she filed her suit in Reno, Nevada:** "Robert Lehman Is Sued," *New York Times*, May 2, 1934.

116   **She had "hob-nobbed with the smart polo set":** Gossip item in the *American*, April 30, 1934, in Robert Lehman/Lehman Brothers Collection.

117   **"I seldom saw Lehman":** Edward L. Bernays, *Biography of an Idea* (New York: Simon & Schuster, 1965), p. 493.

117   **"Stick to straight whiskey or sherry":** Doctor's written advice to Bobbie Lehman, December 14, 1934. See Robert Lehman/Lehman Brothers Collection.

118 **"The people of the State of New York":** Nevins, p. 169.

119 **Lehman's reforms in New York . . . beyond those of Washington:** Ingalls, p. 251.

119 **"between being a business man, and a liberal":** Ibid., p. 255.

120 **"[A]s they all got involved in politics":** Libo, p. 236.

120 **In May 1936, Arthur Lehman died suddenly:** Obituary of Arthur Lehman, *New York Times*, May 16, 1936; reprinted in Libo, p. 143.

120 **"killed by the forces of merciless reaction":** Nevins, p. 172.

120 **"the freedom to live fully and prosper greatly":** Ingalls, p. 250.

121 **"Banking House Advises SEC That Wider Curbs Are Desirable":** *New York Times*, November 11, 1936.

121 **perfected "the use of the cathode ray tube":** See Du Mont Broadcasting Corporation in Lehman Brothers Collection.

122 **"insomnia and easy fatigability":** Doctor's report on Bobbie Lehman, March 8, 1938, in Robert Lehman/Lehman Brothers Collection.

122 **Philip Morris . . . "[A]ll preferred stock sold":** Letter from Robert Lehman to Philip Lehman, June 28, 1938, Robert Lehman/Lehman Brothers Collection.

125–26 **Leo Szilard . . . Albert Einstein . . . Alexander Sachs:** Walter Isaacson, "Chain Reaction," *Discover*, March 18, 2008.

127 **"emotional alarm":** Nevins, p. 213.

128 **"State A.F.L. Comes Out for Roosevelt":** Joseph Shaplen, *New York Times*, August 22, 1940.

128 **"as I know you can show them":** Nevins, pp. 211–12.

Chapter 6: A Little News and a Little Noise

130 **"to inspect banana lands in Guatemala":** Bobbie Lehman letter with application for passport, October 18, 1942. See Robert Lehman/Lehman Brothers Collection, Baker Library, Harvard Business School, www.library.hbs.edu/hc/lehman.

130 **Sam Zemurray:** Peter Chapman, *Bananas: How the United Fruit Company Shaped the World* (New York: Canongate, 2007), chapter 4 passim; see also Cuyamel Fruit Company, in Lehman Brothers Collection, Harvard Business School, www.library.hbs.edu/hc/lehman.

132 **The New York budget was in surplus by $80 million:** "Life and Legacy of Herbert H. Lehman," Columbia University Libraries, www.columbia.edu.

132 **Relief and Rehabilitation Administration, or UNRRA:** Allan Nevins, *Herbert H. Lehman and His Era* (New York: Charles Scribner's Sons, 1963), chapter 11 passim.

134 **"We will get there, somehow.":** *The Handbook of Texas Online*, Halliburton Company, www.tshaonline.org.

135 **"world planning, world WPA-ing":** Nevins, p. 234.

135 **"What sort of Europe we should have had":** Ibid., p. 286.

136 **"They are tired":** Ibid., p. 306.

137 **"preferably drip coffee":** Written advice from Bobbie Lehman's doctors, October 7, 1948. See Robert Lehman/Lehman Brothers Collection.

137 **"an awfully good bet for success":** Frank J. Manheim letter to Bobbie Lehman, October 23, 1947. See Robert Lehman/Lehman Brothers Collection.

138 **"pulls no punches":** From review of *Streetcar Named Desire, Variety*, November 5, 1947. See Robert Lehman/Lehman Brothers Collection.

138 **Bobbie had received regular checks:** Letter from Frank J. Manheim to Bobbie Lehman, August 23, 1948. See Robert Lehman/Lehman Collection.

139 **John Foster Dulles . . . was the more successful:** David Halberstam, *The Fifties* (New York: Fawcett Books, 1993), p. 395.

139 **"the whole people as distinguished from special interests":** Nevins, p. 310.

139 **"I know he is no Communist":** Halberstam, p. 56.

140 **"I hope to make a little news":** *Washington Post* article, January 5, 1950, cited in Nevins, p. 312.

141 **"McCarthy was a dream story":** Halberstam, p. 55.

142 **"whether it be barge traffic on [the] Long Island Sound ":** Nevins, p. 315.

143 **McCarthy resisted requests:** Nevins, p. 338.

144 **"Yet he gets the votes!":** *New York Post* article, October 20, 1950, cited in Nevins, p. 330.

145 **"far more engrossed":** From copy of statement of Ruth Owen Lehman's lawyer in Bobbie's Lehman's files, July 9, 1951. See Robert Lehman/Lehman Brothers Collection.

145 **"She Becomes Bride of Cousin of Senator":** Brief news item in *New York Times*, July 12, 1952.

146 **"same pattern that has been followed":** Nevins, p. 345.

146 **exchange of letters . . . between Herbert and Judge Albert Cohn:** With thanks to Carolyn Smith, the Herbert Lehman archive, Columbia University, New York.

147 **"the immense power of the new medium":** Lawrence Van Gelder, "Crash Kills G. David Schine, 69, McCarthy-Era Figure," *New York Times*, June 21, 1996.

148 **CIA/United Fruit Company coup in Guatemala:** For further background, see Chapman, chapters 9 and 10; full details can be found in Stephen Schlesinger and Stephen Kinzer, *Bitter Fruit: The Story of the American Coup in Guatemala* (Boston: Harvard University, David Rockefeller Center for Latin American Studies, 1999).

149 **"showering even further glory upon the House of Lehman":** Stephen Birmingham, *Our Crowd: The Great Jewish Families of New York* (London: Futura, 1985), p. 386.

150 **"[W]e are all shocked and disturbed":** Bobbie Lehman to Charles Wilson, early 1953 (date unclear), Wilson confirmation hearings in January. See Robert Lehman/Lehman Brothers Collection.

150 **"Mr. Mazur. This was a 'toughie' ":** Note added to Mazur on copy of Lehman's follow-up letter to Wilson. See Robert Lehman/Lehman Collection.

150 **Halliburton's earnings of $26 million:** See Halliburton in Lehman Brothers Collection.

150 *Forbes* **magazine calculated:** *Forbes*, August 1, 1955. Note in Bobbie Lehman's records. See Robert Lehman/Lehman Brothers Collection.

151 **"special attitudes form a continuity":** T. A. Wise, "The House of Lehman: A Banker's Art," *Fortune*, December 1957.

152 **"Goldman Sachs . . . a firm with a few good clients":** Lisa Endlich, *Goldman Sachs: The Culture of Success* (London: Warner Books, 2000), pp. 86–87.

152 **"I get tired of people":** Joseph Wechsberg, *The Merchant Bankers* (New York: Pocket Books, 1966), p. 231.

153 **"I blinked my eyes when I heard that":** Obituary of Robert Lehman, *New York Times*, August 10, 1969.

153 **By 1965, Litton Industries' shares stood at $150:** Wechsburg, p. 229.

153 **Lehman "rejoiced as loudly" at the decision:** Nevins, p. 367.

154 **Thank you, Eisenhower wrote back:** Letter to Bobbie Lehman, June 10, 1955. See Robert Lehman/Lehman Brothers Collection.

154 **"It can become a consuming interest":** Bobbie Lehman letter to *Fortune* magazine, October 1955. See Robert Lehman/Lehman Brothers Collection.

155 **Ahmet Ertegun, owner of the Atlantic label:** Halberstam, p. 471.

156 **Roy Cohn, writing from his home:** Letter from Roy Cohn, January 3, 1956. See Robert Lehman/Lehman Brothers Collection.

156–57 **"Grabbing and greed can go on for just so long":** Nevins, p. 368.

157 **"creating doubt among the American people":** Nevins, p. 437, citing *New York Times*, February 18, 1956.

158 **"[Y]ou have won the admiration of all of us":** Nevins, p. 370.

Chapter 7: "Aristocrat of the Autocrats"

159 **"modest check":** Letter from Bobbie Lehman to First Aid for Hungary, December 4, 1956. See Robert Lehman/Lehman Brothers Collection, Baker Library, Harvard Business School, www.library.hbs.edu/hc/lehman.

160 **Goldwater . . . siren song of socialism:** "Republicans: The Backward Look," *Time*, April 22, 1957.

161 **finance of $35 million:** See European Coal and Steel Community in Lehman Brothers Collection, Harvard Business School, www.library.hbs.edu/hc/lehman.

162 **The Orangerie showed 293 of the 1,000 pieces:** Obituary of Robert Lehman, *New York Times*, August 10, 1969.

163 **"a terrible blow":** Geisst, p. 299.

163 **"The House of Lehman: A Banker's Art":** *Fortune* magazine, December 1957.

164 **Among those writing back:** Letter to Bobbie Lehman from King Umberto of Italy, December 2, 1958. See Robert Lehman/Lehman Brothers Collection.

164 **"aristocrat of the autocrats":** Stephen Birmingham, *Our Crowd: The Great Jewish Families of New York* (London: Futura, 1985), p. 435.

164 **"He'd talk to his horse trainer first thing":** Obituary of Robert Lehman.

165 **"[I]t would be our purpose":** Letter from Lehman Brothers to Bank of America, January 20, 1956. See Robert Lehman/Lehman Brothers Collection.

165 **short note in February 1959:** Bobbie Lehman to Leonard Florsheim. See Robert Lehman/Lehman Brothers Collection.

166 **"grave social problem":** Peter Chapman, *Bananas: How the United Fruit Company Shaped the World* (New York: Canongate, 2007), p. 152.

167 **six hundred guests attended a reception:** Allan S. Kaplan, *Lehman Brothers 1850–1984: A Chronicle*, 1985. Compilation of press reports and some other documents relating to Lehman Brothers kept at the University Club library, W. 54 Street and Fifth Avenue, New York.

169 **Thomas Sunderland, the president of the United Fruit:** Letter from Sunderland to Bobbie Lehman, May 4, 1961. Lehman proposed Sunderland for membership in the Council on Foreign Relations in a letter on May 15, 1961. See Robert Lehman/Lehman Brothers Collection.

170 **possibly useful merger of Coca-Cola and the Folgers Coffee Company:** Internal Lehman Brothers memorandum, January 10, 1962. See Robert Lehman/Lehman Brothers Collection.

170 **"have a cocktail together":** Letter from R. W. Woodruff to Bobbie Lehman, March 10, 1962. See Robert Lehman/Lehman Brothers Collection.

171 **"1,000 artistically and socially prominent New Yorkers":** From a *New York Times* report, October 15, 1962. See Kaplan's compilation, *Lehman Brothers 1850–1984: A Chronicle.*

171 **"loose management and a lack of attention to detail began":** Charles Geisst, *The Last Partnerships: Inside the Great Wall Street Money Dynasties* (New York: McGraw-Hill, 2001), p. 77.

171 **"management by committee":** Joseph Wechsberg, *The Merchant Bankers* (New York: Pocket Books, 1966), p. 257.

172 **"General Clay's comments":** Letter from Joseph Eckhouse to Bobbie Lehman, March 31, 1965. See Robert Lehman/Lehman Brothers Collection.

173 **"in which I expect to keep my pills":** Undated letter from Bobbie Lehman to André Meyer. See Robert Lehman/Lehman Brothers Collection.

173 **bedraggled but delighted:** From a *Wall Street Journal* report, July 16, 1963. See Kaplan's compilation, *Lehman Brothers 1850–1984: A Chronicle.*

175 **"You looked upon Lehman":** Ken Auletta, *Greed and Glory on Wall Street: The Fall of the House of Lehman* (New York: Overlook Press, 2001), p. 46.

175 **"the room":** Geisst, p. 250.

175 **"fearsome foursome":** Ibid., p. 223.

176 **"[H]e has used wisdom and compassion":** Obituary of Herbert Lehman, *New York Times*, December 6, 1963. See also Kenneth Libo, ed., *Lots of Lehmans: The Family of Mayer Lehman of Lehman Brothers Remembered by His Descendants* (New York: Center for Jewish History, 2007).

177 **tour of his art collection:** Letter from William Blackie, president of Caterpillar, July 21, and from Harmon S. Eberhard, chairman, November 3, 1964, to Bobbie Lehman. See Robert Lehman/Lehman Brothers Collection.

178 **LBJ's victory:** Bobbie Lehman's statement reported in *Albany Times Union*, November 6, 1964. See Robert Lehman/Lehman Brothers Collection.

178 **"When will Red China":** Wechsberg, p. 253.

179 **"[H]e wouldn't do it":** Libo, p. 158.

180 **"I still cherish the memory":** Wechsberg, pp. 259–60.

180 **"[T]o begin with, Bobbie isn't going to die":** Birmingham, p. 437.

180 **Juan Trippe's last board meeting:** Marylin Bender and Selig Altschul, *The Chosen Instrument: Pan Am, Juan Trippe, and the Rise and Fall of an American Entrepreneur* (New York: Simon & Schuster, 1982), p. 514.

181 **"He said Lehman was an old man":** Thomas McCann, *An American Company: The Tragedy of United Fruit* (New York: Crown Publishers, 1976), pp. 118–19.

182 **"Economics is basically sociological":** From *New York Times* report, January 1, 1969. See Kaplan's compilation, *Lehman Brothers 1850–1984: A Chronicle.*

182   **Securities and Exchange Commission:** From *New York Times* report, February 2, 1969. See Kaplan's compilation, *Lehman Brothers 1850–1984: A Chronicle.*

182   **"two of the most sophisticated":** From Lehman Brothers internal monthly publication. July 1969. See Kaplan's compilation, *Lehman Brothers 1850–1984: A Chronicle.*

Chapter 8: Traders

184   **"economic Kissinger":** Peter G. Peterson, *The Education of an American Dreamer: How a Son of Greek Immigrants Learned His Way from a Nebraska Diner to Washington, Wall Street, and Beyond.* (New York: Twelve, 2009), p. 147.

185   **Nixon saw him as a "leaker":** Ken Auletta, *Greed and Glory on Wall Street: The Fall of the House of Lehman* (New York: Overlook Press, 2001), p. 39.

185   **DON'T EAT WITH THE GREEK:** Peterson, p. 50.

185   **"Nordic stock in someplace like Sweden":** Ibid.

185   **Peterson's education had suffered a setback:** Ibid., p. 44.

186   **"movie parties":** Auletta, p. 39.

186   **"White Knight":** Marylin Bender, "The White Knight at Lehman Brothers," *New York Times,* November 11, 1973.

187   **Peterson was shocked by his first meeting with Joseph Thomas:** Peterson, p. 222.

188   **Nixon had solicited . . . from ITT:** Ibid.

189   **Banca Commerciale Italiana:** Peterson, p. 227.

190   **"Rumpled was the kindest way to describe him":** Ibid., p. 257.

190   **His father owned a factory:** Auletta, p. 45.

190   **"fucking-a-well":** Ibid, p. 13.

190   **"the kind of Jew who should":** Auletta., p. 10.

191   **"almost unbearably intense":** Andrew Gowers, "Exposed: The man who brought the world to its knees," *Sunday Times* (London), December 14, 2008.

191   **"creative entrepreneurial work":** Auletta, p. 54.

191   **The opening of Bobbie's wing:** List prepared by Peggy Cronin for VIP reception at the Metropolitan Museum of Art, May 12, 1975. See Robert Lehman/ Lehman Brothers Collection, Baker Library, Harvard Business School, www .library.hbs.edu/hc/lehman.

191   **The opening made a media splash:** Byron Belt, "Last Great Collection Goes Public," *Long Island Press,* May 18, 1975.

192   **"a sensation of great wealth, of money lavishly poured":** Thomas B. Hess, "The Lehman, a Lemon?" *New York,* August 11, 1975.

193   **Glucksman, like many former Democrats:** Auletta, p. 51.

194   **He kept thinking:** Justin Schack, "Restoring the House of Lehman," Institutional Investor.com, May 12, 2005.

195   **"I tend to look on international":** Auletta, p. 61.

196   **"stress interview":** Michael Lewis, *Liar's Poker* (London: Hodder & Stoughton, 1989), p. 25.

199   **"How did you make money . . . ?":** Auletta, p. 158.

199   **"peddling the firm":** Ibid., p. 183.

200 **"I wept"**: Ibid., p. 243.

200 **Dick Fuld was distraught**: Ibid., p. 209.

200 **"Frankly, there is no Lehman anymore"**: James Sterngold, "Shearson Lehman Seeks New Image," *International Herald Tribune*, June 29–30, 1985.

202 **"Big Swinging Dick"**: Lewis, pp. 42–43.

203 **"parasite"**: Ibid., p. 182.

203 **Jacques Gelardin, head of Shearson Lehman**: Clive Wolman, *Financial Times*, "Shearson bounces back after its Big Bang shake-out," November 8, 1988.

204 **A solid C-grade student at Columbia**: Bryan Burrough and John Helyar, *Barbarians at the Gate: The Fall of RJR Nabisco* (London: Arrow Books, 1990; New York: Harper & Row, 1990), p. 201.

204 **"admitted he was a good administrator"**: John Cassidy, "Shearson's Chainsaw Massacre," *Sunday Times* (London), February 4, 1990.

204 **while at his weekend mansion on Long Island**: Auletta, p. 188.

205 **"By 1980 the average"**: Martin D. Shafiroff and Robert Shook, *Successful Telephone Selling in the '80s* (New York: Harper & Row, 1982), pp. xiv, 1.

205 **"bullpen one-quarter the size"**: "Have You Been Cold-Called?" *Fortune*, December 16, 1991.

206 **Litton Industries sued Shearson Lehman**: William Hall, "Litton files $30m suit on insider trading," *Financial Times*, August 21, 1986.

207 **"almost unanimous in their enthusiasm"**: Anatole Kaletsky, "Boost for American Express shares," *Financial Times*, March 3, 1987.

207 **"globalization"**: Karen Slater and Steve Swartz, "American Express Considers Partial Sale of Shearson Unit," *Wall Street Journal*, March 2, 1987.

208 **"[W]e didn't know he owned them"**: Lewis, pp. 129–30.

209 **Shearson Lehman . . . drug tests**: *Financial Times*, Brief item, April 18, 1987.

209 **"There isn't a typewriter in the place"**: *Financial Times*, Observer column, July 31, 1987.

209 **Elaine Garzarelli, a Shearson Lehman stock market analyst**: James B. Stewart, "Shearson's Garzarelli Gains Fame for Predicting Wall Street's Crash," *Wall Street Journal*, October 29, 1987.

210 **"believing his press cuttings"**: John Cassidy, "Shearson's Chainsaw Massacre," *Sunday Times* (London), February 4, 1990.

210 **"At forty, he discovered the Louvre"**: Burrough and Helyar, pp. 201–2.

210 **Its directors appeared in the media**: "Shearson's Chainsaw Massacre."

Chapter 9: "Call Me Dick"

212 **"a walking museum piece"**: John Cassidy, "Shearson's Chainsaw Massacre," *Sunday Times* (London), February 4, 1990.

212 **Sixty Lehman Brothers analysts**: William Power, "Shearson Soothsayers Make Surprising Forecasts for '90s," *Wall Street Journal*, February 2, 1990.

213 **"It is about time"**: Janet Bush and Alan Friedman, "The Humbling of Wall Street," *Financial Times*, March 1, 1990.

213 **Amid rapturous cheers**: Janet Bush, "Broking Brothers Divided but Still United," *Financial Times*, June 8, 1990.

213 **"Lehman stood for excellence":** William Power, "Shearson Plans to Resurrect Lehman Name in Hope of Reviving More Than Memories," *Wall Street Journal,* June 5, 1990.

214 **"was once a great name":** Ibid.

214 **"Our product is money":** "Amex takes Shearson on board," *Observer* (London), August 12, 1990.

214 **Wolfe's Sherman McCoy:** Michael Lewis, "The Death of Sherman McCoy," *New York Times* Web site, August 18, 1996.

215 **New York Stock Exchange fined the firm:** William Power, "Shearson Agrees to a $750,000 Fine by the New York Stock Exchange," *Wall Street Journal,* April 3, 1991.

215 **American Express was making brokers:** William Power and Michael Siconolfi, "Shearson Is Recuperating but Still Fighting for Identity," *Wall Street Journal,* June 17, 1991.

216 **on the phone to Maxwell:** John Willcock, "Kevin sought Jewish backing," *Times* (London), and John Mason, "Lehmans 'would not delay default notices,'" *Financial Times,* October 31, 1995.

216 **"[W]e are in the Last Chance Saloon":** Norma Cohen, "City told to tighten regulation," *Financial Times,* July 3, 1992.

219 **They . . . met on the morning of December 3:** Martin Walker, *Clinton: The President They Deserve* (London: Vintage, 1997), pp. 168–69.

219 **"You mean to tell me":** Ibid., p. 173.

220 **His rise to the top spot:** "CEO Richard Fuld on Lehman Brothers' Evolution from International Turmoil to Teamwork," Knowledge@Wharton, www.wharton.upenn.edu, published January 10, 2007.

220 **Fuld gave a speech:** Lehman Brothers' staff video, which was used in the BBC2 television documentary *Love of Money: The Bank That Bust the World,* broadcast September 9, 2009.

221 **"the ascension of Mr. Fuld":** Patrick Harverson and Martin Dickson, "Lehman Bros. co-president quits," *Financial Times,* March 30, 1993.

222 **Cabs "lined up in droves":** Kate Rankine, "Lehman gravy train halted," *Daily Telegraph,* March 24, 1994.

222 **"no free lunch":** Patrick Harverson, "Lean times spoil a free lunch on Wall St.," *Financial Times,* September 29, 1994.

223 **"Free at Last":** Leah Nathans Spiro and Pete Engardio, "Lehman Brothers: Free at Last," *BusinessWeek,* May 22, 1995.

224 **"it was about me":** "CEO Richard Fuld on Lehman Brothers' Evolution from International Turmoil to Teamwork."

225 **"football coach":** personal communication, Gary Silverman, *Financial Times* New York office, April 2009.

225 **Pettit possessed a comfortable manner:** Shawn Tully, "Can Lehman Survive?" *Fortune,* December 11, 1995.

225 **Fuld stated more of his business secrets:** "CEO Richard Fuld on Lehman Brothers' Evolution from International Turmoil to Teamwork."

226 **a family holiday:** Steve Fishman, "Burning Down His House," *New York,* November 30, 2008.

226 **"culture clashes":** "Lehman Brothers: Free at Last."

227 **would soon cease trading:** Tracy Corrigan, "Lehman exits commodities," *Financial Times*, November 21, 1996.

228 **Reports said that Fuld:** Keith Dovkants, "The Godfather, a man they call the Gorilla and how a banking legend was lost," *Evening Standard* (London), September 16, 2008.

228 **Fuld worried:** "Lehman's Desperate Housewives," *Vanity Fair*, April 2010, an excerpt from Vicky Ward's *The Devil's Casino: Friendship, Betrayal, and the High Stakes Games Played Inside Lehman Brothers* (New York: John Wiley & Sons, 2010), www.vanityfair.com/business/features/2010/04/lehman-wives-201004.

228 **"irrational exuberance":** Federal Reserve chairman Alan Greenspan speech to the American Enterprise Institute, Washington Hilton, December 5, 1996.

229 **"Dick Fuld sat there in my living room":** Devin Leonard, "How Lehman Brothers Got Its Real Estate Fix," *New York Times*, May 2, 2009.

229 **"swanlike transformation":** Ibid.

230 **rare step for a bank:** Andrew Garfield, "Lehman denies Chapter 11 filing as credit crunch bites," and Richard Tomkins, "Lehman moves to reassure market," *Financial Times*, September 12, 1998.

231 **in 2003, a court case:** Nikki Tait, "Former Lehman banker sues over unpaid bonuses," *Financial Times*, February 7, 2003, and "Lehman Russia decisions 'misled,'" February, 21, 2003; Jill Treanor, "'Mistreated' bond trader sues for £10m," *Guardian*, February 18, 2003, and "Russian spies, phantom profits and office bullies: Welcome to the City of London," February 21, 2003; Becky Barrow, "City banker 'feared for his life with Russians,'" *Daily Telegraph*, February 21, 2003; Jon Ashworth, "Lehman 'used ex-KGB men' to collect debts," *Times* (London), February 21, 2003.

232 **"Cats with their nine lives":** "Lehman Brothers," *Financial Times*, Lex column, December 16, 1998.

232 **"We're just scratching at the surface":** Christopher O'Leary, "Which Lehman Will Emerge? The firm sees a marvellous turnaround, but rivals remain sceptical," *Investment Dealers' Digest*, November 29, 1999.

233 **"the most brilliant":** Lawrence G. McDonald with Patrick Robinson, *A Colossal Failure of Common Sense: The Inside Story of the Collapse of Lehman Brothers* (New York: Crown Business, 2009), p. 3.

234 **better known as Glass-Steagall. . . Senator Phil Gramm of Texas:** Paul Mason, *Meltdown: The End of the Age of Greed* (London and New York: Verso, 2009), pp. 56–58.

234 **Greenspan's influence was also crucial:** Ibid., p. 62.

235 **Pets.com raised . . . Webvan spent $1 billion:** David Gelles, "Caution puts limits on tech excesses," *Financial Times*, March 10, 2010.

236 **Commodity Futures Modernization Act of 2000:** Mason, p. 57.

237 **"do whatever it takes":** Martin Essex, "Morgan Stanley predicts slump," *Sunday Business* (London), January 14, 2001.

237 **£300 million—about $500 million:** Grant Ringshaw, "The wobble that cost £30bn," *Sunday Telegraph*, May 20, 2001.

238 **Dick Fuld was in a reflective mood:** Gary Silverman and Charles Pretzlik, "A cunning player shows his hand," *Financial Times*, August 17, 2001.

Chapter 10: "Sad in Some Respects"

240   **He was a creature of habit:** personal communication, Bryan Zaslow, son of Ira, March 24, 2010.

242   **the Sheraton was a dingy place:** Joseph Tibman, *The Murder of Lehman Brothers* (New York: Brick Tower Books, 2009), p. 47.

242   **"[T]hose bastards got one us":** Ibid., p. 40.

243   **"Wall Street is virtual":** Sarah D. Scalet, "IT Executives from Three Wall Street Companies—Lehman Brothers, Merrill Lynch and American Express—Look Back on 9/11 and Take Stock of Where They Are Now," *CIO*, September 1, 2002, www.cio.com.

244   **"return to a 'formal' business dress policy":** Charles Pretzlik and Juliana Ratner, "Suits are back in fashion at Lehman," *Times* (London), and James Moore, "Lehman staff are asked to dress the part," *Financial Times*, February 7, 2002.

245   **Dick had never liked:** "Lehman's Desperate Housewives," *Vanity Fair*, April 2010, an excerpt from Vicky Ward's *The Devil's Casino: Friendship, Betrayal, and the High Stakes Games Played Inside Lehman Brothers* (New York: John Wiley & Sons, 2010), www.vanityfair.com/business/features/2010/04/lehman-wives-201004.

245   **Lehman Brothers' quarterly results:** Gary Silverman, "Wall St. seeks M&A revival," *Financial Times*, March 21, 2002.

246   **"diversity of the bank's franchise":** Caroline Merrell, "Lehman plunges by 31% in the second quarter," *Times* (London), June 19, 2002.

246   **"We sat in that room":** personal communication, Bryan Zaslow, March 24, 2010.

246   **"booming bond trading":** "Morgan Stanley fails to match rivals," *Financial Times*, December 20, 2002.

246   **"[I]t's not about playing basketball":** Lina Saigol, "Lehman is 'bank of the year,'" *Financial Times*, December 16, 2002.

248   **"financial weapons of mass destruction":** Warren Buffett, annual letter to Berkshire Hathaway shareholders, March 2003.

250   **Lehman Brothers issued details:** Gary Silverman and David Wells, "Investment banks cut jobs despite earnings leap," *Financial Times*, March 21, 2003.

250   **In June 2003, a jury in California:** Diana B. Henriques, "Lehman Aided in Loan Fraud, Jury Says," *New York Times*, June 17, 2003.

251   **leading investment banks:** Tom Bawden, "Wall Street banks raise risk to lift profits," *Times* (London), September 24, 2003.

251   **Such spirit enabled Greenspan:** Alan Greenspan's speech to a meeting of the American Economic Association, San Diego, California, January 3, 2003.

252   **"Lehman Brothers is a great company today":** "Gordon Brown-nosing," *Private Eye*, April 30, 2004.

252   **Lehman Brothers helped Enron:** Bethany Mclean and Peter Elkind, *The Smartest Guys in the Room: The Amazing Rise and Scandalous Fall of Enron* (New York: Portfolio, 2004), p. 202.

252   **Wall Street's leading banks:** Mason, p. 111, citing Stephen Labaton, "Agency's '04 Rule Let Banks Pile Up Debts," *New York Times*, October 3, 2008.

254   **Lehman Brothers' performance:** Justin Schack, "Restoring the House of Lehman," InstitutionalInvestor.com, May 12, 2005.

255   **"nobody gave this guy any hope":** Ibid.

255 **The Blackstone Group:** Peter G. Peterson, *The Education of an American Dreamer* (New York: Twelve, 2009), pp. 274–79.

255 **heaped praise on Lehman Brothers:** Antony Currie, "Can Lehman grow and still succeed?" *Euromoney*, July 2005.

256 **As in the 1840s:** Lawrence G. McDonald with Patrick Robinson, *A Colossal Failure of Common Sense: The Inside Story of the Collapse of Lehman Brothers* (New York: Crown Business, 2009), p. 113.

257 **At the turn of the millennium:** Gillian Tett, *Fool's Gold: How Unrestrained Greed Corrupted a Dream, Shattered Global Markets, and Unleashed a Catastrophe* (London: Little Brown, 2009), p. 112. See also McDonald, pp. 183–84.

258 **MoMA held a reception:** Jenny Anderson, "The Survivor," *New York Times*, October 28, 2007.

258 **Alan Greenspan sounded the alarms:** Paul J. Davies, Gillian Tett, and Saskia Scholtes, "Derivatives dealers tough match," *Financial Times*, September 24, 2006.

258 **Experts . . . credit default swaps:** Michael Lewis, "The financial crisis was predictable, but only a handful saw it coming," *Guardian Weekend*, March 20, 2010.

259 **Matters reached a critical point:** Ben White and David Wighton, "Bear Stearns, Lehman report record earnings," *Financial Times*, December 15, 2006.

259 **Lehman Brothers' conference call:** McDonald, p. 198.

259 **Dick Fuld prophesied the crash:** Andrew Gowers, "Exposed: The man who brought the world to its knees," *Sunday Times* (London), December 14, 2008.

260 **HSBC declared losses:** McDonald, p. 206.

261 **As for Dick Fuld taking money off the table:** Ben White, "Lehman chief executive gains £40.5 pay-out," *Financial Times*, February 27, 2007.

261 **board meeting in March 2007:** Executive Summary, Report of Examiner Anton R. Valukas, U.S. Bankruptcy Court, Southern District of New York, March 2010, p. 4.

261 **"Mike Gelband thought":** McDonald, p. 234.

261 **"You don't want to take a risk":** Steve Fishman, "Burning Down His House," *New York*, November 30, 2008.

261 **this time to the sands of Dubai:** "Exposed: The man who brought the world to its knees."

262 **Peterson and Stephen Schwarzman were enjoying themselves:** Peterson, pp. 302–3.

262 **Lehman Brothers had lately been involved:** McDonald, p. 262.

263 **Lehman Brothers . . . bought Coeur Défense:** Ibid., pp. 231–32.

263 **Walsh found him Archstone:** Henny Sender, Francesco Guerrera, Peter Thal Larsen, and Gary Silverman, "Brinkmanship Was Not Enough to Save Lehman," *Financial Times*, December 15, 2008.

263 **In the summer Lehman Brothers:** Ben White and Victoria Kim, "Lehman to shut subprime unit," *Financial Times*, August 23, 2007.

264 **Northern Rock traced its roots:** Evan Davies, reporting in the BBC2 television documentary *The City Uncovered*, broadcast January 14, 2009.

264 **Chris O'Meara spoke up again:** David Wighton, Ben White, and Jennifer Hughes, "Lehman lifts the lid on asset markdowns," *Financial Times*, September 19, 2007.

264 **Andrew Haldane, the director for financial stability:** "Rethinking the Financial Network," speech delivered at the Financial Student Association, Amsterdam, April 2009. See also Paul J. Davies, "Securitisation, Risk and Governance: Understanding Uncertainty in the Age of Finance," a seminar at the City University, London, May 6–7, 2009.

265 **compared the subprime crisis:** Paul J. Davies, "Why a lack of diversity in banking could be bananas," *Financial Times*, April 17, 2009.

265 **Gowers sensed the temperature:** "Exposed: The man who brought the world to its knees."

266 **the "Save Lehman Act of 2008":** "Brinkmanship Was Not Enough to Save Lehman."

266 **"[W]e don't want another run on a bank":** Helen Power and James Quinn, "Fed calls on banks to aid Lehman," *Daily Telegraph*, March 18, 2008.

266 **Paulson offered informal advice:** Executive Summary, Valukas report, pp. 5, 10; see also McDonald, pp. 306–8.

266 **"When I find a short seller":** *Love of Money: The Bank That Bust the World*, BBC2 television documentary, broadcast September 9, 2009

267 **accountancy methods . . . Repo 105:** Executive Summary, Valukas report, p. 6. See also Francesco Guerrera, Henny Sender, and Patrick Jenkins, "Damning light into inner workings forces Wall Street to search its conscience," and Francesco Guerrera, "Questions over whether Fuld knew of accounting gimmick," *Financial Times*, March 13/14, 2010.

267 **"I don't think it's just financial engineering":** Jennifer Hughes, "Accounting: Fooled Again," *Financial Times*, March 19, 2010.

268 **apparently still convinced:** Andrew Ross Sorkin, *Too Big to Fail* (London: Allen Lane, 2009), p. 129.

268 **"It's hard to see":** Ben Levisohn, "Lehman Looks Like a Target, *Business Week*, June 23, 2008.

268 **King Kong:** Iain Dey, "Crunch time at Lehman," *Sunday Times* (London), August 24, 2008.

268 **"Johnny Carson knew how to walk out at the top":** Greg Farrell, "Fuld faces a tough fight to save his legacy," *Financial Times*, September 11, 2008.

268 **"I will never sell this firm":** Andrew Gowers, "Lehman: consumed by the death spiral," *Sunday Times* (London), December 21, 2008.

269 **Fuld's exit routes:** Jenny Anderson and Ben White, "Wall St.'s Fears on Lehman Bros. Batter Markets," *New York Times*, September 10, 2008.

269 **AIG already faced payouts of $20 billion:** Tom Bawden, "Wall Street shares live as Lehman Brothers loses Korean lifeline," *Times* (London), September 10, 2008.

270 **"We're not going to do a bailout, are we?":** Henry M. Paulson, Jr., *On the Brink: Inside the Race to Stop the Collapse of the Global Financial System* (London: Headline Publishing, 2010), p. 92.

270 **"Dick is in no condition":** Sorkin, p. 303.

271 **"[T]he British":** Paulson, p. 214.

271 **"They were happy to get rid of a competitor":** Personal communication, former leading executive of Lehman Brothers who asked not to be named, July 10, 2009.

271 **Harvey Miller:** BBC2 television documentary *Love of Money: The Bank That Bust the World*.

271   **"financial Armageddon":** Susanne Craig, Jeffrey McCracken, Aaron Lucchetti, and Kate Kelly, "The Weekend That Wall Street Died," *Wall Street Journal*, December 29, 2008.

271   **"I guess this is good-bye":** *"Burning Down His House,"* New York, November 30, 2008.

272   **the Lehman family and their reactions:** Marissa Brostoff, "The Lehmans? They've Moved On. Sad? A Little," *Jewish Daily Forward*, September 26, 2008.

INDEX